CULTURES OF RADICALISM IN
BRITAIN AND IRELAND

Poetry and Song in the Age of Revolution

Series Editors: Michael Brown
John Kirk
Andrew Noble

Titles in this Series

1 United Islands? The Languages of Resistance
John Kirk, Andrew Noble and Michael Brown (eds)

2 Literacy and Orality in Eighteenth-Century Irish Song
Julie Henigan

CULTURES OF RADICALISM IN BRITAIN AND IRELAND

EDITED BY

John Kirk, Michael Brown and Andrew Noble

Routledge
Taylor & Francis Group

LONDON AND NEW YORK

First published 2013 by Pickering & Chatto (Publishers) Limited

Published 2016 by Routledge
2 Park Square, Milton Park, Abingdon, Oxfordshire OX14 4RN
711 Third Avenue, New York, NY 10017, USA

First issued in paperback 2015

Routledge is an imprint of the Taylor & Francis Group, an informa business

© Taylor & Francis 2013
© John Kirk, Michael Brown and Andrew Noble 2013

To the best of the Publisher's knowledge every effort has been made to contact relevant copyright holders and to clear any relevant copyright issues. Any omissions that come to their attention will be remedied in future editions.

All rights reserved, including those of translation into foreign languages. No part of this book may be reprinted or reproduced or utilised in any form or by any electronic, mechanical, or other means, now known or hereafter invented, including photocopying and recording, or in any information storage or retrieval system, without permission in writing from the publishers.

Notice:
Product or corporate names may be trademarks or registered tradem arks, and are used only for identification and explanation without intent to infringe.

BRITISH LIBRARY CATALOGUING IN PUBLICATION DATA

Cultures of radicalism in Britain and Ireland. – (Poetry and song in the age of revolution)
1. Politics and literature – Great Britain – History. 2. Politics and literature – Ireland – History. 3. Radicalism in literature. 4. Radicalism in music.
I. Series II. Kirk, John M. (John Monfries), 1952– editor of compilation. III. Brown, Michael, 1972– editor of compilation. IV. Noble, Andrew, 1939– editor of compilation.
820.9'3581-dc23

ISBN-13: 978-1-138-66204-9 (pbk)
ISBN-13: 978-1-8489-3344-6 (hbk)

Typeset by Pickering & Chatto (Publishers) Limited

CONTENTS

Acknowledgements — vii
List of Figures — ix
List of Contributors — xi

Introduction: Enlightenment and Revolution: A British Problematic
  – *Michael Brown* — 1

Part I: Constituencies
  1 'English Men Went Head to Head with their Own Brethren': The Welsh Ballad-Singers and the War of American Independence
    – *Ffion Mair Jones* — 25
  2 Scottophobia versus Jacobitism: Political Radicalism and the Press in Late Eighteenth-Century Ireland – *Martyn J. Powell* — 49
  3 Lord Daer, Radicalism, Union and the Enlightenment in the 1790s – *Bob Harris* — 63
  4 The Political and Cultural Legacy of Robert Burns in Scotland and Ulster, c. 1796–1859 – *Christopher A. Whatley* — 79
  5 'Blessèd Jubil!': Slavery, Mission and the Millennial Dawn in the Work of William Williams of Pantycelyn – *E. Wyn James* — 95

Part II: The Geography of Utterance
  6 Serial Literature and Radical Poetry in Wales at the End of the Eighteenth Century – *Marion Löffler* — 113
  7 Popular Song, Readers and Language: Printed Anthologies in Irish and Scottish Gaelic, 1780–1820 – *Niall Ó Ciosáin* — 129
  8 Broadside Literature and Popular Political Opinion in Munster, 1800–1820 – *Maura Cronin* — 145
  9 Radical Poetry and the Literary Magazine: Stalking Leigh Hunt in the Republic of Letters – *Dan Wall* — 159

Notes — 169
Works Cited — 215
Index — 243

ACKNOWLEDGEMENTS

The papers in this volume were originally presented at one or other of two symposia entitled *United Islands? Multi-Lingual Radical Poetry* and *Song in Britain and Ireland, 1770–1820* which were held at Queen's University Belfast from 13 to 15 November 2008 and 26 to 29 August 2009 as part of an AHRC Research Networks and Grants Project under the same name. We gratefully acknowledge the financial support of the AHRC for these two symposia. The first symposium doubled-up as the 8th Language and Politics Symposium of the Gaeltacht and Scotstacht within the AHRC Research Institute of Irish and Scottish Studies, University of Aberdeen, to which we are indebted for further substantial funding. Additional funding came from Foras na Gaeilge.

Between the two symposia, there was a total of 120 invited participants – many more participants than are represented in this volume or its companion volume: *United Islands? The Languages of Resistance* edited by John Kirk, Andrew Noble and Michael Brown, in the present series. We wish to acknowledge each of their contributions, especially those who chaired sessions or gave papers in response to our invitations, or acted as rapporteurs. To this last group we are especially indebted to the following at the first symposium: John Barrell, Claire Connolly, Jon Mee and Katie Trumpener; at the second symposium: Michael Scrivener, Fred Lock and Mark Philp. Each of their contributions accumulatively brought together the main inter-connecting strands of this literary and political matrix and greatly sharpened our own thinking.

At each symposium, there was a multi-lingual concert of song of the types which we are dealing with in these essays, and to which Katie Trumpener refers in her Afterword to *United Islands? The Language of Resistance*. There sang, at the first symposium: Ciaran Carson, Maggie MacInnes, accompanied by Brian MacAlpine, Dafydd Idris Edwards and Terry Moylan; at the second symposium Ciaran Carson, Dafydd Idris Edwards, James Flannery and Adam McNaughtan. We are deeply indebted to each of them not only for their renditions but also for sharing with us their extraordinary rich knowledge of this song material.

At each symposium, there was a reception at the Linen Hall Library, Belfast, founded in 1788 as the Belfast Reading Society. In 2008, the reception coincided with the Thomas Moore 2008 Festival Travelling Exhibition 'My Gentle Harp: Thomas Moore's Irish Melodies, 1808–2008', about which John Gray, the then Librarian, and Siobhan Fitzpatrick of the Royal Irish Academy, spoke. In 2009, John Killen, incoming Librarian, spoke of the 'Hidden Gems of Radical Poetry in the Linen Hall Library Poetry Collection' ahead of a tour of the Linen Hall Library Archives. It is always a pleasure to work with the Linen Hall Library and its Librarians, and those present on each happy occasion are indebted for their hospitality as well as their erudition.

For the help of our colleagues, we are grateful especially to Ciaran Carson, Cairns Craig, Donall Ó Baoill and John Thompson.

We are indebted to Pickering & Chatto for agreeing to publish a new series in the area: *Poetry and Song in the Age of Revolution*, of which this volume is the third. The companion volume: *United Islands? The Languages of Resistance,* the first in the series, was published in 2012. See www.pickeringchatto.com/series/poetry_and_song_in_the_age_of_revolution for further details. As our blurb states: 'Scholars working within the disciplines of English, history, music, Celtic Studies and politics will find the series of interest, as will researchers whose wider concerns pertain to cultural history, anthropology and the history of philosophy, communications and linguistics.'

John Kirk, Michael Brown and Andrew Noble
October 2012

LIST OF FIGURES

Figure 4.1: The Burns Memorial at Alloway   91
Figure 7.1: Titles printed in Irish, Scottish Gaelic and Welsh, 1750–1800   133
Figure 7.2: Titles printed in Irish, Scottish Gaelic and Welsh, 1800–1900   133
Figure 7.3: Subscribers to Kenneth MacKenzie's *Orain Ghaidhealach* (1792)   137
Figure 7.4: Some subscribers to Turner's *Comhchruinneacha* (1813)   139

LIST OF CONTRIBUTORS

Michael Brown is Senior Lecturer in Irish and Scottish History at the University of Aberdeen and Acting Director of the Research Institute of Irish and Scottish Studies. As well as being a co-director of the AHRC network grant *United Islands? Multi-Lingual Radical Poetry and Song in Britain and Ireland, 1770–1820* in 2008–9, he has directed an AHRC project on Irish and Scottish Diasporas since 1600 (2006–11). His primary research focus is on comparative Enlightenment, and he is the author of *Francis Hutcheson in Dublin* (Dublin; Four Courts Press, 2002) and *A Political Biography of John Toland* (London, Pickering & Chatto, 2011). He is currently finishing a study entitled *The Irish Enlightenment*.

Maura Cronin is Senior Lecturer in History and co-ordinator of the Oral History Centre at Mary Immaculate College Limerick. She was awarded a Senior Fellowship by the Irish Research Council in the Humanities and Social Sciences in 2004–5 for her project on broadside ballads and news transmission in pre-famine Ireland. Her research interests are in popular culture and politicization in nineteenth-century Ireland, Irish labour history and oral history and memory, and her more recent publications include 'Claiming the Landscape: Popular Balladry in Pre-famine Ireland', in U. N. Bhroiméil and G. Hooper (eds), *Land and Landscape in Nineteenth-Century Ireland* (Dublin: Four Courts Press, 2008), pp. 13–24; *The Death of Fr. John Walsh at Kilgraney: Community Tensions in Pre-famine Carlow* (Dublin: Four Courts Press, 2010) and *Agrarian Protest in Ireland 1750–1960* (Dundalk: Dundalgan Press, 2012).

Bob Harris is Harry Pitt Fellow in History at Worcester College, University of Oxford. Prior to 2006 he was Professor of British History at the University of Dundee. His research interests focus on the political, cultural and social history of Britain and Ireland during the 'long eighteenth century'. His most recent book is *The Scottish People and the French Revolution* (London, Pickering & Chatto, 2008). He is currently completing a book on Scottish towns in the age of Enlightenment, to be published in 2013 by Edinburgh University Press, and has begun a short thematic biography of Lord Daer. He hopes in due course to return to an earlier project on the cultural and social history of gambling in Britain, Ireland and the British Empire between *c.* 1660 and 1860.

E. Wyn James is Reader in the School of Welsh at Cardiff University, where he specializes in Welsh literature and culture of the modern period. His research focuses primarily on areas relating to religion, identity, book history, gender studies and popular culture. He is a leading authority on the hymn, the broadside ballad and the literature of evangelicalism. Dr James is editor of the Ann Griffiths website and the Welsh Ballads website, and contributed the chapter on Wales in *Dissenting Praise: Religious Dissent and the Hymn in England and Wales* (Oxford: Oxford University Press, 2011). He was a Visiting Fellow at the University of Cambridge in 2004, and in 2012 he was a Fulbright Scholar and Visiting Fellow at Harvard University. Dr James is co-director of the Cardiff Centre for Welsh American Studies, where he has a special research interest in the anti-slavery movement and in the literature of the Welsh diaspora in Patagonia.

Ffion Mair Jones is Research Fellow at the University of Wales Centre for Advanced Welsh and Celtic Studies. Her research interests include the popular eighteenth-century Welsh-language genres of the ballad and interlude, and eighteenth-century correspondence. She is co-editor, with G. H. Jenkins and D. C. Jones, of *The Correspondence of Iolo Morganwg*, 3 vols (Cardiff: University of Wales Press, 2007), and author of *'The Bard is a Very Singular Character': Iolo Morganwg, Marginalia and Print Culture* (Cardiff: University of Wales Press, 2010) and *Welsh Ballads of the French Revolution 1793–1815* (Cardiff: University of Wales Press, 2012). Her edition of a Welsh play on the subject of the French Revolution is in the press, and she is now working on an anthology of correspondence in and out of Wales during the Revolutionary decade.

John Kirk is Senior Lecturer in English and Scottish Language at Queen's University Belfast. During 2008–9, with Michael Brown and Andrew Noble, he held an AHRC Research Networks and Workshops Grant for the project which lies behind the present volume: *United Islands? Multi-Lingual Radical Poetry and Song in Britain and Ireland, 1770–1820*. With primary research interests in dialectology and corpus linguistics, his most recent books are (with J. L. Kallen) *SPICE-Ireland: A User's Guide* (Belfast: Cló Ollscoil na Banríona, 2012) and (co-edited with I. MacLeod) *Scots: The Language and its Literature: A Festschrift for J. Derrick McClure* (Amsterdam: Rodopi, 2012).

Marion Löffler is a Research Fellow at the University of Wales Centre for Advanced Welsh and Celtic Studies, Aberystwyth. Her research centres on cultural nationalism and the transfer of ideas and knowledge in the long nineteenth century. Her most recent work encompasses *Welsh Responses to the French Revolution: Press and Public Discourse 1789–1802* (Cardiff, 2012) and a study on 'The Marseillaise in Wales' in the essay collection *'Footsteps of Liberty and Revolt'*, edited by M.-A. Constantine and D. Johnston (Cardiff, 2013). A volume on *Political Pamphlets and Sermons in Wales 1790–1806* is in press. She is currently working on a study on translation in Welsh culture at the time of the French Revolution.

Andrew Noble is a graduate of Aberdeen and Sussex Universities. He was also a Junior Research Fellow at Peterhouse, Cambridge. His teaching career was entirely at Strathclyde University, where he was for a time Head of the English Literature Section. He specialized in teaching American Literature and Romanticism. Before his retirement, he was the Convenor of the Irish-Scottish Academic Initiative. His published research is mainly in Scottish literature and film. His extensive writings on Burns culminated in the publication of the joint-edition with P. S. Hogg of *The Canongate Burns* (2001, 2003). He has recently been appointed Honorary Visiting Senior Lecturer in the School of English, Queen's University Belfast.

Niall Ó Ciosáin is Senior Lecturer in History at the National University of Ireland, Galway. His main research interests are in popular printing and reading, language shift and language change, and he is the author of *Print and Popular Culture in Ireland, 1750–1850* (Basingstoke: Macmillan Press, 1997, paperback edition 2010). His current work focusses on the state as ethnographer and publisher in nineteenth-century Ireland, and a book provisionally entitled *Talking about Beggars: Ireland in official print culture, 1800–1850* is forthcoming from Oxford University Press. He is also engaged in a comparative study of publishing and reading in the Celtic languages between 1700 and 1900, of which the essay in this volume is a part.

Martyn J. Powell is Head of the Department of History and Welsh History at Aberystwyth University, and an Irish political and social historian. His recent publications include *Piss-Pots, Printers and Public Opinion in Eighteenth-Century Dublin* (Dublin: Four Courts Press, 2009) and *Clubs and Societies in Eighteenth-Century Ireland* (Dublin: Four Courts Press, 2010), edited with

James Kelly. He is the general editor of the interdisciplinary journal *Eighteenth-Century Ireland* and is currently working on a study of the maiming of British soldiers by Ireland's urban 'houghers'.

Dan Wall is currently a Teaching Fellow at the University of Aberdeen, where in 2008 he completed a doctoral thesis examining the role of national identity in the work of John Gibson Lockhart. His research interests are concentrated primarily in the fields of eighteenth- and nineteenth-century British and Irish literature, and in particular the political and literary climate of the 1790s, Robert Burns, Romantic poetry (in particular the Keats/Hunt circle) and nineteenth-century periodical culture. He has published a number of articles on related topics, and has recently co-edited (along with Shane Alcobia-Murphy and Lindsay Milligan) a collection of essays entitled *Founder to Shore: More Crosscurrents in Irish and Scottish Studies*, (Aberdeen: AHRC Centre for Irish and Scottish Studies, 2011).

Christopher A. Whatley is Professor of Scottish History at the University of Dundee, where he is also Head of the College of Arts and Social Sciences and a Vice-Principal. He has been co-investigator on two recent AHRC projects: the Beyond Text programme, 'Inventing Tradition and Securing Memory: Robert Burns 1796–1909', led by Murray Pittock (Glasgow); and 'Smaller Scottish Towns in the Enlightenment, 1745–1820', the principal investigator for which was Bob Harris (Oxford). His current research interests are in memory and memorialization in Scotland in the nineteenth century, and Scotland's Whig ideology and impact in the seventeenth and eighteenth centuries. Representative publications include *The Scots and the Union* (Edinburgh: Edinburgh University Press, 2007); *A History of Everyday Life in Scotland 1600–1800* (Edinburgh: Edinburgh University Press, 2010; ed. with E. Foyster), and 'Reformed Religion, Regime Change, Scottish Whigs and the Struggle for the 'Soul' of Scotland, *c.* 1688–*c.* 1788', in *Scottish Historical Review* (April 2013).

INTRODUCTION: ENLIGHTENMENT AND REVOLUTION: A BRITISH PROBLEMATIC

Michael Brown

1794 was a difficult year for the Hurdy Gurdy. He was on trial, accused of ninety-three counts of sedition. The principal charge of which was the playing of the tune, 'Ça Ira', which the judge pronounced

> one of the most flagitious expressions of disloyalty and disaffections – one of the most dangerous attempts to provoke and excite the people to the acts of force and violence, and to overturn the constitution and to promote anarchy and rebellion, I will not scruple to say, the most so that ever I have known.[1]

Given this view – and the testimony of the French Horn to the effect that 'this instrument has played this tune day after day, through the streets of this metropolis' – chances of an acquittal were slim.[2] Despite the assertion of the French Horn that the Hurdy Gurdy had sung a variety of seditious songs, such as 'Go George, I can't endure you' and 'The Modes of Court', the defence refused to answer to the charges, for 'although there may be a libel without writing, as by words, signs or pictures, Yet there is no law to make mere musical sounds libellous'.[3] However, the prosecutor, the Attorney General, deemed it the necessary task of the jury to

> stand forward boldly and honestly, to defend the constitution against Hurdy Gurdy; and by a firm and upright verdict, to check the career of fanatic delusion, set on by diabolic malignity, which if suffered to go one jot further will burst the bounds of all legal and social restraint, and overwhelm the British Empire, the glory of the world, in blood and desolation, and envelope in worse than Egyptian darkness or Egyptian bondage, you and your posterity forever.[4]

The hyperbole of this passage mounted to a climax at which, emotionally drained, words failed him:

> I will call upon you then, by everything sacred and profane which is dear to man, by a manly verdict to teach these abominable, ambitious, atheistical, atrocious, anarchical, barbarous, brawling, babbling, brainless, blasphemous, cruel, conspiring, contemptible, cursed, confounded, damnable, dangerous, destructive, diabolical, deistical, demagogical, execrable, egregious, extravagant, excommunicated, fanatic, fanatical,

furious, factious, fanatical (I believe I said that word before) ferocious, FRENCH. (Here the Attorney General, overcome by his feelings, grew confused and was obliged to sit down).[5]

This alphabetical lexicon of abuse captured the heightened tensions of the year of its composition. 1794 was a year of trials; a year when the state administration moved to repress the United Irish movement which was increasingly moving from a reformist to a revolutionary analysis of Irish circumstances. The initial clampdown came in 1793, when the movement was declared illegal; William Drennan was tried for seditious libel on 29 June 1794, following the spy William Jackson who had been arrested and charged with high treason on 24 April.[6] Other, less prominent figures were also prosecuted, as in the Drogheda case of seven men accused of 'conspiring with others ... to incite an insurrection and rebellion within the realm of Ireland, and ... procuring arms and armed men to levy INSURRECTION, REBELLION, and WAR for the purpose of overturned the established Government and Constitution'.[7] The political trials only polarized opinion further and radicalized the movement by removing moderate voices such as Drennan's from the organizing committee. The United Irish movement associated with the agrarian protest movement, the Defenders, and added an extensive social critique to their essentially political analysis of the wayward condition of Ireland's circumstances.[8] This in turn produced a political echo in the trials for outrages, as in the trial of John Fay for conspiring to murder the Rev. Thomas Butler of Navan, County Meath.[9] The deadly blend of social protest and a physical attack on a representative of the political establishment encapsulated the fear of the middling ranks that the mob was being mobilized to destructive ends.[10]

In the case of the Hurdy Gurdy, the defence protested that the prosecution indicated how the country had reached such a pitch of political delusion that to criticize the social hierarchy was to be open to condemnation. There was, as it were, an 'epidemical fever in the body politic, the symptoms of which were delirium and a horror of everything new.'[11] In contrast, the judge's closing statement proposed that the purpose of the Hurdy Gurdy's actions constituted

> an indirect and treacherous attempt to stir up the Roman Catholics ... to excite them to murmur and to render them discontented with all that the beneficence of their King and the wisdom and goodness of his Parliament have done for them.

In either case the contest was for the hearts and minds of the 'three fourths of the community uninfected', for as the defence lawyer accepted, 'if these did not soon co-operate and put the others under some wholesome regimen, and salutary restraint, the most melancholy consequences must inevitably follow.'[12] The contest was thus one concerning the differing interpretations of the politicization process.

***

The story in France seems relatively simple. The Enlightenment, which flourished in the salons and civil society of the cities, thrived beyond the stern gaze of the absolutist state. It developed a mode of critical discussion and debate that eventually turned away from the foppish pursuits of art, theatre and literary criticism and gave attention to the flawed workings of an increasingly bankrupted state. The mental skills honed in the Enlightenment compelled the Revolution, and formed its essence. This analysis, dating back to de Tocqueville – that the men of letters forged the Republican Revolution in their minds and then in reality – still resonates in the scholarly literature.[13] Despite different concerns and source-bases, and with greater and lesser degrees of nuance, the French meta-narrative remains one of Enlightenment and Revolution, with a causal connection being sought between the two.[14]

The story in Britain seems rather more complicated. The Enlightenment, which spluttered into life in the coffee houses and civil society of the cities, was cosseted by the loving gaze of the parliamentary democracy. It developed an empirical agenda that eventually provided technological advances and theoretical justifications which underpinned the commercial imperialism of an increasingly potent state. The mental skills honed in the Enlightenment compelled the Empire, and formed its essence. This analysis, best enunciated by Christopher Bayley – that the men of letters forged the commercial Empire in their minds and then in reality – still resonates in the scholarly literature.[15] Despite different concerns and source-bases, and with greater and lesser degrees of nuance, the British meta-narrative remains one of Enlightenment and Empire, with a causal connection being sought between the two.

Two states, two stories; there seems little to excite the historian's curiosity. Yet, the final cause of the Enlightenment continues to perplex. If we are to take seriously the notion of a shared European cultural project of Enlightenment, surely we can trace its influences in the political cultures in which it played a part. But the neat causal connections the individual national lens makes plain becomes blurry and indistinct when the view is widened. Or indeed, and here I want to begin my pursuit, when the nation is devolved into its constituent parts.

Just as French historians have long suggested that France was divided along an imaginary line drawn from Geneva to St Malo, and that a culturally adept north was hampered by a slovenly southern sister, so British historians have tussled with what we have learnt to call 'the British problem': the vexed nature of Britain's internal constitution – politically, religiously and linguistically.[16] Faced with this union of multiple identities, historians have struggled to articulate difference and contestation. And in so doing, they have struggled to identify similarity and consensus.

In this process, the connection drawn between Enlightenment and Empire begins to weaken. Linda Colley's now standard *Britons: Forging the Nation* rightly gleaned criticism for leaving aside the Irish condition as evidence that did not fit the theory of a shared pan-Protestant front.[17] So too, Kathleen Wilson's *Sense of the People* speaks to the experience of the north of England far better than it comprehends the Scottish circumstance across the residual border.[18] And the Empire continues to dissolve under the gaze of the particularizing historian. Equally, the connection between Enlightenment and Revolution begins, cautiously, to reassert itself. At first glance this seems to be far from the case. If anything – and this was the survey I intended to offer in this introduction – the British case complicates and confuses any direct causal connection, for the truisms about the three kingdoms are as follows.

- In England, there was no Enlightenment (traditionally explained through reference to the English self-image as a sturdy, practical people with more common sense than abstract ambition). Hence there was no revolution. The nuanced version of this view argued that Empire displaced the nervous energy of the young, and sated their ambition for adventure, or killed it by killing them on a foreign shore.
- In Scotland, there was an Enlightenment (which has gained its place in the scholarly sun in the last half-century, and which was informed by a tolerant and irenic mix of sceptical Whiggery and Moderate Presbyterianism). But there was no Revolution. This is explained by reference to good guidance by the landed gentry, imperial displacement and the removal of party politics to London in 1707.
- In Ireland, there was no Enlightenment (preoccupation with the sectarian confessionalism of the Anglican elite and the penal servitude of the Catholics pre-empted any such developments and trapped Ireland in the seventeenth-century vortex of religious conflict). Yet there was a Revolution. 1798 is therefore only explicable through reference to sectarian hatreds and economic distress, and the United Irish movement is disconnected from its French allies in their ambition and understanding.

However, the inadequacy of this modelling is apparent when examining how Wales fits into its scheme. Though the nation was largely controlled by a hegemony of old landowners and budding industrialists and hence apparently rests easily within the English narrative, it began to develop a public political discourse in its two languages which complicates any attempt to submerge a four-nation context into a tale of three nations.[19] The emergence of Methodism and its contested political ramifications are also of significance here.[20]

However, nowhere has the traditional tripartite story come under greater challenge than in Ireland. While I am busy trying to solve one problem, establishing the case for an Irish Enlightenment, a generation of scholars from Louis Cullen onwards have re-explored the nature and causes of the 1798 Rebellion.[21] Sectarianism gave way to a large extent under the strain, and economics increasingly came under question. In their place emerged a concern for the political culture of the island, and a nuanced picture of Catholic hidden gentry, Presbyterian associationalism and Anglican disenchantment all fused with youthful idealism and militaristic posturing that rushed the country into slaughter.[22]

In Scotland, the picture has also become more detailed. Some initial soundings have been taken into the radical fringes of the Enlightenment movement. So too, the work of Bob Harris, in particular, has fleshed out the bony structure of Scottish radicalism and detailed its links with their Irish and English counterparts.[23] The picture of an un-inflammable public opinion has been challenged and the assumption that much of Scottish civil society was characterized by banal imperialism and unionist-nationalism has been carefully scrutinized.

And in England, Roy Porter tried to compile a case for a vibrant and volatile Enlightenment, grounded on empirical assumptions and developments in natural philosophy, applied technology and mechanistic understanding.[24] At the same time, John Barrell and numerous others have brought forward E. P. Thompson's seminal synthesis of the radical constituency.[25] The English condition, in other words, collapses into national themes and regional variations in a discordant cacophony of competing political voices.

So the picture alters under examination. Instead of one Enlightenment and one Revolution – albeit in different parts of the islands – we can see four Enlightenments and four radical movements. Aesthetically, this is much more satisfying; historically, it is much more accurate. Yet, all this activity begs a question: if the Enlightenment in France produced a Revolution, why were three of the British Enlightenments (the Scottish, the English and the Welsh) born sterile of political potency? And why was the most volatile of the British Enlightenments – the Irish – so filled with political testosterone?

In other words, despite this scholarly endeavour, we seem to come full circle. We are back to the tantalizing Tocquevillean conundrum: what is the connection between the men of letters and the men of action? What is the connection, if any, between Enlightenment and Revolution?

***

There is something important about Cork; its silence is significant. Cork sets the historian a puzzle as in 1798 it does not rise. Yet, in the years before it was a pit of United Irish activism. The county was the birthplace of that most Enlightened of United Irish leaders, Arthur O'Connor – he later married the daughter of the Marquise de Condorcet – and the city was the home of *The Harp of Erin*. Although it failed to see out the month of its foundation, March 1798, it was modelled on O'Connor's outlet, the *Press*, and held as its motto: 'the harp is new strung and will be heard'. Edited by the brothers, John and Henry Sheares, it offered a diet of rousing tub-thumping and bitter vitriol. The administration quickly moved in to quieten it. In contrast, the county was also home to the North Cork militia, whose ferocity in counter-insurgency actions in north Wexford prompted active resistance rather than sullen compliance.[26] Cork was in this sense at the centre of the culture war of the 1790s.

In other words, even where the Rising did not overtly take hold, where intense political division emerged at the local level, it was accompanied by a series of repressive and counter-revolutionary measures. In the case of Cork, for example, the political constellation favoured the loyalist camp, so although society was divided, the outcome was rowdy repression and sullen quiescence, rather than violent upheaval. Cork city had had its United Irish organization decapitated by arrest and imprisonment, and the surrounding countryside was dissuaded from overt activity by the presence of the military.[27]

This analysis of the case of Cork reveals the centrality of a recent addition to the terminological repertoire of Irish historians seeking to explain the 1798 rebellion: 'politicization'. It is this process that accounts for the antagonisms on either side of the divide, engages loyalist and revolutionary in the fate of the cultural and physical conflict, and changes the contests from the strength of ideas to the strength of arms. Politicization matters because it is the point of praxis. Yet, despite the emphasis that has fallen on the term, politicization remains alchemical, not chemical. In the Irish literature it supplies a magical and not a scientific explanation of the metamorphosis of political life in the last quarter of the century. In what remains of this introduction, I want to unlock the spell, examine its ingredients and then conclude by seeing whether the sister kingdoms might be similarly enchanted.

***

At the heart of the category of politicization is the process by which politics comes to take up a central position in the social and cultural imaginary of the citizenry. It alludes to the way in which the realm of politics has risen in importance, and citizens have increasingly presumed that there are 'political' contexts that explain circumstances and provide guidance for future action. It indicates that *homo politicus* is the preconceived actor in the modern drama, and not *homo religiosus* or even *homo ludens*. Yet, just as with these other constructions of the human subject, it is, according to Jacques Ellul, a limited interpretation, but one so prevalent and all-encompassing, as to be a self-perpetuating myth:

> To think of everything as political, to conceal everything by using this word, to place everything in the hands of the state, to appeal to the state in all circumstances, to subordinate the problems of the individual to those of the group, to believe that political affairs are on everybody's level and that everybody is qualified to deal with them – these factors characterise the politicisation of modern man, and, as such, comprise a myth.[28]

The fundamental conceit within this vision of human organization and activity is that 'all problems are political, and solvable only along political lines'.[29] In other words, the process of politicization reduces other realms of human activity to a subsidiary and dependent relationship to the political, offering a simplification of the nature of those domains, and a false presupposition that the problematic inherent to them might be resolved through a reduction of them to political premises. Or as Ellul puts it 'to participate in non-political activities that are nevertheless definitely related to our society is regarded as without value'.[30] Poetry, art, philosophy, literature, sociability and religiosity are all demeaned by being instrumentalized, reduced into political functions by other means. Art for art's sake and life for life's sake are replaced by engagement and activism.

Two forces combined to create a politicized society in the 1790s, namely democratization and mobilization. The first of these involved bringing people into the political fold, the second implied activating the enthusiasm and sympathy of those who were citizens. In both cases the outcome was an enriching of the relationship between the people and the polity. In Ireland, the extent, limit and consequence of the franchise was under review throughout the last quarter of the century. Indeed it was in large part the question of Catholic inclusion in the ranks of the active citizenry that split asunder the Volunteer movement in the early 1780s. The issue remained potent in the 1790s, with the 1793 Catholic Relief Act granting a limited franchise, and was not to be wholly resolved until 1829, when Catholic emancipation – or the right to sit in parliament – was enacted as part of a wider reconfiguration of the British polity's constitution that included the 1828 repeal of the Test and Corporation Acts and the 1832 Reform Act.[31]

As for mobilization, in the eighteenth century, there were prescribed limits to the ways in which people could engage directly with the state. As Gerard O'Brien has summarized,

> the very absence of governing institutions was in itself a form of social control in that it circumscribed the modes of and opportunities for expression of popular views and directed them into narrow and manipulatory channels. Falling within the realms of such control were petitions, instructions to MPs and elections.[32]

Examining each of these in turn, O'Brien was dismissive of their capacity to effect real change, choosing to emphasise instead the limited nature of the electorate, the infrequency of genuinely open contests, and the ease with which petitions and instructions could be manipulated by the parliamentarians to give a gloss of public sanction to pre-determined actions. He concluded by asserting that 'the uncovering of the true effectiveness of public opinion will reveal also how limited was that same effectiveness'.[33]

Yet, there were some signifiers of change. The Dublin mob could at times physically impose themselves on the parliament, and the turning of the Volunteers artillery on the building on 4 November 1779 during a free trade protest symbolizes the way in which a paramilitary force might dictate affairs.[34] While harder to assess, some evidence exists for the independent nature of the instructions forwarded to MPs in the 1770s.[35] Equally, contested elections remained a vent for the expression of political opinion.[36] While dismissed by O'Brien, the shortening of the parliamentary lifespan with the introduction of the Octennial Act in 1768 was a substantive alteration and enhancement in the electorate's capacity to intervene in the running of the state.[37] In the view of a disconsolate John Hely-Hutchinson, the measure had introduced 'a virulent spirit of licentiousness' and had 'added great weight to the democratical scale and will raise the lever of false popularity greater than before'.[38]

Yet, by looking at democratization and mobilization solely is to occlude one half of the equation. Taking this approach is to prioritize the people in the relationship between the people and the polity. There was also a state side to this story, and one which involved increasing levels of bureaucratization, legislation and infiltration into the society at large. While the people were often reluctant to intervene in the running of the state, the state was overanxious to intrude on the people, and there were commensurately numerous ways in which the polity came into contact with the populace.

Particularly effective was the multifaceted architecture of local government. As Toby Barnard has remarked, 'the paraphernalia of juries, petty and grand constables, vestries, overseers of the poor, manorial courts, even informal committees of village worthies brought the relatively modest into government.'[39] And those that appeared before them were also affected by the tentacle-like reach of the Irish polity into the quiet corners of everyday life. The highpoint of the county's year were the two assizes, where visiting judges sat on numerous criminal cases. The jury was also charged with responsibility for maintaining the roads. While this relied on a form of forced labour for much of the century, by the middle of the century the additional monetary levies that the jury could direct to the scheme far outweighed the contribution of penitential work, hence in 1765 the machinery was overhauled, giving more fiscal power to the jury. So too, the jury could levy money to support the upkeep of legal institutions, such as gaols and courthouses, and to pay the wages of court officials. This was earned through a cess, or tax paid by those occupying the land. Outside of Dublin there were thirty-eight assizes – one for each county and one for each of seven urban centres.⁴⁰ These however were the pretext for social (and sexual) intercourse, trading and drunken conviviality. They supplied the occasion for dances, race meetings, parades and parties. The meetings were therefore as much an occasion for the integration of the state into society as it was a visible statement of the polity's power over the populace. But if power descended, opinion arose, for the county grand jury was able to send petitions to the crown, making them a conduit for the expression of discontent and aggravation.⁴¹

Just as crucial was the continuous and highly visible presence of the military amongst the populace. Indeed, unlike the American Colonies, or even Britain itself, Ireland housed a large standing army, turning the country into something of a garrison state. Moreover the standing army was reinforced by a militia during periods of crisis, notably surrounding the Jacobite threat.⁴² The maximum figure had in fact been set by English statute under William III, setting the ceiling at 12,000. Although it often fell below this level in actual terms, perhaps to even as low as half that number, in 1768 a proposal emerged to raise the limit by 3,000, filling out the Irish regiments to the same size as their British counterparts, and hence allowing them to be rotated through the Empire. Paradoxically, this bred opposition to the augmentation bill, as many Protestants were concerned that they would be left undefended in the event of an imperial crisis. While the first bill was defeated by 105 votes to 101 in May 1768, once reassurances had been issued by the administration the measure was enacted by a large majority in October 1769.⁴³ Although regiments were sent from Ireland to America, as Vincent Morley reports 'in 1775 ... the nominal strength of the Irish garrison was 12,533 men, or 28 per cent of the total strength of the British army throughout the empire.'⁴⁴ Holding them was a system of a dozen or so barracks that had been erected in the wake of the War of the Two Kings (1688–91). As well as bringing colour and wealth to the towns in which they were situated, the presence of a nominally foreign force – the Irish themselves were barred from serving in their homeland – gave access in the Irish provinces to imperial news.⁴⁵

The presence of a large-scale military on Irish soil was not entirely beneficial and uncontested. Indeed, in the years surrounding the Volunteering movement, a sporadic, ineffectual but unpleasant mode of violent protest emerged, namely houghing, a practice in which a soldier had his back tendons cut ensuring that he could no longer walk – and hence be of service. So too there was always the potential for most casual, less ritualized violence between civilians and troops, as when a fracas broke out at the Cashel races, apparently because a solider pushed a child out of his way.⁴⁶ Indeed, the presence of a large number of men trained to violence within the body politic was a recipe for social tension, as Morley makes plain, and was resented all the more as the imperial force was incommensurately a burden being placed on the Irish exchequer.

Yet, the prevalence of British troops on Irish soil also draws attention to a central trend in the century, namely the growth in the power and capacity of the state, associated with the eighteenth-century financial revolution.[47] The motor for this revolution was the changes in the military; particularly the growth in the standing army. The result of this burgeoning cost was, in part, the development and incremental growth of a national debt. Begun in 1716 and a consistent element in the exchequer entry book, with a brief interlude in the 1750s, it ran at around £30,000 in the first phase of its existence, and rose to £50,000 in the second.[48] The central consequence of this increase in the national debt was a commensurate rise in the tax take required to service this debt. The Supply Acts of the period repeatedly extended the range of goods that were subjected to government duties.[49] There was also a significant effort to ensure that the Irish state was better equipped to collect the taxes it already levied. This resulted in a slow inflation in the size of the revenue commission. This held around 1,100 people on its staff in 1715, rising to 1,600 in the 1750s.[50]

All of these trends supported the presumption that there are political solutions to economic problems. That assumption also informed the expansion of the Irish polity in aspects of social endeavour that had traditionally been beyond its remit. Indeed, in the 1730s – a crucial decade in the development of an ideology of improvement – two-thirds of the bills presented to the parliament were concerned with social and economic development and control. The 1730s saw the sudden expansion of the toll-road system with some twenty-nine trusts being set up from 1729 to 1741.

Starting in 1721–2, and the grant of monies to the Linen Board, there was a steady growth in specific legislative provisions, with a sudden efflorescence in the 1750s – probably instituted by the discovery that the Irish exchequer was in surplus and funds were now available to undertake long dreamt of schemes of improvement. The 1753–4 session of parliament offered up £38,100 worth of specifically allocated expenditure. By 1765–6, the amount had tripled, reaching £108,496.[51] And as Eoin Magennis notes 'after the "constitutional revolution" of 1782 and the establishment of an independent parliament, the expenditure of public moneys to achieve infrastructural improvement and import substitution reached new heights'.[52]

Nor were economic concerns the sole matter for consideration in this expansion of the state's ambit. According to Neal Garnham, the development of criminal legislation across the century involved

> an apparent movement within parliament to give a new legal force and status to existing practices. Statute law was to be used to reinforce and legitimise the actions of individuals and authorities in Ireland ... Essentially, there seems to have been a conscious shift in the means of the government of Ireland; from government by proclamation to government by law.[53]

Driven in large part by the Castle administration, statute law introduced a transportation system for punishment, and enabled the introduction between 1692 and 1760 of twenty-two measures that involved felonies punishable by death. While not as extensive as the equivalent British system, these covered an array of categories, such as sexual mores – the abduction of women and sex with girls under twelve were outlawed – crimes relating to property – destroying of stock, arson, sinking a ship, destroying a mine – and crimes relating to persons – cutting or maiming an individual.[54]

Nor was the legislative ambition of the state to be easily quenched. Following the granting of legislative independence in 1782 the pace, if anything, accelerated, with a dramatic increase in the parliamentary business of the Irish state occurring. James Kelly has calculated that an average of twenty-one bills per session was enacted under William, and that the amount of legislation hovered at around twenty-one until George III's accession; it then rose significantly. During the period from 1760 to 1782 the average number of Acts was 37.53. Once legislative independence was attained the number burgeoned again as parliament enacted an average of 58.7 bills every session until the Union.[55] If the 1730s saw the intellectual scope of parliamentary power expand, it was the 1760s that saw this ambition actualized in the statutes.

All of these intrusions into the Irish society and economy shaped the population's consciousness of, and reaction to, the polity, placing greater and greater emphasis on the capacity and remit of the state in creating the context for everyday life. In effect, the widening expanse of legal regulation at once narrowed the liberty of the subjects and politicized them, prompting either the attitude that further political action might resolve residual problems, or resistance to the infiltration of the state into areas of life once considered to be none of the state's legitimate business.[56] In either case, the net result of this state expansion was the prioritization of political values, over and above other modes of affiliation and connection.

Once the populace was politicized, in that they accepted social, economic and intellectual problems had 'political' solutions, three stages were undergone, albeit unevenly and with increasing speed: the creation of a political public opinion, the polarization of debate on central issues within the Enlightenment project, and the radicalization of the populace so that violent revolution appeared an acceptable route out of the impasse. Each of these stages will be briefly adumbrated.

***

With the politicization process, the Enlightenment counter publics began to confront the conundrum of politics with increasing regularity. The intrusion of the state into a broad range of arenas where associational life and free debate had come to dominate altered the nature of the discussion, and the character of those realms. But just as the state was now taking an interest in issues of economic improvement, aesthetic enhancement, political economy and polite behaviour, so the counter public was starting to concern itself with politics, formally understood. In other words, just as the state was endeavouring to politicize society, so society was beginning to develop political opinion.

In this, we connect to the French literature of Mona Ozouf, Keith Michael Baker and Arlette Farge, and the concern for an emergent culture of criticism from within the public sphere. Certainly in Ireland, from the 1750s onwards, pamphleteers like Arthur Browne, Richard French and Charles Lucas all availed of legal controversies to promulgate their political positions. Similarly, writers as diverse as the Catholic campaigner Charles O'Conor, the eccentric military man Charles Vallencey and the establishment academic Thomas Leland all projected back into the past in search of the causes of and solutions for current predicaments. However, for each of them, their reading was commensurately shaped by their present concerns – by O'Conor's desire to see Catholic reform, by Vallencey's ambitions to write of an ancient Irish civilization that might compete with English cultural supremacy, and by Leland's irenic hopes to provide a history that Protestant and Catholic might share, rendering the past impotent and scenic, not virile and gothic in character.

In this, the jurisprudence and antiquarianism of the period was polemical and political in kind, suffering from the symptoms and ill effects of overt politicization. Ireland, in other words, had become, in Donald Dozer's formulation, 'a society in which [legal thought and] history is considered to be serviceable mainly as a tool of political action'.[57] In other words jurists and antiquaries of whatever caste and colouration became kinds of official remembrancers, offering up 'a compound of fiction, legend and myth' and acting as the chronicler of a particular partisan brand of legal and historical memory in which 'all policy decisions that have been made in the past by his superiors have been perfect decisions and ... his bureaucratic masters have a record of complete infallibility'.[58] Whether the paymasters were the Catholic Committee, the Royal Irish Academy or Trinity College Dublin, the warping effect was the same – the jurist and antiquary of the third quarter of the eighteenth century regularly politicized the past for immediate rhetorical effect, presenting 'the past in the light of his own purposes and the preoccupations of his own age'.[59]

And these writers were aware that the manners of the people and the sentiments of the state were in such an antagonistic relationship that the polity was conceivably under threat of rebellion. Indeed, from as early as the 1760s, politicians and the literati worried over the possibility that the sentiments of the state and the manners of the people might diverge with terrible consequences. This was the case primarily because of the confessional identity of the state and the religious character of the people. The concern that the Protestant state and the Catholic people might confront each other was a perpetual fear haunting the Irish polity in the eighteenth century, but as the last quarter of the century unfolded, a greater sense of crisis can be seen leaching into the intellectual reflections of the Irish Enlightenment.[60] While the development of political opinion within the Enlightenment counter public did not inherently imply the creation of oppositional attitudes, in this vexed context, the process of politicization and political opinion formation polarized Enlightenment discussion.

***

Polarization was the outcome of a dual process of, paradoxically, the increasing sophistication and simplification of the political debate. The first element in the process is a rise in the number of issues on which divisions are identified and articulated. This accumulation of differences over the course of time both makes the argument between the camps more sophisticated and makes it increasingly difficult to conceptualize. This process results in a necessary simplification, wherein basic principles are enunciated and the different camps are labelled – by themselves or their opponents – so as to cluster particular differences together into more manageable units. Thus the different sides come to mark out different attitudes on a vast array of policy issues, at the same time as they are simplified into an either/or debate in which complex political attitudes are submerged under party labels.

This process can be witnessed in the gestation of Patriot politics over the period from the 1720s to the 1770s.[61] As Patriot politics evolved, from its origins in the economic arguments concerning Wood's halfpence, the agenda thickened and broadened. By the time Henry Grattan and Henry Flood were active, the platform contained a diverse set of demands for free trade, legislative independence and franchise reform, not all of which any given advocate of Patriot politics might wholeheartedly endorse. The Patriot movement had in that regard become a more complex organism, having accumulated a range of policy decisions and statements through the century. Yet, it was also an increasingly simple enemy, with its critics able to identify more ably both the advocates of the programme and target a slower moving, less agile, more burdened beast in the jungle of Irish politics. So too to cohere the complex weave of political stands and ambitions, the Patriots themselves required some level of reduction to primary colours of basic ideas. Pro-Ireland was to mean anti-England, pro-independence meant anti-Castle, pro-Catholic was to mean anti-establishment. Politics was thus reduced to partisan binaries and either/or alternatives. Yet something was hidden within this process of polarization, for within the Volunteer movement was gestating a new kind of politics based upon naturally inherent rights and not on artificially assumed privileges. While this new politics found its focus in the campaign for the Catholic franchise, it also expressed a deepening distrust in the state itself – a suspicion that found articulation in the Renunciation campaign that demanded the British state explicitly disavow any capacity to legislate for Ireland.

The misgivings the Volunteers expressed concerning the power of the British state, and that of its Irish cousin chimes with what John D. Lukacs has identified as a process of profound alienation from the political system, generated through a distain for and distrust of bureaucracy. This is caused in turn by the sense of 'impersonality and powerlessness' that the expanding architecture of government engenders in the population: 'impersonality because of the hugeness of democratic organisations and the myriads of interchangeable human beings who make up most of their personnel; powerlessness, because of the knowledge that votes, appeals, petitions amount to so very little.'[62] According to Lukacs this 'exasperation with bureaucracy' is in its very essence different from the antagonisms between parties. Indeed,

> it is at the same time more superficial and more profound than our dislike of either form of government. The democratic exercise of periodic elections does not compensate people sufficiently against their deep-seated knowledge that they are being ruled by hundreds of thousands of bureaucrats, in every level of government, in every institution, on every level of life.[63]

This is to draw a strong conceptual demarcation line between mere dislike of the government and disillusionment with the kind of politics that the state is responsible for. As Luckas notes this goes along with a process whereby 'people have become distrustful of the kind of men and women who are interested in holding this kind of power at all' –leading to overt and often vicious personal criticism and a politics of contempt.[64]

Yet, as the populace have been politicized, the solution to this sense of alienation is not to reject or ignore the polity. Indeed the growth of the state makes this a redundant idea for all but the most utopian and anarchic of thinkers who wished away the state or yearned in the nineteenth century for its withering. Rather, the answer was to demolish the existing polity, clear the ground and erect something new. As Lukacs, asserts 'toward the end of an age more and more people lose their faith in their institutions: and finally they abandon their belief that these institutions might still be reformed from within'.[65] The desire is then to replace the state with a new mode of political organization, a new way of doing politics, and a new kind of statesman. What is called for is not reform but regeneration.[66] How that transformation occurred is the next problematic to be considered.

***

Just as it is important to demarcate the category of polarization from politicization and public opinion, so it needs to be differentiated from radicalization. In the first place, notice should be given to J. C. D. Clark's anxiety about using the term 'radical' at all with reference to the eighteenth century. To do so, he has argued, is to commit the sin of anachronism for it was 'a new coinage of the 1820s'. As he trenchantly asserts '"radicalism" is a solecism in discussions of the eighteenth century, and that double confusion "bourgeois radicalism" is a solecism upon stilts.'[67] Yet to argue that the late eighteenth century saw a process of political radicalization is not to indicate adherence to any particular ideology. In as much as there were figures who promulgated revolutionary ideas about republicanism and democracy, the ideology to which they were committed to a greater or lesser extent was, as Clark accepts, a variant of Jacobinism.

However, what is being argued here is that both sides of the debate, both the Jacobins and the establishment, began to understand the conflict between them less as a debate within a political system – as was the case with the Volunteers and the Ascendancy in the 1770s and 1780s – and more as a choice between political systems. The victory of the Jacobin republican/democratic agenda precluded any survival of the existing system of monarchy and patronage and vice versa. Rather than existing as a debate within a discourse, the 1790s saw an ontological conflict ensue in which one or other political imaginary would dissolve and die. This departure is described by the term radicalization for it recognizes that what is at stake is something 'primitive, original ... implanted in nature ... [or] serving to origination' to use the definitions offered in Samuel Johnson's *Dictionary of the English Language* and cited by Clark when in search of eighteenth-century usage of the word 'radical'.[68]

In Ireland, the polarization of the 1780s had not been effectively healed, and in fact the rift widened through the decade that followed. The issues which had caused the breach were no longer specific and isolated. Rather the Catholic question in Ireland now served as an entry point into a wider set of commitments concerned with the nature of the state, the relationship between the state and its people, and the structures of government which the state embodied. Republicanism emerged around the commitment to give Catholics rights, while the idea of a Protestant Ascendancy cohered around the issue of protecting privileges. By 1793, and the decision by the government to prohibit the United Irish from openly organizing, the death knell of political debate between the two sides was being sounded. Within the confines of this newly ontological conflict both sides were marked by increasing levels of ideological commitment and a readiness to use more extreme measures, culminating in violence. This necessarily implied raising the stakes from discourse to death. In other words, radicalization did not only imply a change in the nature of the argument, but in the means that were acceptable to conduct it.

One way to trace this trend towards radicalization is to explore the changing rhetoric of protest – the nature of the argument – watching for the emergence of more extreme and self-contained positions. This has been the task conducted in a French context by the historian of Grub Street abuse, Robert Darnton. By 'taking the smut seriously' Darnton has uncovered a long history of priapic prurience about the court that he sees as having slowly de-legitimized the claim to authority the monarchy embodied.[69]

While no history of smut has been written for Ireland, what may have occurred was a quickening process of alienation from the polity and a rejection of the system commensurate with the encroachment of the state into the lives of its citizenry. This alienation was accompanied by a re-imagining of the possibilities of politics, developing an increasingly sophisticated vision of a possible future in which the Protestant Ascendancy gave way to a secular Republic, and British influence was expunged, potentially being replaced by an alliance with France. The process of radicalization was therefore more constructive than destructive, with both sides in the argument developing ontologically different possible futures for the island.

Far from disenchantment, the problem for Ireland was one of re-enchantment; rather than seeing one system being eroded by the acid of abuse and vitriol, the problem was the conviction an alternative possible future engendered in its supporters. To them the Irish system was corrupt but, worse, it was obstructive. Although not chalked up in the insulting billboards of Paris, Irish political development did experience a process of radicalization. By the 1790s, two systems resided in the country, side by side, both with able advocates and committed protagonists, and containing a strong element of neighbourly hostility. The difficulty was that neither side had anything significant in common with the other. Two Irelands now existed in the minds of the Irish populace, and decisions were being forced upon them as to which possible future they wanted to realize.

It is at this juncture that the other aspect to radicalization becomes pertinent, namely the changes in the means that were considered legitimate in pursuing the desired possible future. In this sense radicalization may imply an increasing turn towards violence – either state-sanctioned or illicit – as the ontological argument becomes increasingly agitated without finding any adequate resolution. Compromise over ontological argument is difficult to find and that it was over competing goods aggravated both parties into increasingly aggressive attempts to win – or close down – the argument as a whole.

This is in line with Butler Shaffer's postulate of a strange paradox, namely that 'the effort to impose social order may in fact lead to a breakdown in order'.[70] This occurs as violence 'may be, in part, a product of the frustration that people perceive in connection with their expectations of benefits to be derived from a formal system of law.'[71] While this frustration can be the result of a failure by the state to provide for basic physiological needs – food, shelter and safety – and the 1790s was indeed scarred by agrarian unrest and interpersonal violence caused by social deprivation and anxiety, this is not the primary concern of Shaffer's analysis.[72] Rather, what Shaffer identified was a higher order of frustration, created when the state's increasingly broad legislative activity intrudes on, or nullifies areas of life that were previously the source of human fulfilment. Shaffer posits that:

> To the degree that individuals are free to engage in goal-directed activity in response to these needs, there is a greater likelihood of need satisfaction, leading to a greater sense of self-fulfilment and the opportunity to develop higher order needs. But the degree such activity is interfered with, such as by the imposition of formal restrictions limiting the choices and the actions of the individual, the individual so affected will experience a frustration of his expectations, with the consequence being an increased likelihood of aggression or violence.[73]

At the top of Shaffer's hierarchy of needs are those of 'self-actualisation' defined as 'man's need for intellectual awareness, growth and creativity [which can] involve virtually any area of human conduct, including for example literary or artistic creativity, business or professional competency, and ... the desire to be an ideal mother.'[74] It was this process of self-actualization that the politicization of society stultified through its widening legislative ambit. In this, the expansion of the state into an increasing range of spheres of life both creates an expectation of benefit and frustrates what were once legitimate actions intended to fulfil those ambitions. In this sense the process of politicization produces violence.

Yet this conflict should not be understood as a clash between the regulatory control of an overreaching state and the reactive politics of expression from a community under threat. The dichotomy is not one between a state as an organization and the community as an organism, despite the claim of the Volunteers and then the United Irish to speak for the people.[75] Indeed, in as much as the United Irish offered a rationalist programme for political reform, their politics were more instrumental and organizational in kind than the state's, which was grounded in an historical and empirical claim to legitimacy. Edmund Burke, for instance, was to construct an organic defence of the state from the attacks of the republicans. At stake in the conflict were two versions of the organization of the state, a new mode grounded in rights and an older structure dependent on privilege. In this sense the conflict can be reduced into a fight between those in the system as it stood and those outside of its operation, railing against their exclusion.

Yet even this is a simplification, for the stakes were not merely those of office holding. The target for the republicans was not merely a palace coup in which they replaced the current regime but continued to uphold the basic norms of political power. It was not just exclusion and a desire for recognition that prompted their activism.[76] Rather, what the state was frustrating was in fact an increasingly complete revision of the nature of the state itself. The self-actualization being blocked was partly that of a Catholic community that longed for political recognition and activism. But more volatile and fissile were the Irish Jacobins, who were committed to a republican counter-state that could not self-realize without the demolition of the state as then existed. The scene was set for an ontological conflict between the establishment and republican malcontents. That this conflict was fed by economic frustrations is clear – the United Irish achieved a limited alliance with the agrarian agitators, the Defenders – and it similarly mapped partially onto the ambitions of the Catholic community for political realization. Yet, at the heart of the conflict was a political clash of cultures with republicans being thwarted by an increasingly active and able establishment.

Thus, politicization also produced violence in a second sense. If the populace now deemed that there were political solutions to problems, which in turn were being frustrated by the kind of politics under which they lived they were prone to develop the kind of new political ontology. That occurred in the 1790s, with the emergence of republicanism, and it was prompted to utilize violence to effect its establishment, giving political expression to political discontent. Politicization may produce social violence, but it also produces the context for political violence. And that was to be the tragic narrative of the 1790s, where the United Irish began by speculating about a new mode of political organization, petitioning for moderate reform from within. Effectively driven out of the political debate as the establishment rallied around the politics of privilege, the republican movement was then banned, and forced underground in 1794. This inspired them to adopt an increasingly violent means of pursuing their objectives. This protracted frustration of ambition and increased extremity of approach culminated in the rebellion of 1798. Violence spilled out across the countryside and left 20,000 dead before the slaughter abated.

***

So the story is not simple. It may be that in breaking down the compound category of politicization into its constituent elements actually gets us little closer to the big bang of revolution. In recognizing the creation of public opinion, its subsequent polarization and the radicalization of discourse we might merely be halving the distance between us and the event, but never actually reaching into the moment of combustion, when violence is resorted to and political activism rescinded. Yet we might be getting closer to the praxis of revolution, and connecting the intellectual investment in Enlightenment with the physical cost of Revolution. Understanding the various events that went to make up the crash in European cultural and political life helps us accident investigators to map the trajectory of particular objects during the catastrophe.

Two questions remain. First, the argument presented here is Irish in its content. How far might this narrative pertain to England, Scotland and Wales? Might their political cultures have undergone some of the processes identified here, but either held back from others or been diverted into other channels? Bob Harris has written recently of how 'the public sphere in Edinburgh did not become "politicised"' and 'given ... the close control on political life exerted "from above" it is doubtful whether a politics characterised by independence and popular involvement of any real depth and resilience could ever have emerged in eighteenth-century Scotland'.[77] So too, the empire might have acted as a political prophylactic after all, sending the disaffected and disillusioned abroad, even before the wave of political exiles tracked by Michael Durey set sail for the Americas.

One postulate to ponder. Might it be that Ireland followed France down the road of political enlightenment and into a trajectory of revolution? That was their tale of radicalization. Might Britain – England, Scotland and Wales – have radicalized in opposition, taking a commercial Enlightenment that lent itself towards imperial expansion? It is certainly true that Ireland was impeded in its access to empire. If this is correct, we need to be careful in dismissing the idea that one or other community did not politicize or indeed radicalize, but rather realize that they may have done so in different ways and towards differing ends. Scotland, for instance, provides much of the ideological energy underpinning empire and the social controls Dundas exercised may need to be understood as a counterpoint to ensure to those external investments. Ireland tacked towards republicanism, Scotland towards loyalism. England fractured into two competing camps and Wales, as recent work indicates, stored tensions within its body politic. The whole of the Atlantic Archipelago became a debating chamber of these possible futures.

Second, is it possible to track these processes? In thinking about this, the Hurdy Gurdy comes once again to mind. The contention of this collection is that something is to be learnt about the processes of politicization – in all of their multivalent complexity – by attending to the mode of distribution of political ideas. Nothing brought the community together more than the fraternal occasionality of reciting verse and singing songs. Poems and songs provided an intoxicating and combustible mix of ideas, entertainment and camaraderie: democratic in reach, memorable in content, and exhilarating in their blend of solidarity and sociability. It is for these same reasons that the authorities were so anxious to prosecute the Hurdy Gurdy. As the Attorney General recognized, the instrument had the capacity

> to promote far and wide the principles of anarchy and fanaticism; for there is not a street nor lane where it has not been heard; nor a shoe boy who does not whistle it

['Ça Ira'] as he polishes your boots; nor a newsman who does not introduce it as a symphony to fill up the intervals between 'Bloody News' and 'Chronicle of Liberty'.[78]

The extent of this process of politicization is nicely illustrated in the conclusion of the first essay in this collection. There **Ffion Mair Jones** describes a Welsh ballad from the epoch of the American Revolution in which the author narrates a political debate between a farmer's wife and a shopkeeper's wife. 'By opening our ears to this conversation' between two rural women, Jones argues, we can begin to reveal 'the broadening of the public sphere'.[79] It also captures two of the central issues of this collection: the development of political constituencies – both republican and loyalist – and the intimate geographies of utterance that related the emotional networks of political support to an analysis of the parochial condition.

Thus, Jones at once traces the manner in which news of the American crisis shaped and reshaped the political expression of balladeers in the Welsh language. Initially, the conflict was placed into the genre of religious war, with the Presbyterian character of the colonies finding sympathy among the Methodist and dissenting communities of the principality, and the American cause given an airing even by ballad singers, whose sympathies were largely with the Church of England. Subsequent to the entry of France into the war in 1778, the comprehension of the war moved into the framework of international relations being connected instead to the 'regular and uncompromising battling between two of Europe's greatest powers – Protestant Britain and Catholic France'; a change in vantage point that enabled the loyalist element in the population to find its voice.[80]

A similar shift in perspective, albeit over a longer period of time, can be traced through **Martyn Powell's** essay on the virulence of Scottophobia in Irish political discourse, from anti-Jacobite musings of the early century through to the rejection of Lord Bute in the 1760s. Therein Powell expertly dissects the vexed relationship between the Scottish Whigs and the Irish Patriots, arguing how the tropes of anti-Scottish prejudices were deployed to indicate the difference between the Irish devotion to British liberty and a proposed tendency of the Scottish political culture to advocate centralization of power and harbour tyranny. This analysis extended, as Powell documents, into a rendering of the American conflict of the 1770s as a 'Scotch war': one waged against a Scottish-led subversion of the British constitution into a French-style absolutist tyranny.[81] Crucially however, there was more to this phenomenon than this. 'Hostility towards the Scots', Powell suggests, 'was not simply the jealousy of a rival sibling fighting for crumbs – trade concessions, political favours – from the colonial mother.' At its core he identifies a debate over the value of religious toleration. The anti-Catholic campaign, supported by Scottish Presbyterians in the period, supplied a flattering contrast for Irish Patriots to their own emergent 'willingness to forget past enmities and unite in the cause of parliamentary reform.'[82] That this portrait of Irish Enlightenment contained an element of self-deceit was to become clear when the Volunteers split over the issue of the Catholic franchise in the 1780s and polarized opinion across the 1790s.

Powell further concludes that 'it was the outbreak of the French Revolution that enabled the Scots to ... enter into dialogue with English and Irish reformers via the emerging network of corresponding societies'.[83] This is well illustrated in **Bob Harris's** close study of the leading Scottish reformer, Lord Daer, whose pan-British vision of a union of republics provided a counterweight to particular national sentiments.[84] Reconstructing Daer's brief, vibrant life from the scant remaining sources, Harris provides a pen sketch of a leading activist who experienced the full process of politicization delineated above. From his early induction in English radical dissenting culture, he was given to assume a political dimension to religious, social and economic questions, as evinced in his intervention into electoral politics in the late 1780s. Polarization was developing as Daer increasingly engaged in reforming campaigns, notably that surrounding abolition. Radicalization prompted him to join and perhaps lead the Scottish Friends of the People.

Set against Harris's exploration of the career of Lord Daer, the study of Robert Burns's post-revolutionary legacy offered by **Christopher Whatley** highlights how far the Scottish context was fallow land for radical politics to till. Indeed, from the point of his death, Burns acted as a compass for political positioning. As Whatley documents, the centrality of the sentimental impulses on Burns's work, culminating in 'The Cotter's Saturday Night', took precedence over the democratic energies that informed 'The Twa Dogs' that itself inspired revisions by Chartist poets. In this transition from social critic to patriotic paternalist what was at stake was the reimagining of the past to effect the construction of a loyal Scotland. This conceit was vital to the Tory perception of the Scottish contribution to a wider British polity in the mid nineteenth century, although as Whatley makes clear, 'Burns had the capacity to divide as well as to unite. Public memory was pluralist, not monolithic.' The politically abrasive Burns was never fully expunged from the record.[85]

The religious component of Burns's identity, with the democratic intellectualism of his Presbyterian inheritance complicating the appropriation of his memory by ministers in Ulster as 'the "fountainhead of Ulster-Scottish identity"' who 'symbolised a former way of life, and where it was required, a distinct Presbyterian identity in Ireland', highlights how faith provided a rather different focus for political identity than that supplied by social circumstance.[86] Indeed while republicanism offered a secular mode of moral regeneration, the religious counterpoint to this conceit was a conviction in postmillenialism, as the essay by **E. Wyn James** elucidates.

This belief structure provided a narrative of Christ's return only after a period of gospel government. This created the space for humans to help hasten Christ's return by working to spread the Christian creed. In this belief system hymns became not just an expression of Christian faith but a vehicle for the radical moral regeneration of mankind, and a mechanism to bring about the end days. It is in this light that James provides a sustained reading of William Williams of Pantycelyn's Methodist hymn 'O'er those gloomy hills of darkness', regarding it as 'a mature expression of a decade and more of reflection by Pantycelyn on the "Puritan Hope" and the certain success of the Christian gospel worldwide in the "last days".'[87]

The essay also illustrates how evangelical politics focused energy on reshaping local society and the imperial dominion. In the case of Pantycelyn this concern was expressed through his involvement in the colonial mission into Georgia of the Methodist circle surrounding the Countess of Huntingdon. 'O'er those gloomy hills of darkness' was expressive of the increasingly Abolitionist credentials of the circle and had an extended influence in the nineteenth century. Indeed, James contends,

> there had been a slow but steady growth of radicalism in [Welsh Calvinistic] Methodist ranks throughout the first half of the nineteenth century, and one could argue that nothing had put them more on that road than the opposition to transatlantic slavery that had first been articulated in Welsh in the works of William Williams of Pantycelyn.[88]

The personal cost of confronting this kind of social orthodoxy and challenging the political verities of the period has been emphasized by Mark Philp, who has written cogently of the fragility of reform.[89] The psychological importance of developing a community of support accounts for the attention given in later chapters in this volume on the variety of vehicles for the radical voice. Indeed the geography of utterance is central to any understanding of the radical constituencies as they emerged across the islands in this period. One of the central ways in which a disparate radical community might find fraternal encouragement was through renditions of political verse and song. In this, print culture became a vital conduit of the burgeoning radical imaginary.

In retrieving a sense of the regional print cultures in which the radical constituency operated it is helpful to set Jones's dissection of the sources for ballads in Wales alongside **Marion Löffler's** analysis of Welsh-language poetry in the serial publications which were part of the Welsh discourse. As she notes, one result of the fractured communication lines within the country was a dispersion of Welsh poems and songs between titles located on the English side of the border, old almanacs and new, radical but short-lived, Welsh-language periodicals. Their concern was, Löffler argues, to construct a common conception of the national past as well as to transfer a new ideology into an old language. While anti-war sentiments were strongly expressed in the 1790s and the new periodicals carried religious poetry that conveyed political meaning, they also celebrated the British royal family in verse. The apogee of the radical moment here arrived with the publication of a translation of the 'Marseillaise', but by 1796, Löffler notes Wales was 'bereft of an indigenous periodical literature once more.'[90] Without a political or educational focus, the vitality of the fragile radical movement here depended directly on the health of the serials which commented on politics, transmitted ideas and provided emotional support to those espousing the cause. Without the means of communication, the nascent political community withered.

While the scale of publication was dwarfed by material in Welsh, **Niall Ó Ciosáin** makes a substantial case for the political vitality of printed works in Scots Gaelic. Their political character was, however, conservative and evangelical, more than subversive and republican, and the predominant audience, derived from a close study of extant subscription lists was, he concludes, 'overwhelmingly rural in location', and commonly farmers by occupation.[91] The only hint of the radical voice he has heard echo in the corpus, however, concerns a nostalgia for highland dress and custom, and some bitter criticism of the Clearances. Similarly, the efforts of the United Irish to use the Irish language to mobilize support were virtually non-existent. Of *Bolg an tSolair*, their short-lived Irish language periodical, Ó Ciosáin writes on p. 130 of this volume: 'The booklet is an engagement with Gaelic culture, but not an engagement with Irish speakers .... none of the texts has any overt political content, let alone the revolutionary ideas contained in the English-language propaganda of the United Irishmen'. The variegated nature of the politics of language in this decade are perhaps nowhere better illustrated than in Duncan Campbell's *Nuadh Orain Ghailach*, a Scots Gaelic song collection published by a soldier in the Fencibles while stationed in Cork. Politics, language and verse here convene to develop a rich music of loyalism.

The cautious conclusions offered by Ó Ciosáin are echoed in **Maura Cronin's** study of the spread and influence of political broadsides in Munster in the post-Union decades. Despite the heritage of radicalism left by the United Irish, the decapitation of the movement in the months before the Rising and the subsequent entrenchment of loyalist views espoused in such works as Richard Musgrave's denunciatory *Memoirs of the Different Rebellions in Ireland* (1801) ensured that the populace remained resolutely unmoved by radical exhortations. As Cronin recognizes, 'radicalisation was only surface deep. Catchphrases about reform and equality were no indication of any fundamental changes in popular attitudes'.[92] Indeed, despite the circulation of such iconic texts as the United Irish songbook, *Paddy's Resource* (first issued in 1795), Cronin is adamant that 'religious animosities and competition for land proved far more important than any new-fangled ideas about the rights of man.'[93] In this the essays by Ó Ciosáin and Cronin, taken together, are valuable reminders that however far the process of politicization may have left compelling textual evidence, high politics was still very much the preserve of a mobilized elite in the early nineteenth century.

The conservative forces in British society were by no means unaware of the subversive deployment by radicals of ephemeral elements in the wider print culture, and the campaign to alter the aesthetic sensibility of readers as a precursor to their political reformation. As **Dan Wall's** article documents, the Whig vehicle, the *Edinburgh Review* (founded 1802) was to have its market dominance and its artistic judgement challenged by a Tory voice that found a home in *Blackwood's Edinburgh Magazine* (founded 1817). In focusing on the moral as well as literary failures of Leigh Hunt, *Blackwood's* endeavoured to dismantle the public reputation of the 'Cockney School' of poets, and reframe the debate away from the political failings of the regime and instead around the moral turpitude of the radical voice.

One of the striking aspects of Wall's essay is, however, the anxiety that *Blackwood's* exuded that the republicans had won the propaganda, if not the political war. The willingness to accept Shelley's *Revolt of Islam* as a literary success at the same time as castigating Hunt's *Rimini* hints at how poetry had become a vehicle for utopian ideals. The failure of this vision of a republican fraternity spanning the islands – a United Republics of Britain and Ireland – was not a given, as *Blackwood's* knew, and conservatives needed to remain watchful across the literary battlefield.

The republican crusade in retrospect seems foolhardy perhaps, but it was an age in which the foolhardy seemed to be fated to succeed. Colonial America had seceded; monarchical France had collapsed; utopian visions proliferated and seemed tantalizingly close to realization. The slave trade was under terminal threat; the reform of the electoral system seemed imminent; the government was addressing the sectarian character of the state while confronting the atheist politics of the Jacobin regime. Social, economic and religious questions all seemed soluble, if the state could be redesigned and redirected. And to achieve this Hurdy Gurdy was to be put to use, playing a new tune for a new future. Even upon being declared guilty, the Hurdy Gurdy roused itself to a performance of resistance. Affidavits testified that he had 'played the most disrespectful and opprobrious tunes, against the King, Constitution, the Church, and the Law; and levelled many personal invectives against the Judges, the Jury and the witnesses'.[94] He subsequently declared, that despite his imprisonment,

> that so long as a peg shall be left in his barrel, he shall never in any wise change his tunes – but continue to play such free airs as he hath been accustomed to play, in honour of LIBERTY, and in furtherance of the RIGHTS OF MAN.[95]

Politicized and radicalized, the Hurdy Gurdy was still playing a revolutionary air.

1 'ENGLAND'S MEN WENT HEAD TO HEAD WITH THEIR OWN BRETHREN': THE WELSH BALLAD-SINGERS AND THE WAR OF AMERICAN INDEPENDENCE[1]

Ffion Mair Jones

Introduction

London, 1776. David Samwell (Dafydd Ddu Feddyg), who later came to fame as the surgeon on Captain Cooke's last voyage, penned a poem about the tumultuous events of the day.[2] By that time, the troubles brewing between Great Britain and her colonies in America since the 1760s regarding 'taxation without representation', as the popular slogan put it, were coming to a head. The first shots of what is now called the American War of Independence were fired in the towns of Lexington and Concord in Massachusetts in May 1775; by the summer of 1776, the Americans had issued their declaration of independence, and British troops under the leadership of William Howe had reached New York, ready to begin an intense military campaign.[3] Understandably, there was great interest in these events among the public in Britain, especially so in London, where strong objections were voiced against the coercive measures of Lord North's government by a group of political radicals. They believed that: 'As we would not suffer any man, or body of men to establish arbitrary power over us, we cannot acquiesce in any attempt to force it upon any part of our fellow-subjects.'[4]

This statement strongly reflects the concept of a British Constitution which was prevalent after the Glorious Revolution of 1688, responding, in many respects, to what was seen as the tyranny of Stuart rule. David Samwell's poem addresses this question of an Englishman's freedom within the Constitution and laws of Great Britain. He acknowledges fully that a king who misuses his position to oppress his people should be punished:

Ped fae ef yn cynnal ryw Ormes anwadal
Ni a ddylem ei ddial yn hafal i hon.

> (If [the king] should undertake some kind of wanton oppression
> we should wreak vengeance upon him in accordance with [the law].)

Samwell's view was that the current government (of which the king was head) was 'upholding the law' and that, therefore, there was no justification in accusing either George III or his servants of any wrongdoing.[5] Yet this was exactly what he saw happening in the London of 1776. His poem represents the voices of radicals railing against the government and trying to persuade and encourage others, more naive than themselves, to do likewise. Pleaders for 'Freedom', as they considered themselves, went 'among the innocent, to cause trouble, boldly and in defiance of the peace', and Samwell could only lament the fact that the 'stupidity of the ordinary man / could benefit others of such dubious behaviour'.[6] Extensive 'speech-making' was to be found in 'every tavern', and the shoemaker and other artisans were to be seen 'contending for the stories of / lying newspapers every morning, dreadful thing'.[7]

Only two copies of Samwell's poem survive. One is in the manuscript collection of Edward Jones (Bardd y Brenin), and it is easy to see that he – a man who later denounced the stonemason Edward Williams (Iolo Morganwg) to the authorities as a dangerous radical – would have appreciated Samwell's fears and anxieties about the extraordinary expansion of the public sphere in the London of the period. The other surviving version of the poem includes a note of introduction:

> Y Pennillion canlynol a wnaeth Dafydd ddû yn y Flwyddyn 1776 yn Llunden pan oedd fath chwerw ymddadlu yn Llundain drwy'r Deyrnas ynghylch Rhyfel America.
>
> (The following stanzas were composed by Dafydd Ddu in London in the year 1776 when there was such bitter contention in London throughout the kingdom regarding the American war.)

It appears that Samwell changed his view of the situation after writing the original note, amending it to suggest that there was contention not only in London but throughout the entire kingdom regarding this war. We do not know whether the poem reached Wales at the time it was created, but it appears that Samwell, by the time he had completed it, was of the opinion that the war was firing people's imaginations beyond the capital. His view would have resonated with two important twentieth-century Welsh historians. Both R. T. Jenkins and Gwyn Alf Williams argued that Wales woke up, politically, for the first time during the American Revolutionary period. These two, and others after them, acknowledge the part played by the Welsh ballad in this awakening.[8] Conversely, Stephen Conway, the author of a recent volume on the effect of the American war on the constituent parts of Britain, argues that 'Wales, though divided, was perhaps less excited by the conflict than any other country in the British Isles'.[9] This chapter moves from Samwell's London to Wales to consider the evidence for Welsh interest in the war, concentrating on the ballads which secured the attention of Jenkins and Williams, but discussing also a range of works in various other genres which developed alongside the ballads and may have influenced them.

Translated Pamphlets, 1775–6

The first ballad relating to the war was published in 1776. It is a poem complaining about a dearth of tobacco resulting from the dispute.[10] At least three further ballads were sung the following year.[11] The ballad-singers, however, were not the first Welsh people to take an interest in the American conflict. Welsh translators had been at work since 1775. During that year, William Pine, a bookseller in Bristol, published an anonymous Welsh translation of the Scotsman William Smith's *A Sermon On The Present Situation Of American Affairs*, originally published in the same year at Philadelphia.[12] Smith's work had swiftly crossed the Atlantic to Britain and Ireland where it was reprinted (again in 1775) in London, Dublin, Belfast, Cork and Bristol. In 1776 another edition appeared in Edinburgh. This pamphlet thus quickly spread to the four nations of the British Isles, and Wales was no exception.[13]

William Smith, ordained as a minister of the Church of England, was a provost at Philadelphia College.[14] His pamphlet, as befits a sermon, begins with a Biblical story, portraying the relationship of the Israelites and the Gileads in the Old Testament. Two and a half Israelite tribes settled on the eastern bank of the river Jordan (in a territory which became known as Gilead), opposite the other Israelite tribes, who inhabited the western bank. In order to celebrate their happiness in reaching the land of Gilead, these tribes began to raise a high altar, 'as an everlasting symbol of the fact that they belonged to the same nation, and were entitled to the same national and religious rights as their brothers among the other tribes'.[15] Unfortunately, the Israelites of the west bank misconstrued what had happened and raised 'a cry against them without delay. The hotheads of that day did not hesitate to call them rebels against the living God ... [and] because of this the entire audience of brother-tribes, who resided in Canaan, gathered together for war against their own flesh and blood'.[16] The relevance of the story is evident to anyone by now, but to emphasize his point, Smith laments in parenthesis '(and, alas, my God, that the example has been followed among the brother-tribes of our Israel in the mother country)'.[17] There is clear sympathy here for the colonists of America (the 'American Gilead'), whose 'act ... of godliness and love' was 'misconstrued' by the inhabitants of their mother country, the 'Britannic Israel'.[18]

The sermon goes on to show how faithful and partisan towards Britain her American colonies are. It traces the history of the settlement, when the Americans showed real courage by pioneering in a deserted land, 'taking no heed of the inconvenience of our situation', and refusing to be 'stifled by fear'.[19] It shows how they responded to Britain's plea for military aid, fighting alongside the mother-country during the Seven Years' War, and doing so with such bravery as to win the praise of their mother-country as well as a substantial monetary prize.[20] The Americans' 'altars' are all testimony to their 'unity and love' towards Britain, according to Smith, and their refusal to repay taxes as demanded during the 1760s was not an act of disrespect towards Britain but a sign of their understanding of and adherence to the British 'altar', namely the Constitution established following the Glorious Revolution of 1688.[21] This Constitution noted the right of Britons to freedom and representation: 'even our refusal [to pay taxes] was ample proof of our respect towards the altar itself'.[22] After describing the conflict in these terms, Smith goes on to express, with real emotion, his grief at seeing plans for war afoot between 'brothers'.[23] The threat from beyond the 'free' British nation state – that posed by the Catholic European states – here raises its head, Smith arguing strongly for the 'reunion ... of the members' of the Empire 'as the only safety-net for freedom and Protestantism' in the face of 'those kingdoms who are the enemies of freedom, truth and mercy'.[24]

In the final section of his sermon, delivered as an address to Congress, Smith sets out the dilemma which now faces the American people. He is not in favour of lying down and letting the privileges and 'freedom' so revered by open-minded Englishmen of the day be put aside. The Americans should be sure that 'this vast land, in ages to come, will be filled and adorned with virtuous and wise people; enjoying FREEDOM and all its associated blessings', and not 'covered with a species of men worse than the savages of the desert, since they once "knew what pertained to their happiness and peace but had suffered them to be hidden from their view"'.[25] Thinking forward to the future like this was one of the tactics of radicals such as Thomas Paine, who argued that independence was inevitable, and that the current generation should ensure it for the sake of those to follow them:

> I once felt all that kind of anger, which a man ought to feel, against the mean principles that are held by the Tories. A noted one, who kept a tavern at Amboy, was standing at his door, with as pretty a child in his hand, about eight or nine years old, as most I ever saw; and after speaking his mind as freely as he thought was prudent, finished with this unfatherly expression, 'Well, give me peace in my days.' Not a man lives on the continent, but fully believes that separation must some time or other finally take place, and a generous parent would have said, 'if there must be trouble, let it be in my days, that my child may have peace;' and this single reflection, well applied, is sufficient to awaken every man to duty.[26]

Smith, however, backs away from this view, recommending that his listeners should accept 'that the power of every state, under God, is contained in their UNITY' and that the two sides should accept the 'faults, and even the differing beliefs' of each other.[27] Despite this loyal ending, his sermon raises questions about the relationship of both Britain and America with the Constitution – the alleged instrument of 'Freedom' – expressing criticism of the behaviour of the British government, but at the same time a strong resistance to war.

In 1776, an anonymous Welsh translation appeared of a pamphlet entitled *The Rise, Progress, and Present State Of The Dispute Between The People of America, And the Administration*, also produced anonymously, and probably composed a year earlier.[28] The translator's address to his native Welsh audience explains that 'there is a great deal of talk about the war between this country and America, many not knowing its true cause'.[29] He suggested that 'the account would be of benefit to the Welsh in their own language' and noted 'that the language that I put in it will be comprehensible to everyone'.[30] The printer of the work, Dafydd Jones of Trefriw, however, clearly felt that an apology was needed for the poor quality of the typesetting. He noted in stanzas at the end of the first part of the pamphlet that 'there were not enough letters / to do this without fault'.[31] This technical deficiency contributes to making this pamphlet poorer in quality and considerably less lucid than that published by William Pine in Bristol. It is much more controversial in its contents, too, and makes no attempt to adopt the allegedly unbiased attitude of Smith (who understood that he had been called to address Congress as one who was 'above all party politics').[32] It originated in Britain, rather than in America and, although its author remained anonymous, a note on the cover of the pamphlet states that he was 'the Bishop of —'. The voices of Church of England clergymen were, on the whole, strongly raised against the 'revolt' of the Americans, but there were some exceptions, among them Jonathan Shipley, who had been Bishop of St. Asaph since 1769. Shipley produced a sermon for one of the meetings of the Society for the Propagation of the Gospel in 1773.[33] This was composed in very moderate language, and purposely rejected any temptation to blame the executive for the troubles in America. Shipley nonetheless suggested that Britain should not exert excessive control over her American colonies, and that she should base her rule on friendship and understanding of the potential for a mutually profitable relationship. The following year, Shipley wrote a speech intended for the members of the House of Lords, arguing, this time in a more openly critical tone, that Britain was mistreating her colonies, and had sacrificed a previously happy relationship, which had depended on such things as trade which was beneficial to both sides.[34] Shipley's ideas were widely circulated through imprints of the *Sermon* and the *Speech* in the form of pamphlets in both Britain and America, the effort to publish aided (especially in America) by Benjamin Franklin. Franklin was particularly interested in influencing public opinion on both sides of the Atlantic, trying to promote the cause against Britain among his fellow-Americans on the one hand and, on the other, attempting to persuade the British of the justice of the colonists' protest against the government of Great Britain.[35] Franklin's influence on Shipley was strong: he was a close friend of the Archbishop and spent time at the latter's home in Twyford, Hampshire.[36] Some believed that Franklin was the true author of Shipley's *Speech*. There was similar confusion regarding the authorship of *The Rise, Progress, and Present State Of The Dispute*. Several names have been suggested, Shipley's among them. Thomas R. Adams, in a bibliographical survey of the pamphlets composed during the period of the dispute between Great Britain and America, argues that Franklin was certainly involved with the latter pamphlet, which is staunchly anti-ministerial and extremely critical of Britain's attitude towards her north American colonies.[37] Adams also suggests that if Shipley was the author, he could have arranged a Welsh translation of the work for his own diocese. Unfortunately, it is not possible to make any definite claims about the authorship of *The Rise, Progress, and Present State Of The Dispute*. As far as can be judged from the translation, it is a much more amorphous composition than Shipley's other works; it does not contain the arguments central to his other two pamphlets; and the language is much more fiery, even when compared to the second of Shipley's other pamphlets, which continues to take up a moderate and careful stance towards the American dispute.

If the pamphlet did not reach the translator through Shipley's hand ('Since these pages came to my hand in the English tongue'), it seems likely that there was another person of some standing who was working in favour of the American cause in north Wales.[38] Some credit can be given to Dafydd Jones for realizing that this was a pamphlet that would sell. It is not difficult to imagine that sections of the second part, where the testimony of soldiers at the battles of Concord and Lexington are reproduced, would have been attractive to the audience which Jones wished to capture.[39]

The Earlier Ballads, 1775–8

Very few pamphlets were translated into Welsh, considering the sheer volume of material produced on either side of the Atlantic.[40] Nonetheless, the ballads composed early in the period of the troubles suggest that the extensive debate about the rights and duties of the British government and the Americans alike left its mark on rural Wales. It appears that the ballad-writers familiarized themselves with both sides of the argument, attempting to present a balanced picture of the dispute rather than prioritizing one side over the other. A ballad pamphlet containing the work of the poet Hugh Jones of Llangwm in Denbighshire, possibly published in 1777, opens with a poem in the voice of the mother country, Britain, and is followed by another poem presented as the 'response' of the child, America.[41] Hugh Jones chose to engage with the central metaphor of the dispute – that which saw the relationship between Britain and her colonies in North America as that of a mother and child. This is a metaphor employed and discussed by pamphleteers on both sides, almost without exception. In the first poem, the 'Mother', Britain, makes her complaint. She has been a very generous parent to the Dissenting dregs (as they are here portrayed) who left her shores in order to colonize America. She instated Church of England personnel in America and aided in protecting the youthful colonies from the military threat of France and Spain during the Seven Years' War. She was generous also in sending merchandise such as wheat, butter, cheese, iron and lead to America, although she did so often at the expense of her own needy population. The ungrateful response of the Americans to this generosity was to initiate a war. The following lines probably refer to the first shots of the conflict, fired at Concord and Lexington north of Boston:

> Dinistro fy ngwŷr oedd pur i chwi hyd ange
> Efo'r gwnn ag efo'r cledde y bore yn ddi bwyll,
> Mawr dwyll a fu'r daith,
> Lladd gwragedd a phlant, llawer cant yr ydwi'n ofni
> A'n gelanedd y leni, drygioni drwy grêd,
> Yr ydwi'n gweled y gwaith,
> Ow! lladd fy holl wŷr trwy nerth plwm a dûr,
> Y rhain oedd ichwi'n bûr, ow fy Offisers mwŷnion,
> Sy a'u gwaed fel lli'r afon, nid cyfion mo'm cûr.

> (You destroyed my men who were true to you till death
> with the rifle and the sword in the morning, without stopping to think.
> It was an act of great deceit
> to kill women and children – several hundreds, I fear,
> shall fall dead this year, evil [spreading] through Christendom.
> I can see the deed!
> Oh! the killing of all my men by the power of lead and steel,
> the blood of those who were true to you, oh my sweet officers,
> flows like a river (my pain does not do it justice).)

Hugh Jones could have learned a little about these events from reading *Dechreuad, cynnydd, a chyflwr presenol, y dadl rhwng pobl America a'r llywodraeth*, which represents the testimony of soldiers on both sides, including the American Elijah Sanderson, who was, he says

> ar dir cyffredin Lexington, boreu y 19 Ebrill rhagddywededig ... ac a welais gorph helaeth o'r rheolaidd Fyddinoedd, yn cychwyn at gwmpeini Lexington ... mi a glywais un o'r rheolaidd, yr hwn a gymmerais ei fod yn Swyddwr yn d'wedyd, ("damn them ni a'u cawn hwy.) ac yn fuan y rheolaidd, a waeddasant yn uchel, a redasant, ac a saethasant at gwmpeini Lexington, pa rain ni saethasant unwaith, cyn i'r rheolaidd saethu attynt hwy.
> Wyth o gwmpeini Lexington a laddwyd ... ac amryw archollwyd.[42]

(on common ground at Lexington on the morning of 19 April in the aforementioned year [1775] ... and saw a substantial body of the regular army making for the Lexington company... . I heard one of the regulars, whom I took to be an officer, saying 'Damn them, we'll get them!', and soon the regulars shouted out loud, ran and shot at the Lexington company, who did not once draw fire before they were fired at by the regulars.

Eight among the Lexington company were killed ... and many were injured.)

Hugh Jones could also have been influenced by newspaper reports regarding these events. In a study of the way in which the war was reported in British newspapers, Troy Bickham has suggested that reports of this conflict at Lexington and Concord were strongly biased by patriot American influence. Indeed, it was this version of events which reached Britain first. Reports offered outrageous estimates of the numbers killed and maimed (which is perhaps reflected in the words 'to kill women and children' in the ballad). Hugh Jones shows an awareness of losses to the king's army – or the 'regulars', to use the pamphlet's term – as well, however. Three British soldiers died in Concord and nine were injured; only one injury befell the troops at Lexington.[43] After this beginning a serious war was inevitable. The poet faces this reality and considers what advice he should give to his audience 'should war come'.[44] This suggests that the poem belongs to a period before its likely publication date of 1777. The poet reflects on preparations for war, speaking to a domestic Welsh audience, although he does so in the guise of an address by Britain to her colonies. His advice is for the Welsh to pray for God's aid and support, since, in war, 'Christ can give us comfort like the ship of Peter'; and 'the hand of the Almighty, anointed one, / is strong and merciful to us'.[45] The Welsh have no need to fear the arms of America, which is unable to 'blind us or to overcome us in conflict'.[46]

The second poem in the same pamphlet belongs clearly to the year 1777, and was composed expressly for the purpose of 'answering' the first poem.[47] It is obviously related to the first ballad, although the latter may have been conceived originally as a poem in its own right, especially if we take into account the possible gap between the composition dates of the two (the second half of 1775 and perhaps the second half of 1777). The second poem claims to be the work of a 'young Man who lives in America', and makes a clear attempt to answer the 'points' raised by the figure of the Mother in the first poem.[48] For example, the American child argues that his people gave honourable payment to Britain for 'your corn and your butter, reluctant ardour, and your cheese', by sending back to the mother-country 'sugar, prattle-leaves or tea; / rum, brandy and wine'.[49] Nevertheless, he notes with astonishment that the Britons are bold enough now to attempt to 'put a tax upon every county in the land of America'.[50] The 'young man' presents America's cause for anger towards Britain very strongly.[51] The Americans are largely a people turned out of Britain because of their religious beliefs; Britain let them pioneer in an uncivilized land, full of threatening Indians; she showed them further disrespect by using their land as a dumping ground for the crooks of her own society – people found guilty of murder or other crimes. By referring to the practice of transporting criminals to America, the ballad-writer expresses a genuine complaint in the New World: in May 1751, Benjamin Franklin had suggested in 'Rattlesnakes for felons' that America should send rattlesnakes to Britain in payment for the criminals she sent to America.[52] The greatest injustice from the young man's point of view is that Britain, once it realized the value and wealth of America, began to show friendliness towards its people, expecting countless favours from them in return. The narrator is not foolish enough to give in to their flattery. Instead, he states his intention of using the American population of British criminals as weapons in a war against the mother-country:

> Pob lleidar ceffyle a phoccede a phob cêr,
> O Loeger dros ddyfnder a ddaeth,
> Cyn talo ni drethi y rheini wna i rhann,
> Fe guran pan gofian ddau gwaeth.

> (Every horse-thief, tackle-thief and pickpocket
> who came over the sea from England,
> will play their part before we pay taxes –
> strike twice as hard when they remember.)

He is relentless and ferocious in his attitude towards England, encouraging his own people to go to battle against the English:

> Dowch byddwch yn bûr i drîn arfe dûr,
> Ceiff Lloeger ar ddyrnod gryn gafod o gûr,
> I gwŷr chwerw a garcharwn neu a laddwn trwy lîd,
> A'u herlid, traws ofid, tro sur;
> Rhown iddyn safn goch, mi lladdwn fel moch,
> Mewn gwaed y cânt orwedd, bydd rhyfedd eu rhoch,
> Ow'r loewgoch hên Loeger, ceiph llawer o'ch llu,
> I bradychu a'u trybaeddu tra bôch.

> (Come, be loyal in handling steel weapons!
> At a strike England shall have a real shower of pain;
> with fury we shall imprison or murder her bitter men
> and pursue them – what a cruel care, what a sour turn of events!
> We shall make their jaws red, we shall kill them like pigs,
> in blood they shall lie, their grunting will amaze.
> Oh, shining, redcoated old England, many of your army
> shall be betrayed and shattered as you live!)

Then, in the final stanza the young man, whose attack had hitherto concentrated solely on England, turns to address Wales too. The proposed war will have an impact on American trade with Wales ('Welsh corn shall not come to this land, I swear'), and the threat of destruction and death is made real to a Welsh audience.[53] Either through the grief that will befall families from losing members involved in fighting for the king in America, or through the possibility that the hostile Americans could stage a landing on Welsh soil, the poem's Welsh audience face danger: 'There shall be a slaughter, ugly shouting, that will terrorize every army, / every Welsh person, every family, every father'.[54] As well as introducing elements of the political dispute between the two sides, this poem also makes the reality of war between Britain and America alive to its Welsh audience, and even raises the possibility that Britain's enemies could land on her territory and threaten her people and property directly.

Almanacs, 1777–9

In 1778 Hugh Jones sang again on the subject of the war, this time with a very balanced awareness within the compass of a single poem of the deficiencies of both sides. 'It was not one party ... that sinned against Jesus' to cause this war, he said, but 'The two parties daggled and went awry and darkened their names'.[55] England was beset by 'opinions and falsehood' (the word 'Opiniwne' in the original refers to the evils of Dissent, which encouraged people to become opinionated), and the Americans by 'inconsiderate stubbornness'.[56] By 1778 Hugh Jones was aware of the fiery nature of the debate against the war. He knew that, as a poet, he was one of the spokespersons of his society on the matter, in competition with many a 'dear astrologer' and other poets who had and continued to attempt to interpret the events of the war and to foresee how it would develop.[57] The almanac-writers had been referring to America with increasing interest since 1777 when John Prys prophesied that a particular eclipse of the sun during the year would be 'terrifying to many lands in America. There shall be great commotion regarding wars and the deaths of renowned men in those parts of this world, because the eclipse is in their meridian'.[58] In the same year, Mathew William published an almanac entitled *Britanus Merlinus Liberatus: Sef, Amgylchiadau Tymhorol ac Wybrennol: Neu , Almanac am y Flwyddyn o Oed ein Iachawdwr, 1777*, in Carmarthen, the first to be printed by him. The American war was on his agenda as well, with a reference to it in the 'Register' stating that two years had passed since 'the war between England and America started'.[59] He also included a poem by W. Williams, which 'pray[s] intently for peace between England and America'.[60] Williams was concerned that 'Old France and Spain expect to have some prey yonder' (a threat to which we will return below),[61] and felt very strongly that the Americans needed to acknowledge their long-lasting debt to England and should make peace with her:

O ymostyngwch bellach, gwenewch eryd sychau o'ch cledd,
Mae yspryd brenin Lloegr o hyd yn dewis hedd.

(Oh! yield yourselves now; make ploughshares of your sword;
the spirit of the King of England always chooses peace.)

This lack of sympathy with the American cause suggests that Williams had loyalist leanings. Although conciliatory in tone, his final stanza names the various religious sects at work in Welsh communities, suggesting that he saw the sympathy of Dissenters with the Americans as a potential evil:

Dewch *fabtists*, dewch *ddisenters*, dewch *gwacers* yn gytun,
Ac eglwys Lloegr ffurfiol, a'i *methodists* yn un;
I wylo wrth yr orsedd ar frys i ddifodd tân,
A lysg, os ni ddiffoddir, holl Ewrop fawr yn lân.

(Come Baptists, come Dissenters, come Quakers in accord,
and the formal Church of England, and her Methodists as one;
to cry by the throne in haste to extinguish the fire
which will, unless quenched, utterly burn great Europe in its entirety.)

In 1778 Mathew William provided a description of the geography of the American colonies, 'Since every class of man has his eyes on the current unnatural war [there]';[62] and also an estimate of the 'cost of the war up to 1777', which he set at £5,000,000, a sum '… collected from the inhabitants of the kingdom through tax, tolls, stamps, &c.'.[63] By 1778, William's almanac had sellers in north Wales for the first time, in addition to his established agents in the south of the country, able to advance the process of forging a more inclusive, all-Welsh response to the American crisis.

The most intriguing example of an astrologer's efforts to deal with the topic of the war appears in John Prys's almanac for 1779.[64] In his conclusions regarding the 'Four Quarters of the Year', Prys quotes several dark couplets, offering his own expertise in interpreting them.[65] The first is by 'One of the astrological writers of England', and is translated into Welsh as follows by Prys:[66]

Llygredig Lloeger o Adwyth,
Cymru yn llawn o'r un llwyth.

(England is corrupted by evil,
 Wales is full of the same load.)

Prys suggests that the meaning of the couplet is

fod y deyrnas sef Lloeger a Chymru dan orddwyad drwmlwyth drethiad er's rhai blynyddoedd, ond i Dduw byddo'r diolch mae pawb etto yn cyrraidd talu yn rhesymol diddig ... a gobeithio y cynhaliant yw talu felly rhag llaw, ac nid mynaid ben yn erfydd ym mysc eu gilydd fel ac yr aethant yn *America*, ac i'r hên ddaroganau gymeryd eu lle. (Mai Lloeger hên, a'i llygra ei hûn.)

(that the kingdom, namely England and Wales, has been under the oppression of a heavy weight of taxation for some years, but, thanks be to God, everyone still manages to pay reasonably contentedly ... and let us hope that they shall continue to pay them [i.e. the taxes] thus hereafter and shall not go head to head among themselves as they have done in America, allowing the old prophesies to be realized (that Old England shall corrupt itself).)

The implication in the couplet quoted ('that Old England shall corrupt itself') is that the country's demise is the responsibility of its own people; indeed, the couplet may originate in an earlier situation of civil war. A variant form appears in the work of the Civil War poet, Wiliam Phylip, who lamented the self-destruction of the England of his day: 'And strong England corrupting its power'.[67] Having considered the possibility that it is the moral deficiency of the population at large which threatens the destruction of England (offering the couplet as a kind of prophesy of another civil war), Prys changes tack:

> Ond rhai eraill sy'n dywedyd fel hyn,
>   Mai pen brig a dyscgedigion,
>   Lloeger ei hun sy'n llygru hon,
>   Trwyth oer lwyth, trethi ar lêd,
>   Troi'n ddilwydd dramor ddeilied
>   Hyn ar led fi ddyweda,
>   Wnaeth wŷr croes yn 'Merica.

> (But others say like this,
>   that it is the mighty and learned men
>   of England itself that corrupt her;
>   it was a cold tribal concoction of taxes far and wide,
>   and the ill-fated expulsion of citizens abroad,
>   (this I say far and wide),
>   that made men angry in America.)

His message now is that the destruction of England is not caused by an internal corruption arising from the deficiencies of the ordinary people, but rather by the policies of the British government.

Prys's work attempts to interpret truisms, prophecies and scraps of poetry of uncertain origin. Hugh Jones's poem 'Cerdd newydd ym mherthynas y rhyfel presennol yr America, yn gosod allan mai oferedd yw daroganau a brudiau ac yn dangos mai ordinhad Duw yw'r cwbl', decries prophecies and interpretations of this kind:

> Medd gair yr Ysgrythure, 'Drygionus yw'r drogane, eirie oerion',
> Rhai'n sôn am dri o seithie sy'n oedran Aer uchelne', gole gwiwlon;
> Medd un, 'Lloger hen a'i llygra ei hun'; medd y llall, 'Mae goleuni yn arwydd inni
> Fod Crist o ddifri' yn mynd i dorri dyn';
> Pwy ŵyr yn yr oesoedd yma pa beth arwydda yr un?
> Duw mawr, pan altro ei wedd a'i wawr, a feder chwalu'r byd o'i ddeutu,

Pob gwlad a theulu na chân' aneddu un awr
Pryd na bo dri o seithie nac wythe, oer leinie, ar lawr.[68]

(The word of the Scriptures says, 'The prophecies are evil, cold words',
some say three sevens is the age of the Heir of high Heaven, that kindly light;
one says, 'Old England will corrupt itself'; another says 'There is a light which is a sign for us
that Christ is truly going to bring down man';
who knows in this day and age what any of these mean?
Great God, when he alters his appearance and his mien, can destroy the world around him;
neither country nor family can live one hour
whether there be three sevens or eights, cold words, on earth.)

In his opinion, there is no place for prophecies. Men should rather accept the war as sent by God, 'who has decreed killing and murder' with the intention of 'making us pure so as to bring about our improvement'.[69] This is Hugh Jones's contribution to a public debate which he sees as increasingly complex and pluralistic.

The Broadening of the Conflict, 1778

In the summer of 1778 the nature of the war changed entirely when France joined on the side of the Americans, the exact outcome that W. Williams, the poet quoted from Mathew William's almanac, had feared. In many respects, singing about the American war became easier after this change. There had been regular and uncompromising battling between two of Europe's greatest powers – Protestant Britain and Catholic France – throughout the eighteenth century and before; so when France joined the war on America's side, it was possible to avoid the difficulty of singing about war between brothers, and look at the conflict instead as one in a series of European wars. The ease with which the American war could be interpreted in this way can be seen from a copy made by David Ellis, vicar of Amlwch (and later Criceth) of a matin carol composed by Hugh Hughes (Y Bardd Coch o Fôn) in 1755 – during the Seven Years' War.[70] The poem complains about the sins of the Britons, encouraging them to 'desist from their pride, which is too great'.[71] And yet there is no doubt that God is more than prepared to support Britain against French hosts in the poet's opinion:

Duw cynnal ein lluoedd, ar Dir ac ar Foroedd
A threfna'n byddinoedd trwy'r siroedd a'i sain;
Dy law fendigedig fo'n ffrwyno'r llu ffreinig,
Rhag bod yn frawedig i Frydain.

(God, keep our men, on land and on sea,
and arrange our armies with their speeches through the counties;
may your glorious hand rein in the French host
lest they should cause terror to Britain.)

David Ellis, a diligent collector, was noted for his biased comments on the poems he transcribed. In another context, Iolo Morganwg had questioned the impartiality of Ellis's opinion in notes on poems collected by him. Iolo claimed that this vicar, as one of the servants of the Church of England, decided on the value of a poet's work on the basis of his religious affiliations, and that as a rule he would dismiss Dissenter-poets.[72] The note which Ellis wrote at the end of Hugh Hughes's poem suggests the same kind of High Church and Conservative prejudice in his attitude towards the American war:

> N.B. – Y Carol hwn a wnaed yn nechrau'r Rhyfel 1755 ac a ail 'sgrifennwyd yn amser y Rhyfel tostaf, sef Gwrthryfel Traeturiaid America, a'r Gelynion tauog o Ffrainc ac Hispaen yn cymmeryd eu plaid hwynt yn y fl. 1780. gennyf fi Dafydd Ellis, Curad Amlwch yn Swydd Fôn.
>
> (N.B. – This carol was sung at the beginning of the war in 1755 and was rewritten at the time of the bitterest war, namely the revolt of the American traitors and the slavish enemies from France and Spain who took their part, in the year 1780, by me Dafydd Ellis, curate of Amlwch in Anglesey.)

In the British press there were now regular attempts to portray the war in the light of old European rivalries between Britain on the one hand and France and Spain on the other.[73] In a ballad commemorating the landing of the American privateer, John Paul Jones (born in Scotland), at Whitehaven in Cumbria in April 1778, this new dimension is presented forcefully.[74] The indignation of people throughout Britain was ignited by Paul Jones's attack, and numerous reports about the event appeared in newspapers throughout the kingdom.[75] Ellis Roberts's ballad on the topic was an attempt to inform his monolingual Welsh audience in north Wales of the event and of the danger posed by the activities of Paul Jones, who was intent on wreaking revenge upon the British 'because of the American war':[76]

> Mae Cymru wael dôn yn arfon a mo[n]
> Heb glwed fawr son
> Am Bol Sion yn siwr
> Na chanfod mor llu sy ar gefn y Mor du
> Tu ag atyn nhw'n gry am dynny hyd y dwr.
>
> (There are Welshmen, sad to say, in Caernarvonshire and Anglesey
> who have doubtless heard very little
> about Paul Jones;
> nor have they seen the host on the ridge of the dark sea
> which is about to draw forcefully towards them across the water.)

This ballad's appeal lies in the portrayal of the threat and in the novelty of the news which it imparts. Paul Jones is portrayed as a lackey of the French king –

one of a line of hated tyrants portrayed as servants of the 'Great Prince', Belial, in the Welsh literary tradition from the days of Huw Morys and Ellis Wynne onwards.[77] According to Ellis Roberts, Paul Jones was given refuge by Louis XVI, 'King of the Underworld' and a descendant of Louis XIV, the 'Roi Soleil' who had so incensed Ellis Wynne and his generation.[78] He was provided with better weapons than he possessed at the beginning of his evil campaign against the harbours of Britain, namely 'Fireworks and shining black powder / to burn black-headed Wales to smithereens'.[79] Like the young man in the ballad by Hugh Jones, Llangwm (see above), Paul Jones is seen by Ellis Roberts as posing a threat specifically against Wales. From reading contemporary accounts which noted Jones's intention 'to alarm the coasts of Wales, Ireland, the Western parts of Scotland and the North', it appears that the poet was responding to common fears.[80] The threat to what is local and well-known is furthered in the portrayal of the hostile relationship between the Machiavellian figure of Louis XVI and Wales:

> Rhoes iddo'r Llonge cryfa
> A haid or lladron pene
> Aflawena oedd yn y Wlâd
> Rhoes fendith i pol yno
> Dy[m]unodd lwyddiant iddo
> I lâdd pob Cymro ai brifo a brâd.
>
> (Louis gave Paul Jones the sturdiest of ships
> and a host of the worst and cruellest thieves
> in the country.
> He gave Paul his blessing there
> and wished him success
> in killing and maiming every Welshman through treachery.)

France's support of Paul Jones was known from the time of his attack on Whitehaven onwards.[81] The nature of the relationship intensified during 1779 (after the publication of this ballad), when reports began to circulate of his alleged visits to Louis XVI's palace at Versailles, and of the way in which he was honoured by the king and queen.[82] By 1780, Jones, 'now the most general topic of conversation', was being portrayed as a romantic hero, *à l'aise* feasting, writing poems and paying court to the ladies in Versailles.[83] Ellis Roberts, however, saw things differently. His ballad centres on depicting Jones as a direct French threat against Wales. England is only once named in the poem, and the meaning of that reference is not clear.

Having terrified his audience, Ellis Roberts goes on to persuade them of their ability to resist this dual threat from Jones and his 'Father', Louis. He had heard that Jones was born in Anglesey but that he had been transported to America as a criminal. Should he land in his own patrimony, therefore, he could be hanged for his earlier crimes:

> Er î fod on ŵr crŷ ag yn lleidr mawr hŷ
> Ni bydd ar un ll[?u] ddim pallu am ladd po[l]
> Ni hwyrach mynn y crwytgi
> Ddw'd etto iŵ Wlâd i grogi
> Am ddrygionî dreidi drŵg
> Am gadw meddwl creulon
> I ladd i hen gym'dogion
> Ag yn ei Galon y mae'r gŵg.
>
> (Although he is a strong man and a big, bold thief,
> no host will desist from murdering Paul.
> Perhaps the foul rover
> wishes to return to his land to hang
> for his misdemeanours and evil pranks,
> or harbours cruel thoughts
> of killing former neighbours –
> there is wrath in his heart.)

The poem ends by maintaining that 'blessed God can protect the old Britons / so that this intention is not carried out'.[84]

Militia and Impressment Ballads, 1778–83

Britain, land of the old Britons, could thus unite against the Catholic French enemy, whereas it had been harder to do so when the war against America was an internal, civil war. The years from 1778 onwards were notable for the increase in military recruitment, made necessary to answer the call for soldiers to fight against the disloyal Americans. The militia were embodied for the first time in the five Welsh counties of Merioneth, Anglesey, Montgomeryshire, Cardigan and Radnor, and Welsh ballad-writers reflected the new process of military recruitment in their poems. There is much less deference to the process itself and to the forces of church and king in these poems than in the ballads of 1790–1815, when large-scale militarization next took place.[85] One poem by Ellis Roberts mocks those taken away as soldiers: they are the traditional idlers who get their deserts at last by being led away by the constables of the army or navy, and forced, for once, to do some work.[86] Like the Chérubin of Beaumarchais and Mozart's Cherubino, these men are teased by the poet:

> Yyfydion [sic.] penffolion diffydd,
> Sydd yn hoffi cael diogi bob dydd,
> Trwm newydd mewn sadrwydd mawr sydd,
> Pwy bynnag rai beunydd sy'n rhydd,
> Ni chan mwy lonydd yn y wlad,
> I bori yn rhwydd mo'u bara rhad,
> Mae amal Gwnstabl drwg eu nad,
> A'u nwyde brys am wneud eu brad.

(Foolish-headed, faithless madmen,
who like to laze around every day,
grave news and great sadness is nigh –
those who are free all day long
will no longer be left in peace in the countryside
to graze without effort on their cheap bread.
Many a constable, with wretched cry
and swift passions, will want to see them betrayed.)

At other times, it is those who were left behind that are teased. A poem by the same author makes the figure of the ballad-seller – who would have declaimed it aloud in fairs and marketplaces before selling copies of it to the listeners – the subject of ridicule, scorning also his typical female audience. The latter have been left by their lovers who have enlisted as soldiers. So desirous are they, however, of finding a man that even a useless cripple like the seller now attracts their attention:

Bydd saith yn fuan agŵedd egwan
At un Crupl [?swil] yn droppian
Neu'n calyn Dynan di nerth
Mewn odfa bur ddi ymadferth
Rhowch drisswll iddo o drafferth
Yn gydnerth bod ag un.[87]

(Just then, seven girls – what a feeble sight! –
Dump themselves beside one [?poor] cripple,
or follow a puny wretch
to a quite hopeless dalliance.
Give him three shillings for his troubles,
robustly, every one.)

On another day, however, Ellis Roberts could express anger about the practice of enforced recruitment, or impressment. In a poem published in 1780, he describes very vividly the actions of a naval captain named 'Trodn', who landed in Anglesey and began taking men prisoner to his ships at Porth Cemaes and Amlwch.[88] It appears that the captain's fortunes deteriorated after that. The people rose in riot against him, and he had to flee back to sea, 'Lest he should be killed dead' and 'his throat broken'.[89] It is obvious where the poet's sympathies lie:

Na ddelo byth mo'i ffasiwn,
Ir lan ar wndwn lu di-râs,
Y pethe anhydyn Cethin câs,
Rhai na waeth ganddyn ar un trô,
O bethe'r fall pa beth a fô,
Na phwy mewn brô fo'n brifo,
Ar ol un dyn a gaffo,
Yn brysur yno i bresio,
Nid ŷw'r wyneb prês yn prisio,

Ond am y Caffo iw ddwylo ddŷn,
Ai daflu i letty drwg ei lun.

(May none of his sort from that graceless regiment
of perverse, hideous, cruel creatures
Ever come to shore and set foot on open land.
They care not a jot
what evil powers might exist,
nor who back home should be hurting
after a man has been taken
and swiftly pressganged.
That brazen face does not care,
as long as he should get hold of his man
and throw him into squalid lodging.)

Anxieties about the activities of the pressgangs were common in the period. Warnings of their arrival in various areas would appear in newspapers,[90] and although it is not likely that this ballad was created for that purpose, the fact that it goes on to describe a chain of communities (at Llandygái, Llanllechid, Conwy, Abermaw and Llanfair) who came to hear about the threat posed by Trodn and his men suggests the interdependence of coastal communities and the ability of their members to spread the word about such threats in order to protect their people and their livelihoods. There is very little love lost for the British state here. Rather, communities are portrayed as being threatened by the national political order, and having to fight for their own survival.

In some cases, ordinary people were aided by higher members of society in campaigns against the practice of enforced recruitment. Although Thomas Pennant, the renowned naturalist, wrote in October 1775, 'I detest the Americans', he was just as unremitting in his condemnation of the British government for its conduct in the war against them.[91] In his *American Annals*, he criticized the behaviour of British officers in America between 1775 and 1778, portraying the campaign against the American rebels as a series of disasters from a British perspective, and concluding by calling for an enquiry into the actions of General Howe.[92] He was equally critical of the behaviour of the Justices of the Peace who implemented the government's policies for recruitment to the militia back home. In *Free Thoughts on the Militia Laws* (1781), he attempted to explain to his 'Dear countrymen' the details of laws relating to the militia, so that they should not be deceived by unscrupulous officers.[93] Militia members were chosen by ballot. If a man chosen was either not free or not willing (perhaps because of family duties or health reasons) to take on the work, he had the right to offer another suitable man in his place. Pennant suggests, however, that there was a strong tendency among Justices to reject deputies offered, and this without good reason. Justices would then, sometimes, command the man originally chosen to pay them the sum of ten pounds for failing to find a deputy. In some cases, the man originally chosen was unable to pay such a sum, and this could lead to his being punished for 'the crime of poverty', as Pennant puts it. The background to Pennant's essay, written in October of 1781, lies in his own experiences.[94] During the summer of that year, he acted on behalf of men mistreated in this way. Pennant assisted John Jones from the parish of Bodfari who had offered the Justices five deputies after deciding that his health was not good enough to permit him to serve in the militia following his selection by ballot. Each of the five were rejected, although they were all 'able & unexceptionable in all respects'.[95] John Jones had been fiercely accosted by the head of the militia; his offer to pay the ten pounds' fine instead of providing a deputy was also rejected and he was made to pay over twelve pounds instead. To add insult to injury, the five men Jones had offered as deputies were taken anyway as members of either the militia or the regular army. However, Pennant succeeded in securing the judgement of prominent lawyers at Lincoln's Inn that the behaviour of the Justices and officers involved in this and one other similar case had been unacceptable.[96]

Although no ballads on this theme survive, it is noteworthy that responses to military service are far from supportive, whether in the work of Thomas Pennant or of ballad-writers such as Ellis Roberts. The picture is much less uniform than that seen in the French Revolutionary and Napoleonic periods. During the time of the American war, it was still permissible to write about the opposition of rural society to the power of central government.[97]

Further Pamphlets, 1781–2

A poem by Hugh Jones has already shown a tendency within the Welsh response to the American war to look inwards and blame the shortcomings of the British for the dispute.[98] This tendency can be witnessed in the responses of Anglicans and Dissenters alike within the wider British community. Beilby Porteus, Archbishop of Chester, saw the war as the result of 'impiety and irreligion, of dissipation and extravagance [which] by provoking the anger of an offended God, has, I am convinced, been the principal, the radical cause of our present misfortunes'.[99] According to the Dissenter, Joshua Toulmin, 'War is a *Judgment of God*. The American war had been caused by 'The dissipation and luxury of the age; the increase of all places of diversion and amusement throughout the kingdom, and the excessive spirit of gaming'.[100] Similar voices were to be heard in Wales. In 1781, John Ross of Carmarthen published a translation by Peter Williams of an anonymous English pamphlet entitled *Galwad Gan Wyr Eglwysig, Ar Bawb ffyddlon, i gyd-synio mewn Gweddi, yn enwedig Tra parhao'r Rhyfel presennol*. The pamphlet's principle argument is that men are chastized by God for their sins and that the punishment often comes in the form of war, as in the case of the

Seven Years' War and the current war against America and its allies. The only way to subdue the enemy is to turn to God in prayer and penitence, rejecting sins of all kinds. It is the individual's responsibility to examine his own behaviour and see his sins as part of the 'guilt of the state': 'Looking upon our sin as part of the sin of the state will teach us to cry upon the Lord's chastisement for blessing'.[101] It is argued that there are 'men in many a corner of the kingdom ... who are as alien to the life and power of Christianity as those in the wilderness of Africa or the grasslands of Arabia'.[102] Unless those among the inhabitants of Britain who know about God prostrate themselves in prayer, there is a real danger that the French and Spanish enemies will land on British soil, 'stab our friends, tear our children to pieces, kill the young men and rape our wives before our eyes!', let alone re-establish 'Popery and servitude' in the country at the expense of 'our religion and freedom'.[103] A year later, in 1782, Hugh Jones of Maesglasau published an original pamphlet which discusses similar themes, naming specific sins which he believed to have developed as a result of the prosperity of Great Britain in the aftermath of the Seven Years' War, among them miserliness, pride, drunkenness and laziness.[104] He addresses his work to a rural Welsh audience, bringing his critique of their behaviour alive through examples such as the following which disparages drunkenness:

> Pa gynnifer o honoch chwi y Cymry, wedi gwerthu eich dâ a'ch ydau yn y farchnad am bris uchel, a arhosech yn y tafarn-dai ar hŷd y nos gwed'yn, a thrannoeth ysgatfydd; yn sottio ac yn meddwi, yn gloddesta ac yn gwallgofi; ac yn tynny cynnifer o bechodau am eich pen, a oedd o wallt ar eich coryn.[105]

> (How many of you, the Welsh, after selling your cattle and your corn in the market for a high price, would hang around in the pubs through the ensuing evening and the following day, perhaps, boozing and getting drunk, feasting and raving, and drawing as many sins upon yourselves as you had of hairs on your head?)

Singing about men's sins is one of the characteristics of the balladry relating to the American war. One ballad by Hugh Jones, Llangwm, published in 1779 is narrated by the figure of Pride.[106] As if speaking from the stage of a contemporary interlude, this allegorical figure pumps out his contention that the American war originated in the pride of the British people – especially that of their leaders and their women. A pair of ballads by Ellis Roberts and Hugh Jones (one published in 1779, the other undated) tell of a bright light in the skies which, they suggest, is a sign from God that he shall soon be visiting Britain and bringing destruction to its people, as he did in Jerusalem during the Jewish revolt of AD 66.[107] Men must rely on God, says Ellis Roberts, and not upon their own strength in reversing this dire situation:

O Bryden ystyr dithe, heb Dduw nad nerth y cledde
Na chryfion longe na murie mawr,
A ystopia i'r lan d'elynion.

(Oh, Britain, be mindful that, without God, neither the power of the sword
nor strong ships nor great ramparts
will keep your enemies from the shore.)

By praying to God and 'improving our lives, all of us, inhabitants of undefiled Britain' an end may hopefully be seen to the threat represented by the fiery skies.[108]

Conclusion

The latter pair of poems reveal one important fact about the close to fifty Welsh ballads that have survived relating to the American war and its effects on Wales. Two ballad-writers – Hugh Jones and Ellis Roberts – dominate the scene. The latter, author of more than thirty ballads on the topic, was by far the more prolific of the two.[109]

This pattern changed significantly during the period of the French Revolution. Ellis Roberts died in 1789, as the Revolution was beginning. Hugh Jones had already died in December 1782.[110] The field opened widely, therefore, for new ballad-writers – many of them completely unheard of by us today.[111] There were developments in the field of publishing too, with more printers, scattered more widely across Wales, publishing ballads. There are only eight locations where we know that ballads on the American war were published: these are Brecon, Bala, Chester, Carmarthen, Machynlleth, Trefriw and Wrexham. The majority of the texts by far emerged from Dafydd Jones's Trefriw press.[112]

To conclude, however, we shall break the mould by presenting a poem by a third ballad-writer, more famous than either of the two hitherto discussed. Only one ballad by Thomas Edwards (Twm o'r Nant) relates directly to the American war. It presents the event from a different standpoint from those already discussed. There were three contemporary editions of 'Ymddiddan rhwng Gwraig yr Hwsmon a Gwraig y Shiopwr' (A dialogue between the farmer's wife and the shopkeeper's wife) in ballad form: one by Thomas Huxley of Chester (undated), another by Dafydd Jones of Trefriw (1780) and a third by E. Evans, Brecon (1781). Manuscript copies have also been preserved, and the ballad is seen, too, in Cain Jones's 1783 almanac, all of which testify to its popularity.[113] The poet overhears a conversation between the two women named in the title and gradually, after an introduction in his own voice, the exchange becomes alive before us, with the women speaking for themselves. The farmer's wife complains. The world has changed. Instead of the simplicity of the past, when food and clothes were plain, she now lives in a world of pride and ostentatiousness, where there is not enough to be had. The shopkeeper's wife is more positive. Her livelihood depends on new fashions, of course, and she encourages the farmer's wife to take delight in the handsome appearance of her sons and daughters and in their graceful behaviour following years of polish 'at school'.[114] The farmer's wife is not to be comforted, however. She turns her attention to the current war, which prevents the 'lovely merchants' from taking 'anything in exchange for corn from this side of the sea'.[115] She has also heard the proverb mentioned above about England bringing corruption upon itself ('There is a proverb that is manifestly true, / that old England shall corrupt itself / – that is her fault'), and she attributes this corruption to the love of luxury.[116] The shopkeeper's wife can sympathize with her companion in her anxiety about the war. She knows that the people of Chester are enraged because of the trading restrictions, and goods such as tobacco, sugar, fruit and tea are harder to come by than they used to be.[117] The shortage of tea, at least, can be overcome by the actions of 'very sly smugglers' who can 'make their way into houses to sell tea', according to the farmer's wife.[118] But these miscreants have not been named in order to be denigrated. The farmer's wife believes that 'smuggling' is an apposite term to describe the actions of the state as well:

> A pheth yw Smyglo hefyd,
> Wrth Benaethiaid, sy'n ymwneuthyd,
> I ddwyn ein tir an bywyd,
> Gan godi Rhyfel gwaedlyd,
> A bwlio'r byd. Rebelwyr baw.
>
> (And what is smuggling, besides,
> compared to the actions of the rulers, who endeavour
> to steel our land and our lives,
> raising a bloody war
> and bullying the world, despicable rebels.)

The shopkeeper's wife agrees with her hurriedly, then suggests that they should bring their conversation to an end, since 'a green bush has eyes, / and a dry field has ears of flesh':[119]

> Nid allwn ddweyd mon pwrpas
> Rhag ofn bŷdd Cnawon atcas,
> Yn gweiddi ar ol Gwrageddas,
> Am daflu geiriau diflas.
>
> (We cannot speak our minds
> lest foul rogues
> should call us gossips
> for saying unpalatable words.)

There is an awareness here of the daring of the critique made of the government for going to war to the detriment of its own people. By opening our ears to this conversation – which was witnessed, of course, by scores of listeners and readers

– Twm o'r Nant shows the broadening of the public sphere in Wales during the period of the American war. Dafydd's Samwell's fears have been realized: even women in Wales are discussing and expressing criticism (to the real interest of their audience) in this new age.[120]

2 SCOTTOPHOBIA VERSUS JACOBITISM: POLITICAL RADICALISM AND THE PRESS IN LATE EIGHTEENTH-CENTURY IRELAND

Martyn J. Powell

I

In historiographical terms, neither Jacobitism nor Scottophobia have featured heavily in the historiography of late eighteenth-century Ireland until relatively recently. In terms of the former, the native Irish did not rise in 1745 and the accepted historical narrative is one of a process of Catholic rehabilitation until the seismic shock of 1789. As for Scottophobia, or anti-Scottish sentiment, this has been addressed in the British context as a result of interest in John Wilkes and his skirmishes with Bute, but, with the notable exception of work on Jonathan Swift,[1] there has not been any concerted attempt to explore the phenomenon in Ireland. Indeed, when thinking of the second half of the eighteenth century, with its influential work in the British context by Brewer and Colley, there has in the Irish case been more coverage in work with a literary slant on the 'forger' James Macpherson.[2]

The avalanche of publications marking the bicentenary of the 1798 rebellion has gone some way towards shaping a new debate on Irish–Scottish connections in this period. Works have been published on interlinking Scottish and Irish radicalisms in the 1790s and, in more general terms, the reassessment of the role of Thomas Paine and the French Revolution in politicizing the United Irishmen, and even their Defender allies, must have a knock-on effect upon our judgement of older traditions of native Catholic discontent.[3] At the same time the growth of 'new British history', and the reaction against some of that movement's traits (such as a revival of interest in British constitutional history and a teleological approach to British state formation), has encouraged a degree of pan-Celticism in modern historiography: a unity in the Celtic postcolonial experience which pushes historians towards the analysis of hegemonic relationships with the imperial English centre.[4] While comparative 'Celtic' historiography must be welcomed, historians must be wary of the dangers of simplifying and disguising much more complicated relationships. I have written elsewhere on Celtic rivalry during periods of imperial crisis in the second half of the eighteenth century,[5] and in this essay I would like to reflect further on one dialectic, the relationship between Ireland and Scotland, and, more particularly, the extent of Scottophobia in Irish political discourse outside of Ulster. As we shall see, such an investigation also pulls in England, and in this case not as imperial enforcer, but rather sharer in, and possibly even originator of, radical political beliefs.

Snippets on Scottophobia and Jacobitism can be discovered in a multitude of Irish sources, from private correspondence to Gaelic poetry. In the case of the latter, the work of Vincent Morley and others has led to a vigorous (and still rumbling) debate over the nature and extent of Jacobite sympathies in late eighteenth-century Ireland. This is not something that I would wish to prolong, and the source base utilized here – English-language periodical and pamphlet publications – offers, I hope, a different perspective on Irish attitudes towards Scotland. Arguably, in the second half of the century it is in Irish patriotic newspapers and accompanying pamphlet and handbill ephemera that the Scottophobic refrain is strongest. From the 1760s to the late 1780s patriotic newspapers like the *Freeman's Journal*, *Hibernian Journal* and *Dublin Evening Post* took a line that was avowedly hostile towards Scotland's position in the British polity and the wider Empire. The imperial dimension is significant, as it both sharpened hostility towards the Scots and offered possibilities of a Whiggish coalition between radicals in Ireland, England and the American colonies.[6] Ireland's position within the mercantile British Empire also coloured its views on Scotland. It regarded the trade advantages that its neighbour had gained through the Union of 1707 with jealousy, particularly given Scotland's ungratefulness manifested in the rebellions of 1715 and 1745, as Swift illustrated in 'The Story of the Injured Lady', published in 1746. Imperial developments also give this essay its (loose) chronology, bookended as it is by the end of the Seven Years War and the beginning of the French Revolution. Within this period I intend to dwell on a number of distinct episodes that saw Scottophobia rear its head, namely the rise of John Wilkes and Wilkite politics, the reaction to the American War of Independence, which also encompassed hostile responses to the writers Richard Twiss and James Macpherson, and finally, the radicalization of politics and popular protest in the mid 1780s.

II

The Duke of Cumberland ensured that Scottish abandonment of Jacobitism would be quick, and long-lasting. The appointment of Lord Bute, first as Secretary of State and then as Prime Minister, brought the Scots to the heart of the political system barely fifty years after union, but as Linda Colley, John

Brewer and, most recently, Adam Rounce have pointed out, this development was far from welcome, and the success of John Wilkes and his followers owed much to their anti-Scottish rhetoric.[7] Yet there has perhaps been a tendency to see the Wilkite phenomenon as peculiarly English – partly because it was so anti-Scottish in nature. In the 1760s and 1770s Irish patriots were, like Wilkes, engaged in what they perceived as a struggle against an over-mighty executive, careless of the sensitivities of parliament and the 'people'. In the Irish case, matters reached a climax during the administration of Lord Townshend (1767–72), and the Wilkite comparisons were facilitated by the fact that both Townshend and his chief secretary, Sir George Macartney, were connected with Lord Bute, supposedly George III's *eminence grise*.

Although some Irish parliamentary politicians no doubt had their reservations over Wilkes, popular political sentiment was firmly behind him. The nature of the Wilkites' Whiggism certainly suited. Wilkite propaganda, anti-Stuart, anti-Catholic and directed at a corrupt executive subverting the liberties of both parliament and the press, was grist to the mill of Irish patriots. There were certainly factors that led to anti-Butite and pro-Wilkite feeling that resonated less in Ireland, such as ministerial faction fighting, rumours that Bute was enjoying carnal relations with the king's mother, and Bute's cider tax which so inflamed passions in the west country.[8] Nevertheless the English link was important. The Wilkite agitations resulted in the formation of a number of clubs in Dublin sympathetic to John Wilkes, including the Liberty Tree Blues, the Old Nol Club and the 45 Club.[9] One Irish newspaper gushed that 'it was entirely owing to the spirited associations of the people of England, that the doctrine of general warrants, the remains of a tyrannical star-chamber, was totally set aside in the case of John Wilkes'.[10] Ireland also had native associational traditions, and an older club, the Free Citizens of Dublin, formed during the travails of Dublin demagogue Charles Lucas in the late 1740s, became a keen supporter of Wilkes.[11]

It must be acknowledged that some of the sentiment emanating from the Free Citizens and others that might be perceived as anti-Scottish, was actually more about anti-Catholicism, and this applies to much of the material directed at the Stuarts and their Jacobite officers in squibs, broadsides and toasts.[12] The Free Citizens drank toasts to the anniversary of the battle of Culloden, '16 April 1746', and to 'the memory of the late Duke of Cumberland'. Indeed the anniversary of Culloden became a fixture in the Protestant commemorative calendar, and Sir Laurence Parsons erected a column in Birr to commemorate Cumberland's victory.[13] Some of this content, however, moved beyond anti-Catholic Whiggism and general praise for Wilkes, and took on board the Scottophobic raillery of the Wilkite newspaper the *North Briton*. There were particular toasts aimed at those deemed to be Butites in the British government, such as 'may his Majesty confide in the old supporters of his Family, and no longer place a confidence in those who attempted to deprive his Grand-father of the Throne',[14] and a jibe directed at the inveterate enemy of Wilkes, the lord chief justice, Lord Mansfield: 'may the man *who bared his knee to the Pretender*, and whose counsels have divided the British empire, be *brought to his knees on a scaffold*'.[15] Outside of toasts, which offered a pithy and ritualistic credo for Ireland's patriotic clubmen, there are plenty of other examples of Irish Wilkite coverage in the press that was anti-Scottish in tone. In 1763 the *Freeman's Journal* reported on an attempt to assassinate Wilkes by Alexander Dun, a Scotsman, and included copies of letters relating to the incident.[16] The *Freeman's Journal* also reported that Scottish newspapers had refused to print advertisements placed by the Society of the Bill of Rights,[17] and termed the arrest of the printer John Almon as a measure worthy of the Stuarts.[18]

General warrants and the freedom of the press doubtless concerned leading Irish Whigs like Charles Lucas and his successor as Dublin's favoured city-radical, Sir Edward Newenham. But as I have hinted, there were some slight differences between the Scottophobia witnessed in England during the Wilkite agitations, and the version that developed in Ireland. The perception of Scotland as a country of low taxation, and thus a meagre contributor to government coffers, was not as prominent in Irish satires as in their English counterparts – Ireland had its own issues with poverty and had no land tax.[19] In Ireland support for Wilkes crystallized around hostility towards a Scottish-driven imperial mission. With the support of the Chatham and North ministries Lord Townshend, as Irish viceroy, launched a largely successful attempt to reassert British control over the Irish political system. His personal connections with Bute, and those of Sir George Macartney, Bute's son-in-law, meant that his venture was perceived as an attempt to export Butite, Scottish influence over Ireland.[20] Consequently, during one of Townshend's public relations exercises, the coaches of government peers were smeared with potato; daubings that allegedly formed the number 45 (of the Wilkite *North Briton* newspaper).[21] In parliament there was a concerted attempt to stymie the award of a pension on the Irish establishment to Jeremiah Dyson, the procedural expert who had schemed against Wilkes. Overlapping with the Castle party that Townshend built up with personal loyalty to the viceroy was a section of government supporters associated with Bute and the Duke of Bedford. This group, regarded as antagonistic towards the American colonies, was actually termed 'the Scotch' and, in the faction's less prosperous times, the patriotic *Hibernian Journal* expressed its delight at the fact that 'the Scotch are not in favour at the Castle – alas poor Sawney!'[22]

III

The presence of large numbers of Ulster Scots in the northern counties in combination with latent Stuart sympathies among sections of the lower orders meant that anti-Scottish feeling in Ireland would never be universal. Nevertheless anti-Scottish sentiment in patriotic thought proved to be resilient, and was given a fillip by the outbreak of the American War of Independence, termed by Irish newspapers as a 'Scotch war', a view that was shared by other Whigs in the Atlantic world. In England, senior Whig politicians, including Newcastle, Shelburne and Rockingham, made Scottophobic remarks, and given the plethora of anti-Scottish toasts, squibs, caricatures, effigy burnings and even physical violence, it is clear that the populace did not require much steering to take a similar view.[23] In the American colonies John Adams observed that notwithstanding the Scottish Enlightenment, the Scots 'have not the most worthy ideas of liberty'.[24] The New England clergyman Ezra Styles noted in 1777 that 'The Policy of Scotland & all the governmental Ideas of the Body of that People, are abhorrent to all Ideas of civil Liberty & are full of rigorous tyrannical Superiorities & subordinations.' Moreover, he contended that

> the whole of this war is so far chargeable to the Scotch Councils, & to the scotch as a Nation (for they have nationally come into it) as that had it not been for them, this quarrel had never happened.[25]

Philadelphia's Benjamin Rush, who studied in Edinburgh, was critical of Bute and the historian William Robertson, and had doubts about David Hume, but, as a member of Edinburgh's Revolution Club he was well aware that there were Commonwealthmen in Scotland who would find common cause with Whigs in America and Ireland.[26] These subtleties seemed not to have spread beyond America's political class, and a range of prejudices were directed against the Scots in the colonies, focusing upon their Jacobite inclinations, linguistic barbarism and their poverty, which made them vulnerable to the temptations held out by political corruption.[27] Scots incomers were unpopular due to their reputation as staunch loyalists, and it was alleged that Scottish refusal to agree with non-importation agreements in Boston had led to a resolution to 'banish all the Scotchmen'.[28]

In Ireland concerns remained much the same as in the mid eighteenth century. The Scots continued to be styled as Jacobite crypto-Catholics, hence the continued celebrations of Culloden; when threatened with invasion in 1779 a body of gentlemen from Cork decided to call their armed society the Culloden Volunteers.[29] The most popular insults levelled during the American war can loosely be divided into four broad (and occasionally contradictory) satirical arcs focusing upon political corruption and the danger to the constitution; 'old'-Whiggism (which also meant anti-Catholicism); Scottish religious intolerance in the aftermath of the Gordon riots; and Scottish migration to Britain and the jobbery that came in its wake.

In the case of the first of these, just as in mainland party politics the Butite bogeyman had a remarkable longevity – even after Bute had ceased to play any meaningful role in political life – so in Ireland Bute's name continued to be invoked as a byword for ministerial despotism. A writer in the *Dublin Evening Post* bemoaned the fact that 'since the accession of George III we are debilitated by luxury, and governed by Scotchmen'.[30] From the – perhaps convenient – perspective of Irish writers, Bute, in combination with Lord Mansfield, had exercised his influence over George III to bring Britain and Ireland into an unwanted war with the American colonies. With this in mind Dublin's Free Citizens added 'A speedy downfall to the present Jacobite administration' to their litany of toasts.[31] Irish commentators had no doubt that Bute and Mansfield carried the Scottish nation with them. '[I]t is too obvious', said the *Hibernian Journal*, 'that the Adulation of a B[ut]e and a M[ansfiel]d precedes the worship of their God.'[32]

Bute and the alleged double cabinet were simply the highest profile examples of Scottish political malfeasance. Joseph Pollock, a leading Volunteer writer, commented upon the 'potent body of corruption' emanating from Scots MPs since the Union. And the likeminded Frederick Jebb agreed that 'the principles of these Scotchmen have contributed very much to the ruin of the British empire'.[33] In 1775, replying to an address from the anti-Jacobite club, the Aldermen of Skinner's Alley, recommending him as a candidate for the County Dublin seat, Sir Edward Newenham affirmed his opposition to 'the present Butean system'.[34] More specifically the *Dublin Morning Post* claimed that 'one main cause of the American War was the insolent, petulant and despotic treatment of Sawney (Alexander) Wedderburne, the then Attorney General of England to Dr Franklin'. The newspaper went on to cite *North Briton* contributor Charles Churchill's lines on Wedderburne: 'A prim pert prater of the Scottish race, Fraud in his heart, and famine in his face'. The *Dublin Morning Post* used the word 'Scottish' to replace the 'northern' in the original, perhaps to ensure their readers were well aware of the national point being made.[35]

Observations of this nature were neatly packaged by the *Hibernian Journal* in an insulting lexicon: the 'Royal Scotch Political Dictionary'. Sample entries being: *Absolute Monarchy* – 'The only perfect Form of Government ever yet introduced into the world'; *British Constitution* – 'Is nothing but a Bladder full of wind' and *Unconditional Submission* – 'The only Terms, on which a k—g should ever make Peace with his Enemies'.[36] An Irish commentator on the progress of the American war blamed the calamity on 'Scotch contractors and placemen', and, similarly, one of Burke's key charges against Warren Hastings during his impeachment in 1785 was the manner in which he distributed a fount of corruption to thirsty Scottish contractors and placemen. He was allied with another Irishman, Richard Brinsley Sheridan, whose journalistic output in Henry Bate's *Morning Herald* may well have included some of the Scottophobic articles appearing in its pages.[37]

A substantial amount of the anti-Scottish output was part of what might be termed an Atlantic world Whiggery. In this sense Whigs in England, Ireland and the American colonies were united in a struggle against what they perceived to be Scottish-backed royal despotism. The definition of *Vermin and Scum of the Earth* in the 'Royal Scotch Political Dictionary' can be viewed in very general terms. It was 'One in Ten of the Scotch – Nine in Ten of the English – Nineteen in Twenty of the Irish, and Ninety-nine in the Hundred of the Americans'.[38] But this tallying was also about political virtue and Whiggery, concerns that were uppermost in an impassioned letter published in the *Hibernian Journal* in opposition to the war. It suggested that the Caledonians 'seem to vie with each other in the cruel, ruinous, and destructive Business of fettering our fellow Subjects in America; of Subjugating a brave and loyal, and a free People to absolute Slavery and Bondage'. The enemy was dancing reels, 'their Daggers fresh reeking from the Sacrifice of Freedom'. 'The Ball that pierces the Bosom of an American Whig, tickled the Heart of a Highlander', and in a final piece of hyperbole: 'The Groans of Liberty are sweeter and more melodious now to *Scotchmen*, than even the grunts of their favourite *Bagpipe*.' In contrast 'every Whig in England and Ireland' sympathized with 'the sufferings of the innocent, injured, insulted Sons of Liberty in America'. Common cause was effectively being made with Whigs throughout the Empire: Americans, Englishmen and Irishmen were cut from the same political cloth.[39] Whiggish concerns were also evident in many of the fictional tales appearing in the Irish press. It was alleged that 'some Scots lords have employed their interest to have the Names of sundry of his Majesty's Ships changed. The Culloden to the New-York; The Boyne to the White Plains; the Sterling Castle to the Hell-gates'.[40]

The survival of anti-Jacobite sentiment as a logical adjunct of the 'old' Whiggism that played such a key part in Irish patriotic life is indicated by the longevity of Williamite clubs like Dublin's Aldermen of Skinner's Alley. However although this particular society was able to retain the affections of United Irishmen until 1793, there was unease about its pantomimical rituals, and it is clear that some voices within the Irish patriot movement had begun to regard Catholicism as less of a threat.[41] The Relief Acts of 1778 and 1782 were not uncontested, but those in parliament, in the Volunteer movement and in the press who looked to rehabilitate Ireland's Catholics, displayed a degree of self-satisfaction over the newly emerging nation's religious tolerance. Irish reformers pointed to their disciplined, liberal programme in contrast with the dominant popular movement emerging in Scotland.[42] Referring to Lord George Gordon's Protestant Association, a letter in the *Limerick Chronicle* noted that 'the Scotch are playing the enthusiastic pranks of John Knox's days'. In the riots 'neither eminence of station or dignity of character were regarded by people, armed with enthusiastic fury and religious madness'.[43] Another writer in the same newspaper boasted that in relation to the Irish Catholic relief bill of 1778,

> most of the Protestants throughout the kingdom thought the relaxation of the popery laws a liberal, harmless, and expedient measure; and those who differed in opinion with them, though they strenuously opposed it, did it in a Christian, manly, and constitutional manner. How different is the conduct of the Scottish nation?

After noting that the inquisition was falling out of favour in Spain and Portugal, and that Malta allowed a Turkish mosque in its capital the piece went on:

> Is it then in Scotland alone, among the most favoured subjects of an indulgent Monarch, that the bloody standard of persecution is unfurled; outrage, violence, fury, and all the horrid concomitants of religious fury let loose; houses rifled, temples for divine service raised, and libraries, with more than Saracenic rage destroyed.[44]

Long uncomfortable with the tag of most uncivilized of Celtic regions, Irish writers, with more than a degree of smugness, were casting Scotland as the savage 'other'.

On the same theme a *Freeman's Journal* writer called for a caricature of the Dungannon Convention in which Irish Volunteers advocated Catholic relief, comparing it with Lord George Gordon and his followers:

> Irish artist, my fancy affords a canvas for your pencil. If Hogarth has transfused his spirit into you, take the hint and delineate the contrasted scenes. Place on one side of the motley groupe, the Dungannon Delegates with beams of glory playing around their heads, diffusing the rays of toleration and freedom. Paint the Scotchmen with his bible, in the attitude of Diabolo Predicator, or the Devil turned preacher. Believe me it will sell well.[45]

Pan-Whiggism in this case is illustrated by the fact that John Wilkes was a vocal critic of the Scottish Protestant Association in the British Commons.[46] This episode also saw Edmund Burke become embroiled in a paper war with the blind Scottish poet and rabid anti-Catholic, Thomas Blacklock, who was patronized by another Scotsman, James Boswell.

As the American War progressed, Ireland was developing the confidence to move towards a more independent status. Yet even the end of the war would not shake suspicion of the Scots. The *Volunteer Evening Post*, ultra-loyalist, and not particularly sympathetic to Irish Catholics, attacked the University of Edinburgh for opposing a prospective Irish College of Medicine. The Scots allegedly intended to scupper the scheme by petitioning the spiritual members of the House of Lords. Apparently the Irish medical school would be open to Catholics, so it was intended to use the bishops' hatred of popery, which, the Scottish minute noted, 'we heartily applaud'. The Scottish medics lambasted the notion of 'permitting

Roman Catholics, those pests of society, dupes of superstition, and enemies of all good government, to become Professors of Physic'. The letter ended with a reference to the violence sparked by Scotland's Protestant Association: 'We have lately in this country set a splendid example of our abhorrence of such abominations.'[47] In later issues of the same newspaper Lord George Gordon was described as 'that bigoted lunatic' and 'the *Scotch fanatick* of conflagration memory'.[48]

However, other articles hint at another agenda lurking behind the anti-Gordon rhetoric, and that was hostility towards radical Presbyterianism, which, notwithstanding political and commercial jealousies, was a key explanation for Swift's Scottophobia.[49] On Catholic relief the *Volunteer Evening Post* questioned:

> Who violently opposed it, set fire to the city of London, and would have thrown every Catholic into the flames? – the Presbyterians of Scotland and England. Who objected to the privileges already granted in Ireland to the Catholics? – Lord George Gordon, and his protestant, alias Presbyterian, Association.[50]

In this case it should be emphasized that the editorial aims were less about reassuring Catholics – most likely a miniscule proportion of this particular newspaper's readership – and more about making the case for Protestant Ascendancy. But whatever the motives, there was a shift in the iconography of the troublesome Scot – from rebellious Jacobite to revolutionary Presbyterian, a fact illustrated in a satirical letter on the controversial Carrickfergus by-election of 1784, in which the author, 'Sawney Slicer', bemoaned the defeat of the opposition MP Waddell Cunningham and 'the good old cause'.[51]

The final area of anti-Scottish resentment is rather more tangible, and focuses upon the visible presence of Scotsmen in Dublin, echoing similar concerns about Scots on the make in London, and Bute's alleged system of replacing English office-holders with their penniless neighbours.[52] Wilkes alleged that 'No Scot ever exerted himself but for a Scot. This was an odious, and a national character.' And despite the sizeable presence of the Irish in London – targets in riots in the 1730s and 1780 – Wilkes exempted them from similar abuse.[53] In Ireland, disagreements over the American war in his local coffee house with Scottish physicians led a Dublin barber to call, somewhat facetiously, for the medics to be forced to pay the anti-Catholic quarterage tax.[54] Marrying a Scottish presence with parliamentary corruption, the *Dublin Evening Post* claimed that a gentleman from Dumbarton had set up a business in Dublin's Fleet Lane selling 'speeches of all kinds and on all occasions' to MPs, 'made at an hour's warning'.[55] Other jibes directed at migrant Scots included the Volunteer writer Frederick Jebb's complaints at the vices that the Scots brought with them: '[r]eligious hypocrisy, servility of manners, and political depravity'.[56] The *Dublin Morning Post*, echoing English satirists, in an alphabetical satire offered the 'itch' as a 'Scotch Importation'.[57]

IV

The extent and use of anti-Scottish sentiment, stretching beyond the political tussles of the 1760s and 1770s – Wilkes, Townshend, America – is illustrated by the fact that Scottophobia appeared in the most abstruse episodes that garnered newspaper interest in this period. Readers of Irish newspapers in the second half of 1776 would have been struck not only by the escalation of hostilities between Britain and the American colonies, but also by an outpouring of national outrage directed at the tourist Richard Twiss, who had produced a splendidly spiteful Irish travelogue which mocked the manners and morals, art and architecture of the Irish, and reserved special attention for the inhabitants of Connacht (savages) and the legs of Ireland's women (fat).[58] Most of the anti-Twiss ephemera was published in newspapers and pamphlets, with the notable exception of a chamber pot with Twiss's image emblazoned within, an item which caught the imagination of the Irish public and gave hack writers another theme for their anti-Twiss polemics.

Given that Twiss was English and that his closest family connections were in Holland, where his father had set up business, any commentary on Scotland would not have been germane to either Twiss or the tour, and yet the Scottish dimension in the anti-Twiss reaction is noteworthy. For example, in a fake gallows speech printed in the *Hibernian Journal* and then taken up by several other newspapers, Twiss acknowledged that his father was Scottish, and named Sawney Twiss. His involvement in the Jacobite rebellion had forced him to flee to Holland.[59] Part of the explanation for the inclusion of such jibes lies in the identities of the hack writers who took up their pens in opposition to Twiss. For example, William Preston, friend of the leading Patriot peer Lord Charlemont and a member of the patriotic association the Monks of the Screw, was the author of two very popular anti-Twiss epic poems. However he was also producing satires directed at Britain's prosecution of the war against the American colonies. Preston included a number of anti-Scots jibes in his *A Congratulatory Poem on the Late Successes of the British Arms* of 1776 and *The Female Congress* of 1779, the latter referring to '[t]he voice of gain, which *Scotchmen* always hear'.[60]

A more concerted effort to combine Twiss, the Scots and ministerial corruption came in the form of the anonymous Dublin-published epic poem *Fidêfract*. This piece, directed at Lord North and his ministerial colleagues, contained plenty of anti-Scottish sentiment. There were hostile references to the absolutist Stuarts, historic betrayals and the increasing numbers of Scots evident in London society.[61] The Scots were also treated to the scatological barbs that characterized much of the anti-Twiss literature, and had their leitmotif in the form of the Twiss-pot. The inability of Scots to disguise their true nature was expressed in, 'So Urine empty'd in a Rill, Is nothing else but Urine still'. 'Mac' was ultimately 'a Vermin-eaten Log, The pissing Post of ev'ry Dog'.[62]

James Macpherson, the discoverer of works by Ossian, was a more obvious target for Scottophobic impulses within Irish patriotism. He was of interest to Irish patriots for two reasons. First, Macpherson was patronized by Bute and was eventually made secretary to the governor of Florida. This had already brought him to the notice of the Wilkites, and more particularly Wilkes's friend and collaborator Charles Churchill, who was an unexpected ally of Samuel Johnson in questioning the authenticity of Macpherson's work.[63] Second, the nature of Macpherson's Ossianic ballads threatened to undermine Irish cultural prowess. Macpherson sought to rehabilitate the Scottish highlanders by making them the original Britons, and this required downgrading any Irish claim to the title.[64] His work provoked replies from both Catholics and Protestants, some of whom had already been offended by comments made by David Hume.[65] The Catholic antiquarian Charles O'Conor of Belanagare claimed that 'no Gentleman, or Sharper, ever knew less of the Trade of an able Imposter, than the most memorable Mr James Mac Pherson'.[66] *Faulkner's Dublin Journal* attempted to undermine the publication of Macpherson's *Fingal* in 1762 by alleging that a planned Irish version would 'set forth all the blunders and absurdities in the edition now printing in London'.[67]

In 1776 the *Hibernian Journal* published a number of pieces critical of Macpherson; one writer accusing him of 'lessening the Merit of our Glorious Deliverer'.[68] Even the single letter defending him acknowledged that the hostility directed at him 'seems to be grounded on his being a scotchman and of the name Macpherson'.[69] Like Twiss, Macpherson was a fabricator, guilty of slandering Irish history and traditions.[70] This explains why a writer in the *Hibernian Magazine* suggested that Twiss' F. R. S. was a more suitable acronym for 'Forger of Romantic Slanders'.[71] Macpherson may have been accused of forgery, and his juxtaposition of the barbarous Irish with civilized Celt was certainly provocative, but the tone of articles in the *Hibernian Journal* suggests that his Scottishness – and the Scottishness of his patron Lord Bute – was as much of a problem as his mythmaking and his approach to source material.[72] It should also be noted that the willingness of the *Hibernian Journal* to return to a debate that had started in the 1760s can be explained by the fact that 1776 was the year of the publication of the Dublin edition of Macpherson's *The Rights of Great Britain Asserted against the Claims of America*, thus further cementing the link between Scottishness and imperial centralization in the minds of Irish Patriots.

One final point worth making on the anti-Scots trope in the cultural arena is that though clearly prevalent in the work of William Preston and other Dublin writers, the Ulster Scots living in the north of Ireland – in this period a hotbed of radical patriotism – and Macpherson fans elsewhere in Atlantic world Whiggery (Thomas Jefferson for example)[73] make it dangerous to generalize. Indeed one of the interesting features of the anti-Twiss backlash was the slight regional variations. For example the version of the gallows speech published in the *Londonderry Journal* referred to Twiss's father as 'Richard' rather than 'Sawney' Twiss. Whilst in the *Belfast News Letter* 'AN IMPARTIAL SCOTSMAN' wrote to condemn the writings of tourists to Scotland and Ireland. He also looked forward to purchasing his own piss-pot.[74]

V

The abandonment of Jacobitism by the Irish political elite was determined by the fact that the Protestant land grab depended upon the Williamite settlement. Recent work by Eamonn Ó Ciardha and Vincent Morley points to the survival of Jacobitism in Gaelic culture, both domestically and in the Irish regiments active in France and Spain.[75] Morley argues that the lower orders did not follow the example of the Catholic elite and shy away from the Jacobite connection.[76] But David Hayton and Sean Connolly, among others, have misgivings about any real political significance.[77] There is no doubt that even very late into the eighteenth century the wearing of white cockades, the playing of Jacobite airs and toasts to the Old and Young Pretenders offered an indication of, at the very least, a sentimental attachment towards Jacobitism, while the combination of explicit commentary on the American war with Jacobite language in vernacular poetry may be deemed to bring Jacobitism up to date, and either bolstered sympathy towards the colonies or was grafted onto it.[78] But even if we reject Louis Cullen's view that an *aisling* was 'a literary form; not a message for the people',[79] it is probably best to show caution before attributing very direct political agency to Gaelic poetry. Evidence might yet be forthcoming – and here Morley's continued work is of critical importance – but the riotous cause and effect that we can connect to newspapers and handbills in England and Ireland does not seem to be present.

I would argue that the tenor of Dublin protest in the 1770s and 1780s – with its focus upon parliamentary reform and the liberty of the press – had moved far beyond the Jacobite creed and into radical territory. The nature of aristocratic rule in Ireland – and the wider British polity – was debated in the pages of the press after the rejection of reform bills.[80] The *Hibernian Journal* expected the Scots to be firmly behind the ministry in the British general election, on the grounds that '[t]heir peasantry are the slaves of the landholders, because they weigh nothing in the scale of representation'.[81] Even the loyalist *Volunteer Evening Post* welcomed Scottish attempts to make their 'despotic magistracy' more accountable in 1786.[82] And yet there are odd reports that might connect radical urban politics to Jacobitism. A malicious satire claimed that new radical Volunteer recruits planned to wear 'milk white' cockades.[83] Handy Pemberton, a Dublin lawyer and member of the common council, turned up to a meeting of Dublin's aggregate committee in June 1784 sporting 'a large bunch of white ribband' in his hat. His civic colleagues were outraged and the sheriff forced him to remove this 'mark of disloyalty'. Pemberton had already courted controversy by writing a letter published in the *Volunteers Journal* in which he expressed his admiration of Louis XVI and appeared to condone the houghing of soldiers. Yet in both of these cases, there is no mention of Jacobitism, and it is much more likely that the white cockade was a sign of support for the Bourbon monarchy. Pemberton said it was in honour of the Volunteers being instituted, while elsewhere he was accused of having 'hoisted *Gallic* colours'.[84]

Even where white cockades of the Jacobite variety were still in evidence in the last quarter of the century, it surely said more about disaffection with the political status quo than any real hankering for a Stuart restoration. Pro-American, even pro-revolutionary French feeling was simply a continuation of sectarianism using whichever political language was current. The Protestant Ultra Patrick Duigenan felt that pro-Stuart feeling in Catholic Ireland had only ever been an attachment of convenience.[85] And if we come back to the theme of anti-Scottishness, then it is also clear that Gaelic poets had no great love of English-speaking lowland Scots; on a number of occasions seeing the American War of Independence as a civil war that would, happily, weaken both England and Scotland.[86] Similarly Catholic Defenders associated their Protestant enemies with the Scottish covenanters who had given up Charles I.[87]

VI

Although Christopher Wyvill had pushed, unsuccessfully, for an alliance between English and Scottish reformers in 1782, it was the outbreak of the French Revolution that enabled the Scots to bypass Whig prejudices and enter into dialogue with English and Irish reformers via the emerging network of corresponding societies.[88] But how should we interpret the flowering of Scottophobia within Irish patriot discourse prior to this point? We can, certainly, dismiss the phenomenon as a replanting of English ideas about the Scots in a colonial class. But I think that this would be to diminish the sophistication of Irish patriotism in the late eighteenth century. Irish patriots felt that they had, as revitalized Whigs, become the superior brand, akin to their American cousins and their radical brethren in England. Hostility towards the Scots was not simply the jealousy of a rival sibling fighting for crumbs – trade concessions, political favours – from the colonial mother. There were a host of other tensions developing out of a new kind of political radicalism that was about opposition to the centre. And the Scots – thanks to the likes of Bute, Mansfield and Wedderburn – were regarded by Irish patriotic newspapers as a ruling force, and, as such, a threat to the independence of the press. If we turn back to 'The Royal Scotch Political Dictionary', the definition for *newspaper* is 'originally intended for the Circulation of Fact, and the Propagation of dangerous Notion of Liberty and such; but by proper Management they are now made to counteract those very Evils'; lines that were most likely influenced by Wilkite politics and Lord Townshend's patronage of the *Dublin Mercury*, a newspaper that is explicitly mentioned later in the piece.[89]

Oddly, given its history, one of the key areas in which Scotland was failing – in Irish patriotic eyes – was enlightenment. Religious intolerance was the key here, and the *Volunteer Evening Post* took the (Presbyterian) Scots to task for their hostile reaction to the publication of John Home's *Douglas*; claiming that only the Irish students at Edinburgh University had prevented the theatre from being pulled down.[90] Even when the Irish example was followed – as in premiums offered along the lines of the Dublin Society, the same government-sponsored newspaper snidely remarked that 'it must be very obvious how powerfully a little money will operate, to make them indefatigable in the pursuit of a national advantage'.[91] In this light, it is worth noting that while Irish patriotism could conceivably embrace a breathtaking range of political shades – especially in its improving guise – there did not seem to be any great divergence on the fun that could be had with Scots-baiting. Here though, the *Volunteer Evening Post*'s approach did mark a shift in the kind of Scots satirized – no longer were they disloyal Catholic Jacobites, but rather radical, even revolutionary, Presbyterians. In contrast these radicals, Presbyterian or not, were demonstrating a willingness to forget past enmities and unite in the cause of parliamentary reform. In Roscommon in 1784 reformers drank toasts to radicals in Scotland as well as their allies in England and Ireland.[92]

As for Jacobitism in the age of reform and revolution, it is doubtful whether Irish patriotism was sufficiently elastic to encompass it. Jacobitism did have some sort of value as an oppositional creed, and certainly survived in confrontational healths, even if these toasts failed to inform action beyond the occasional barroom fracas. Political links are not easily proven, but arguably those combining Jacobite and pro-American propaganda within a Gaelic *milieu* were the natural bedfellows of the sectarian Defenders, and, when the United Irishmen (many of whom were from an 'old' Whig intellectual background) came looking for an alliance, this 'elasticity' question came into play, bringing Jacobitism and Scotophobic traditions together in a heady and unstable brew.

3 LORD DAER, RADICALISM, UNION AND THE ENLIGHTENMENT IN THE 1790s

Bob Harris

I watch'd the symptoms o' the Great,
The gentle pride, the lordly state,
The arrogant assuming;
The fient a pride, nae pride had he,
Nor sauce, nor state, that I could see,
Mair than an honest ploughman.

Then from his Lordship I shall learn,
Henceforth to meet with unconcern
One rank as weel's another;
Nae honest, worthy man need care
To meet with noble youthful Daer,
For he but meets a brother.
'Lines on Meeting with Lord Daer'

The above verses were penned by Robert Burns after he had met Basil William Douglas, Lord Daer, eldest son of the fourth Earl of Selkirk, at Dugald Stewart's country house in Catrine, Ayrshire, on 23 October 1786. Daer was twenty-three years old. Endowed with abundant reserves of curiosity and intellectual energy, he was deeply immersed in Enlightenment learning and culture. He had just returned from France, where he had met the Marquis de Condorcet. Another of his French contacts was Antoine Laurent Lavoisier, who, together with Joseph Priestley, was in the 1780s forging a new understanding of the composition of the material world.[1] As Richard Holmes has recently written, this was 'a great new and revolutionary age of chemical experiment'.[2] Chemistry held out the promise of rapid intellectual progress, as well as, in the eyes of some, portending great social and political transformation. Just a few years after the meeting in Catrine, and a year before his laboratory went up in the flames of political reaction, Priestley would exultantly declare in his *Experiments and Observations on Different Kinds of Air*, 'the English hierarchy (if there be anything unsound in its constitution) has equal reason even to tremble at an air pump, or an electrical machine'.[3] That Daer should have been caught up in the heady currents of enthusiasm and hope surrounding this developing world of scientific discovery was entirely in keeping with his character, although his interest had, as we will see later, another, more self-interested motivation. In the early 1790s, as in the case of Burns, but only more openly, as his social status and wealth allowed, Daer embraced the cause of radical political reform. Yet, as the life was remorselessly crushed from the reform movement in Scotland by Lord Braxfield and his colleagues on the Scottish bench, so Daer's own life was fast ebbing away. Travelling to Madeira and warmer air, he died at Ivybridge, Devon on 5 March 1795.[4] Few among the elite may have admired his politics, but no one doubted his integrity and honesty. The only plausible charge against him was imprudence.

One purpose of this essay is to draw Lord Daer out from among the shadows, where he has too long rested, in order that he and his politics are better understood. His was a fascinating intellectual and political journey, and one which raises significant questions about how far the Scottish Enlightenment was capable of nurturing 'radical idealism' alongside the complacent loyalism and social conservatism with which it has become commonly identified.[5] However, Daer also provides a powerful lens through which to examine the British dimension to radical politics in the early 1790s. Some years ago, Linda Colley observed that a feature of a great deal of radicalism in Britain in the 1790s was, in so far as it was coloured at all by national feeling, that it was British rather than English, Scottish or Welsh.[6] The story of how radicalism was made to be British, in practical as well (or as much) as ideological terms, has never been fully told.[7] The events of the British convention which met in Edinburgh in late 1793 are fairly well known.[8] They were both an end and not an end to this narrative; what they were not was its beginning.

Daer is best known to political historians as the author of a remarkable letter to the young opposition Whig politician, Charles Grey, written on 17 January 1793.[9] The letter appears to have been written in response to one which Grey had sent to William Skirving, who was the secretary of the Edinburgh Friends of the People, the main coordinating body in Scottish reform politics in the early 1790s. Grey had expressed scepticism about the depth of support south of the border for a petitioning campaign in favour of reform to support his forthcoming motion on the subject in the Commons. The main thrust of Daer's message to Grey was the need for him and his fellow Whig reformers to keep up the momentum behind the petitioning drive since this would be crucial to the morale of reformers 'at a distance'; in other words, to those remote from London.[10] Daer was, nevertheless, extremely sensitive to the national issues which he saw as being involved. No divide, he hoped, would emerge between the campaigns for reform north and south of the border. Daer was an acerbic critic of the Union of 1707 and its consequences for Scottish liberty and morals. The Union may have brought unity in government, but not in sentiment or understanding. 'We have', he declared to Grey, 'suffered the misery which is perhaps inevitable to a lesser and remote country in a junction where the Governing powers are united, but the Nations are not united'.[11] What he thought reform would bring is somewhat ambiguous, but there are hints that he conceived of it as producing a new type of union, at the same as eradicating the corruption which disfigured the British body politic.[12] In order to achieve this, he advocated a convention of radicals in England similar to the one which had recently met in Edinburgh. At the new convention, delegates from Scotland would attend as representatives of their individual societies.

Reform was, therefore, in Daer's eyes a means to more complete union; but equally it might prove a route to disunion. 'One of the greatest Bonds of Union betwixt the two nations at present is that the Reformers here feel that they have need to lean upon you', he wrote, adding, however, 'If it be possible once to teach them that they can take the lead many may be for bidding you farewell'.[13] It is a political message which resists simple explanation.

We need to start, however, by examining in more detail Daer's life and political experiences before 1792. While much of this is unfortunately visible only in fragments, the circumstances of his education are fairly well documented.[14] Selkirk sent Daer and his brothers to school at Palgrave near Diss on the Norfolk–Suffolk border. A progressive dissenting establishment, it was run between 1774 and 1785 by Rochement and Anna Letitia Barbauld.[15] Mrs Barbauld's family, the Aikins, were originally from Kirkcudbright, which may explain the presence of the Douglas siblings at the school. Daer was to become her particular favourite at the school. In 1787, some years after he had left, she wrote to her brother, John Aikin, 'He was before the finest boy; he is now the finest young man I know.'[16] Another pupil was Benjamin Vaughan, who, like Daer, would go on to study at university in Edinburgh, visit France to witness the early stages of the French Revolution, and espouse the cause of political reform in the early 1790s. Vaughan also shared many of Daer's intellectual interests.[17]

In joining the community at Palgrave, Daer gained an entrée into the heart of English rational dissenting culture. John Aikin, Joseph Priestley and William Enfield all sent their sons to the school. As with other dissenting educational establishments, the curriculum emphasized practical learning. Mrs Barbauld taught geography, history, public speaking and English composition. Daer would have heard much also of the dissenting notion of patriotic citizenship, which stressed the obligations of those of property and 'enlightened minds' to superintend the welfare of all parts of the community. It was a conception of patriotism which looked to, but also well beyond nation, which saw 'every private partiality' and even 'patriotism itself' subsumed and finally occluded in the cause of 'universal philanthropy'.[18] It was an ideal which Daer appears to have thoroughly internalized, and which guided his actions during the rest of his short life.

After Palgrave, Daer enrolled at the University of Edinburgh for the 1781–2 and 1782–3 sessions. In the Scottish capital he lodged with Dugald Stewart, who in 1772 had replaced his father in the mathematics classroom, before following him three years later as professor of mathematics. In 1778, Stewart temporarily took over from Adam Ferguson as the teacher of moral philosophy at the university, and would do so again in the 1784–5 academic session. When Ferguson finally retired as professor of moral philosophy early in 1785, Stewart was elected to the chair.[19]

The extent of Stewart's influence on Daer's intellectual and political formation can only be guessed at.[20] That they were fairly close is indisputable. Stewart appears to have been a fairly frequent visitor to St Mary's Isle, the family home of the Earls of Selkirk, before and after Daer's death.[21] In 1789 Daer accompanied Stewart to Paris to witness the meeting of the Estates General.[22] Thomas Jefferson, American ambassador in the city in 1789, later recalled:

> I became immediately intimate with Stuart, calling mutually on each other almost daily, during their stay at Paris, which was of some months. Ld Dare [sic] was a young man of imagination, with occasional flashes indicating deep penetration, but of much caprice and little judgement.[23]

It is tempting to assume that Stewart helped further to instil in Daer conviction in the progressive direction of history, an internationalist outlook, but also a moralistic view of enlightenment as a commitment to cultivating personal virtue and advancing the public good.[24] From 1793, Stewart, temperamentally averse to controversy, tempered and to an extent disguised his reformist political views, a move which led Bruce Lenman to describe him some years ago as 'the most cautious of Whigs'.[25] Criticism, actual and potential, disposed Stewart from 1793 to communicate in 'hints, asides, and circumlocutions'.[26] But in reality, his political stance seems to have held in balance several potentially contradictory elements, belief in the 'general and infallible progress of human reason', but also suspicion about 'indiscriminate zeal against established institutions', which perhaps explains why historians have found it possible to portray his political disposition and outlook in rather different terms. In 1789, however, his enthusiasm for events in France was unrestrained by caution, and would continue so well into 1792.[27] Daer fully shared in this excitement. How much, if at all, this owed to Stewart's influence is unknowable; it is just as conceivable that each influenced the other in their reactions.

At Edinburgh, Daer's interest in science also further deepened and broadened. He was among those who attended the first natural history class given by Professor John Walker in 1782.[28] He was closely involved in the creation of the Natural History Museum under Walker's keepership, making a donation of material to the museum and entering the subscription to purchase Alexander Weir's large collection of natural specimens.[29] Daer was also a pupil of Joseph Black, and an interest in the rapidly developing science of pneumatic chemistry would bring him into contact in the early 1790s with Thomas Beddoes, another of Black's pupils, and conceivably Joseph Priestley.[30] In 1789, through Daer, Lavoisier sent a copy of his *Traité Élémentaire de Chimie*, the epochal work in which he rejected the theory of phlogiston as the agent of combustion in the air, to Thomas Charles Hope, erstwhile fellow student of Daer, and from 1787 professor of chemistry at Edinburgh. Hope informed Black in regard to this work, in terms which strongly imply Daer's closeness to Black: 'According to my promise I should have transmitted it to you for perusal instantly, did I not conceive by the Channel thro which it has come that in every probability you have got a copy of it.'[31] In March 1784, Daer was elected to membership of the Chapter House Philosopical Society in London, known on occasion simply as the Chemical Society, although he is known to have attended their meetings only once.[32] Many of the members of this group had, like Daer and Hope, studied with Black. Enthusiasts for technological innovation, chemical experiment and scientific debate, they lived a version of enlightenment that was truly international in its reach, utilitarian, and often socially reformist. 'The Coffee House crowd', as Larry Stewart has put it, 'emanated a reforming pneumatology'.[33]

Daer's interest in the 'chemical revolution' of the 1780s had a further, personal motive. He suffered from consumption, like his younger brother, John, who died in Florence in 1797. In the early 1790s, Daer turned to Beddoes, then running his Pneumatic Medical Institute in Bristol, in search of a possible cure in the breathing of 'factitious airs' (artificial gases). As the disease advanced inexorably, so he became more desperate, grasping at any solution which appeared to offer itself.[34] Restlessness was a family trait, amply displayed by another of Daer's brothers, Thomas, later fifth Earl of Selkirk, who would long struggle under the weight of the memory of his brilliant older brother.[35] Prior to 1792, Thomas appears to have shared Daer's political sympathies, albeit always with a degree of reserve. In the mid 1800s, he decisively broke with the family tradition of opposition Whiggery and reform.[36] Divergence between the two brothers' political paths was in part simply a consequence of timing, and the impact of the waves of political reaction provoked by the French Revolution in Scotland and Britain. It may also be further indicative, however, of the different political possibilities present within the Scottish Enlightenment.

By the mid 1780s, Daer found himself, therefore, near to the heart of enlightenment Edinburgh. He was a member of the Edinburgh Speculative Society, in which capacity he briefly came into contact with the future United Irishman, Dr Thomas Addis Emmet.[37] The most eminent and important among the Edinburgh student societies, the Speculative met on a weekly basis. Designed to improve public speaking and literary composition, meetings were divided into two parts. In the first a paper was read and discussed, while in the second there was a debate on a separate topic.[38] On 30 March 1784, Daer delivered a discourse on 'the ground and tendency of the benevolent system of philosophy'.[39]

Questions debated by the society in this period included whether the means by which the Irish were pursuing parliamentary reform were 'warrantable', whether the Union was of advantage to Scotland, as well as several issues arising directly from the political crisis which was then engulfing Westminster politics with the king's dismissal of the Fox–North coalition, such as, on 3 February, 'Can the late exertion of secret influence in the House of Peers be justified'. The society's minutes record voting totals only, so we can only surmise on which sides Daer gave his vote, although it seems inconceivable that he was not among the minority of five who opposed the motion that the Union had brought benefit to Scotland. In view of his later political activism, it seems notable that Daer was one of several members who protested in April against the failure of a proposal 'to mark against a member's name in the Minutes on the side on which he voted' in debates. The letter of dissent, signed by Daer and six others, declared: 'We Dissent – Because no Reasons are alleged against it, – and we enter this Protest, that it may remain registered which of the gentlemen present this evening, were ashamed to have their opinions known to future times.'[40] Along with Dugald Stewart, John Playfair, William Robertson junior and Henry Mackenzie, who would become an arch loyalist and presiding figure over the anti-radical press in Edinburgh in the 1790s, Daer was involved in an attempt to revive the Poker Club in the mid 1780s. In 1785, he became a fellow of the Royal Society of Edinburgh.[41]

Some time prior to early March 1785, Daer left Edinburgh.[42] For several years thereafter, his energies were consumed primarily by the task of managing the family estates in the south-west of Scotland, a role handed to him by his father in 1786. The latter could claim some distinction as an early agricultural improver in south-west Scotland, but his record in this context was totally eclipsed by his son. Daer's approach to agricultural and estate improvement was typically energetic and far-reaching; it was also stamped by an ability and will to keep in view a wider vision of local development.[43] He began a heavy programme of tree planting. He took a lead in seeking improvements to the road network in the county of Wigton and Stewartry of Kirkcudbright. Daer's politics were profoundly at odds with the vast majority of local landowners, but his improving activities and sense of public duty won him widespread recognition, and at the same time a reputation as a heroic improver which long outlived his death.[44] Daer also took a very close interest in the development of the town of Kirkcudbright. At various points during the eighteenth century, the town council and the earls of Selkirk fought one another over issues of rights and property. At no point, however, was the relationship more harmonious and constructive than when Daer was elected provost in 1789 and 1790. In this capacity, he helped institute a major programme of town improvement, which involved development of the harbour and creation of two new streets, Castle Street and Union

Street. It was a programme of development which was extended further in the early 1800s, but along lines laid down in 1790.[45]

If Daer's role as an improving Scottish landowner occupied much of his time between 1786 and 1790, he continued to nurture his other interests. He made several visits to France, as already noted. He was intermittently present in London, where from the later 1780s his father had a house in Upper Brook Street. As well as the Chapter House Philosophical Society, Daer was a member of the Society for the Improvement of Arts, Manufactures and Commerce, as well as the Association for Promoting the Discovery of the Interior Parts of Africa, established in 1788.[46]

Through his father's influence Daer was also drawn in the later 1780s into electoral politics, a move which propelled him into the orbit of the opposition Whigs at Westminster. Reforming the system for electing Scottish peers had been a cause of the fourth earl's from the 1770s.[47] Daer's first intervention in national (here meaning British) politics was in 1784 as an intermediary between his father and the ministry regarding reform plans of his father. It was his father's determination to establish his electoral interest which was probably the initial reason behind Daer's efforts to get his name added to the electoral roll for the counties of Wigton and Stewartry of Kirkcudbright. An attempt in 1789 was rebuffed by the freeholders on the grounds that he was the eldest son of a peer. To have done otherwise, it was argued, would have been contrary to the 'inveterate usage of Scotland' and destroyed the 'happy equilibrium' which existed between the 'component orders of the state'.[48] In the same year, he contemplated attempting to stand as a candidate for Glasgow burghs, made vacant by the elevation of Ilay Campbell to the post of Lord President of the Court of Session. In the general election in the following year he stood as an opposition Whig candidate in two English constituencies, Canterbury and Poole.[49] In the Poole contest, in alliance with Lord Haddo, he aligned himself with the interest of the 'commonalty', arguing that the right of election resided in those paying scot and lot and not the mayor and burgesses, as his opponents stated. In both constituencies he fought determined and seemingly popular campaigns.[50] Neither delivered victory, however; and petitions to parliament protesting against the returns failed to overturn the results. In the following year he finally managed to have himself enrolled as a freeholder in Kirkcudbright, by a majority of above three to one at the Michaelmas Head Court. This was very quickly overturned, however, by the Court of Session.[51] Struck off the roll of freeholders and found liable for court expenses, Daer unsuccessfully appealed to the House of Lords. The burden of his case was that by seeking enrolment he was not introducing an innovation to the constitution, but recovering an older right; but as one pamphlet, perhaps written by Daer, artfully declared:

> It is not meant to introduce arguments from expediency; to ask, whether it is reasonable to exclude, for a time, from the legislative body, men, who, by their birth, must one day make part of it? to exclude them at a time of life when they can be

most useful, because they may be included after an uncertain period? or, Whether a distinction ought to be made between the sons of English and Scots peers, whilst Mr Hatsell's proposition is indisputable, that 'it is of great importance that young noblemen should pass through the House of Commons to the House of Lords, as a school in which they hear the first principles of the constitution ably and freely debated, and where they acquire ideas of freedom and independence, and contract habits of business'?[52]

In other words, it would open up new political opportunities for young noblemen such as Daer. Daer also became closely involved at the beginning of the 1790s in debates about reform of the county franchise in the Stewartry of Kirkcudbright and at the national level, attending meetings of delegates from the counties on the subject in Edinburgh of delegates in July and December 1792.

Daer was also a committed abolitionist. He was, for example, present at the famous meeting to draw up a petition against the slave trade which took place in Edinburgh in early March 1792, chaired by the opposition Whig Henry Erskine.[53] One English female sympathizer with reform causes wrote in her diary in the spring of 1792 of Daer's 'glorious ardour in the cause of liberty', describing him as 'one of the very few men of rank who exerted themselves in the cause of Abolition in Edinburgh'.[54]

There is much here that is unsurprising in the career of a Scottish reformer of the early 1790s. The early leaders of the Scottish parliamentary reform movement in Scotland in the summer and autumn of 1792 came from the ranks of advanced Whigs, burgh and county reformers and abolitionists.[55] It was broadly the path followed by another figure within British reform circles who played a key role north of the border in 1792–3 – Colonel Norman Macleod of Macleod.[56] Macleod had succeeded his grandfather as chief of the clan Macleod in 1772, but shortly thereafter had gone to America and then India to carve out a military career. On his return from India in 1789, he had got himself elected as MP for Inverness at the 1790 general election. In his lurch towards opposition Whiggery and reform in 1791 there was a large element of personal frustration at Dundas and the ministry's apparently blocking the resumption of a military career in India.[57] Nevertheless, whatever its cause, he became an important intermediary between the Edinburgh Friends of the People and the Whig Association of the Friends of the People, the opposition Whig body formed in April 1792 under the leadership of Grey, Lauderdale, Sheridan and Philip Francis. Macleod, who joined the Glasgow Associated Friends of the Constitution and of the People, was a member of another body which linked opposition Whigs and reformers in London, the Friends of the Liberty of the Press. He was present in Edinburgh in late October–November 1792 and again in January 1793, when he attended meetings of several radical societies. When he was in London he seems to have corresponded quite frequently with the Edinburgh Friends of the People.[58] In

May 1793, he presented the Edinburgh petition in support of Grey's motion in the Commons on parliamentary reform. His commitment to the Scottish Friends of the People continued after the spring of 1793, when many advanced Whigs dropped away from the cause of reform, and he showed solidarity with the Scottish radicals into the autumn. It was under his franking privilege as an MP that the *Edinburgh Gazetteer*, one of two Edinburgh radical newspapers formed in the autumn of 1792, was sent free through the post. In January 1793, it was reported from Edinburgh that without the influence of Daer and Macleod 'the Friends of the People could not go on'.[59]

Daer was, therefore, an advanced Whig with a foot in both Scottish and English reform camps. Yet, his political outlook and reactions to events in France and Britain in the early 1790s can only be fully appreciated in terms of his education, interactions with English rational dissent, enthusiasm for scientific enlightenment, restless curiosity and an egalitarianism rooted in a profound sense of duty to the 'public good'. Equally importantly, by at least 1792, and perhaps a bit earlier, he had a place at the heart of metropolitan radicalism.

He was, in the first place, present at the meeting of advanced reformers held at the Crown and Anchor tavern in July 1791 to mark the second anniversary of the fall of the Bastille.[60] More significantly, Daer was one of several Scots who in the following year became members of the London Corresponding Society (LCS), a body in which émigré Scottish artisans were well represented, not least through its first secretary, Thomas Hardy. It was to Daer that Hardy wrote in July 1792 asking for information about the spread of liberty north of the border.[61] In the autumn of 1792, Walter Berry was introduced to a meeting of the LCS by Thomas Christie, son of Montrose merchant Alexander Christie, and nephew of William Christie, Unitarian minister at St Cyrus in Angus. Berry was an Edinburgh bookseller, and one of two men responsible for the publication of the *Caledonian Chronicle*, the second and more short-lived of the two Edinburgh radical papers of the early 1790s. Hardy wrote, again in a letter to Daer, that the LCS had been 'highly pleased with the informations' that Berry had 'communicated' from Scotland. He went on:

> If you now judge it proper and have opportunity to promote a correspondence between any of the societies in Scotland and the London Corresponding Society it will tend to cement us together for by uniting we shall become stronger and a threefold cord is not easily broken – It appears absolutely necessary by communicating with each other we shall know one another's mind and act with one heart in the same important cause.[62]

What he meant by a three-fold cord is somewhat unclear, although it may have been a reference to Ireland.

Daer became a member of several other metropolitan reform and radical bodies. Like Macleod, he was a signatory to the initial declaration of the Whig Association of the Friends of the People, as well as being present at meetings of the Friends of the Liberty of the Press.[63] He joined the Society for Constitutional Information (SCI), which by the first half of 1792 was acting as the co-ordinating body in metropolitan radicalism before this role was taken over by the LCS later in the year. Daer's membership of the SCI was proposed by the veteran reformer Major John Cartwright and seconded by Thomas Paine.[64] As far as we can tell from the society's minutes, he was an active member in 1792–3. In 1793, for example, he was nominated one of the stewards for an anniversary dinner of the society. Another of his actions was to nominate and see elected John Millar, professor of civil law at the University of Glasgow, as an honorary member in the previous summer.[65]

Daer was thus extremely well placed to help thread together several parts of the British reform movement in the early 1790s. He was present at the first general convention of Scottish radicals in Edinburgh in early December 1792, as well as the third and British conventions, and, as we have seen, was a keen advocate of cooperation with reform societies in London and 'the supporters of freedom at a distance'. His radicalism, moreover, went well beyond the conservative reformism of the Whig Association of the Friends of the People, and indeed a good proportion of the initial Scottish reform leadership. In early May 1792, he chaired a meeting at the White Hart Tavern, Holborn, of delegates from the SCI, the Southwark Society of the Friends of the People, and the London Society of the Friends of the People – the latter two not to be confused with the Whig Association of the Friends of the People – which agreed to publish in the press a 'Declaration of the Constitutional Rights of the King, Lords and Commons of Great Britain', among which were universal suffrage and annual parliaments.[66] By this period, Daer was being described as one of the capital's leading 'Jacobins' in the conservative metropolitan press.[67] The same contemporary diarist, quoted from earlier on p. 70, who praised his 'ardour for liberty' also wrote in her diary in the early summer of 1792, 'Lord Daer has been much in France he is a member of the Jacobin club, whose opinions and proceedings he says are much misrepresented in England'.[68] The anxiety which opposition Whigs and many Scottish reformers showed to distance themselves and their cause from events in France was not shared by Daer.

As we saw, Daer was in Paris in 1789 to witness the opening phases of the Revolution, including the fall of the Bastille. He was in France again between April and July 1791, as a member of a party comprising two of his younger siblings, Thomas and John, and his brother-in-law, Sir James Hall of Dunglass.[69] They were later joined in Paris by Daer's father.

Hall's diary is the only account to survive of the trip in 1791.[70] Mentions of Daer are infrequent, and shed little additional light on his personality or views. In several of its entries, we catch, nevertheless, fleeting glimpses of a man swept up in the explosion of excited political talk and speculation in the French capital. The trip coincided with the French royal family's flight to Varennes and subsequent upsurge of republican enthusiasm and feeling in Paris. Daer appears to have been the first of those on the trip to attend meetings of the Jacobins.[71] He was also a frequent attender at debates in the national assembly. Brown suggests that Hall's diary documents a change in its author's political views in a more radical direction as he strove to comprehend the nature and tendency of the events to which he was witness. Daer may well have pushed him in this direction, although there is no proof of this. The diary does reveal clearly, however, that it was in France in 1791 that Daer first met Paine, accompanying him back to England in early July.[72]

The political detonation in Daer's mind caused by witnessing the dramatic events in Paris in the early summer of 1791 may be inferred from his subsequent actions. That it confirmed him in his commitment to radical political reform and gave much sharper definition to his egalitarian instincts seems indisputable.[73] A striking feature of his interventions in the radical convention politics of 1792–3 is how far he looked to import into British radical political *praxis* systems which he had seen in operation in the French National Assembly, as a way of helping to prevent 'aristocratical dependence' and create a fully democratic style of politics.[74]

Daer's role in Scottish and British reform politics in the early 1790s also exposes the web of connections being forged between Scottish and English radicals from at least 1792, a process which, as we have begun to see, can be traced back to relationships and networks in operation from the previous decade. This nexus extended much more widely than between the Scottish Friends of the People and the Whig Association of the Friends of the People. It was William Skirving, one of the main architects of the British convention, who at the first Scottish general convention proposed, albeit unsuccessfully, a series of far-reaching measures designed to achieve much closer and continuous cooperation and communication between the Scottish Friends of the People and their counterparts in London and England.[75] It was a proposal which, as we have seen, Daer echoed in his letter to Grey in January 1793.

There is not scope here to rehearse in any detail the story of the British convention, which, in any case, has been very ably and fully discussed in John Barrell's *Imagining the King's Death*.[76] Two aspects of this meeting, however, do merit brief comment. The first is the commonly expressed view that the Scottish radicals were led into a new extremism at the convention by the presence and intervention of the English delegates – Maurice Margarot and Joseph Gerrald from the LCS, Charles Sinclair from the SCI and Matthew Brown from the

Sheffield Society for Constitutional Information.[77] The arrival of Margarot, Gerrald and Sinclair in the Scottish capital in the first week of November galvanized Scottish radicals, causing, in the first place, Skirving and the Edinburgh general committee to recall the third convention for 19 November. Margarot and his English colleagues played crucial roles in guiding this reconvened convention to adopt several controversial measures and initiatives, notably the idea of the emergency convention, but also, at Daer's suggestion, the organization of business into French-style divisions. The key question, however, is how far Margarot and the other English delegates were working with rather than against the grain of Scottish radicalism at this stage.

There is no simple answer to this question since the views of Scottish radicals at this stage remained quite diverse. Some were alienated by the trajectory of radical politics in late 1793, the turning away from the moderate stance which had characterized Scottish radical politics up to that point. The need to continue to avoid confrontational tactics and 'violent measures' was urged on Skirving by several individuals prior to the meeting of the third convention. On the other hand, even before the arrival of the English delegates, the Scottish radicals had finally declared unambiguously that the political reform sought was universal suffrage and annual parliaments. The vote on this at the third convention was unanimous, with several delegates arguing that this move would be strongly supported by their constituents. The political views of those who made this decision were hardened, even transformed, by their experiences of radical politics in the previous twelve months, but also by intense loyalist, government and judicial hostility from the autumn of 1792.

Union with their English counterparts, the other key aspect of the British convention, was also enthusiastically supported by Scottish radicals in late 1793; and this is the second point which requires emphasis. Plans for closer cooperation between radicals in different parts of Britain appear to have been widely discussed in the autumn of 1793. In September, one radical wrote from Cromarty of the advantages which union promised to the cause. 'This union betwixt the two nations', he enthused, 'shall not, like the former [i.e. the Union of 1707] be effected by the distribution of sordid gold; but result from the genuine impulses of Patriotism, uniformly tending to one centre.'[78] This vision of a new union, a union of the people, was almost certainly what Daer had in mind earlier in 1793. When the proposal for union was made at the re-called third convention, it received unanimous support. Daer was one of the delegates who sat on the committee of union appointed by the convention. One of the divisions, or 'sections', in which the delegates met in the mornings, drew up a document entitled 'Hints on the Question of Union'. The first of these hints read:

That the people of Great Britain (disclaiming every distinction of Scots & English) from this Period, & forever, doe unite themselves into one Mass, & in an Indissoluble Union, Bold appeal to this Island & to the Universe; that they demand the restoration of the Rights, from which demand they shall never depart.

In order to achieve this end, the division recommended that delegates from national conventions in England and Scotland meet twice yearly on the banks of the River Tweed. This would be a symbolic meeting place 'where the Ashes of their Ancestors now Lye', ancestors who had been condemned to die because of the 'caprice of the few in the Paltry Feuds of Court Etiquette'. It was also suggested that a weekly communication be opened up between 'South' and 'North' either by letter or in person so that 'Occurrences maybe known from one end of the Kingdom to the other' in order to 'strengthen & instruct every individual of this great but one indivisible Mass'.[79]

The suppression by the authorities of the British convention and subsequent sedition trials in 1794 of Margarot, Sinclair, Gerrald and Skirving marked the end of the open phase of radicalism in Scotland in the 1790s. It drove a small minority of Scottish radicals to contemplate insurrection as the only means to rescue or continue to pursue the radical cause, one result of which was the so-called Watt or pike plot, associated with the Edinburgh wine merchant and former government informer, Robert Watt.[80] Daer by this stage was dying and removed from events in Scotland, although an obituary in the opposition Whig paper the *Morning Chronicle* claimed that he repudiated his former political allies once they embraced violence as the means of reform.[81] There is no corroboration for this, and it certainly suited the opposition Whigs to say this in 1795.[82] Links, meanwhile, between Scottish and English radicals appear to have become fractured and very sporadic, certainly until 1795–6, when efforts were made to rejoin the connection to, certainly, the LCS.[83] By this point, however, the relationship to Ireland and Irish radicalism had assumed a new importance, symptomatic of which was the formation of the United Scotsmen. In the earlier 1790s, there were links with the United Irishmen, not least through Thomas Muir, but they were probably rather less important than is suggested in various recent accounts of Scottish reform politics in this period.[84] At the end of October 1793, Robert Dundas received one report on the third convention, which referred to a letter from the 'four united societys of Ireland', which supposedly claimed that there were 200,000 in Ireland ready to join with the Scottish radicals. According to the author of this report, one of the dominant personalities at this convention, Alexander Callendar, 'was agt having any connection with them'.[85]

So, how should we view Daer's political career and the unfolding pattern of relationships and attitudes which this paper has outlined? One obvious point to make is that, while not without precedent, what was taking place in the 1790s was a point of departure in reform politics. Wilkite radicalism was English not

British; effigies of Wilkes were still, apparently, being burnt in Edinburgh into the early nineteenth century.[86] Attempts were made by the Rev. Christopher Wyvill and the Association Movement in 1782–3 to forge alliances with the emergent burgh and county reform movements in Scotland, but these did not amount to terribly much. There are hints that the formation and activities of the SCI had some influence on reformers in Scotland, as they did, indeed, in Ireland. We should perhaps not give too much weight to this; if it was symptomatic of anything it was probably the growing influence of print in the later eighteenth century as a force drawing the different parts of the British Isles into much closer political proximity. In any case, what stands out is not the links between Scottish and English reform in the 1780s, but rather, through individuals like John Jebb, those between Ireland and England.[87]

Secondly, Scottish radicals, as with reformers and radicals elsewhere in the British Isles in the 1790s, tended to see themselves as members of a cause that transcended nation, but which looked to nations (in this instance Britain) as the vehicles of political, moral and social regeneration. As the case of Lord Daer shows, there were threads within enlightenment culture in Scotland in the later eighteenth century which strongly expedited this tendency, at an intellectual level, but also in terms of forging connections across national boundaries, and shaping perspectives which looked well beyond nation. Enlightenment for Daer, as for his teacher Dugald Stewart, was at one and the same time patriotic, pragmatic and idealist. Politics for Daer seems to have been in part an extension of the business of 'improvement'. To adapt an idea of Vaclav Havel, it was a form of 'practical morality', a 'service to the truth' and humanity.[88] Enlightenment was a protean, shifting set of realities, and is ill suited to tight definition; Edinburgh in the 1780s was not simply the breeding ground of anxious loyalism.

Finally, union was for Britain's late eighteenth-century radicals, first and foremost, a political strategy. The full title of the committee on union formed at the British convention was the committee 'for framing a Precious Unnion between Englishmen & Scotchmen as the most effectual measure for attaining the rights of the People'.[89] For Scots, as Daer noted in his letter to Grey in early 1793, union had the additional advantage of providing necessary leadership from elsewhere. Union offered the hope also of better protection against the forces of repression. As Skirving poignantly observed in April 1794 from aboard the ship, the 'Surprise', which was due to transport him to Botany Bay: 'Uniting Love is the strength, as well as solace of mankind.' His advice to his fellow radicals could not have been more unambiguous: 'Cement by reciprocal kind communications, the Union of hearts, of interest, of measures, which have solemnly been resolved. By so doing, you will escape the destruction which is coming on all the earth.'[90] For some, the early 1790s also presented, or seemed to present, an opportunity to eclipse the Union of 1707, to produce a genuine union bred of shared goals and attitudes; a people's union, in short, and not a corrupt bargain arranged between elites, as the 1707 settlement was often portrayed. This, it seems, was Daer's view. Daer, it is worth noting in this context, was completely opposed to Thomas Muir's attempts to introduce into the first general convention an address from the United Irishmen which contained an appeal to Scottish nationalist sentiment. As the minutes of this convention noted, 'Lord Daer was against the paper being answered or even lying on the table'.[91] Most influential Scottish radicals in the 1790s were British or even Anglo-British radicals who happened to be Scots; and to this extent, their history is one which is best viewed in a British context. To suggest that Daer was a nationalist, as some have sought to do, is to misunderstand both the man and his visionary politics.[92]

4 THE POLITICAL AND CULTURAL LEGACY OF ROBERT BURNS IN SCOTLAND AND ULSTER, c. 1796–1859

Christopher A. Whatley

Introduction

Robert Burns, Scotland's self-proclaimed national bard, was mourned, and his birth and life celebrated, at suppers or 'festivals' held on or around 25 January (his birthday) from the start of the nineteenth century. Like the first, held in 1801 at Alloway, near Ayr, Burns's birthplace (but on 21 July, the fifth anniversary of his death), most took place in Scotland, although by no means exclusively, and over time a pattern was established whereby Burns's birthday was celebrated annually, and internationally.[1] On 25 January 1859, the centenary of Burns's birth, there was hardly a town, village or hamlet in Lowland Scotland where some kind of celebration marking the occasion was not organized. The project was orchestrated by Burns enthusiasts in Glasgow in 1858 who sent invitations to participate in it around the globe. One contemporary counted 676 local festivals in Scotland alone. There were also dinners, soirees, lectures, exhibitions and concerts in many other parts of the world where Burns's works were read – participants often interconnected by means of the new electric telegraph.[2] Ulster, with its strong social, economic, religious, cultural and linguistic ties with south-west Scotland, was one of these places, although the orchestrated campaign of celebration reached out to the farthest extremities of the British Empire as well as the United States. That the nineteenth century was the heyday throughout Europe of the Romantic cult of the national hero, and of national milestones, jubilees and anniversaries, serves as a warning against exaggerating the significance of the outpouring of public enthusiasm for Robert Burns.[3] Even so, contemporaries were struck by the depth of the fervour there was for Burns, particularly in Scotland; the term 'Burnomania' was coined in 1811 to describe the poet's popularity and celebrity.[4]

What is also clear, however, is that Burns's legacy was fiercely contested. Burns as a poet and song adaptor had multiple voices; the protean Scot.[5] Neither was his memory produced spontaneously; it was mediated and manufactured, the sum of disparate parts.[6] Consequently, it was difficult to claim him unambiguously for any particular set of values or a single political ideology, although in the 250 years since his death many have tried so to do.[7] Of the tensions this created in Scotland, the most public was between radicals and conservatives. Of Ulster too, it has been recognized that Burns was an important influence in the 1790s, primarily amongst communities of handloom weavers in the counties of Antrim and Down. Amongst the factors that attracted radically-inclined weavers to Burns were his 'egalitarian and democratic sentiments, his outspoken pro-Americanism' and his depiction of Westminster as a corrupt political system.[8] Yet whilst some of Ulster's 'rhyming weavers' were to participate in the 1798 Rising, by no means did all of them associate with, let alone join, the United Irishmen.[9] Recent work has shown that Burns was also promoted as 'the inspiration and figurehead for a whole school of conservative poets, editors and patrons ... and might be described as the tutelary poet of conservative as much as radical Ulster'.[10] This essay extends the time-frame beyond the 1790s, and is concerned with how Burns was portrayed, exploited and received in both Scotland and Ulster, in the half century or so after his death.

Contested Memory

In Scotland, notwithstanding Burns's well-known radical associations, it was the Tories and their allies (including Whigs such as Lord Francis Jeffrey), who led the way in commandeering and shaping in their own interests the memory of Burns. Their aim was to counter the social unrest they feared was resulting from the linked processes of rampant industrialization and rapid urbanization.[11] Following the revolutions in Europe, not only France's in 1789 but also the widespread revolts of 1830, Scotland's dominant classes suffered from periodic intimations of the dangers posed by disaffection.[12] Tories were especially fearful of what they perceived to be the threat of militant radicalism.[13] In 1819 Sir Walter Scott defined the Radicals of that period as 'a set of blackguards a hundred times more mischievous and absurd than our old friends in 1794 and 1795'.[14] The inclination of Scott and others of his stamp was to look backwards to rural paternalism for a model of social relations appropriate for the industrial age. It was amongst the Scottish peasantry that a sense of loyalty to their social superiors was still to be found, unlike the inhabitants of the manufacturing districts, where in years of bad trade the large numbers of unemployed – 'a separate class, a new state' – provided 'excellent materials for the demagogue'.[15] But Tory idealism also had to compete with the growing influence of those strands of radicalism in Scotland that in the 1830s and 1840s were channelled into 'moral force' Chartism, and demands for political change that would ameliorate working class distress.[16] Values and principles articulated in Burns's work, as well as selective interpretations of aspects of Burns's life, were appropriated by radically-inclined Scots in the first half of the nineteenth century. Manifested first in Chartism, many of the same values were held equally dear by the Chartists' successors, the radical Liberals. It was this form of popular liberalism, anti-aristocratic and centring on notions of oppression and injustice, to which large sections of the respectable working class turned after 1848, often in alliance with the petty bourgeoisie and the middle classes.[17] Thus, despite their best efforts, conservatives in Scotland were unable to corral Burns's legacy in the service of the political and social status quo against what many of them saw as the dangers of unbridled 'democratic ambition'.

Social historians and historians of labour and popular politics in early nineteenth-century Scotland have had little or nothing to say about Burns's influence.[18] This is not so in regard to Ulster, where for some time it has been established that Burns was not only widely read, but also influential – as noted on the previous page – amongst the Ulster-Scots weaver poets of the region. For many of them Burns was a heroic figure and a role model. He was considered to be a brother bard, and admired as a patriot and champion of liberty.[19] The strength of Burns's appeal in Ulster is hinted at by the fact that it was in Belfast that the first edition of Burns's works was published outside Scotland, in September 1787, while the United Irishmen's *Northern Star* too had a 'fondness' for printing the poems of Burns.[20] Yet in Scotland most historians have tended to focus on and explain the enthusiasm there was for Burns after the Disruption of 1843, and into the twentieth century.[21] This is despite the fact that in the early years of the nineteenth century there was acute alarm in some circles about how pervasive and damaging to public morals and social stability was the popularity of what one critic called 'the worse than trash of Burns'.[22] The political significance of Burns's legacy, well before the century's end (when, it has been asserted, Burns's influence was at its height) has been largely overlooked.[23] Perhaps too much importance has been attached to the fact that Burns was promoted as a role model by advocates of laissez-faire liberalism, a hegemonic 'paradigm of Scottish bourgeois virtue'.[24] He was certainly adopted in this manner by Scotland's manufacturing and commercial elite, as he was in Belfast, Ulster's burgeoning industrial centre, and a major port.[25] Burns, however, was revered across the classes – on both sides of the North Channel.[26] In Scotland as in Ulster there is evidence that he was held in especially high regard by the mainly skilled and literate, independent, usually Protestant and largely sober segments of the respectable working classes. Not infrequently, they were also members of freemason's lodges. Indeed, that Burns himself had been a freemason may have been one of the factors that drew the Ulster weaver poets to Burns.[27] The celebrants of the first 1801 Burns supper, in

Alloway, were freemasons. Processions of freemasons were prominent at most of the events celebrating Burns in the first half of the nineteenth century in both lowland Scotland and Ulster. They featured prominently at many of the dinners, soirées and other centennial festivities in 1859: thus at Haddington, near Edinburgh, one of those presiding at the dinner was Robert Richardson, Master of the town's lodge, while 'a considerable number of the company wore the insignia of the Masonic body'.[28] Lodges of freemasons in Scotland, however, seem rarely to have been as self-consciously egalitarian as their Ulster counterparts; indeed in Scotland, where in the provinces lodge membership included high proportions of the gentry and urban elites – along with tradesmen – discussion of political and religious subjects may even have been discouraged.[29] But we should be careful not to exaggerate Burns's influence in Ulster. Whilst it is undoubtedly true that Burns inspired many Ulster-Scots poets to think, write and publish in the vernacular, there was a bardic tradition in Ulster which predated Burns. That tradition included the writing of satirical and subversive verse. Like the radical poetry that followed, it was located in an Irish setting, directed at Irish injustices, and expressed in the writers' own voices.[30] And, as Liam McIlvanney has made clear, the limits to 'bardolatry' were exposed further when Burns joined the Dumfries Volunteers, apparently deserting his erstwhile radical admirers across the North Channel.[31]

Nevertheless, there is ample evidence that Burns's works were widely known. In Belfast, there were further editions of the 1787 collection of poems referred to on p. 81 – a copy of the Edinburgh edition. Another sixteen editions had appeared in Ulster by 1826. By 1805, less than ten years after Burns's death, James Currie's *Works of Robert Burns* had reached its fifth edition and sold more than 10,000 copies. An eighth edition had been published by 1820.[32] The *Works* could be borrowed too, from several of the 200-plus subscription libraries that were founded in provincial Scotland between 1800 and 1830, and through which much Enlightenment writing, including Burns, was disseminated and discussed. While the instigators of subscription libraries tended to be drawn from the urban elites, there was working-class involvement too. Handloom weavers were an occupational group who had their own small but heavily used subscription libraries.[33] Indeed reading rooms for and reading societies of the labouring classes are said to have 'proliferated' during the period of the French Revolution.[34] As has been seen, newspapers too published Burns's poems. Literacy levels were relatively high in the Presbyterian communities of Lowland Scotland and Ulster, reading ability especially so, with the Bible and Burns being the two books most often found in the households of ordinary people.[35] Beyond the rapidly extending but still relatively confined orbit of the subscription and circulating libraries, cheap editions of Burns's works and the unauthorized appearance of some of his poems and songs in chapbooks costing a penny, and in equally cheap broadsheets, meant that Burns was becoming accessible to thousands of ordinary people. In Scotland, as many as 200,000 chapbooks may have been sold annually – and were available virtually everywhere, transported into the smallest hamlets by peddlers, hawkers and chapmen.[36] And just as Burns himself had acquired many of the songs he collected by listening – mainly to women – acquaintance with Burns happened too by word of mouth, as was later recalled by Andrew Somerville, the son of a Berwickshire agricultural worker, who heard several of Burns's poems and songs before reading them.[37] In Ulster too, where there was also an enduring song culture, many of Burns's songs were heard before they were seen in print.[38]

What may be important here is that at least some of Burns's work was received unmediated by Tory commentators and censorious editors (discussed below on pp. 85 and 88).[39] Heard or read thus, the effects could be profound, with readers from comparatively humble backgrounds testifying to their elation on first becoming acquainted with Burns.[40] Reading context was important for certain kinds of poetry. As John Barrell has argued, read in periodicals intent on fostering a popular radical culture, pastoral sentimentality could take on a sharp subversive edge.[41] Thus a poem such as 'The Twa Dogs', which was the first to be seen by readers who opened the frequently reprinted Kilmarnock edition, could be interpreted as an exemplification of peasant contentment. Equally it could be read as a questioning of social hierarchy;[42] or, more crudely, as an attack on landlord greed, and indifference, and a celebration of the spiritually richer lives of the far from docile cottar class.[43] In this as in other poems representative of what Colin Kidd has termed 'the politics of sentiment', Burns gave voice to the poor, hungry and the hitherto powerless.[44] His verses not only offered empathy, succour and support, but also articulated the rumbling resentments that may have lain beneath the sullen and eerie silence that in Scotland accompanied the processes of rural commercialization, proletarianization and clearance.[45] Autobiographical evidence provides further support for the proposition that from an early date, Burns's songs had a powerful appeal, and provided moral underpinning and inspiration for radically inclined artisans. In his *Recollections* of 1844, William Thom, the handloom weaver poet of the north-east, and a Chartist agitator, described the relentlessly dull, soul-destroying environment of the weaving shed in which he had been employed in Aberdeen, and recorded his indebtedness to the gloom-lifting 'Song Spirits as they walked in melody from loom to loom'. When 'the breast was filled with everything but hope and happiness', he recalled, 'a vigorous chorus of "A man's a man for a' that"' cheered the 'fagged' weavers.[46]

In Scotland Burns's best-known poetry-writing contemporaries were the handloom weavers, a disproportionate number of whom were located in Renfrewshire – the county town of which was the rapidly expanding textile manufacturing centre of Paisley.[47] Not dissimilar to his reception in Ulster in the later 1780s and 1790s, in terms of subject matter, poetic form, the use of vernacular language and his sentiments, Burns inspired many to follow in his footsteps, with poets from Paisley and its surrounds producing a hefty body of radical verse which clearly owes much to his influence.[48] Just how many people from backgrounds of this kind owed their ventures into poetry writing to Burns is unknown, although it has been claimed that in the early nineteenth century almost 'every village in Scotland' could boast its local imitator.[49] Working class versifiers included Perthshire's Robert Nicoll, James Taylor in Fenwick, Ayrshire and Andrew Fisher, a Chartist from Larkhall in Lanarkshire, who consciously adopted the role of bard of the local mining community.[50] England too had its share of Burns-inspired worker poets.[51]

In some cases direct links can be traced from Burns's poetry to that of his imitators and thence through traditional dissent to the sharper political programme of the Chartist movement. Thom provides an example of this. Another is the Glasgow operative weaver Alexander Rodger's 'The Twa Weavers', which borrows heavily from the dualistic format of Burns's 'The Twa Dogs', where Luath and Caesar debate and compare the lives of cottar and landlord. In Rodger's poem the two discussants, Robin and Tammas, highlight the plight of the handloom weavers who '*live* naewhere' but 'starve at Tollcross', before expatiating on a litany of complaints about corrupt politicians, bankers, monopolists, machinery and canting churchmen. The poem closes with the patriotic reflection on 'Poor Britain! How sadly thou glories decline', before conceding that the weavers' prospects are 'most gloomy and black': 'Unless the BLACK Box to the flames we consign / And begin a new score, like our fathers langsyne.'[52]

Also indicative of Burns's impact amongst artisans, tradesmen, small employers and shopkeepers, are fragments of evidence which suggest that the emerging tradition of keeping alive in a formal sense the memory of Robert Burns was not solely the preserve of Scotland's aristocrats, Tories and other members of the social elite who organized and attended most of the early dinners to mark Burns's birthday.[53] Thus whilst men of this rank applauded Burns's advocacy of independence, this – especially independence from the state but also from aristocratic rule – was equally important to large numbers of working people, including plebeian radicals, and practised through a plethora of mutual aid societies, including trade unions.[54] In 1820, the year of the so-called Radical War in Scotland, in the weaving village of Kilbarchan, a New Burns Club was formed, partly as a reaction to the alleged 'aristocratic' nature of Burns suppers held there hitherto.[55] Only bread and cheese and water were consumed at the new club's suppers – a menu designed to deny the government tax revenue and force it to 'submit to the views of the inhabitants'. Although less is known about the Burns Club of Ayr, that in 1836 its president was Dr John Taylor, Ayrshire's Chartist revolutionary, suggests that at least some of its members may have had radical leanings too, although his later calls for violence, albeit more rhetorical than real, probably left most them behind.[56]

Commemoration

Despite Burns's undoubted popular appeal, much of the initial impetus to commemorate and celebrate Burns came from Scottish aristocrats and others of relatively high social standing – bankers, merchants, lawyers and the like, whether in Scotland, England or parts of Britain's overseas empire, India in particular. In North America too Burns was avidly read.[57] The committee established in 1819 for a national memorial to Burns in Edinburgh was chaired by the Duke of Atholl, whilst amongst the 'noblemen and gentlemen' present were Lord Keith, and Charles Forbes, MP, sometime head of Forbes & Co, of Bombay.[58] It was certainly not Burns's radicalism such men wished to memorialize. The sponsors of the Edinburgh memorial were keen to promote Burns as a product of Scotland's superior educational system, and of a Presbyterian polity.[59] In Dumfries, 'the committee and noblemen and gentlemen connected with the south of Scotland' who were behind the move to erect the mausoleum over the poet's grave had felt it necessary to play down Burns's political views in order to persuade the Duke of Buccleuch to participate. Instead they stressed the advantages to the county town of the increase in visitors – literary tourists and reverent pilgrims – that might result from such an attraction.[60]

Burns's early biographers and editors of his works too turned a blind eye to Burns's most scathing social commentaries, along with his politics. 'I suppose it will be thought prudent to avoid all political allusions in the life', wrote James Currie, before taking on the task of being Burns's first major, and posthumous, biographer.[61] Similarly, in the preface to his *Reliques of Robert Burns*, published in 1808, R. H. Cromek declared it proper to omit any of Burns's compositions which displayed 'a spirit of resentment, the result of the moment', or those the publication of which, 'although in these days perfectly harmless, might render the Editor obnoxious to the letter, though not to the spirit of the law.'[62] Other critics in the same mould – Edinburgh University's Professor John Wilson for example, an outspoken enemy of parliamentary reform – expressed disbelief that the man who wrote 'The Cotter's Saturday Night' could also have been a Jacobin. Wilson explained Burns's attachment to democracy as fleeting, born of a Byronic desire to shock, whilst also dismissing the charge as one exaggerated by Dumfries's Tories.[63] At core, Wilson declared, Burns was a patriot, his song 'Does Haughty Gaul' embodying more political wisdom, and appealing more effectively to the 'noblest principles of patriotism in the British heart', than any orator either inside or outside parliament. Indeed in the years immediately after his death, and during the ongoing conflict with France, Burns was frequently used to galvanize the powerful pro-British patriotic sentiment that had emerged in the wake of the threat of French invasion, his songs bowdlerized and embellished in the ubiquitous song chapbooks of the early nineteenth century.[64] This was not simply a passing phase. Burns and British-ness were often conjoined by leading nineteenth-century celebrants of the poet, albeit that he was lauded primarily as the saviour of Scottish language, song and national pride.[65]

Tories and 'The Cotter's Saturday Night'

Burns's patriotic poetry, song and sentiments – British as well as those that aroused Scottish nationalistic ardour – united Scotland's Whigs and Tories and induced something of a cross-class consensus. Some of his other work, however – or even the same work read differently, clearly had the capacity to unsettle. Initially it may seem perverse to conflate 'The Cotter's Saturday Night' with anything other than social tranquillity. With its portrayal of a humble rural household at the head of which was a pious patriarch, 'The Cotter's Saturday Night' was a Scottish manifestation of industrializing Europe's 'discovery' of the stoical peasant, with commentators like Currie praising the poem for its representation of 'a form of naturalised civil society operating harmoniously with minimum state intervention'.[66] Not only in Scotland but throughout Europe it was in the 'frugal life and noble labour' of the peasantry that the 'virtues of goodness, humility, loyalty, piety and natural wisdom' were to be found.[67] The attributes which were intrinsic to this version of rural society, headed by the aristocracy and held together by the bonds of interdependence, paternalism and deference, Scotland's leading conservatives wished to inculcate into the hearts and minds of Scotland's present-day country and small town dwellers, tomorrow's big city migrants. The patriotic flourish of the two final stanzas of the poem wherein a 'virtuous Populace' might rise and 'stand a wall of fire around their much- / lov'd ISLE', and God was implored 'never, never' to 'SCOTIA'S realm desert', could appeal equally to Scot and Briton. Because it offered such a powerful recipe for social contentment within a secure homeland, the poem became, in effect, a manifesto for Scotland's conservative elite.[68]

This was the primary ideological thrust of speakers at the Ayr Burns Festival in August 1844. Instigated by John Wilson, the Earl of Eglinton and Sir Archibald Alison, the Tory Sheriff of Lanarkshire, ostensibly the festival was organized to honour Burns's three surviving sons, two of whom had now returned to Scotland after many years overseas in the service of the East India Company. Homage was to be paid by 'an admiring and repentant people' – assuaging the widespread sense of guilt there was that the nation's bard had been permitted to end his days in penury, pain and as a pariah cast out by his former lionizers. The location was chosen with care: near the place of Burns's birth, and in full view of Thomas Hamilton's delicately classical Alloway monument to the poet, completed in 1823 (see Figure 4.1 on p. 91).

Yet, as indicated, in the forefront of the minds of the organizers of the festival was the hope that it would serve to reinforce the bulwark of aristocratic paternalism in Scotland, and thereby counter the baneful effects of modernity.[69] This goes a long way towards explaining why several of the speeches that were delivered to the well-heeled audience who were crowded into the great tented pavilion at

Ayr acknowledged the industry and frugality but also the piety and patriotism of the Scottish peasantry. The source of their 'beautiful attribute of contentment', asserted Sir David Hunter-Blair of Blairquhan, proprietor of an estate to the east of Ayr, was to be found in the Scottish rural worker's household – as depicted by Burns in 'The Cotter's Saturday Night'. The choice of 'The Cotter's Saturday Night' as the festival's manifesto was masterly in another respect too. Albeit in an idealized fashion, with its emphasis on the family unit at the head of which was the hard-working, pious patriarch, the poem represented a way of life that was still recognizable, certainly to Ayrshire's rural population, and with which they could readily identify, and empathize – a point to which we will return below.

But the poem seems to have been familiar to and to have resonated with ordinary people elsewhere too, especially in rural and small-town Scotland.[70] Both in Ayrshire and across the North Channel there could still be detected in the homes of small tenant farmers, village tradesmen and agricultural workers 'a serious tone of conversation, where readings from the family Bible were commonplace, the Sabbath was observed, and children were reared with an appreciation of the importance of honesty and obedience, good service and thrift'.[71] But earnestness in (Presbyterian) religion, especially where there was a strong dissenting tradition, could be combined with an equally sincerely held belief in the cause of political radicalism. This was notably so in handloom weaving communities, where an over-supply of labour, mechanization and the introduction of female labour were leading to the loss on the part of older male weavers of their former status as highly-paid, privileged artisans.[72] At least in part, and despite much telling revisionism and a reassessment of the worth of Ulster's 'rhyming weavers' as poets in their own right (rather than simply being imitators of Burns), New Light Presbyterianism remains a decisive factor in accounting for the radicalism of some of their number – primarily in the Protestant-dominated eastern portion of the province.[73]

Their attractiveness to Scottish Tories notwithstanding, the virtues celebrated in 'The Cotter's Saturday Night', of moral worth, integrity, independent labour and rural living, also had a powerful appeal for mid nineteenth-century British radicals.[74] It was the familiarity of the scenes portrayed and evoked by Burns, and the nostalgia this induced amongst those for whom this was a world that was disappearing or had only recently disappeared, in the cases of those now inhabiting manufacturing towns like Glasgow and Belfast, that appears partly to explain Burn's immense popularity in the nineteenth century.[75] Burns's poetry was rooted in the social life of the countryside and the smaller towns, and captured communal events like dances, fairs and festivals.[76] With their stress too on unaffected simplicity, and references to the nobility of the poor, Burns's poems provided a profoundly attractive image for the former country-dwellers who now inhabited the teeming towns of the early and mid-nineteenth century.[77] A recurring theme in urban culture in early and mid-Victorian Scotland, which also resonated in radical circles, was of a lost Arcadia, an imagined rural idyll that contrasted with the cramped environment of the manufacturing town, with its regimentation of work and space, little of which was open, or green.[78] It was no coincidence that in its later stages Chartism became associated with plans for small-scale land ownership, with Feargus O'Connor envisaging a return to the land as the means of securing independence for working-class families. Popular agrarianism had long been a strand within radical politics, while since 1839 Owenites (followers of Robert Owen) had run a model community farm – 'Harmony' – in Hampshire.[79]

Yet embedded within the text of 'The Cotter's Saturday Night' were more overt challenges for those who sought to employ the poem as a checklist of domestic and societal harmony. Not only were there lines in the poem that were critical of the kirk. Potentially more corrosive were lines from the third last stanza, including:

> Princes and lords are but the breath of kings,
> 'An honest man's the noble work of GOD:'
> And *certes*, in fair Virtue's heavenly road,
> The *Cottage* leaves the *Palace* far behind:

The sentiments expressed here could be read as a mini-hymn on the nobility of the smaller tenants and husbandmen on Scotland's Lowland farms. Professor Wilson of course was well aware of this and had condemned the poem's levelling sentiments.[80] For Wilson and his associates, that Burns had produced such lines, and a poem such as 'The Address of Beelzebub', an anti-landlord, anti-aristocratic diatribe composed in 1786 but held back from publication until 1818, was deeply regrettable.[81]

Radical Reactions

In consolidating a renewed sense of Scottish-ness amongst those present (but within the framework of the British Union the primacy of which was announced symbolically by several prominently-located Union flags), the Ayr festival was undoubtedly a success.[82] In other ways it was rather less so. So unhappy was the well-heeled audience of 1,800 or so in the tented pavilion both with the length of Wilson's speech and about his references to Burns's moral 'frailties' – spoken in the presence of members of Burns's family – that he was booed off the stage.[83] In this respect the responses to Burns in Scotland and Ulster were different, at least to a degree. While there were those in Scotland who welcomed Wilson's strictures, there appears to have been a sizeable body of evangelical Protestant opinion in Belfast (which Burns's eldest son visited to much acclaim later in 1844) that was less inclined to overlook Burns's moral laxity and thought Wilson had not gone far enough.[84] To critics in both Scotland and Ulster the *Belfast*

News-Letter responded by conceding that a number of Burns's acts 'no moralist will admire', but at the same time asserting the right of 'Scotchmen' to revere the genius of Burns and to celebrate him as a national hero.[85]

In terms of reaction to the festival, equally instructive is the reflection by a London journalist present at Ayr, that even if there had been no pavilion with its 'tasteful draperies ... and elevated galleries', 'the manifestation of respect on the part of *the people* towards *their poet*, would have been accomplished' and the '*heart-beatings* of Scotland, as thoroughly accomplished'. This may be a reference to the inclusion amongst the banners held aloft by those in the procession of 'the ancient historic flag of Scotland', but more likely to an eight-foot high thistle near the marchers' tail, which when it became visible, induced 'loud and unrestrained' applause on the part of those watching.[86] Struck too by the unprecedented fervour of the crowd, the same writer noted that the arrangements for the procession had been 'the PEOPLE's arrangements', a reference to the fact that a series of sub-committees had been established by the festival's organizers to arrange particular activities.[87] In determining the composition, order and appearance of the Ayr procession, Professor Wilson seems to have been influential, not least in echoing in the Ayr proceedings some of the flavour of the spectacular medieval tournament of 1839 that had been held in the grounds of Eglinton castle, in which Wilson and the Earl of Eglinton had also been key figures.[88] Visually striking, and in keeping with Tory visions of a feudalized Celtic Scotland (and harking back to Eglinton in 1839), were the presence in the 30,000–50,000-strong, three-deep, mile-long procession that preceded the festival, of tartan-bedecked bag-pipers and others dressed as Highland chieftains – as well as characters drawn from Burns's poems.

But if this is clearly indicative of the influence of the festival's organizers, it is highly unlikely that Wilson and his associates would have readily sanctioned the decision that the procession would move, as it did, to the tune of 'A man's a man'. The genesis of this song, probably composed by Burns in 1794, was Thomas Paine's *Rights of Man*.[89] While a version of the song had appeared in print in Belfast in 1796, it had not been published in Scotland until 1805, almost ten years after Burns's death. But by 1844 it had become an established part of the radical song canon in Scotland.[90] More direct evidence in explaining the reception there was on the part of those in the procession at Ayr for Burns's sons as well as for Burns's memory, is to be found in the report of a conversation at the festival between the editor of the *Glasgow Argus* and his companion on the question of why Burns was preferred to Walter Scott. The two men agreed that of a number of reasons for Burns's appeal, the most important lay in the perception of Burns as 'a man of the people ... a sturdy lover and preacher of independence'. Scott by contrast was 'too far above the crowd to attract their affections'.[91] Above all though, Burns was 'a democrat to the bone'.

Britain's radicals were quick to make their views on the Ayr festival known, picking over and contesting the arguments of the speakers – in particular those of Wilson, who had long been the *bete noire* of Scotland's political reformers. He had his critics in Ulster too.[92] As we have seen already, there was nothing new by 1844 in the recruitment by radicals of Burns for their cause. By the end of the 1830s Burns was being included in the pantheon of Scottish, English, French and American liberty-espousing radical philosophers and writers lionized by the Chartists, not only in Scotland but also south of the border.[93] Nor was the editor of Glasgow's *Chartist Circular*, William Thompson, alone in harnessing the poetry of the Romantics for the cause of liberty, and against tyranny.[94] What was different, however, was his positioning in the poetic vanguard in Scotland of Burns, whose works were to be taught in the Chartist schools Thompson was then advocating.[95] Itinerant Chartist lecturers were amongst the thousands of self-styled pilgrims – including several from Ulster – to the 'land of Burns', and the sites associated with the deceased but revered poet, in Ayr, Dumfries, Mauchline and Maybole.

In Scotland the attack on the festival was led by the Rev. Patrick Brewster, Paisley's Chartist minister.[96] The event's organizers were denounced as hypocrites, honouring Burns in 1844, but ignoring him when he was alive (other than for a brief spell when Burns had been fêted in Edinburgh) and, during his final years in Dumfries, in need of support. Do not 'feast upon your poet's grave', thundered the *Northern Star*, 'having first starved him into it'.[97] The charge was a potent one, replicated in Ulster by the editor of the *Belfast News-Letter* who proclaimed that 'If the aristocracy of Scotland had done for Burns, during his lifetime, only a fraction of the part bestowed upon his memory, he might yet have been a living man.'[98] Not dissimilar were the comments of a Chartist lecturer, Julian Harney, who had visited the Burns monument in Alloway the previous year (see Figure 4.1).

Harney readily acknowledged that this was a fitting altar to Burns. Yet according to its Chartist critic it did not reflect well on the class that had erected it: whoever recalls Burns's deathbed appeal for five pounds, he wrote, will regard 'this cold stone pile as a monument to the meanness, as well as pride, of the Scottish aristocracy.'[99] Scrutinized and criticized too were the festival arrangements, not least the separation of the banqueters in the great marquee and the majority of those present who remained outside in the rain for the best part of three hours, to dance or engage otherwise in 'rational amusements'.[100] The *Northern Star* was in no doubt about Burns's importance for reformers:

> wherever the sons of freedom are gathered ... 'A man's a man for a' that' [will] electrify them with the love of equality, while 'Scots wha hae' will inspire them to do and dare all for liberty. The writings of Burns embrace every human heart: hence, despite his nationality, the universal homage paid to his name.[101]

Figure 4.1: The Burns Memorial at Alloway. Designed by Thomas Hamilton, inaugurated in 1823, and instigated by Robert Burns's Tory admirers in Ayrshire, the memorial attracted and met with the approval of thousands of nineteenth-century pilgrims (including many from Ulster) to the site, which was near the poet's birthplace. For Chartist admirers of Burns such as Julian Harney, however, it was a 'cold stone pile' and a 'monument to the meanness as well as the pride, of the Scottish aristocracy' (*Northern Star*, 26 August 1843). Image: Christopher A. Whatley

1844 and 1859 in Scotland and Ulster

By 1844 Burns's memory had become a major cultural force in Scottish society; what Alex Tyrell, following Pierre Nora, has called a 'lieu de memoire'.[102] Burns was celebrated – at Ayr in 1844 as at other public ceremonials – as representing the 'quintessence' of the (Scottish) nation. But as the example of Ayr has also made clear, Burns had the capacity to divide as well as to unite. Public memory was pluralist, not monolithic. Yet in recognition perhaps of the dangers of social division should Burns be hijacked by the promoters of a single cause, in both Scotland and Ulster efforts were made to present Burns as a unifying force. With reference to a public breakfast held in Belfast in honour of Robert Burns (Burns's eldest son) in September 1844, the reformist *Belfast News-Letter* delighted in reporting that those present had

> included men of all religious and political classes – Protestants, R. Catholics, Presbyterians, Unitarians and Quakers ... Repealers, Anti-repealers, Whigs, Tories and radicals, all associated together in the utmost cordiality for the purpose of doing united homage to the genius of Robert Burns.[103]

Similarly, of the centenary celebrations in Scotland of Burns's birth, in January 1859, the Rev. George Gilfillan of Dundee – politically a moderate radical – wrote that they had been supported by all ranks, 'high and low, all creeds and denominations, all varieties of opinion and of caste – nobles, cotters, cotton lords, artisans, churchmen, dissenters, teetotallers, men of mason lodges, and many Englishmen, Irishmen, and foreigners', and 'not in riot and revelry' but 'in calm, sober, though merry and multitudinous assemblies.'[104] Gilfillan, however, had either forgotten, or chosen to overlook, the clergymen and teetotallers who in 1859, as earlier, had deplored the Burns cult and his elevation to the status of secular saint. In a sermon on the theme of 'Herod's birthday was kept', which would have been equally well-received had it been delivered to a similar audience in Ulster, the Rev. Macdowall of Alloa denounced Burns as 'a despiser of evangelical religion' and the Burns celebrations as 'a species of idolatry' which were 'in direct opposition to the will of God'.[105] Indeed, Gilfillan himself had earlier been critical of Burns for his attacks on what Gilfillan termed 'the old Presbyterian spirit', and for failing to celebrate the Covenanters (who by the 1840s had been incorporated as part of the Chartists' heroic heritage): 'What a loss this has been! Had our greatest national poet possessed but in a small degree the religious spirit of his country, what poems might have expressed and immortalised it!'[106]

Gilfillan said nothing either about one of the most momentous gatherings to celebrate Burns in 1859, a dinner in Glasgow's City Hall attended by around 800 people, when the city's uncompromising chief legal officer Archibald Alison had reluctantly conceded that Burns had indeed been a Radical. It was a concession savoured by those who regarded Burns as 'the poet of the people' or even 'the poor man's poet'. 'Blundering' Alison's concession might have been (he had tried to explain away Burns's politics by suggesting that this was a juvenile aberration, a corollary of poetic genius), but it was welcome nonetheless. In the eyes of Alison's detractors, patrician patrons of Burns's memory 'did not care to confess that the ploughman's honest radicalism – that his contempt for the mere guinea stamp – was the quality which had warmed the heart of the nation to him.'[107] Burns, the *Illustrated London News* declared, had 'held up his head among the highest in the land', and spoken to them as an equal; he stood, a 'Ploughman and Exciseman', as the 'Poet of the Scotch', 'the representative of one great democratic idea and formula'.[108] Interestingly, Burns's importance for the working classes in Scotland was recognized in 1864 by Dublin's building labourers, who were bidding to form a general union. A Mr M'Corry, the secretary for the meeting organized for this purpose, called on his brother workers to exert themselves 'in their own cause' as they could expect little help from Dublin's social elite. In Scotland, M'Corry declared to cheers, there was not a labourer 'but flung back with contempt any slight sought to be put on him by the class above him, when he thought of Robert Burns.'[109]

In Ulster too, as in other parts of Ireland, the Burns centenary attracted considerable attention, with a poetry competition being organized by the *Northern Whig*, and festivals and dinners held in Armagh, Dublin, Dundalk, Gort, Limerick, Newry and Tralee. In Belfast there were two large dinners. As in a number of Scottish towns, although not everywhere, there was marked social segregation in the arrangements for the festivities. One of the Belfast dinners, held in the Music Hall, comprised 'Upwards of two hundred gentlemen and a hundred ladies' (including Burns's granddaughter and great-granddaughter), along with the city's social and cultural elites. Owing almost certainly to the audience's belief in the primacy of Protestant virtues, there were 'loud cheers' when in his address Professor G. L. Craik alluded to 'the resolute and indomitable, spirit of Scotch enterprise, Scotch energy, and Scotch industry', even if some observers felt that Craik had rather overdone the Scottish dimension.[110] The other dinner, in the Corn Exchange, was attended mainly by the respectable working classes – numbering around 400 individuals.[111] At this event, unsurprisingly, more was made of Burns's appeal for working people. The stance taken by speakers who addressed this theme was very similar to that adopted by George Gilfillan in Dundee who was cheered by a sizeable audience of 2,000 people when he declared that Burns was the poet of the people, 'not the slavish poet of the aristocracy, as Southey, Scott, and Wordsworth, to some extent all were … he told the people wherein their great strength, like his own, lay, namely, in themselves.'[112]

Temperance was a major issue in Ulster, with the organizers of the Music Hall banquet being heavily criticized for serving alcohol;[113] none was served at the Corn Exchange soirée. At Perth in Scotland, by contrast, the organizers of the City Hall celebration acknowledged temperance concerns by allowing only porter to be drunk, except for a 'small quantity of spirits' – three dozen bottles amongst 900 attendees. But that was as far as they were prepared to go; teetotallers present had simply to make the best of it.[114] Elsewhere, the efforts of Free Church ministers to block the celebrations were largely ignored, although many events were liquor-free.

At both Belfast gatherings, clergymen were prominent amongst the speakers – more so than at most of the celebrations in Scotland; indeed at the Corn Exchange most of the speakers were Presbyterian churchmen. Perhaps for this reason there was a focus in both venues upon Ulster's Scottish connections, with particular emphasis at the Corn Exchange being placed upon the province's Scottish Presbyterian – and Covenanting – foundations, foreshadowing what would become the 'Ulster unionist construction of Ulster-Scottishness in the latter part of the century'. In this guise, for conservative Belfast, Burns was the 'fountainhead of Ulster-Scottish identity' and an acceptable representative of 'Presbyterian literary and religious sensibility (as long as he was adequately edited)'.[115] Thus Burns was necessarily celebrated somewhat differently in Ulster than in Scotland. For the descendants of the many thousands of Scots who had migrated to and settled in Ulster, Burns symbolized a former way of life, and where it was required, a distinct Presbyterian identity in Ireland. Yet as we have seen, in both Ulster and Scotland Burns was appropriated as a model who could serve middle-class and even upper-class interests which, in terms of the primacy of the values of self-help and independence, and an anti-aristocratic stance in politics, coincided with those of many artisans. Even so, whilst the legacy – and memory – of Burns continued to be contested, increasingly, on both sides of the North Channel, Burns was championed by and as the working people's bard, the voice of popular radicalism.

5 'BLESSÈD JUBIL!': SLAVERY, MISSION AND THE MILLENNIAL DAWN IN THE WORK OF WILLIAM WILLIAMS OF PANTYCELYN

E. Wyn James

In London, on 26 August 1743, a young Englishman could be seen escorting a friend into 11 Downing Street. His friend was a young Welshman who had recently arrived on a visit to the capital from his native Breconshire. The purpose of the visit was not to introduce the Welshman to the Chancellor of the Exchequer, since 11 Downing Street had not yet become the Chancellor's official residence. Rather, it was for him to meet for the first time 'a Lady of quality', as the Welshman would describe her in his journal.[1] What bound the three together was that they had all experienced evangelical conversion a few years previously and were all becoming increasingly prominent as leaders of the Methodist Revival – part of an evangelical awakening which had begun more or less simultaneously in Wales, England, Scotland, New England and continental Europe around the 1730s,[2] and which has been described as 'an international movement of such significant proportions that the history of Western civilization is still permeated by its ramifications'.[3]

Who, then, were the three that met in Downing Street on that day in August 1743? The Welshman was Howel Harris, the dynamic young Methodist leader from Trefeca near Talgarth in Breconshire. His English companion was Charles Wesley, the great Methodist hymn-writer. And the 'Lady of quality'? She was Selina Hastings, Countess of Huntingdon, a member of the English aristocracy, who would become a very influential patron of the Methodist movement until her death in 1791, aged eighty-three. In the words of the Countess's biographer, Edwin Welch, that day in London in 1743 'was to be the beginning of a long and somewhat tumultuous friendship' between Howel Harris and the Countess of Huntingdon[4] – which is not really surprising, since all Harris's friendships seem to have been tumultuous, even with people far less determined and domineering than Lady Huntingdon!

The 1750s was a doldrum period in the relationship between Howel Harris and Lady Huntingdon, and indeed in the history of Welsh Methodism in general. Harris's estrangement from his fellow Methodists during that period saw him retreat to his home in Trefeca and create there an exclusive, monastic-like religious community not dissimilar to the Moravian community at Herrnhut, on the estate of Count Zinzendorf in Saxony.[5] For her part, the 1750s saw Lady Huntingdon preoccupied with family responsibilities. However, the early 1760s witnessed marked changes in the situation. A new wave of spiritual vitality hit the Welsh Methodists in this period.[6] This second major stage in the development of the Evangelical Revival in Wales coincided with the healing, to a large degree, of the breach between Harris and his fellow Methodists. It also coincided with Lady Huntingdon becoming relatively free from her family responsibilities and being able to give herself more fully to the Methodist movement. In November 1763 Harris and Lady Huntingdon met for the first time since the breach of the 1750s, and for the next ten years, until Harris's death in 1773, they would work together closely.[7]

Harris almost immediately began impressing on the Countess the need for an academy to train preachers, and in 1768 she opened a college at Trefeca with that in view.[8] This brought the Countess into regular contact not only with Howel Harris, but also with others of the Welsh Methodists, including William Williams (1717–91) of Pantycelyn – a farm some four miles east of Llandovery in north Carmarthenshire. Usually referred to in Welsh cultural circles as 'Williams Pantycelyn' – or simply 'Pantycelyn' – Williams is probably the best known outside Wales of all the Welsh Methodists, mainly through his popular English hymn, 'Guide me, O thou great Jehovah, / Pilgrim through this barren land', which was first published as a leaflet *c.* 1772, entitled *A Favourite Hymn, sung by Lady Huntingdon's Young Collegians. Printed by the desire of many Christian friends.*[9] Following his evangelical conversion in the late 1730s as a twenty-year-old student, Williams would become one of the most able Methodist leaders of his generation. He had been raised among Nonconformists and was attending a Dissenting academy in Breconshire when he was converted under the preaching of Howel Harris. He had apparently been intent on becoming a doctor, and his writings show that he retained a keen interest in matters medical and scientific throughout his life; but after his conversion Williams joined the Anglican church, intent on becoming a priest. However, opposition from Church authorities to his evangelicalism led to him leaving his curacies in 1744, and from then until his death in 1791, aged seventy-three – he died, incidentally, in the same year as both John Wesley and the Countess of Huntingdon – Williams conducted an itinerant ministry among the Welsh Methodists from his home at Pantycelyn, travelling over 2,500 miles annually on horseback the length and breadth of Wales, preaching and pastoring the Methodist flock. Little wonder then that 'pilgrim' and 'pilgrimage' are dominant themes and images in his hymns.

In addition to his work as preacher and pastor, between 1744 and his death Williams Pantycelyn published over ninety books and pamphlets, almost all in Welsh – which was the only language of the majority of Welsh people in the eighteenth century. A wide variety of material flowed from his pen, including two epic poems and a number of important prose works (among them a substantial volume on world religions and a book on marriage guidance), all geared to instruct the Methodist converts, to establish them in their faith and to help them better understand their spiritual experiences and condition. Although Williams was a productive writer from the mid-1740s onward, the main body of his work, and the work of his maturity – both in poetry and prose – belongs to the fifteen years which began with the second great wave of the Evangelical Revival in Wales, the so-called Llangeitho Revival of 1762, an awakening which was especially noted for its 'spirit of singing, rejoicing and leaping for joy', which led to the Welsh Methodists being nicknamed 'Welsh Jumpers'.[10] It is difficult to overemphasize the importance of Pantycelyn's literary corpus and its influence on the religious and cultural life of Wales. With it began 'a preoccupation with spiritual experience and personal salvation', and with 'self-searching and self-discovery ... [and] the realization of an ideal good', that would be a dominant feature of Welsh literature, both 'sacred' and 'secular', for the next two centuries.[11] Despite the significance of the corpus as a whole, and the importance of his epics and his prose works in particular, pride of place must be given to his hymns. Williams is the father of the Welsh hymn,[12] with over 850 Welsh-language hymns to his credit – about a quarter of the total number of Welsh hymns written during the great flowering of hymnody which Wales experienced in the eighteenth century. He also wrote over a hundred English hymns, bringing his total output to around 1,000 hymns in all. However, Williams's English hymns are not as successful as those in Welsh. In general they lack the vigour and lyrical beauty of their Welsh counterparts, and his only really popular English hymn is 'Guide me, O thou great Jehovah', although others are still to be found in English-language hymnals.[13]

Many of Williams's English hymns appear to have been written at the request of Lady Huntingdon. Although their paths had crossed as early as 1748, it is with the establishment of Trefeca College in 1768 that Williams Pantycelyn and the Countess of Huntingdon seem to have become well acquainted. He was one of the preachers at the first anniversary services of the college in August 1769, and preached regularly at those anniversary services in the years that followed.[14] Such was her regard for Williams that the Countess is on record as frequently stating that 'everything considered, Wales had no greater man of whom to boast'.[15] Shortly after founding the college at Trefeca, Lady Huntingdon had another important responsibility placed upon her, following the death of the great Methodist preacher and leader, George Whitefield (1714–70). Although the Methodists are often portrayed as only having concern for people's souls and spiritual welfare, it is important to emphasize that they also had social concerns and a vision for social justice. Howel Harris, for example, planned to found an orphan house in Wales as early as 1736, the year after his conversion and, although Harris's plans came to naught, in the same period George Whitefield established an orphanage in North America – at Bethesda in Georgia, ten miles from Savannah.[16] On his death in 1770, Whitefield bequeathed that orphanage to the care of Lady Huntington, 'buildings, lands, negroes, books, furniture and every other thing whatsoever'.[17]

George Whitefield not only kept slaves at Bethesda, but had actually supported the extension of slavery to the state of Georgia for economic reasons,[18] and Lady Huntingdon continued the practice at Bethesda after she inherited responsibility for the orphanage. The term 'ambivalent' is frequently used to describe the attitude of the first generation of Evangelicals to slavery,[19] and it would seem that the position of someone like Lady Huntingdon was to accept that slavery was part of the warp and woof of the international social and economic order, which would prove very difficult, if not impossible, to eradicate until the coming of the Millennium, and that 'it was better to keep slaves in a comfortable and Christian setting than to release them into a harsh and pagan world'.[20] Despite Whitefield owning slaves, it is worth remembering that he has been called 'the first great friend of the American negro' because of his campaigning for the humane treatment of black slaves and for their evangelization and education.[21] Indeed, the poem that first brought the black slave poet, Phillis Wheatley of Boston, to prominence was her elegy for George Whitefield, which received wide circulation on broadsides and in pamphlets in America and Britain. In that elegy she emphasizes how Whitefield would urge everyone, whatever the colour of their skin, to accept Christ:

> Take HIM [he said] ye *Africans*, he longs for you;
> Impartial SAVIOUR, is his title due;
> If you will chuse to walk in grace's road,
> You shall be sons, and kings, and priests to GOD.[22]

Williams Pantycelyn, in his Welsh-language elegy on the death of Whitefield, also emphasizes the way he took the 'blessed holy gospel over to the Negroes and to the Indians', to black as well as white.[23] Furthermore, although one can agree that in one sense 'anti-slavery was not intrinsic to Evangelicalism',[24] by its very nature the Evangelical Revival of the eighteenth century – with its emphasis on the 'new birth', on justification by faith and on preaching the gospel 'among all nations ... unto the uttermost part of the earth' (Luke 24:47; Acts 1:8) – would sow the seeds of the demise of institutional slavery; since, as the Apostle Paul states in the New Testament, there is in Christ neither Jew nor Greek, bond nor free, male nor female, but all are one in Christ Jesus (Galatians 3:28). One sees an example of this in a sermon on Luke 4:18 preached in Cambridge in 1788 by the influential Baptist minister Robert Robinson, in which he imagines how a slaveholder must have felt in one of the early Christian churches during the Lord's Supper:

> Let us imagine a primitive assembly of Christian slaveholders and slaves, *not now*, in this instance, *as slaves, but above slaves, brethren beloved in the Lord* [Philemon 1:16], all sitting at the same table, eating the same bread, drinking the same cup, in remembrance of their common benefactor [Jesus Christ], who had said, *the Lord sent me to preach deliverance to captives* [Luke 4:18] ... How must a slaveholder feel, when in the assembly a charitable deacon proclaimed: *Remember them that are in bonds, as bound with them* [Hebrews 13:3]?[25]

Increasingly during the eighteenth century, black slaves were converting to evangelical Christianity in large numbers.[26] In that century, religion was an extremely important element in defining identity and the 'other'. As Roxann Wheeler has noted:

> Skin color was not the only – or even primary – register of human difference for much of the eighteenth century ... Religion, in fact, was arguably the most important category of difference for Britons' understanding of themselves at various times during the century ... In eighteenth-century texts, Christianity often functions like a proto-racial ideology ... To be a Christian was to be fully human.[27]

This was especially true of Evangelicals, for as David Bebbington has emphasized, 'The line between those who had undergone the [conversion] experience and those who had not was [for Evangelicals] the sharpest in the world. It marked the boundary between a Christian and a pagan.'[28] And this 'birth of a vibrant black Evangelicalism', together with the increasing influence of Enlightment values, would play a significant role in rallying Evangelicals to the abolitionist cause[29] – so much so that one can argue that it was the next generation of Evangelicals (and those sympathetic to evangelicalism), people like Granville Sharp, Thomas Clarkson, William Wilberforce and the 'Clapham Sect', who provided the backbone of the campaign to secure the necessary institutional changes which would ban Britain's slave trade by the beginning of the nineteenth century, and subsequently the institution of slavery in Jamaica and other British territories in the 1830s.[30]

One of Williams Pantycelyn's better-known English hymns, 'O'er those gloomy hills of darkness', contains a specific reference to 'the Negro':

> Let the Indian, let the Negro,
>   Let the rude Barbarian see
> That divine and glorious Conquest
>   Once obtain'd on Calvary.

It may be that the reference was inspired in part at least by the black slaves at Whitefield's Georgian orphanage, since the hymn seems to have close connections with the Countess of Huntingdon and her missionary endeavours. It first appeared in print in Pantycelyn's second collection of English hymns, *Gloria in Excelsis: or Hymns of Praise to God and the Lamb*, printed in Carmarthen in 1772; and it is said that that collection was specifically published at the request of the Countess of Huntingdon, in order for her to send it to be used in the orphanage in Georgia.[31] Tradition has it that the hymn was written at Llwyn-gwair mansion, between Nevern and Newport in north Pembrokeshire. The Bowen family of Llwyn-gwair was sympathetic to the Methodist cause.[32] John Wesley, for example, stayed at Llwyn-gwair on seven occasions during his journeys in south Wales between 1772 and 1790.[33] It is said that James, the son of Squire George Bowen (1722–1810), was converted in 1786 after hearing one of Williams Pantycelyn's verses being sung fervently by a girl on the road in Trecastell, Breconshire, as he passed by in his carriage;[34] and when the Welsh Methodist Association was held at Nevern in the October of that year, about sixty members of the Association were given beds at Llwyn-gwair, with around 120 being provided with meals.[35] According to tradition, on one occasion when Williams Pantycelyn was staying at Llwyn-gwair, George Bowen asked him to compose some verses about the Preseli hills, and the hymn 'O'er those gloomy hills of darkness' is said to be the fruit of that request. The tradition can be traced back to the beginning of the nineteenth century, and it is claimed that at one time a copy of the hymn in Pantycelyn's own hand was in the possession of the Bowen family.[36] Whatever one makes of the tradition, anyone who is familiar with Llwyn-gwair – now the Llwyn-gwair Manor Holiday Park – will be able to confirm that Williams Pantycelyn, looking out from a bedroom window in the front of the mansion, would have seen Carn Ingli mountain rising steeply in the distance. However, there exists a parallel tradition which can also be traced back to the early nineteenth century, which links the composition of the hymn not with Llwyn-gwair in Pembrokeshire but with the Rhondda valley in Glamorgan. According to that tradition Williams Pantycelyn was travelling on horseback through the Rhondda valley, which in pre-industrial times was densely wooded and sparsely populated. He was on his way to visit relatives at Gyfylchi, a farm near the village of Pont-rhyd-y-fen in the adjoining Afan valley. As he travelled, a request by the Countess of Huntingdon for him to compose a missionary hymn for a particular occasion weighed heavily on his mind. It was a rather stormy day, and as he passed near the ruins of the old Cistercian foundation at Pen-rhys, he could see rising threateningly in the distance the mountains over which he would have to cross in order to reach the Afan valley. Tradition has it that it was that view which inspired him to begin composing 'O'er those gloomy hills of darkness', and that by the time he reached the comfort of Gyfylchi farm, the hymn had been completed and was ready to be sent to the Countess. Although concrete evidence for the family ties between Williams Pantycelyn and the Rees family of Gyfylchi has proved elusive, there are local traditions which maintain that he did indeed have close family connections in the area, through his sister and his mother's sister; and he certainly visited the locality regularly to preach, including (significantly perhaps) a visit in 1771, the year prior to the first publication of 'O'er those gloomy hills of darkness'.[37] The mountain range facing

Williams in the Rhondda valley would have been darker and more threatening than Carn Ingli; and the fact that Lady Huntingdon's request for a missionary hymn is mentioned in the context of the Rhondda valley tradition does perhaps give it more credence than that of Llwyn-gwair, since Lady Huntingdon did indeed send a number of her students on missionary ventures around the time of the hymn's composition. However, Lady Huntingdon's name can also be connected to the Pembrokeshire tradition, for in August and September 1771 she accompanied Daniel Rowland and Williams Pantycelyn on a preaching tour of south Wales, following the third anniversary services of her college at Trefeca at the end of August; and one of the places they stayed on their travels was Llwyn-gwair![38] One is tempted, of course, to reject both traditions as being topographical tales forming part of the rich corpus of Methodist folklore. However, on the basis that there is often a spark of fire amidst the smoke of Methodist folk tales, it is not beyond the bounds of belief to suggest the following: that Pantycelyn wrote the hymn at the request of Lady Huntingdon; that he wrote it while journeying through the Rhondda and Afan valleys in 1771; that he gave a copy to Lady Huntingdon during their preaching tour in the late August and September of that year, making a copy of the hymn for George Bowen at his request during their time at Llwyn-gwair in mid-September.

Interesting though these traditions may be, the identification of the mountain range which may have inspired the hymn is ultimately, of course, of little import in the context of the hymn itself, since one must always remember that the hills in the first line of the hymn are to be understood spiritually rather than literally. Here is the text of the hymn as it first appeared, in *Gloria in Excelsis* (1772):

> O'er those gloomy Hills of Darkness
>   Look my Soul, be still and gaze,
> All the Promises do travel[39]
>   On a glorious Day of Grace,
>   Blessed Jubil, &c.
>   Let thy glorious Morning dawn.
>
> Let the Indian, let the Negro,
>   Let the rude Barbarian see
> That divine and glorious Conquest
>   Once obtain'd on *Calvary*;
>   Let the Gospel, &c.
>   Word resound from Pole to Pole.
>
> Kingdoms wide that sit in Darkness,
>   Let them have the glorious Light,[40]
> And from Eastern Coast to Western
>   May the Morning chace the Night,
>   And Redemption, &c.
>   Freely purchas'd win the Day.

> May the glorious Days approaching,
>   From eternal Darkness dawn,
> And the everlasting Gospel
>   Spread abroad thy holy Name.
>   Thousand Years, &c.
>   Soon appear, make no Delay.
>
> Lord, I long to see that Morning
>   When thy Gospel shall abound,
> And thy Grace get full Possession
>   Of the happy promis'd Ground;
>   All the Borders, &c.
>   Of the great Immanuel's Land.[41]
>
> Fly abroad, eternal Gospel,
>   Win and conquer, never cease;
> May thy eternal wide Dominions
>   Multiply, and still increase;
>   May thy Scepter, &c.
>   Sway the enlight'ned World around.
>
> O let Moab yield and tremble,
>   Let Philistia never boast,[42]
> And let India proud be scatt'red
>   With their numerable Host;
>   And the Glory, &c.
>   Iesus only be to thee.

The hymn is a prayer for the worldwide success of the Christian gospel. Its main characteristic is its confident longing. A strong desire for the success of the gospel is expressed throughout, as can be seen in the constant repetition of 'let' and 'may'; but side by side with that longing, there is a confidence that the gospel will ultimately succeed, that God's promises will be fulfilled. This is reflected in the imagery of the hymn, the most obvious being light *versus* darkness (verses 1, 3, 4, 5, 6) and battle and warfare (verses 2, 3, 5, 6, 7): a glorious day of grace will chase the night, as surely as the sun travels from east to west; the eternal gospel will win and conquer. That, then, is the great theme which runs through this hymn: the certain victory of the gospel as a result of 'that divine and glorious conquest once obtained [by Christ] on Calvary'. It is also worth noting the strong appeal to the visual that runs through the hymn ('look', 'gaze', 'see', 'appear'); the way the hymn personifies the jubilee, the gospel, grace and redemption; and the repetition of the word 'glorious' in the first four verses, reaching a climax in the 'glory' afforded to Jesus alone in the last couplet of the hymn.

    One of the great Welsh-language volumes of the twentieth-century – and certainly one of the most influential and controversial – is Saunders Lewis's critical analysis of Pantycelyn's work, *Williams Pantycelyn* (1927). While acknowledging its undoubted brilliance, it must also be emphasized that its portrayal of Pantycelyn is basically flawed, since (as R. Tudur Jones showed in his Henry Lewis Memorial Lecture, *Saunders Lewis a Williams Pantycelyn*, in 1987), rather than attempting, like Saunders Lewis, to fit Williams into the mould of classical Catholic mystical theology – the threefold 'way' of purification, illumination and union – it is far more appropriate to place his spiritual thought and experience in the context of Puritan theology, since Pantycelyn may rightly be regarded as a full-blooded heir of the Puritans.[43] This is perhaps nowhere clearer to be seen than in his eschatology, for as both 'O'er those gloomy hills of darkness' and Williams's other writings amply attest, in his eschatology Williams Pantycelyn embraced what has been termed the 'Puritan Hope'.

When it comes to matters regarding the end of the world, the final judgement and the second coming of Christ, anyone who has the slightest acquaintance with the work of that breathtaking Welsh Puritan prose-writer, Morgan Llwyd (1619–59), will know that there was a wide spectrum of beliefs and opinions on such matters abroad in Britain during the Puritan period. Morgan Llwyd was a premillennialist, who believed in the imminent return of Christ to conquer evil and to reign physically on earth for a thousand years.[44] However, as Iain H. Murray has demonstrated in his volume, *The Puritan Hope* (1971), it was a particular brand of postmillennialism, espoused by a significant section of mainstream Puritans, that would become the dominant outlook in these matters within British evangelical thought and belief for over two hundred years, until the middle of the nineteenth century;[45] and it is that eschatology which is to be found in the work of Williams Pantycelyn.

There are many variants in the detail of the 'Puritan Hope', but its main elements may be summarized (if perhaps oversimply!) as follows. Their interpretation of the prophecies of Scripture – the 'promises' of the first verse of 'O'er those gloomy hills of darkness' – led postmillennialists such as Williams Pantycelyn to believe, not in a sudden, imminent end to the world, but rather in an extended 'last-days' period which would begin with a marked success of the Christian gospel worldwide. This would continue 'until the fulness of the Gentiles be come in' (Romans 11:25), which would then be followed by the destruction of the Antichrist (namely heresy and 'all the errant churches in the world'); the conversion of the Jews to Christianity; the binding of Satan and the destruction of all false religions. Following this there would be a long period – the Millennium, or 'Thousand Years' of 'O'er those gloomy hills of darkness' – when the Christian gospel would hold sway everywhere, when Christ's kingdom would be established throughout the world, and when the earth would 'be full of the knowledge of the Lord, as the waters cover the sea' (Isaiah 11:9). Then, after this blessed period, Satan would be released from bondage and Christ would return visibly to defeat Satan, to judge 'the quick and the dead', and to wind up the present order and bring in a new heaven and a new earth (Revelation 20:7–21:1).[46]

That then is an outline of the 'last days' as Williams perceived them. Millenarianism flourishes especially during periods of turbulence, both political and religious, not to mention times of wars and natural disasters such as earthquakes.[47] Such periods and events heighten the expectation that the end of the world, or a period of radical change in society, is at hand. The Methodist Revival itself fuelled such flames because of the way it was transforming religious adherence and challenging established structures, both directly and indirectly, during the eighteenth century. The emphasis on the Millennium in Methodist circles in that period is attested in a volume by Theophilus Evans (1693–1767), an Anglican clergyman who wrote a popular and influential history of early Britain, *Drych y Prif Oesoedd* ('Mirror of the First Ages'). Evans was surrounded by Methodists – he was, for example, chaplain to the Breconshire squire, Marmaduke Gwynne of Garth, the father-in-law of Charles Wesley – yet he was very hostile to all expressions of religious 'enthusiasm'. In 1752 he launched an attack on Methodists and other 'enthusiasts' in a volume entitled *The History of Modern Enthusiasm*. In it he states that Methodists such as John Wesley and George Whitefield believed that 'God has raised them up to usher in the glorious *Millenium*'.[48] Although he does not name Williams Pantycelyn, it is far from impossible that he also had him in mind, since Pantycelyn had served as his curate between 1740 and 1744. Certainly the 'Puritan Hope' is in evidence throughout Pantycelyn's writings. For example, in a letter to Howel Harris, written in December 1745 during the Jacobite rising, Williams could say:

> In the midst of wars and tumults, my dear brother, stand still and you shall see the salvation of God. How long before this rebellion cease, or how far God will permit them to go, I know not. I am apt to believe a popish pretender will not prevail long. The church of God will be more glorious in the time to come. Glorious promises are not fulfilled. Is the gospel preached through the whole world, as promised in the gospel by our Saviour himself? No, no! All America as yet never heard such things. Has the great Babylon fallen? No, no! Its time I hope is at hand. Has the poor ignorant sinful and reproachful Jews been called (Rom. 11). No; but 'tis certain to come. Has the devil been bound for 1,000 years (Rev. 19)? I suppose not. Has the fulness of the Gentiles come in? Has the glorious promises of Isaiah, Ezekiel, Revelation been fulfilled? No, no! Dear brother, pray for them. We have great reason to expect these things in short. Dark cloud in the morning is no proof the day is far; hard travailing pain is no sign the delivery is far; wars, famine, pestilence, kings raging one against another, is no sign the glorious day of the gospel is far off. Who knows but Christ's kingdom of peace may come of the shaking [of] empires, kingdoms, states, &c. Many prayers are gone up now of late and formerly that the idolatrous Church of Rome

should be pulled down, Jews converted, and Mohametanism rooted up. May these things come to pass. Amen. Amen. Amen.[49]

And he writes in a similar vein toward the end of his life, in a letter to Thomas Charles of Bala in September 1787, immediately prior to the French Revolution:

> For the harvest is great, and the Lord of the harvest will have labourers for his harvest. For the fulness of the Gentiles shall come in, viz. the Gentiles round the globe, black, white, yellow, orange, tawny, shall hear of a crucified Saviour and shall believe in him; and then all Israel, the twelve scattered tribes that inhabit the farthest and remotest part of the world, shall be gathered as sheep unto the sheepfold of the gospel, as may be seen [from] Isaiah 11:9–12. And as the fall of the Jews became the riches of the Gentile world, how much more riches will the Gentile world gain by their fulness (Romans 11:15)? For if the casting away of the Jewish world became a reconciling of the Gentile world, what shall the receiving of the Jewish world be, but life from the dead ... Thus all the Gentile world shall receive the gospel and believe. Then drowsiness shall fall on them; and in the time of their drowsiness, decay and backsliding, the Jews shall awake round the globe and believe; and then the sleeping Gentile church shall be roused up by the zeal, love and faith and catch the fire, so that the whole world will be on a blaze.[50]

However, the most frequent expression of the postmillennial hope in Pantycelyn's work is to be found in the 1760s and 1770s. During this period the worldwide success of the Christian gospel seems to occupy Williams increasingly. This is, in part, due to the 'Llangeitho Revival', that second great wave of revival which hit the Welsh Methodists in the early 1760s. Pantycelyn's view of gospel expansion is closely linked to his theology of revival. As his Puritan predecessors, Pantycelyn believed 'that the kingdom of Christ would spread and triumph through the powerful operations of the Holy Spirit poured out upon the Church in revivals'.[51] In other words, he expected the worldwide expansion of the Christian church to come, not so much by sending missionaries abroad to places previously untouched by the gospel, but rather through a ripple effect linked with times of spiritual blessing or revival.[52] Until the 1760s Pantycelyn seems to have taken a similar stance to the Lutheran pietist scholar, J. A. Bengel (1687–1752), who could say:

> The approach of better times for Christianity may be compared to the gradual peep of verdure through the dissolving snow, with here and there a green patch more or less conspicuous. The large wintry covering spread over all the nations ... will be broken through at the proper time ... [But] at present the age of missions to the heathen and to the Jews is not fully arrived.[53]

However, the 'Llangeitho Revival' of the early 1760s engendered in Pantycelyn the hope that a wider success of the gospel was imminent.

His increasing occupation with the worldwide success of the gospel was also fuelled by the fact that in the 1760s and 1770s Pantycelyn was engaged in an ambitious publishing project, *Pantheologia, neu Hanes Holl Grefyddau'r Byd* ('Pantheologia, or a History of All the Religions of the World'), a 654-page volume which appeared in seven parts between 1762 and 1778/9. It is a book full to the brim of information, not only about various faiths and beliefs, but also the history, geography and customs of the countries in which those faiths pertained. Although he can sometimes express criticism of other religious standpoints and practices, the book is generally educational rather than devotional or polemic in tone. Pantycelyn was scathing in his condemnation of the ignorance of the Welsh. A white monoglot Welsh male is about as ignorant as a white monkey in India, he says in an advertisement for the book in 1764, and the aim of the volume was to dispel some of that ignorance. As such it is a prime example of Williams Pantycelyn being an heir of the Enlightenment as well as a child of the Evangelical Awakening of the eighteenth century.

In the present context, it is significant that the sections of the work which deal with religions other than Christianity appeared in the years between 1762 and 1769. Little wonder then that the worldwide success of the gospel seems to have weighed particularly heavy on Pantycelyn during those years. This is reflected in his hymn output. Most of Pantycelyn's hymns concentrate on the salvation and spiritual pilgrimage of the individual believer. As Dewi Arwel Hughes has rightly commented, the central theme of Pantycelyn's hymns is a 'personal eschatology' rather than a more general one. However, it is surely significant that, even though the percentage of hymns on the worldwide success of the gospel remains fairly small in *Ffarwel Weledig, Groesaw Anweledig Bethau* ('Farewell Visible, Welcome Invisible Things'), the collection of his hymns which Williams published in three parts between 1763 and 1769, such hymns occur in markedly greater numbers than in his earlier hymn collections. It should be added that *Pantheologia* includes a number of references to the 'Puritan Hope', and it is also worth noting that the first part of that volume, which appeared in 1762, contains in the section on Guinea in West Africa the first published condemnation in Welsh of the slave trade.[54]

The following years, between 1769 and 1772, witnessed efforts on the part of Lady Huntingdon, during the early years of her college, to send some of the Trefeca students as missionaries to the East Indies and to Georgia in America.[55] Then in 1774, but advertised as early as 1771, we see Williams Pantycelyn publishing his fullest expression of the 'Puritan Hope', in his lively pamphlet, *Aurora Borealis*, subtitled 'The Light in the North, as a Sign of the Success of the Gospel in the Last Days (or, The *Shekinah* of the Thousand Years)'. In it he argues that God uses great wonders in the heavens and on earth as signs of judgement or, more frequently, of salvation and blessing (such as the rainbow after the Flood or the star which led the Magi to the young Jesus). After elaborating on a number of such biblical examples, he then says that according to Scripture great signs in the heavens will precede the establishment of Christ's kingdom on earth in the 'last days', and that he was convinced that the remarkable way in which the northern lights were now to be seen over Britain was a sign that the millennial dawn was imminent. Pantycelyn's main reason for believing this, he says, was the evangelical revival which had begun about forty years previously in Europe and North America, shortly after the lights had begun to be visible in the north. He saw, in the way those lights, in all the colours of the rainbow, danced and interweaved playfully and peacefully together in the sky, a representation of the joyful rejoicing of Christian believers; and as those northern lights were now spreading ever southward, so he was convinced that the religious revival that had begun in the northern hemisphere would spread throughout the globe.[56] 'I am ready to believe', he concludes, 'that summer is at hand': '*Yr wyf yn barod i gredu bod haf gerllaw*.'[57]

That then is the overall context of the composition of the hymn 'O'er those gloomy hills of darkness', which may be regarded as a mature expression of a decade and more of reflection by Pantycelyn on the 'Puritan Hope' and the certain success of the Christian gospel worldwide in the 'last days' – a hymn which (as has already been suggested) could well have been written about 1771, to be sung at a valedictory service for some of the Countess of Huntingdon's Trefeca students as they left for missionary work overseas, and specifically perhaps for those going to Georgia.

Whether that be the case or no, it is worth emphasizing how Pantycelyn's missionary awareness must have been heightened by his contact with Lady Huntingdon, her interests and activities, and in particular perhaps with relation to Native Americans and black slaves in the American colonies. The Native Americans had long been regarded as a mission field by Protestants, since they were one of the few groups of 'heathens' actually living in close proximity to them; and the evangelistic efforts and pastoral work of the Puritan, John Eliot, among Native Americans in the mid seventeenth century,[58] and the missionary activities of David Brainerd among them in the mid eighteenth century (mediated to the Christian public through Jonathan Edwards's exceptionally popular biography, first published in 1749), were both extremely influential in inspiring and promoting missionary work in general, and not just among Native Americans. The Countess of Huntingdon had a sustained interest in the spiritual welfare of Native Americans, as indicated, for example, by her support, financial and otherwise, for the work of Samson Occom (1723–92), a pioneer Native American minister and author who visited Britain from 1766 to 1768,[59] and by her proposal to George Washington in 1782 for an ambitious plan for their evangelization.[60] It is not surprising, therefore, to see the group of students that was sent from Trefeca in late 1772 to establish a missionary base at the Bethesda orphanage in Georgia, being specifically charged by the Countess with the task of missionary work among the 'Heathen Nations' (i.e. the Native Americans).[61] This may explain why

Pantycelyn included the reference to 'the Indian' in the second verse of 'O'er those gloomy hills of darkness'. Although the students' missionary work was hindered by a number of factors, including the American War of Independence,[62] they would make promising contacts with the Cherokee in particular.[63]

The second verse of 'O'er those gloomy hills of darkness' also includes a reference to 'the Negro'. The missionary party sent to Georgia in 1772 was expected to continue George Whitefield's evangelizing work among the black slaves, and although this did not proceed particularly smoothly, a number of slaves were converted.[64] As has already been noted, one could argue that the Countess's position, like that of George Whitefield, was compromised because of her involvement in the slave trade and because of the actions of some of her representatives at Bethesda; but it is also important to emphasize the significant role she played in promoting the publication of the earliest 'narratives' of converted black slaves. She was involved in the publication of the first slave narrative in English, by Ukawsaw Gronniosaw, in 1772 – translated into Welsh by Williams Pantycelyn in 1779 – and in 1773 she supported the publication of a volume of poetry by the Boston slave girl, Phillis Wheatley – an important landmark in black and female publishing.[65] Both these volumes were dedicated to the Countess and coincided with the period of her missionary enterprise in Georgia. She would also encourage in the 1780s the publication of the influential slave narratives of Olaudah Equiano and Quobna Ottobah Cugoana, together with *A Narrative of the Lord's Wonderful Dealings with John Marrant, A Black*, which was first published around the time of Marrant's ordination in 1785 as a minister in the Countess of Huntingdon's Connexion.[66] These narratives would prove a very significant genre in the campaign against slavery, emphasizing as they did the full humanity of black people, the inhumane treatment afforded them as slaves, and their ability to respond in faith and repentance to the Christian gospel and to be 'born again'. It is also worth noting that the Countess had a number of black preachers in her Connexion (including David Margate, who, having been a student at Trefeca, was sent to join the missionary group in Georgia in 1774),[67] and that there were significant numbers of adherents of the Countess of Huntingdon's Connexion among the black people who sailed from Nova Scotia for Sierra Leone in the early 1790s, as part of the attempt by members of the 'Clapham Sect' and others to create a new homeland in Africa for freed slaves.[68]

It hardly needs to be stated that the last decades of the eighteenth century were revolutionary times. One has only to cite the American War of Independence and the French Revolution to be reminded of that. It was a period which witnessed a marked growth in radicalism, and it also saw a significant growth in millenarianism, both religious and secular, especially as the end of the century approached. In a Welsh context, for example, one could mention the 'Signs of the Times' columns that appeared in one of the first Welsh-language periodicals, edited by Morgan John Rhys in 1793–4;[69] or the plans of the Romantic poet, Robert Southey, to establish a 'Pantisocracy' in Wales in the 1790s;[70] or the deep influence of Joanna Southcott on the prominent Welsh lexicographer, William Owen Pughe (1759–1835), between about 1803 and her death in 1814.[71] Their enemies often accused the Methodists of being a seditious element in society, and claimed that they disseminated the doctrines of Jacobinism and the works of Tom Paine. Like Williams Pantycelyn in his letter to Howel Harris in 1745, during the Jacobite rising, Thomas Charles and others of the next generation of Welsh Methodist leaders would fiercely protest their loyalty to king and country in the aftermath of the French Revolution;[72] and indeed, despite its millenarianism, its Calvinism and its clashes with the Anglican establishment, Welsh Methodism in this period was, in general, a force for promoting political quietism and conservatism. However, there were two causes that were gaining momentum in the latter decades of the eighteenth century, both fuelled to a large degree by the radicalism, evangelicalism and millenarianism of the period, with which the Methodists engaged positively, and which would gradually feed the latent radicalism in their ranks. Those were the missionary movement and the campaign to abolish the slave trade.

The modern Protestant overseas missionary movement began in earnest in Britain with the formation of the 'Particular Baptist Society for the Propagation of the Gospel Amongst the Heathen' by William Carey and others in 1792, followed in 1795 by the formation of perhaps the most influential of all the early missionary societies, 'The Missionary Society' (later renamed the London Missionary Society), which brought together evangelical Christians from a wide spectrum of church affiliations and backgrounds, including the Welsh Methodists. Williams Pantycelyn and the Countess of Huntingdon did not live to see this dynamic new phase in overseas mission work, as both had died in 1791. It has been argued that Pantycelyn was a visionary and a theorist rather than an activist in matters of overseas mission.[73] Although an overstatement, as may be seen from his support for the Countess of Huntingdon's missionary endeavours in the 1770s, there is an element of truth in that argument. Yet it can also be argued that Pantycelyn the visionary theorist made a key contribution to the development of the overseas missionary movement by promoting through his writings the postmillennial vision of the worldwide success of the Christian gospel as epitomized in the 'Puritan Hope'. It was fitting, then, that the great congregation, including over two hundred ordained ministers, which gathered at Lady Huntingdon's Spa Fields Chapel in London on 22 September 1795 for the inaugural meeting of the London Missionary Society, should sing as their opening hymn Pantycelyn's 'O'er those gloomy hills of darkness', amidst great emotion.[74]

The Protestant overseas missionary movement that developed from those beginnings would transform the religious map of the world.[75] The nineteenth century did indeed see Protestant Christianity spread like the 'northern lights' to all parts of the globe, as Williams had intimated in his *Aurora Borealis*; however it did not usher in the Millennial Age that Pantycelyn had believed was at hand. Indeed, as the nineteenth century progressed there would be a marked decline in the numbers who adhered to Pantycelyn's postmillennial 'Puritan Hope'. By the end of the century, the growth of liberal theology, a confidence in scientific and technological advancements and the belief in evolutionary progress would see many embrace a 'social gospel', a secularization of the 'Puritan Hope' aimed at promoting a kingdom of heaven on earth through social reform, while those more conservative in their theology tended increasingly toward a premillennialist position which emphasized personal conversion and regarded attempts at wider social change as futile, since their expectation was that the world would go from bad to worse until the imminent, personal advent of Christ. In evangelical circles, therefore, the optimism of postmillennialism gave way increasingly to the pessimism of premillennialism.[76] Interestingly, Brian Stanley in his book, *The Bible and the Flag* (1990), links the growth of premillennialism in the nineteenth century with the growth of Romanticism.[77] The Enlightenment and the Evangelical Revival of the eighteenth century have often been juxtaposed as two opposing forces – Evangelicalism being portrayed as a religion of enthusiasm, emotion and personal salvation as compared to the more moralistic, rational religion one associates with Enlightenment thinkers. However, in recent years, increasing emphasis has been placed on the fact that Evangelicalism not only reacted against the Enlightenment, but was in some ways wedded to it.[78] This is certainly true of Williams Pantycelyn, as witnessed for example by his great interest in medicine and science; and in one sense, the postmillennial convictions of Pantycelyn and his fellow evangelicals and their belief in the steady advance of Christian civilization in an orderly, progressive manner, may be regarded as an aspect of Enlightenment thinking – as opposed to the immediate and dramatic personal return of Christ as the only means of achieving the goal, which characterizes premillennial thought.

The missionary movement and the campaign to abolish slavery were closely linked. Both were fuelled by millenarian expectations, and strong impetus was given to both movements by the French Revolution, through the hope it engendered that the old political and religious order was breaking down and a new age of freedom and equality was dawning. Furthermore, the longing which is at the heart of the postmillennial vision – a yearning for a worldwide utopia where the Christian gospel and social justice hold sway – was an important factor in nurturing evangelical support for the abolition movement, since central to the fulfilment of that longing was the evangelization of peoples in every part of the world, regardless of cultural setting, geographical location or skin colour; and it is implicit in the act of evangelizing that its object is fully human, an immortal soul created in the image of God and for whom Christ died. It is no surprise, therefore, to find that key figures in the anti-slavery campaign, such as William Wilberforce and Granville Sharp in England and Morgan John Rhys in Wales, were also keen supporters of the overseas missionary movement.[79] Vocabulary and imagery also linked the two movements, and made for ambiguous discourse. Spiritual redemption is often conveyed in hymns, and in Christian literature in general, through imagery which originates in biblical events involving release from physical slavery. The term 'jubilee' is a case in point. In 'O'er those gloomy hills of darkness', Pantycelyn uses it to refer to the worldwide success of the Christian gospel in the 'last days', but its origins lie in the Old Testament practice of proclaiming a jubilee in Israel every fifty years, when slaves were released (Leviticus 25), and Williams Pantycelyn would have been very aware of that. Similarly, the dominant imagery which Pantycelyn utilizes in his hymns to portray the Christian's pilgrimage through this world is drawn from the biblical story of the Israelites' release from slavery in Egypt and their subsequent journeying through the desert to the 'Promised Land' of Canaan. To quote Adam Potkay:

> The ambiguity between spiritual and political liberation inheres, in part, in the very idiom of Christian soteriology. Since the gospel writers first presented Jesus as a new and greater Moses, Christian salvation has routinely been allegorized as freedom from Egyptian captivity.[80]

The campaign to abolish the slave trade began in earnest in Wales in the early 1790s with the publication in Welsh of pamphlets and poetry by the radical Baptist, Morgan John Rhys, and the Methodist, Edward Barnes, encouraging people join in a popular boycott of the use of sugar produced by slave labour in the Caribbean.[81] Most of the material published in Welsh in support of the anti-slavery campaigns of the late eighteenth and early nineteenth centuries was written from a Christian standpoint, and even that most politically quiet and conservative of all Welsh Methodist leaders, John Elias (1774–1841), gave his full support both to the campaign for the abolition of the slave trade at the turn of the century and to the subsequent campaign in the 1820s and 1830s to abolish the institution of slavery in Jamaica and other British territories.[82] Those attending the Welsh Methodist Association meeting in Machynlleth in April 1795 were reminded of their duty, in such perilous times, to 'be subject unto the ... powers that be', which are ordained of God (Romans 13:1); and they were also told that 'Organizing earthly governments, without our ever being called to that, ... is great foolishness, and one of the snares of the devil'.[83] However, although they did not feel called to political involvement and reform, the Welsh Methodists were happy to bring public pressure for the abolition of the slave trade, since they regarded it as a moral rather than a political matter. With hindsight, one can see that this willingness on the part of Methodists, and evangelicals in general, to become involved in the abolition campaigns of the late eighteenth and early nineteenth centuries, was an important watershed in the matter of political action. It was the thin end of the wedge. For once one starts bringing pressure to bear in the public sphere in matters relating to moral issues, where does one stop? R. T. Jenkins claimed that one of the great turning points in the history of Welsh politics was the radicalization of the Welsh Calvinistic Methodists in the mid nineteenth century.[84] The phenomenal growth of Calvinistic Methodism, and of evangelical Nonconformity in general, during the first half of the nineteenth century meant that by mid-century Nonconformity had become the dominant element in Welsh society. The radicalization of the Methodists was therefore a key factor in creating the radical Wales of the second half of the nineteenth century. That radicalization grew apace after the death of John Elias in 1841, but there had been a slow but steady grow of radicalism in Methodist ranks throughout the first half of the nineteenth century, and one could argue that nothing had put them more on that road than the opposition to transatlantic slavery that had first been articulated in Welsh in the works of William Williams of Pantycelyn.

As with the overseas missionary movement, it could be argued that Williams Pantycelyn was more of a visionary and theorist than an activist as regards the abolition of slavery. Yet, as in the case of the missionary movement, it could also be argued that Pantycelyn the visionary theorist, through his prose and poetry, made a key contribution in preparing the ground for the abolition movement that would begin in earnest towards the end of his life. And as the congregation in Spa Fields Chapel would sing Pantycelyn's 'O'er those gloomy hills of darkness' with great emotion at the inaugural meeting of the London Missionary Society in September 1795, so too the former slaves who sailed from Nova Scotia to Sierra Leone in the early 1790s gained much comfort and inspiration from singing that very same hymn, since 'O'er those gloomy hills of darkness', with its references to freedom and redemption, and its hope of a millennial dawn and a blessed jubilee, was among the most popular of the hymns sung by them during their voyage to Africa.[85]

In a number of ways, therefore, Williams Pantycelyn may be regarded as an important forerunner of both the overseas missionary movement and the abolition movement, and as such he was also a forerunner of the radical Wales that had come into existence by the second half of the nineteenth century. The vision expressed in 'O'er those gloomy hills of darkness' would indeed have far-reaching consequences for Welsh life and culture.

6 SERIAL LITERATURE AND RADICAL POETRY IN WALES AT THE END OF THE EIGHTEENTH CENTURY

Marion Löffler

> Here lies puried under these stones,
> Shon ap William ap Shinkin ap Shones:
> Hur was porn in Wales; hur was kilt in France,
> Hur went to Cot by a ferry creat mischance.
> W. T. M.[1]

The 'Epitaph Copied from a Tombstone in Wales' illustrates the challenges posed by the concept of serial literature and radical song in Wales towards the end of the eighteenth century, but it also indicates the rewards which crossing borders may bring. It was not published in Wales itself but in England and the identity of 'W. T. M.' remains unknown. Yet the newspaper in which it appeared – the *Chester Chronicle* – was part of the Welsh public discourse, the poem referenced Welshmen in more than one way,[2] and it reflected the anti-war sentiments which characterized Welsh and English language radical song from Wales in the 1790s.

The concept of Wales in the 1790s itself was complex. Incorporated by the Acts of Union of 1536 and 1543 and thus officially a part of England, the Principality of Wales, though retaining a separate cultural identity and language, lacked the characteristics of a political nation. Without a capital, major cities or a university it was also missing the requirements for the rise of a public sphere. The scarcity of sizeable towns restrained even the development of Terry Eagleton's 'counter-public sphere' of corresponding societies, political associations and Dissenting churches sustained by an artisan class.[3] By 1801, Swansea alone had developed something akin to an urban culture, yet it counted just 6,099 inhabitants.[4] Only Carmarthen with a population of 5,548 came anything close in numbers and sophistication. Few pockets of industrialization, mainly in the north-east and the south of the country, encroached on its rural landscape and mountain wilderness. The largest of these, the industrial parish of Merthyr Tydfil, still only counted 7,705 inhabitants.[5] Disturbances and riots centred mostly on the bread and wages which had incited unrest through the eighteenth century, on enclosures and on the activities of the press gangs.[6] Political radicalism was a minority project undertaken by a fragile network of Welsh Dissenters between London, Wales and America, not a sustained mass movement such as that engendered by the English LCS, or a revolutionary organization like the Society of United Irishmen.[7] Welsh radicals did not have the means to publish series of radical songbooks,[8] or plaster the walls of Swansea and Carmarthen with satirical handbills.[9] Their radical inventory centred on translating and writing political poetry and prose, which they published in pamphlets, exchanged within the extended privacy of their manuscript culture, performed in subversive religious services and at revived cultural festivals like the eisteddfod, and, significantly, included in the serial literature which constituted a large part of the public discourse in Wales.[10]

Until 1804, when the Swansea *Cambrian* was founded, no newspaper was published in Wales itself,[11] but that does not mean that the Welsh middling sorts, those most receptive to radical and reformist ideas, did not come by the latest news. Even in 1738, Robert Pritchard, a sea captain from Pentraeth on Anglesey, wrote in a poem that it was 'the pleasure of many a *Welshman* to read the English news of *Chester* or *London*' ('Pleser llawer *Cymro* yw darllain, Newyddion seisnig *Caer* neu *Lundain*').[12] Ballads in north Wales mentioned that newspapers were received 'every second day' ('bob yn ail [d]dydd').[13] The letters and notebooks of Welsh radicals such as the stonemason Edward Williams (Iolo Morganwg) in Glamorgan, the weaver Thomas Evans (Tomos Glyn Cothi) in Carmarthenshire and the cobbler John Davies (Siôn Dafydd y Crydd) in Cardiganshire, show that metropolitan as well as provincial serials were sold in Welsh shops and that the radical material they contained was read and copied avidly and repeatedly.[14] The Welshmen gathered in the displaced public sphere of the Gwyneddigion and Cymreigyddion societies in London contributed radical poetry to metropolitan serial publications,[15] but they also sent it back home to Wales by contributing to the newly resurrected eisteddfod competitions and publishing in the provincial newspapers, almanacs and periodicals circulating in Wales.[16]

The English provincial papers located close to the Welsh border formed a major part of the public discourse of Wales. Weeklies like the *Hereford Journal*, the *Shrewsbury Chronicle* and the *Chester Chronicle* relied heavily on their Welsh readership and had carved up the Welsh market between them.[17] The *Hereford Journal*, the English provincial paper with 'by far the greatest unrivalled area of distribution',[18] covered the whole of south and mid Wales. The *Shrewsbury Chronicle*, the most widely read paper in mid and north Wales, was so successful that a rival *Salopian Journal* was set up to gain a share of the market. The loyalist *Adam's Weekly Courant* and the *Chester Chronicle* vied for control of north Wales, from the eastern border with England to the isle of Anglesey. While much loyalist Welsh poetry was published in the *Shrewsbury Chronicle*,[19] the *Chester Chronicle* was the mouthpiece of Welsh radicals. It published reports of the eisteddfod meetings held by the Gwyneddigion society in parts of Wales as well as Welsh and English language poetry by well-known bards such as Richard Llwyd (Bard of Snowdon), David Thomas (Dafydd Ddu Eryri), Iolo Morganwg and John Jones (Jac Glan-y-gors).[20] The complex historical poetry of the 'Anglo-British' Bard of Snowdon awaits interpretation by Elizabeth Edwards and Dafydd Ddu Eryri was a staunch loyalist,[21] but other poets contributed material relevant for this chapter. Iolo Morganwg published a version of his anti-war 'Ode on converting a sword into a pruning-hook' here. He had first performed it at his third public gorsedd meeting of the bards – 'the heralds and ministers of peace' of old Britain – on Primrose Hill on 22 September 1793.[22] A prodigiously foot-noted version was included in *Poems, Lyric and Pastoral*, his attempt to establish himself as a labouring poet in English literary circles at the beginning of 1794.[23] The *Chester Chronicle* version of July 1794, shorn of the footnotes and a stanza shorter, transported his radical sentiments back to Wales. The 'Ode on converting a sword into a pruning-hook' was fashioned after Isaiah 2:4, which inspires peace movements to this day, but was more radical than purely pacifist. It did not call so much for converting weapons into agricultural implements as for wresting them from the hands of 'despot King[s]' in order to end the reign of 'tyrant oppression'. The priests and mobs invoked by the 'sceptred band ... of ev'ry land' in support of the current wars were condemned. God, the 'eternal Prince of Peace', alone would lead man back to reason and a peaceful, free life in tune with nature:

> Dark Error's code no more enthrals,
> Its vile infatuations end;
> Aloud the trump of Reason calls;
> The nations hear! The worlds attend!
> Detesting now the craft of Kings,
> Man from his hand the weapon flings,
> Hides it in whelming deeps afar,
> And learns no more the trade of War;
> But lives with Nature, on th' uncity'd plain:
> Long has this earth a captive mourn'd,
> But days of old are now return'd;
> We Pride's rude arm no longer feel,
> No longer bleed beneath Oppression's heel;
> For Truth to Love and Peace restores the world again.[24]

The poems which 'Tom Paine's Denbighshire henchman', Jac Glan-y-gors, contributed to the *Chester Chronicle* were less highbrow than the sharply, even obsessively, revised work of Iolo Morganwg, but he made up for this with topicality, social awareness and satirical appeal.[25] Jac Glan-y-gors had migrated to London, where he became a leading member of the Gwyneddigion society, in the late 1780s. From 1793 he ran the Canterbury Arms in Southwark, but local accounts insist that he was forced into hiding in his native Denbighshire following the publication of his republican pamphlet *Seren tan Gwmmwl* (*A Star under a Cloud*) in October 1795.[26] His presence in north-east Wales may explain why the editor of the *Chester Chronicle*, the 'rueful Jacobin' William Cowdroy, published a series of poems by him from early 1796 onwards.[27] When yet another public fast day in support of the war was announced for 9 March 1796, the *Chester Chronicle* printed 'A Welsh hymn, to be sung on the fast-day', a satirical Welsh poem by Jac Glan-y-gors disguised by means of an innocent English heading.[28] A week later, however, the paper showed its radical colours by publishing an English version, most probably Jac's own translation:

> Translation of the Welsh Hymn, Inserted in our Last.
>
> Ye hapless Sons of humble life,
> Who ne'er aspire to feast,
> Now distant eye the bread you want,
> But must not dare to taste.
>
> The Royal Mandate now ordains,
> For sin an expiation,
> To fast, for that's the cheapest way,
> To feed a starving nation.
>
> Our Bishops of exalted rank
> will feast on butter'd fish –
> Can this evasion save the soul,
> Mere changing of a dish?
>
> Let all in Britain's ample bounds,
> For George's welfare pray;—
> That Heav'n may crush the horrid crew
> That would their Sovereign slay.[29]
>
> Yet powerful chiefs, RELIGION – FAITH –
> Own not such sanguine features;
> 'Tis vain, they cry, to ask for aid
> To kill your fellow creatures.
>
> Remember ONE, who, void of wrath,
> Could Malchas's ear replace;
> Who taught us, as his Father's will,
> LOVE, CHARITY and PEACE.[30]

This co-operative use of Welsh and English in the *Chester Chronicle* and the rare, almost simultaneous, self-translation of poetry raise questions of the bilingual writing and translating skills of Welsh poets at the time, and make this text especially interesting.[31] In 1809, Jac Glan-y-gors attempted to avail himself of the

North Wales Gazette, the second newspaper published in Wales, to bring out another anti-fast day poem, but it was rejected, as he noted in his manuscript, by the 'cowardly gentleman' ('y gŵr boneddig cadnoaidd') who edited it.[32]

Apart from radical poetry by well-known bards, the *Chester Chronicle* also featured authors who preferred to remain unknown by providing their initials or a general location only. During the hungry summer of 1795 anti-war poetry and prose from north and mid Wales together condemned the war against France as the source of Welsh suffering. On 21 August 1795, for instance, an anonymous poem from Denbigh and a letter by 'Juvenis' from Welshpool appeared side by side.[33] In a bleak reinterpretation of the pastoral, the poet's 'painful Muse' reveals north Wales as a landscape whose 'humble poor', driven by unbearable hardships, face tragedy:

> For want of bread the infant cries;
> The father hangs his head;
> The mother fills the air with sighs,
> And wou'd her child were dead!
>
> Rather than see its infant form
> Become a pray to thee,
> 'I'd hurl it headlong to the storm,
> And die in misery!'
>
> Such, haughty War, thy poignant woes,
> To thee such scenes belong;
> The painful Muse wou'd thee disclose
> In simple, artless song.[34]

'Juvenis' complemented the poem by engaging in a more abstract religious condemnation of this war as anti-Christian. The *Chester Chronicle*, which claimed sales of 1,700 copies every week in the 1790s,[35] was both a significant channel of radicalism into Wales and a vital medium of communication for a wide range of Welsh writers. It was, however, not the only serial in Wales to feature radical song.

Welsh almanacs, which had appeared since 1680, furnished a second public arena. At least five different Welsh-language almanacs were published in Shrewsbury, Chester, Trefriw, Brecon and Carmarthen in the second half of the eighteenth century.[36] In addition to communicating astronomical and astrological information, they contributed to the development of a sense of national terrain by publishing the distances between various Welsh market towns and maps suggesting routes to reach them, but also by giving the details of all the fairs held in Welsh counties.[37] Their lineages of Welsh royal dynasties down to shadowy founder figures kept alive a sense of the historical depth of the Welsh nation.[38] Last but not least, these almanacs served as repositories of Welsh poetry, old and new. Their editors were unable to respond swiftly to topical events, but they published ballads deploring the strenures of the war with America,[39] and poems in praise of this new world composed by those who had emigrated there. '*Cywydd* of the story of Pennsylvania in America' ('*Cywydd* o hanes Pensylfania yn America'),[40] sent by Hugh Gryffydd, 'a man born and raised in Merionethshire', was an early advertisement of the religious freedom, the justice and the material advantages enjoyed by the new Welsh Americans:

> Brawdgarwch bwriad gwrawl
> Sydd yn eu mysg hyddysg hawl,
> A swyddogion dyfnion daith
> I rannu i bawb ar unwaith,
> Cyfiawnder uniawnder a wnân
> Er naws ceraint nis gwyran,
> Da y gwelan a di gilwg
> Roi barn drom yn erbyn drwg,
> A rhoi swccwr dyfdwr dawn
> Wyr onest i rhai uniawn,
> Gwlad i bawb golud a budd
> Air groywfaith er eu grefydd,
> I gael llonydd ddedwydd ddawn
> Hoywedd achles heddychlawn,
> Gwlad anfelus gofus gur
> I'r rhai swga rhy segur,
> Gwlad ethol glyd i weithiwr
> A chyflog serchog yn siwr.[41]

> (Brotherly love, heroic aim
> Is in their midst a learned right,
> And far-travelling officials
> To share to everyone at once,
> Justice, righteousness they undertake
> They don't deviate for the sake of kindred
> They see well and without frown
> Give heavy judgment against evil,
> And give the profound gift of nourishment
> Of honest men to the righteous,
> A country wealth and good for all
> A clear word whatever their religion,
> To have peace a happy gift
> Healthy peaceful protection,
> A country of bitter memorable pain
> For the slovenly and too lazy,
> A choice comfortable country for a worker
> With a fine salary, for sure.)

Satirical poetry printed separately or embedded in prose took aim at drunk and negligent priests, and condemned the debts incurred through subsequent wars and the taxes raised to support them.[42] In 1796, John Harris of Carmarthen published a poetic attack on William Pitt's tax on dogs.[43] The fragment, 'The Dream of John of the Hill, Llandeilo Fawr, and his Dog Cupid' ('Breuddwyd Sion o'r Bryn, Llandilo-Fawr, a'i Gi Ciwpit') featured a monologue in which the poet's faithful companion, faced with strangulation, asked to 'extend a bait to Billy Pitt' ('ystyn bait i Bily Pit') instead, and called on all to hunt him down and 'Dent, too' ('Dent hefyd').[44] The land surveyor Mathew William ended his predictions for the same year with a short bilingual poem which imbued the preceding prose with political meaning. The only English verse in this otherwise Welsh text connected Jesus and Thomas Paine:

> Good will no public grievance can devise;
> Real religion *wills* – no strain'd supplies,
> All christians, were sincere, pursue one plan,
> Peace – taught by *One*, who bought the *rights of man*.[45]

Dafydd Risiart, a Welsh Dissenter from Llandybïe, Carmarthenshire, who was rumoured to sympathize with the French Revolution, similarly connected religion, and especially anti-Catholicism, with contemporary politics by depicting Thomas Paine as an instrument of God whose deeds should be judged by God alone. The poet proclaimed his loyalty to England, yet he still rejected the 'all earthly princes' ('holl dywysogion daear') and condemned the 'bloodthirsty *Capet* family' ('[t]eulu'r *Capets* gwaedlyd'). For Welsh radicals, God was the sole judge of man and Jesus Christ, man's 'eldest Brother' ('hynaf Frawd'), his only compass point.[46]

Welsh poets in their metropolis London and at home utilized the English newspapers published along Offa's Dyke and the yearly Welsh almanacs to voice political opinion and publish radical song. Significantly, however, they also attempted to establish their own periodical press. The first Welsh periodical *Tlysau'r Hen Oesoedd* (*Gems of the Old Times*) had appeared as early as 1735, and from then until the end of the Napoleonic Wars sixteen journals were published in Wales, most of them in the Welsh language.[47] The translation of the Bible into Welsh in 1588 and the distribution of tens of thousands of family and pocket bibles from 1620, *in tandem* with the pioneering system of circulating schools established by the Anglican priest Griffith Jones of Llanddowror from 1731 onwards, had led to the development of a flourishing native print culture aimed mainly at the religious needs of its labouring and middling classes.[48] Publications in the Welsh language were designed to protect the Welsh flock from the dangers of 'Atheism, Deism, Infidelity, Arianism, Popery',[49] but this evolved print and reading culture also provided an infrastructure for the production and dissemination of secular and dissenting literature. In 1770, the Unitarian Josiah Rees of Gelligron near Neath, south Wales, attempted a second periodical, *Trysorfa Gwybodaeth, neu Eurgrawn Cymraeg* (*Treasury of Knowledge, or Welsh*

Magazine).⁵⁰ The corrections to the proof for its first title page illustrate how Welsh intellectuals adapted Enlightenment concepts and radical ideas in a process which encompassed linguistic patriotism. Borrowing the English term, Rees had intended his periodical to be a 'Magazine', but this was criticized by Richard Morris, a navy officer, and 'father' of the first patriotic Cymrodorion society in London:⁵¹ 'Magazin: an abominable word to be introduced in a new work in the language: ought by no means to be admitted. Several compounds may be expressive to this purpose; but I think Eurgrawn as proper as any.'⁵²

His suggestion *Eurgrawn*, or 'Golden Collection' as he wrote in a later letter, would be the title of many a periodical until the end of the nineteenth century.⁵³ England had provided a cultural concept, but Welsh intellectuals in London and Wales made it their own by way of translation. If this fortnightly publication had survived, it would have been a truly national venture, but it failed after only fifteen numbers, the publisher noting that he had already incurred a loss of £100 and regretting that he could not afford to continue.⁵⁴

The *Eurgrawn* had, however, provided the blueprint for three Welsh Dissenters, whom the French Revolution galvanized into publishing radical journals twenty-three years later. In 1793/4, the Baptist minister Morgan John Rhys published five issues of *Cylch-grawn Cynmraeg; Neu Drysorfa Gwybodaeth* (*The Welsh Magazine; Or Treasury of Knowledge*). It was followed, in 1795, by three numbers of *Miscellaneous Repository: Neu, Y Drysorfa Gymmysgedig* (*The Miscellaneous Repository: Or, The Mixed Treasury*), edited by Tomos Glyn Cothi, the first Unitarian minister in Wales, and in 1796, by *Y Geirgrawn: Neu Drysorfa Gwybodaeth* (*The Magazine: Or Treasury of Knowledge*), edited by David Davies of Holywell, which ran to nine numbers.⁵⁵ All three editors were Dissenters from south-west Wales whose radicalism brought them into conflict with the Established Church and the state. Morgan John Rhys, educated at the Baptist College, Bristol, was an ardent anti-slavery campaigner who had travelled to France in 1791.⁵⁶ He emigrated to America shortly after publishing an anti-war sermon, *Cyngor Gamaliel* (*Gamaliel's Advice*), and an appeal for emigration to America, *Y Drefn o Gynnal Crefydd yn Unol-Daleithiau America* (*The Order of Keeping the Faith in the United-States of America*) in 1794.⁵⁷ The weaver Tomos Glyn Cothi spent most of his life in the tiny hamlet of Brechfa, Carmarthenshire, yet he corresponded with Theophilus Lindsey, whose support enabled him to build the first Unitarian chapel in Wales. He had already translated Joseph Priestley's *An Appeal to the Serious and Candid Professors of Christianity* into Welsh, thus earning himself the nickname 'little Priestley' ('Priestley bach'), when he set up his intensely religious, but highly radical periodical. In 1802, he was sentenced to two years in prison, 'during which time to stand twice in the pillory' for allegedly singing a seditious song at a local festivity, and bound over to keep the peace for seven years after his release.⁵⁸ The least is known about David Davies, the editor of the Chester-published *Geirgrawn*. Born at Llanybydder, Carmarthenshire, he trained at the Dissenting academy in Swansea and ministered at Holywell church, north Wales, from 1790 until 1800 when he disappeared for two years before his appointment as the minister of Stoneway church in Bridgnorth in 1803. According to the radical pamphleteer Thomas Roberts, Llwynrhudol, *Y Geirgrawn* had ceased publication because some 'knaves' ('gnafiaid') threatened to drive the editor out of the country for publishing texts which struck 'at the root of oppression' ('at wreiddyn Gorthrymder').[59]

All three editors pursued a Welsh Enlightenment project which invited contributions from all quarters. Prominent churchmen, such as the schoolmaster David Thomas (Dafydd Ddu Eryri) and Rector Peter Bailey Williams (Peris), were given space for their work in defence of church and state, and *Y Geirgrawn* staged the acrimonious discussion of Jac Glan-y-gors's Paineite pamphlet *Seren Tan Gwmmwl* (*A Star Under a Cloud*). The editors ensured, however, that loyalist contributions were answered by radical replies or contrasting editorial remarks and footnotes.[60] Patriotic concern for the Welsh language was a main part of the Welsh Enlightenment and therefore of these periodicals.[61] Editorials appealed to intellectuals to publish in 'the mother tongue' ('y famiaith') rather than in 'the stranger' ('yr estrones') English, and to the common people to purchase and read Welsh literature. The controversial spelling reforms of William Owen Pughe were partially implemented and vigorously discussed. Essays on Welsh rhetoric and style drew on the work of those famous Welsh renaissance scholars who had translated the Bible into Welsh and composed the first Welsh dictionaries. Secondly, both radicalism and loyalism were expressed via contributions on the history and philosophy of Christianity, which also featured biographies of Protestants and Dissenters from Andrew Dudith to Gilbert Wakefield. Essays on the history of Christianity denounced tithes as alien to early church doctrine and challenged the claim to God-given governance of the people made by religious and secular authorities. A strong anti-Catholic element ran through most essays, with recent events in France cited as evidence of God's judgement on the sins of Catholicism. Dissenting Christianity, particularly Unitarianism, was explained to those still shackled by the Trinity, and Luther and Calvin were cited in defence of the doctrine of the *One* God. A third strand in the periodicals imbued Welsh history with political meaning. Essays on the decline of liberty focused on the imposition of the Saxon's 'iron yoke' ('iau haiarnaidd') on the Briton, though the Saxon, in time, was punished with his own, Norman, yoke.[62] The distant past represented a mythical Wales governed by an enlightened nobility and enjoying religious liberty, the future lay in the religious toleration of the new America. Letters from America and descriptions of its political and religious system received pride of place in the periodicals. Past and present were combined in the story of Welsh Prince Madoc's discovery of America in the thirteenth century, which had recently been revived and was part of the pro-American message advertised in the pages of *Cylch-grawn Cymraeg*. All three periodicals were strongly anti-war in their message. They contained no poetry or prose extolling war, but plenty of anti-war material.

Each of the three periodicals published, indeed their editors called for, poetry on the subjects outlined above in a variety of genres. Their repertoire included reprints from the canon of Welsh classics, winning entries to the eisteddfod meetings and poems which had been recited at Iolo Morganwg's gorsedd assemblies in London, elegies on great Welshmen, and religious poetry. Formally, the poetry encompassed highly formalized classical Welsh compositions written in *cynghanedd*,[63] religious hymns, short poems in praise of editors, publishers, fellow bards and the Welsh language, as well fugitive pieces embedded in prose to accentuate its radicalism. Morgan John Rhys, for instance, interlarded his 'Signs of the Times' ('Arwyddion yr Amserau') with an *englyn* in praise of liberty, which may have been composed by Jac Glan-y-gors:

> Trwy'r byd, nid tristyd y tro, cu ryddid,
> Caredig a lwyddo;
> Rhag i gwmmwl dwl yn do
>   A chaddug ei orchuddio.[64]
>
> (May dear liberty prosper throughout the world,
> happy event;
> lest a dense cloud of darkness
>   should cover it over.)[65]

Short poems expressed joy at the appearance of the periodicals as instruments for the education of the common people, for honing the native language and for uniting Wales, as the closing stanza of the '*Englynion* to the Geirgrawn' ('*Englynion* i'r Geirgrawn') by 'Poeta Rusticus' shows:

> Yn gain, trwy'r dwyrain, a'r De – a llawen
> Drwy'r gorllewin ynte,
> Bid dy daith groyw-iaith gre;
> Y gogledd, a phob gwagle.[66]
>
> (Artful, through the east, and the south – and happily
> Also through the west,
> May your clear and strong-phrased journey be;
> In the north, and every empty space.)

Some poets understood the periodicals' avowed aim of 'defending the truth' ('amddiffyn y gwirionedd') as an invitation to contribute work in defence of established religious doctrine.[67] Promising titles, such as 'Reflections on the Age of Man' ('Ystyriaeth ar Oes Dyn'), 'Ode on Liberty' ('Awdl ar Ryddid') and 'Ode on Truth' ('Awdl ar Wirionedd'), are therefore disappointingly misleading.[68] Dafydd Ddu Eryri's 'Ode on Liberty', for instance, prefaced with a line from Joseph Addison's *Cato* (1712), was old Whig and had most recently been quoted by Edmund Burke.[69] It rejoiced in the freedom enjoyed by the British as compared to the French, the Spanish, the Indians and the people of Africa, and culminated in a paean to King George:

> Dan Sior, ein llawn-bor, a'n llyw,
> Gwawr Rhyddid a geir heddyw,
> Gwawr odiaeth gywir adeg,
> A gwawr deg o gariad yw.[70]
>
> (Under George, our full-sovereign, and our leader,
> The Dawn of Liberty is begotten today,
> Dawn at an excellent time,
> And a fair dawn of love it is.)

Other poems reveal their radicalism upon a close reading, at times of the footnotes. The anonymous author of a poetic address to the editor of *Cylch-grawn Cynmraeg* attacked Catholic priests in the verse, but in a long footnote, he also censured Anglicans. Above all, he made sure that his religious text was applied to the secular sphere:

> Gellir cymmwyso'r farddoniaeth at draws-lywodraeth *ddinasaidd* yn gystal âg *eglwysaidd*. – Y mae rhyddid dinasaidd ac eglwysaidd yn wastad yn cyd-fyned; ac yn sefyll, neu syrthio gyd â'u gilydd: er nad oes un berthynas (fel y breuddwydia rhai) rhwng eglwys a llywodraeth wladol: etto mae awdwr rhyddid wedi cysylltu, hawl naturiol, ac ysprydol, ei greaduriaid mor agos, yn y byd hwn, fel na ellir byth mo'i gwahanu.[71]
>
> (The poetry may be applied to *political* as well as *religious* tyranny. – Political and religious liberty always go together; and stand or fall with each other: although there is no relationship (as some dream) between church and state government; nevertheless the author of liberty has linked together the natural and spiritual rights of his creatures so closely, in this world, that they can never be separated.)

The radical poetry of the Welsh periodicals thus echoed the close link between religion and politics present in the songs which were published in the 'Welsh' provincial papers and the almanacs.

History was pursued in the form of poetry, too. In its second issue, *Cylchgrawn Cynmraeg* reprinted the classic poem 'On the Court of Ivor the Generous' ('Ar Lŷs Ifor Hael') which Evan Evans (Ieuan Brydydd Hir) had written in 1780 on the occasion of a visit to the ruined court of the medieval patron of Welsh art, Ifor Hael. Bemoaning the loss of a native nobility, Ieuan Brydydd Hir contemplated their 'houses in the sand' ('teiau yn y tywod') now overgrown by brambles and home only to the owl, symbols of cultural glory lost.[72] Although Iolo Morganwg, his companion on this visit, also composed an ode to Ifor Hael by adapting the work of the medieval poet Dafydd ap Gwilym,[73] he graced the pages of *Cylch-grawn Cynmraeg* with a poem on an unspecified Welsh prince whom he criticized for straying from the path of the just ruler, corrupted by power and wealth. Like the 'Ode on converting a sword into a pruning-hook', this *cywydd* had been recited at the third gorsedd of the Bards of the Isle of Britain in London, in the presence, it is claimed, of 'throngs of Welshmen and Englishmen of London, and in their midst the Prince of Wales' ('lluoedd o Gymry a Saeson Llundain, ac yn eu plith Tywysog Cymru').[74] This classical poem sounded a clear message to all rulers not to turn from generous keeper of peace to 'oppressor and crusher of the weak' ('gortrechwr, gwasgwr y gwan').[75]

The material which Tomos Glyn Cothi contributed to his own *Miscellaneous Repository* ranks among the frankest expressions of radicalism written and published in Wales in the 1790s and illuminates the complex process of translating the French Revolution into the Welsh language.[76] His 'HYMN to be sung on a day of fast by the friends of mankind' ('HYMN i'w chanu ar ddydd ympryd gan gyfeillion dynolryw') sent a strongly anti-war message, condemning 'predators wallowing in blood' (''sglyfaethwyr sy'n ymdroi mewn gwa'd') and sympathizing with oppressed 'brothers' ('brodyr') in every country. In eighteen translated and newly created stanzas he demanded that these 'monsters' ('anghenfilod') may pay with their blood for destroying the world. Stanzas five to eleven of the hymn bear a resemblance to lines from stanzas five, eight, nine and ten of 'An Hymn for the Fast Day to be Sung by the Friends of Mankind' which had appeared anonymously in *Politics for the People*,[77] but Tomos Glyn Cothi had added his own voice to that of the English poet. He called on God himself to liberate man and facilitate his return to nature:

> 9 Yn bendramwnwgl bwr i lawr,
> Holl dreiswyr byd mewn munud awr;
> O! gwasgar, Hollalluog Dad,
> Y rhai sy'n pesgi ar ddynol-waed.
>
> 10 Yna daw heddwch i bob gradd,
> Yn lle gorthrymder llym a lladd;
> A'r holl fyd fel cyd-blant yn byw,
> Yn deulu mawr i ti ein Duw.
>
> 11 Yna caiff caethion fyn'd yn rhydd,
> O'u bron, 'nol bod yn hir yn brudd,
> A mwynhau'r breintiau hyfryd hael,
> Appwyntiodd nattur i ddyn gael.[78]
>
> (9 Throw down headlong
> all the tyrants of the world in an instant;
> Oh! disperse, Almighty Father,
> those who grow fat on human blood.

10 Then peace will come to every station,
instead of harsh oppression and killing;
and all the world will live as fellow-children,
as a big family for you our God.

11 Then slaves will be allowed to go free,
altogether, after long sadness,
and enjoy the lovely, generous rights
which nature appointed for man to have.)

It does not surprise that one of the accusations brought against Tomos Glyn Cothi in 1802 was changing the wording of the official texts prescribed for the religious services to be held on the public fast days.[79] In the Welsh literary and religious context, which was less blood-soaked and more abstract in its condemnation of war and oppression than the English tradition, this 'hymn' was an exceptional piece that must have shocked his flock in rural west Wales. It indicates the depth of Tomos Glyn Cothi's conviction and his anger at the distortion of the original Christian message. Despite the many differences between his work and the writings of Jac Glan-y-gors, who was rumoured to be an atheist, it is striking that both stretched the genre of the hymn well beyond its traditional limits.

The creative potential of radical English sources is confirmed by the free adaptation of one of the most iconic cultural artefacts of the French Revolution, 'La Marseillaise'.[80] In May 1796, a poem bearing the title 'Song of Liberty' ('Cân Rhyddid') appeared in the fourth number of *Y Geirgrawn*, sent in by 'Gwilym'.[81] A paratext consisting of introduction, new title, first line of the original and a footnote advertised the translator's political credentials, informed the readers of the revolutionary power of this song and highlighted the act of translation.[82] 'Gwilym' appropriated the 'Marseillaise' for Wales by a process of cultural adaptation which reconstructed it as a 'Song of Liberty' using English and French sources.[83] He translated three stanzas from the four-stanza English version circulating in England, Ireland and America since 1793, followed by an adaptation of the original French stanza four which may have been perceived as too dangerous to publish in English because it directly threatened oppressors. The Welsh song closed with a translation of the French stanza seven, footnoted to explain that this was usually sung by children.[84] So thorough was the transformation that the song would be unrecognizable, had it not been prefaced by an explanation of its importance and the first line of the original, 'Allonz enfants de la patriæ'. The first stanza and the chorus are indicative of the changes made throughout the text:

CHWI feibion Rhyddid daeth yr amser,
Ac wele myrdd yn galw i ma's!
O clywch ruddfannau plant gorthrymder,
Yn gwawdd i wisgo'r cleddyf glas!
A gaiff hyll dreiswyr, llawn drwg fwriad,

A'u byddin lôg (hull arfog lu!)
Ladd a dinystrio ar bob tû,
Er gwaedu o Ryddid, hêdd a chariad?

I'r maes! – I'r maes rai dewr!
Ein llawn ymroad fydd,
Ymlaen! – Ymlaen! awn oll yn un,
Am farw, neu fyw'n *rhydd*![85]

(For you sons of Liberty the time has come,
and see the myriads calling out!
Oh, hear the groans of the children of oppression,
an invitation to take up the grey sword!
Shall ugly tyrants, full of ill intention,
and their hired army (an ugly armed mob!)
get to kill and destroy everywhere,
to bleed Liberty, peace and love?

To the field! – To the field brave ones!
This our full devotion be,
forward! Forward! Let's all go as one,
to die or to live *free*!)

The French 'children of the Fatherland' ('enfants de la Patrie') became the 'sons of Liberty' ('meibion Rhyddid'), since 'fatherland' ('patrie') had been transformed into the more abstract 'liberty' ('rhyddid') throughout. There was no threat of fatal injury to 'sons and consorts' ('fils et ... compagnes') – as in the English and French versions – but in mortal danger were the very principles of 'Liberty, peace and love' ('R[h]yddid, hêdd a chariad'). In the chorus, Welsh citizens were not called to 'Let impure blood / Water our furrows!' ('Qu'un sang impure / Abreuve nos sillons!'), but to 'go as one / To die or to live *free*!' ('awn oll yn un, / Am farw, neu fyw'n rhydd!'). Overall, the Welsh lyrics appealed more to general moral principles than bloody patriotism. This 'Song of Liberty' was copied into manuscripts, where news stanzas and choruses were added, a close translation back into English was attempted, and it was sung at the 'bid ale' which led to the conviction of Tomos Glyn Cothi for sedition.[86] The song and its journey exemplify the far-reaching influence of published material in a deeply rural, early modern culture.

The publication of the Welsh version of the 'Marseillaise' possibly marked the zenith of radical song in Welsh serial publications during the 1790s, but it was also part of its swansong. Soon after, this chapter in radical Welsh publishing closed with an equally powerful, but classical, poem by the Baptist minister Dafydd Saunders of Lampeter, mid Wales, which combined a condemnation of the current war with a paean to free America.[87] In his 'Look at the present war;

and on the emigration of men to *America*, together with the advantage of going there' ('Golwg ar yr Rhyfel presenol; Ac ar fynediad dynion i *America*, ynghyd a'r fantais o fyned yno') Saunders meditated on the 'lying spirit' ('yspryd celwyddog') which was misleading King George and his advisers and had turned the Britons into slayers in the name of God. He wondered whether it was the French threat, after all, which made this war a necessity and empathized deeply with the common soldier in his fearful exposure to violence and bloodshed. He pointedly asked why all reports focused on the sensationalist, like the guillotine, thus neglecting 'Humanity' ('Tiriondeb'). His suggested solution was emigration to America, where 'Humanity' had found its bastion:

'Rwy fi'n barnu'n fynych,
O'm rhan i fy hunan,
Wrth ganfod y drefn,
I hwn fyn'd i ryw fàn,
'R hyd wyneb y dyfn-for:
'R ydwyf fi'n ofnus,
Ei fyn'd ymhell enbyd
'R hyd llwybr *Columbus*,
At *Washington* anwyl,
'R hwn sy, on' tê, 'n hynod
I 'mddiffyn *Tiriondeb*,
A'i hoffi trwy Undod?
O mor hoff yw'r elw,
Ymrown i ffarwèlo –
Mwy, wyr da, tan ganu,
Mordwywn tu ag yno![88]

I often judge,
on my own part,
in beholding the order,
that it went somewhere,
over the face of the ocean:
I am fearful
that it went awfully far
on the path of *Columbus*,
to dear *Washington*,
he who is remarkable, is he not,
defending *Humanity*
and celebrating it through Unity?
Oh, so marvellous is the gain,
let us say farewell –
now, good men, while singing,
let's voyage over yonder!)

The fragmented form of this masterpiece sends an additional message of loss. Only the first part was published with the conclusion promised 'in the next' ('yn y nesaf'). Like its predecessors, however, *Y Geirgrawn* came to an abrupt end and thus the remainder of the poem remains unknown. Dafydd Saunders himself left Lampeter, albeit for a Baptist congregation in industrial Merthyr Tydfil, not for America.

None of the radical periodicals lasted beyond 1796, which left Wales bereft of an indigenous periodical literature once more. In the last quarter of the eighteenth century Wales had the roads, the postal service, the printing houses, the booksellers, the writers and, most probably, the readers, to sustain at least one periodical which could have provided a medium for public discussion and radical song.[89] Yet Welsh printers and publishers survived by publishing religious fare and loyalist ballads, only rarely affording to venture on to the economically *and* politically risky territory of the radical serial. Between 1799 and 1814, eleven more short-lived periodicals and two newspapers were published in Wales, but the conservative backlash ensured that none of them was radical in any way. 'Shon ap William ap Shinkin ap Shones' and his compatriots would have to wait another twenty years for the golden age of the Welsh periodical press to arrive.[90]

7 POPULAR SONG, READERS AND LANGUAGE: PRINTED ANTHOLOGIES IN IRISH AND SCOTTISH GAELIC, 1780–1820

Niall Ó Ciosáin

In recent writing on the radical political movements of the 1790s in Ireland, the United Irishmen in particular, a new emphasis has been placed on their mobilization of popular printed propaganda in their campaigns for politicization and change. The first scholar to address this issue comprehensively was James Donnelly in 1980, according to whom 'the unique degree of support which [the United Irishmen] enjoyed was also largely owing to the effectiveness, the appeal of their propaganda.'[1] Donnelly's article explored the various genres within this propaganda, such as ballads, prophecies and satires, and its variety of material formats, from the newspaper to the single printed sheet.

Donnelly's example was followed, and the subject further developed, in the 1990s by Nancy Curtin and Kevin Whelan.[2] All of these authors, while emphasizing the importance of printed propaganda as a vehicle for politicization, were at the same time aware of the limitations of such a campaign and the obstacles it faced. Foremost among these was the determined opposition of the state. There were continual seizures of printed material and arrests for distribution of seditious publications, and the offices of the United Irish newspaper, the *Northern Star*, were destroyed by the Monaghan Militia in 1797. The obstacles were also cultural and material, however, notably in the realms of literacy and language.

Printed propaganda depended on literacy for its effect, and reading ability was unevenly spread among the United Irishmen's target audience, in particular those whom Tone called 'the men of no property'. Reading ability was high in the commercialized and Presbyterian north-east, where United Irish publications made their initial impact and where subscribers to the *Northern Star* were concentrated. Elsewhere it was lower, and was lowest of all along the west coast. Moreover, the cost of buying the publications would also have limited their circulation among the majority of the population.

All the above writers demonstrated the ways in which the propaganda campaign overcame this barrier. The principal way in which this was done was by exploiting the practice of reading out loud, typical of societies with partial or restricted literacy. The United Irishmen encouraged public reading, both on formal occasions, such as after religious services on Sunday, and informal ones. Within the texts themselves, they mobilized genres which were suitable for absorption and transmission within an oral culture, such as catechisms and ballads.[3]

The second major barrier was that of language. United Irish propaganda was in English whereas Irish was the spoken language among the majority of the population in the 1790s, and the only language of a substantial section. Opinions are divided on the permeability of this barrier. Donnelly suggests that 'even those who spoke Irish exclusively ... were not closed off from United Irish propaganda' but does not expand any further on the issue. Tom Dunne, in contrast, argues that the Gaelic poetry and song of the period shows little United Irish influence. Garrett Fitzgerald's maps of language ability among the generation who would have been in their twenties during the 1790s show few areas in which Irish was not spoken, although clearly many Irish speakers would have understood and spoken English. It is striking, however, that two of the areas in which no Irish whatever was spoken, Wexford and east Ulster, were the areas that saw the most substantial rebellions in 1798 itself.[4]

The United Irishmen were not unaware of the linguistic difficulty. A short item in their newspaper, the *Northern Star*, in April 1795 addressed the question of Irish, urging their members to learn it: 'By our understanding and speaking it, we could more easily and effectually communicate our sentiments and instructions to all our countrymen; and thus mutually improve and conciliate each other's affections.'[5] There is little evidence, however, that they made any systematic effort to break through this barrier, to communicate with Irish speakers in the same way as with English speakers. It is true, on the one hand, that the practices of public reading would in many areas have included translation. On the other hand, however, the use of rhyming and metrical genres such as ballads would have made translation more difficult, certainly less simultaneous. Most striking of all, the United Irishmen produced no popular printed propaganda in Irish.

Their principal publication in Irish was the booklet *Bolg an tSolair*, published in Belfast in 1795.[6] The booklet is an engagement with Gaelic culture, but not an engagement with Irish speakers. The title page and the introduction are entirely in English, and these are followed by a forty-three page grammar and vocabulary designed for learners. Then come twelve pages of elementary dialogue and four pages of biblical passages, thirty pages of Irish saga literature and some love songs by Carolan and others, taken from Charlotte Brooke's *Reliques of Irish Poetry* (1789). All these are given in English as well as in Irish, the English coming first in most cases. The assumed reader, in other words, is not an Irish speaker but someone without Irish who wishes to learn it for antiquarian or literary purposes. Moreover, none of the texts has any overt political content, let alone the revolutionary ideas contained in the English-language propaganda of the United Irishmen.

If the radical political movements of 1790s Ireland made little attempt to communicate in Irish, the same is not true of the conservative and counter-revolutionary propaganda movements that were active in the aftermath of the rebellion of 1798. A good deal of the publishing in Irish which was undertaken in the first half of the nineteenth century formed part of this conservative reaction. One of the most influential strands in this project was a diagnosis of rebellion and radicalism which saw them as a result of the absence of religion. The response was to evangelize, and often to evangelize in the everyday language of the population. This approach was sketched out already in 1799 by Whitley Stokes, a Trinity College professor of medicine who himself had been a member of the United Irishmen in their earlier, more moderate, manifestation. The rebellion, according to Stokes, was partly due to the circulation among the ordinary people of what he called 'pernicious' reading material:

> The first and most essential step to be taken now is to disseminate the scriptures in the Irish language, or rather such portions of them as shall come within the purchase of the people. It will be said that very few indeed can read Irish; but this must have been the case of every language, before printed books were in common circulation. It must have been so in the highlands of Scotland, Wales and the Isle of Man, where the Bible has been published in the native dialects and extensively circulated.[7]

Stokes' first project in this direction was the publication of a bilingual edition of St Luke's Gospel in 1799 with the assistance of Patrick Lynch, a Belfast teacher of Irish who had also produced *Bolg an tSolair* for the United Irishmen, and it was printed in Dublin by William Watson, who had been a founder in 1792 of the principal counter-revolutionary propaganda organization, the Association for Discountenancing Vice, as well as its printer. Stokes was followed in the early decades of the nineteenth century by a series of educational and publishing organizations which distributed Bibles and moral tracts, mostly in English but also in Irish. The principal group which operated in Irish was the Society for the Education of the Native Irish through the medium of their own language, founded in 1818 as an offshoot of the Association for Discountenancing Vice.[8]

In the context of this volume, there are two related aspects of Stokes' statement which bear emphasis. The first is that conservative, later counter-revolutionary, religious publication in the Celtic languages was undertaken throughout Britain and Ireland, that it was, in other words, a 'four nations' project (five if you include Manx); the second is the implication that publishing and literacy in the other languages were more advanced than in Irish. By extension, there was also a greater readership in those other languages.

This four nations context becomes clearer if we look at another aspect of the background of these religious publishing organizations. They were not only a specific local reaction to the revolutionary ferment of the 1790s and the rebellion of 1798 in Ireland, but also part of a wave of evangelical activity that swept the Protestant anglophone world at that time. Some of the Irish groups were branches of international organizations, such as the British and Foreign Bible Society and the Religious Tract Society, both based in London. In the case of those groups which operated in Irish, much of their impetus came from Scotland and Wales. The inspiration for the publication of an Irish-language Bible in 1811 by the British and Foreign Bible Society came from the Welsh minister Thomas Charles, who had toured Ireland in 1807.[9]

The input from evangelicals in Scotland was more substantial, given the similarities of the Irish and Gaelic languages.[10] The foundation of a Baptist missionary society in Ireland owed much to the Scot Christopher Anderson, who visited Ireland in 1814 and four years later published a short history of scripture printing in Irish.[11] Another Scottish visitor was the Presbyterian divine Daniel Dewar, a Gaelic speaker who had published a book of hymns in Gaelic in 1806 and would later be a co-author of a popular Gaelic dictionary. Dewar preached in Irish during his visit and drew on his experiences for his *Observations on the Character, Customs, and Superstitions of the Irish* (1812), in which he urged a campaign of publishing in Irish. As he put it:

> A native Irishman in the county of — when he read, for the first time in his life, a New Testament, which a benevolent gentleman put into his hands, exclaimed, 'If I believe this, it is impossible for me to remain a rebel.' Behold the means which a beneficent providence has appointed to make good men and good citizens![12]

This dynamic continued throughout the first half of the nineteenth century. During the 1830s, Norman McLeod, a Presbyterian minister, co-editor with Dewar of the Gaelic dictionary and the most prolific author in Gaelic of the nineteenth century, undertook preaching tours of Ireland. He was invited by the Synod of Ulster to prepare an Irish edition of the Book of Psalms, which had been a fundamental text within Gaelic culture in Scotland since its first edition in 1659. McLeod's Irish edition was published in 1836.[13]

The second noteworthy aspect of Stokes' statement is its implication that literacy and publishing in Irish were far more restricted than in Gaelic, Welsh and perhaps even Manx. This observation is a frequent one in the evangelical literature and in writing about the Celtic languages throughout the nineteenth century. It is borne out by the comparative amounts of printed production in the second half of the eighteenth century. This is most effectively represented visually in Figure 7.1 and 7.2:[14]

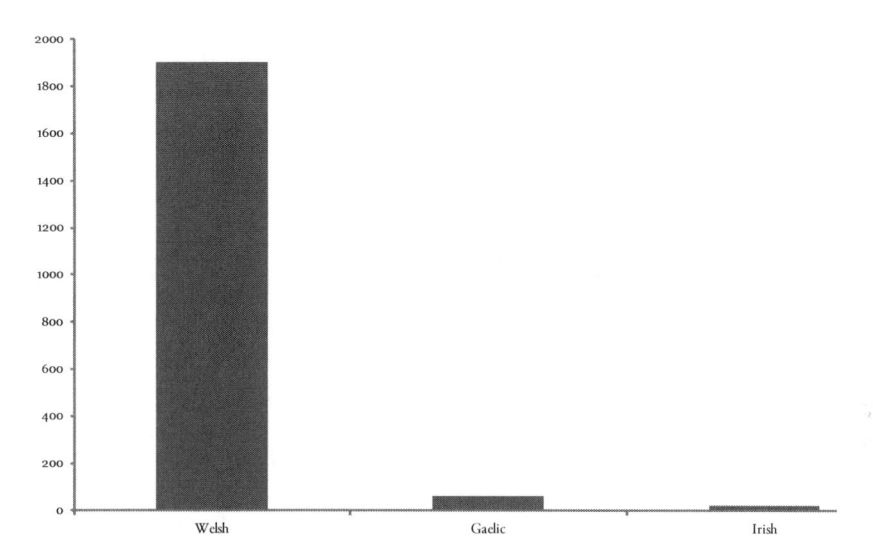

Figure 7.1: Titles printed in Irish, Scottish Gaelic and Welsh, 1750–1800

The same pattern persisted through the nineteenth century:

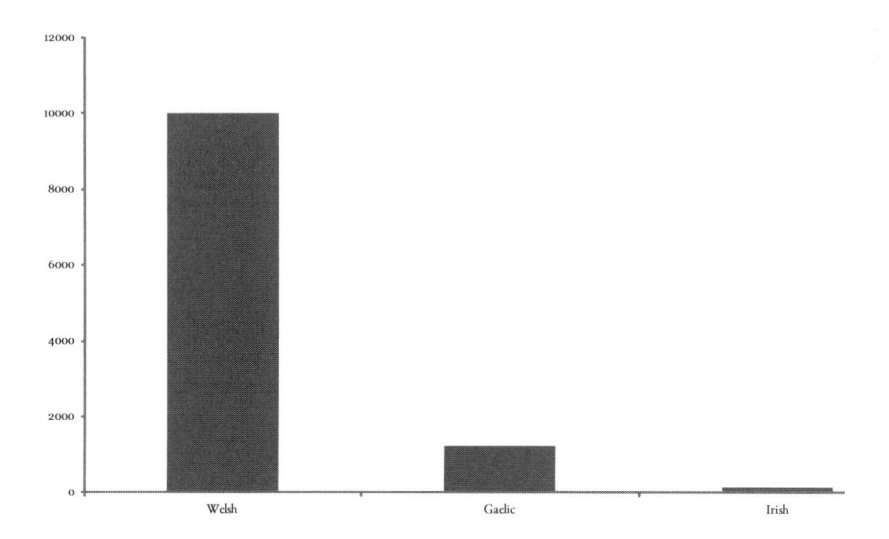

Figure 7.2: Titles printed in Irish, Scottish Gaelic and Welsh, 1800–1900

The contrast between Irish and the other languages is made more remarkable still when the size of the different language communities is taken into account. In 1800 there were two or three million Irish speakers compared to perhaps half a million speakers of Gaelic or Welsh. There were, certainly, readers of manuscripts in all of the languages, particularly in Irish, but given the fact that a printed book is produced in runs of hundreds and even thousands, and is consequently much cheaper and more accessible, printed production is a better guide to the size of readership. It is more than likely, therefore, that the number of readers in Gaelic was many times larger than the number of readers in Irish. What can we tell about the respective reading communities of Irish and of Gaelic from the printed production?

The first thing to note is that readers of Gaelic had a wider range of genres available to them than did readers of Irish, and by implication a greater range of styles of reading. The most popular genre in both languages, however, was the same – religious verse or hymns. The best seller in Irish was the *Pious Miscellany*, a collection of hymns from east Munster by Timothy O'Sullivan (Tadhg Gaelach Ó Súilleabháin), which had eighteen editions between 1802 and 1845. Its equivalents in Gaelic were the collections of Dugald Buchanan, *Laoidhe Spioradail*, first published in 1767, and Peter Grant, *Dain Spioradail*, which first appeared in 1815, both of which were regularly reprinted into the twentieth century.[15]

There were entire genres, however, in Gaelic which had no equivalent in Irish. The 1830s and 1840s, for example, saw the appearance of a number of monthly periodicals in Gaelic, such as *An Teachdaire Gaelach* (1829–31) and *Cuairteir nan Gleann* (1840–3). These were founded and edited, and to a large extent written, by Norman MacLeod. Their content can be broadly described as 'improvement literature', covering topics such as thrift and temperance, and there was a strong emphasis on emigration in the *Cuairteir*. In these periodicals, MacLeod elaborated a form, the prose dialogue, which had not previously existed in Gaelic writing, though it had been typical of earlier improvement or counter-revolutionary popular literature in English, such as the tracts of Hannah More. In Irish, by contrast, there was no periodical before 1860 and there was next to no improvement literature, even though there was a vast English-language production of the latter in early nineteenth-century Ireland.[16]

The type of book which was most spectacularly present in Gaelic and missing in Irish, and the one most germane to the topic of this volume, is the anthology of verse or song. It began with the publication in 1751 of *Ais-eiridh na Sean Chánoin Albannaich*, [The Resurrection of the Old Scottish Language], a collection of the poetry of Alastair Mac Mhaighstir Alastair (Alexander McDonald), the first non-religious printed book in Gaelic, published by McDonald himself. This was followed in 1766 by *Comh-chruinneachidh Orannaigh Gaidhealach*, a miscellany of songs which was published by his son Ranald McDonald and had later editions in 1782 and 1809. *Orain Ghaidhealach*, the songs of

Donnchadh Bàn Mac an t-Saoir (Duncan Ban McIntyre), was published in 1768 and reprinted in 1790 and 1804. Similar collections were published regularly from then on, such as *Comh-chruinneachidh orannaigh Gaedhealach agus Bearla*, by Donacha Loudin (1780), *Orain Nuadh Ghaidhealach* (1785), *Sean Dain, agus Orain Ghaidhealach* (1786) and others. These were of two kinds: collections of the work of a single poet, published by themselves, such as those of Alastair Mac Mhaighstir and Duncan Ban; and anthologies of songs, collected orally or from manuscripts. The collection of secular song or verse was therefore well established within Gaelic print culture by the early nineteenth century. In Ireland, by contrast, no Irish-language poet saw his (or her) work in print during the entire eighteenth century, and hardly any during the nineteenth, and no collections of secular verse or songs aimed at an Irish-speaking readership were printed.

Some of the Gaelic collections, moreover, were published by subscription, and an analysis of the printed lists of subscribers can give us some indication of the social and spatial location of a Gaelic-language readership. Some of these lists were lengthy, and show a substantial demand for this literature. The list of subscribers in the second edition of Duncan Ban's songs in 1790, for example, had 1,480 names, that in the third edition (1804) had 600. I have chosen two lists for analysis.[17] The first is that in *Orain Ghaidhealach* (1792) by Coinneach MacCoinnich (Kenneth MacKenzie), a collection of original verse and song by MacKenzie himself, and which contains 980 names. The second is from an anthology which mixes older poetry with recently composed work. This is *Comhchruinneacha do dh'ain taghta Ghaidhealach*, published in 1813 by Padraig Mac-an-Tuairneir (Patrick Turner), which lists an astonishing 1,680 subscribers.[18] To put this number in context, of 194 books in English published by subscription in Dublin between 1730 and 1800, only six had more subscribers than that of Turner.[19] Turner's collection is very classical in flavour, containing mostly love songs and Jacobite poetry from the seventeenth and eighteenth centuries, along with a few more recent songs in traditional style, such as one on the Battle of Egmont, 1799. MacKenzie's, by contrast, is all of his own composition, and its content is more influenced by contemporary concerns. It begins with a trilogy of songs on the Gaelic language, the first in praise of its ancient lineage, the second an elegy for its decline in the eighteenth century and the third in praise of revivalism. There are also songs of various kinds, love songs and a criticism of clearances.

Both books were published in Edinburgh, which was then the centre of Gaelic publishing, and both were dedicated to aristocratic patrons who were also subscribers. MacKenzie's was dedicated to David Stewart Erskine, Duke of Buchan, who during 1790s was a member of the London Society of the Friends of the People, and in 1780 had founded the Society of Antiquaries of Scotland, while Turner's was dedicated to McDonald of the Isles.

Coming to the lists themselves, two striking features emerge from both. The first is the overwhelmingly rural location of the subscribers. This is remarkable because, while Gaelic speakers mostly lived in rural areas, literacy and book-owning everywhere in Europe were much more frequent among town populations. Out of 980 in the MacKenzie book, seventy-nine were in Inverness, thirty-six in Edinburgh, twenty-six in Perth and eleven in Dingwall. There was only one in Glasgow (Daniel McMartin, a gardener), and four in London (three sadlers and a watchmaker). One hundred and fifty of the subscribers were in towns, about 15 per cent of the total. The bulk of the subscribers were located in the rural area between Perth and Inverness, in the districts of Atholl, Badenoch, Strathspey and Rannoch, while I have found only two on the west coast (see Figure 7.3).[20]

It is not a surprise, therefore, to find that MacKenzie collected the subscriptions himself, travelling on foot. This gave rise to the most famous story connected with the book. In a footnote to 'Aoire do dh 'Alastar Mac'antoisich', 'A satire on Alexander McIntosh', MacKenzie recounts the origin of the satire:

> When the Author was going about taking in subscriptions, coming to Cantry Down about dinner-time, he thought that he would not be allowed to go away hungry; but he soon found it otherwise: for when Mr M'Intosh came to the door, he not only denied him his subscription, but desired him to go away from his house.

A later editor takes up the story:

> Our bard, thus unworthily insulted, retaliates in a satire of great merit. In this cynic production he pours forth periods of fire; it is an impetuous torrent of bitter irony and withering declamation, rich in the essential ingredients of its kind; and M'Intosh, who does not appear to have been impenetrable to the arrows of remorse, died, three days after the published satire was in his possession. Distressed at this mournful occurrence, which he well knew the superstition and gossip of his country would father upon him, M'Kenzie went again among his subscribers, recalled the books from such as could be prevailed upon to give them up, and consigned them to the flame.[21]

As this story suggests, the list, which contains sixty-three MacKenzies, can best be described as localized and personalized.

Turner collected subscriptions in the same way as did MacKenzie, and personal travel was probably the easiest way in which rural customers could be reached. (Duncan Ban MacIntyre financed the second and third edition of his songs in the same way, and his failure to be appointed bard to the Highland Society in Edinburgh in 1789 was because of his lengthy absences soliciting subscriptions.[23]) Turner was apparently a well-known figure in the Highlands, and his collection was a source for later scholars of Fenian or Ossianic poetry. One of these was J. F. Campbell of Islay, who wrote in 1872 that:

Figure 7.3: Subscribers to Kenneth MacKenzie's *Orain Ghaidhealach* (1792)[22]

In his old age Turner used to wander about the Islands with his meal bags, cracking jokes and living on the hospitality of the classes who are ever readiest to help each other out in the west ... When Turner was seeking for subscribers, a Bard composed the following quatrain: —

A Phadruig Mhic an Tuarnair
Gur mòr a thug mi luaidh dhut
Na 'n tachradh tu 'n Gleann Ruadh rium
Gun costann uan san drama ruit.[24]

Turner's list is again overwhelmingly rural, and the proportion in the larger towns is exactly the same as in MacKenzie's, 15 per cent. Out of 1,680 subscribers, 135 are in Edinburgh, sixty-eight in Inverness, twenty-seven in Perth and eighteen in Dingwall. A further 10 per cent are in smaller towns such as Tain (fifty-nine), Oban (twenty-nine), Fort William (twenty-eight) and Campbelltown (twenty-six). As these latter towns indicate, however, the geographic spread of Turner's list is much wider than that of MacKenzie. There are subscribers on the west coast and in the Inner Hebrides, including twenty-two in Mull, twenty-one in Islay, ten in Lismore, eight in Coll, eight in Tiree, seven in Skye, six in I-Colmkil and three in Jura. Figure 7.4 shows these clusters of subscribers, 28 per cent of the total.

The second striking feature of the subscribers is their range of social backgrounds. Here we are on slightly less secure ground than with the spatial distribution, since occupations are given for less than half of the names whereas location is given for almost all. (I have included nobility as an occupation.) On the MacKenzie list, occupations are specified for 437 people, 45 per cent of the total. The largest grouping can be described as 'skilled artisan'. The biggest single category is 'wright', of which there are fifty, to which can be added three wheelwrights and two cartwrights, altogether 12 per cent of those whose occupations are given. There are also twenty-one shoemakers (5 per cent), sixteen weavers (3.5 per cent), thirteen smiths and thirteen tailors (3 per cent each), as well as five shepherds, three pipers, one dancing-master and more. Other large groups are the twenty-six reverends (6 per cent), forty-seven soldiers (i.e. names with a military rank specified, making 11 per cent) and thirty-seven merchants (8.5 per cent). Only seven are titled nobility (this includes those described as 'hon.' and eighteen described as 'esq.').

In the Turner list of subscribers, the occupations of 620 people are specified, about 37 per cent of the total. The social and occupational profile is somewhat more wealthy that that of MacKenzie's list, but there is still a substantial popular readership. The biggest category is that of merchant, (ninety-seven, or 16 per cent of those specified), followed by vintners (sixty-eight or 11 per cent). Nobility and 'esquires' together make up ninety-four or 15 per cent while there are fifty-eight reverends, or 9 per cent of those specified. There are still plenty of skilled artisans, however, with forty wrights (6.5 per cent), twenty-six shoemak-

Figure 7.4: Some subscribers to Turner's *Comhchruinneacha* (1813)

ers (4 per cent), fifteen tailors and ten weavers. Sixty-three (10 per cent) of those listed are described as teachers, and there are also some legal professionals, such as twenty-eight writers, four writers to the signet and one advocate.

The majority of the remainder on both lists could well be farmers, but it would require a great deal of prosopographical work to establish this. In his analysis of the Glasgow-based subscribers to the second edition of Duncan Ban MacIntyre's collection, Ronald Black suggests that those without a specified occupation could well have been casual labourers.[25] If those whose occupations were not specified were of a lower social status to the others, it would mean that the readership was even more popular than the given occupations would suggest.

Overall, therefore, it appears that there was a solid and substantial readership for poetry and song in Gaelic. That readership was Gaelic-speaking and sufficiently at ease with printed Gaelic that it did not require a translation or any other obvious form of intermediary between reader and text. It was popular in the sense that it included people of all social levels above the very poor, it was principally rural in location, and it was fairly comprehensively spread throughout the Highlands and islands, outside of the very east and north. While Turner did not have subscribers in the Outer Hebrides, Duncan Ban MacIntyre did, and the list of subscribers to his 1790 edition contains fourteen names in Stornoway along with four in Lewis and four in Harris, as well as thirteen in South Uist, six in North Uist and one in Barra. There was thus a potential constituency for printed political material in Gaelic, of whatever persuasion. The songs that were published, moreover, were not without political content. The songs in praise of Gaelic and Highland dress in the books of MacKenzie and MacIntyre came not long after the repeal of the Acts which forbade the wearing of the latter, while MacKenzie has a bitter song criticizing the clearing of people from the Highlands and their replacement by sheep.[26]

There was no similar potential audience for print in Irish, and, as noted previously, nothing like these books was published in Irish. Some collections of secular poetry and song were, it is true, published from the late eighteenth century on. Charlotte Brooke's *Reliques of Irish Poetry* (1789) contained Fenian lays collected from the oral repertoire and some eighteenth-century songs, and, as we saw above on p. 130, the United Irishmen's *Bolg an tSolair* (1795) reproduced some of these. James Hardiman's *Irish Minstrelsy* (1831) was made up largely of eighteenth-century verse from manuscripts, as were John O'Daly's *Reliques of Irish Jacobite Poetry* (1844) and *The Poets and Poetry of Munster* (1849). These were fundamentally different to the Scottish collections, however. First and foremost, they were directed at anglophone readers. Their title pages were all in English, they all had parallel English translations, a critical apparatus in English and often a guide to the Irish language. *Bolg an tSolair*, as noted above, is probably best thought of as an aid for learners of Irish, and the contemporary critical reception of O'Daly's anthologies also thought of them as primers.[27] In the Scottish books, by contrast, there were no translations, title pages were in Gaelic (sometimes in English as well, but never in English only) and there was no critical or pedagogical apparatus in English. Their intended readers, and almost certainly their actual readers, were Gaelic speakers.

The contrast between the Irish and the Scottish anthologies is dramatically illustrated by comparing the subscription list of Brooke's *Reliques* with the two Scottish lists analysed. The Brooke list has 289 names. Of these, 132 (45 per cent) are described as 'esquire', eighteen (6 per cent) are titled male nobility and ten (3.5 per cent) are titled female nobility. Over half, in other words, can be described as 'élite', and many of the remaining names are their siblings and relatives. There are twenty-seven members of the Royal Irish Academy, thirteen MPs, three fellows of the Royal Society and two of Trinity College Dublin. This is an overwhelmingly upper-class, anglophone, Anglo-Irish group, interested in Ossianic verse for reasons which were predominantly antiquarian and patriotic in the eighteenth-century sense, and emphatically not an Irish-speaking readership.[28]

The different ways in which the subscribers were collected is also worth noting. MacKenzie and Turner, and Duncan Ban MacIntyre before them, collected most of their subscriptions by travelling around the Highlands in person. Brooke, by contrast, mobilized what looks like a network of influential friends and correspondents:

> The accomplished family of Castle-browne, in the county of Kildare, have exerted all the influence of taste, and character, to extend the subscription to this work. The learned author of the Historical Memoirs Of The Irish Bards, and his brother, Samuel Walker, Esq. late of Trinity College, Dublin, have also been equally zealous and successful; and to these two families I am indebted for the greater number of my subscribers, in this kingdom. For the rest, I am obliged to the influence of the Honorable Justice Hellen; Dominick Trant, Esq., Richard Griffith, Esq., the Reverend Edward Ryan, D. D., the Reverend T. B. Meares, and several other friends.[29]

This approach explains, for example, the presence of four subscribers in Prague and six in Italy, including Cardinal Boncompagni, Rome, and Curzio di Marchesi Venuti, Cortona.

There were two Dublin booksellers on Brooke's list, Patrick Byrne and James Moore, both of whom took six copies. While they presumably subscribed as a commercial proposition, it is significant that both were later prominent United Irishmen. Moore seconded the proposal to make Thomas Paine a member of the organization in 1792, while Byrne produced the first Dublin edition of the second part of *The Rights of Man* in 1792 and was jailed for two years after the rebellion of 1798.[30] Other future United Irishmen on the list were William James MacNeven, a Catholic doctor, and Whitley Stokes, doctor and fellow of TCD, later the publisher of St Luke's Gospel in Irish. There was, in other words, a substantial common ground and continuity between the patriotic antiquarianism of the late eighteenth century and the approach of the United Irishmen to the Irish language and Irish Gaelic culture.

This returns us to the question discussed at the outset of this essay, the failure of the United Irishmen to produce printed propaganda in Irish. There are two aspects to this question, the attitude of the United Irishmen to Irish and the nature of print culture in Irish. As regards the first, we can take another look at the short article about Irish in the *Northern Star* which is normally cited as evidence of the United Irishmen's attitude to Irish. The article is essentially an exhortation to the readers of the paper to learn Irish and an advertisement for the principal teacher of Irish in Belfast, Patrick Lynch. It gives three reasons why its readers might want to acquire some knowledge of the language, only one of which related directly to the radical propaganda campaign. As one might expect from the above discussion of Brooke's reliques, one was antiquarian: 'This Language recommends itself to us, by the advantages it affords to the students of Irish and Eastern antiquities, especially to those who wish to acquire the knowledge of Druidical Theology and Worship, as sketched by Caesar and Tacitus.' Another motive, already quoted, was to facilitate communication with Irish speakers for political purposes, for 'improvement' and 'conciliation'. The third was to facilitate communication for commercial reasons, since those who learned Irish 'would then be qualified for carrying on Trade and Manufactures in every part of their native country'.[31] The target audience for this item was clearly the Presbyterian merchant class of Belfast, the founders of the United Irishmen, a group that was culturally and socially far removed from the Irish-speaking majority, and a group that would have found it difficult to produce texts of any kind in Irish.

The second aspect is the nature of print culture in Irish. According to Curtin, the English-language propaganda campaign of the United Irishmen constituted a 'calculated exploitation of a vibrant oral cultural tradition'.[32] While this is true, it would be more accurate to say that they mobilized not so much oral forms as genres within popular print culture that were themselves partly oral in nature, the ballad or songbook, the catechism and the prophecy. Small songbooks or garlands began to be produced in large quantities from the 1780s onwards, and their popularity may well pre-date that of the single-sheet ballad; catechisms were universal among all Christian denominations, and were often the first texts seen after children had learned to read; and printed versions of seventeenth-century Scottish prophecies were a staple of Ulster popular print through the eighteenth century.[33] If the United Irishmen had wished to produce printed propaganda in Irish, what genres were available to them?

One available genre was the catechism. Catechisms were the most frequently printed item in Irish from the 1760s onwards, and were being produced in considerable numbers by the 1790s. According to Whitley Stokes in 1807,

> I am informed by a respectable person, who has good opportunities of being acquainted with the fact he speaks to, that at least 2,000 Irish catechisms are sold annually; he himself sells 500 annually. Irish catechisms are printed not in Dublin only, but in Cork, Strabane and Dundalk, and I suppose in Waterford and Limerick; possibly in many other towns. I know that an edition of 3,000 copies has been struck off at Dundalk, so that it is rather more probable that the annual number sold greatly exceeds 2,000 than falls short of that number.[34]

Dundalk and Strabane were close to areas where the Defenders, allies of the United Irishmen from the mid-1790s, were strong, and books printed in Dublin would have been sold in those areas too. It seems fair to conclude that the catechism could well have served as a template for United Irish publications in Irish as it did for their publications in English. The other two printed genres, however, did not exist in Irish, most notably the songbook, as we have seen. Overall, therefore, the failure of the United Irishmen to produce propaganda in Irish was principally a result of their lack of familiarity with Irish-language culture and by extension Irish-speaking communities, but it was also a result of the nature of print culture in Irish, of the relative absence of both readers and textual models.

As an addendum, it is important to note that the failure of the United Irishmen to produce a corpus of radical texts in Irish does not imply that Irish-speaking communities were not radical themselves. Recent research on the Defenders, the lower-class, largely Catholic agrarian movement with whom the United Irishmen were allied and which had their areas of strength in the Irish-speaking regions of north Leinster and South Ulster, suggests that they were influenced by revolutionary and radical political ideas and were independently in contact with France.[35] On the other hand, there is not necessarily an equation between Gaelic-language culture and opposition to authority or the state. Many of the Scottish Gaelic song collections had a loyalist and military dimension. MacKenzie's *Orain Ghaidhealach* includes two songs in praise of the 42nd Highland regiment (or the Royal Highland regiment), while Duncan Ban MacIntyre's collection has songs for the Argyll and Bredalbane regiments. There were also songs about individual battles during the long war with revolutionary and Napoleonic France. Turner's *Comhchruinneacha* has a song on the Battle of Egmont, 1799, and another substantial anthology published in 1804 has a song praising the Royal Highland regiment's participation in the battles in Egypt a few years earlier.[36]

Most striking of all is a collection of songs in Gaelic which was published in Cork in the year 1798 itself. This is *Nuadh Orain Ghailach* by Duncan Campbell, who, as the title page announces, was a soldier in the second battalion of the Rothsay and Caithness Fencibles.[37] It also was published by subscription, and of the 502 subscribers, all but seventeen were soldiers. These were officers and men of Campbell's own regiment, as well as members of the Elgin Fencibles, the Duke of York's Royal Highlanders, Fraser's Fencible Highlanders, the Argyll Fencible Highlanders, the Bredalbane Fencibles and Reay's Fencible Highlanders. These were all regiments that were being deployed by the state in Ireland during its counter-insurgency campaign in the 1790s, and whose 'loyalty and steadfastness', as Elaine McFarland puts it, 'was a watchword for the authorities'.[38] The Argyll regiment fought against the United Irish army at the Battle of Ballinahinch while Campbell's own Rothsay and Caithness Fencibles participated in the brutal campaign of terror conducted by General Lake in Ulster in 1797. There is one song in English in Campbell's collection and it celebrates the regiment's role in Ireland:

> The sons of Old Scotia each danger can brave
> And with Albion's brave offspring each country can save
> Then the French they may boast, but they ne'er can affright,
> Tho' at Bantry Bay they should land ev'ry night.
>
> The county of Armagh has given us the name
> Which few Reg'ments can boast in the annals of fame
> Then let emulation our bosoms inspire,
> To perform such bold deeds as the brave must admire.[39]

According to McFarland, 'when the long awaited rebellion in Ireland finally broke out at the end of May, Scots played a key role, not as democratic allies, but as members of the crown forces ranged against the United Irishmen'.[40] This was the case before and after the rebellion as well, and it was as true of Gaelic speakers as it was of English speakers.

8 BROADSIDE LITERATURE AND POPULAR POLITICAL OPINION IN MUNSTER, 1800–1820

Maura Cronin

From the early 1790s onwards, in Ireland as on the sister island, an ongoing print war raged between those who supported the political status quo and those who sought to replace it with one shaped by French revolutionary ideas. While French Enlightenment writings had been circulating widely among the elite and upwardly mobile of Irish towns since the early eighteenth century, cheap print was now pressed into service to determine whether an increasingly literate and politically aware population would stay with the values of the old order or move towards the new radical ideas.[1] Competing pamphlets and newspapers battled it out, to be enforced by a veritable deluge of songbooks, broadsides and handbills proclaiming for and against the new ideas.

Pamphlet warfare was nothing new in the realms of political disputation in the two islands but now the London and Dublin publications were supplemented by an increasing number from Belfast – the hub of United Irish print production in the disturbed decade of the 1790s.[2] Though one of Thomas Paine's works was published in Cork in 1797, the output of southern printers, insofar as it was political at all, seems to have been dominated by the conservative rather than the radical.[3] In Cork both Edwards and Haly published a number of works that focused on 'exterminating French principles' (as one 1793 publication expressed it) and particularly challenging Paine's *Age of Reason*.[4] The Limerick and Waterford printers seem to have concentrated more on reproducing for public sale the various pastoral letters addressed by Catholic bishops to their flocks to warn against social and political revolt, particularly in the late 1790s.[5] The same leaning towards the status quo was obvious in the press. In Belfast and Dublin the system was challenged by the *Northern Star* and the *Press,* but in the south it was really only in Cork that a radical press operated. The *Cork Gazette* caused considerable worries to the authorities during its five-year career and even more severe headaches were caused by the *Harp of Erin* that lasted a mere ten days in 1798 before it was suppressed.[6]

Whether pamphlets and newspapers – either conservative or radical – were popular in the broadest sense is, certainly, open to debate. The style of the language used was one barrier to popularization. Typical was the work of one Cork author who addressed his anti-Paine pamphlet to his 'Fellow Citizens', but whose exalted prose suggested that the readership envisaged was an elite one, even the author himself admitting that some of the material covered was 'too metaphysical for many readers'.[7] The bishops' pastorals, too, which were probably simplified, explained and perhaps translated when they were read in the churches, used equally impenetrable language – considerably limiting any popular impact they may have had in pamphlet form. Price was another barrier. Pamphlets in the 1790s appear to have cost between three and six pence on average, while the price of newspapers in the thirty years after 1790 rose from two to five pence per issue, though radical productions like the *Northern Star* cost only half that sum.[8] Such sums were well beyond the means of the lower levels of the population and represented perhaps 50 per cent of a single day's wages for a labourer at the time.[9]

On the other hand, as Nancy Curtin and Gillian O'Brien suggest, price was not an impossible barrier to building up a popular readership.[10] Paine's works were distributed free in Cork in the early 1790s and newspapers seem to have been handed out in a similar manner by United Irish 'emissaries', in even remote parts of Wicklow and Tipperary.[11] Even where free distribution was not involved, the purchase of a newspaper by one individual had a considerable spin-off. Single newspapers were passed around from person to person so that up to ten people may have had access to any one paper purchased, while others were read aloud to an assembled group, thus transmitting the contents (quite possibly distorted) to those who lacked the money or the literacy to access them directly.[12]

The physical bulk of newspapers and (to a lesser extent) of pamphlets was another practical deterrent to their wide circulation, more especially in rural areas. Consequently, the proprietors of newspapers and journals tried various methods of distribution, ranging from regular coach services to the pedlars that sold books, ribbons and novelties through the countryside, a dissemination method used in 1811 by Walter Cox in getting his radical *Irish Magazine* to buyers in the midlands.[13] Cox's pedlar found himself on trial at the King's County assizes for his trouble, but even in less dramatic circumstances newspaper distribution could prove a nightmare. Proprietors and readers of publications as fundamentally different as the radical *Northern Star* and the moderate Protestant *Limerick Chronicle* faced exactly the same problems at opposite ends of the island – undependable agents, faulty packing and non-payment of subscriptions – interrupting the flow of payment inwards and lessening the popular impact of the production.[14]

If language style, cost and bulk combined to impede the dissemination of print media and the popularization of their message, the more effective spread of news and ideas among the broadest possible sector of the population required the downsizing of the printed item. This meant substituting pamphlets and newspapers with single-sheet productions – broadsides, handbills and chapbooks – that required little financial investment, were easily and quickly run off by jobbing printers, and could be distributed over a wide area at minimal cost. The three decades after 1790 saw an increased reliance on the cheap single sheet as an effective popular persuader, a reliance that was shared by radicals and government alike. In the fraught years of the late 1790s and early 1800s, government proclamations – already published in the press – were reprinted as handbills and distributed through the provinces, especially in areas of serious unrest. Military commanders in these years regularly communicated to the Castle the need to keep this dissemination going as the most effective means of maintaining or restoring order and their belief in the handbill's capacity to influence the lower orders was shared by local elites.[15] In April 1798, following the pacification of Ulster, a Limerick-printed sheet published with an eye on the unrest simmering in north Munster, called on 'The People of Ireland, South' to 'return to your peaceful occupations, fly to your clergy and testify your allegiance on the altar'.[16] The futility of such an appeal did little to dampen the elite's belief in the restraining power of print. In 1801, when several members of local 'banditti' that had operated along the Carlow–Wexford border were shot by the Newtownbarry yeomanry, a list of the names of the dead and the circumstances of their death was printed up in Carlow to serve as an example to other such gangs.[17] Similarly, following a period of considerable agrarian unrest in Limerick and Kerry in 1809, one concerned south Tipperary gentleman urged that the administration print brief accounts of the ensuing trials and executions and circulate the handbills through the country as a deterrent to further disturbance.[18]

Those who sought to undermine the political system put equal faith in the power of the single-page print to influence popular opinion and such 'scraps of sedition' became an increasingly common feature of the articulation of both popular protest and radical propaganda in the three decades after 1790.[19] Some one-pagers were at the very bottom of the amateur production league, scrawled by hand on any available scrap of paper. Such was the small notice, about three inches square and in childish script, posted up in Slane in 1803 and proclaiming – 'Bonapart [sic] is our Friend. B [sic] Ready'.[20] This manuscript notice, sparked by local labourers' wage claims against farmers, was obviously an unmediated expression of economic grievance 'from below' rather than a piece of radical political evangelism, but most one-page productions were part of the radical mission to spread ideas *à la française* in rural areas. Run off by jobbing printers, they were economical and easy to produce, reproduce and distribute, their low cost ensured their saleability, and their contents were easily digested by an increasingly, but still not fully, politicized *cosmhuintir*.[21] The single leaf 'newspaper', printed in Carlow and read every Sunday after mass to the 'ignorant country peopel [*sic*]' in Baltinglass in the neighbouring county of Wicklow was apparently one such production but since no copy was forwarded to Dublin Castle its contents can only be surmised.[22] Somewhat more detail was given regarding another apparently similar production that was distributed in Clonmel in 1803 and which, 'together with a great deal more', called for local support for the French whose imminent arrival was expected. The printed paper was transmitted to Dublin, but separately from the covering letter, so that its contents, too, remain as much a mystery as those of the Carlow production.[23]

Such one-page productions with a radicalizing intent may well have continued to appear during the first decades of the nineteenth century, but if they did there is little trace of them in the surviving documentation and it is more likely that, like the Carlow production of 1797 and the Clonmel sheet of 1803, they appeared only in times of intense political activity or when news of political ferment elsewhere – in Britain or on the continent – was widely reported in the Irish press. Such was the situation in the period 1815–19, when the reform campaign of Orator Hunt in England made major headlines in Irish newspapers both radical and conservative, the news spilling over into the realm of handbills and broadsides.[24] In Belfast, reports of Hunt's campaign and of related radical activities were circulated widely through the medium of single-sheet publications reprinted from British originals – subversive pieces like the 'Political Litany' and 'The Political Pig-Stye', along with flyers advertising the *Political Register* and single page reports of radical meetings in Liverpool and other British centres.[25] But if the circulation of such productions – veritable radical newspapers in cut-down form – was to be expected in Belfast, there are also some elusive signs that it was also happening in far less likely milieus in provincial towns and rural areas in the island's south and midlands. In November 1819 a very concerned Protestant clergyman in the south Tipperary village of Fethard, and a more sanguine military man at Cashel, both reported the local sale and circulation of a two-column handbill describing 'The Grand Procession of Mr Hunt into London, surrounded by half a million of people'. The handbill had been offered for sale by 'a miserable looking creature' at the fair of Thurles on 2 November and – whether by the same pedlar or another is not clear – a few days previously at the fair of Nash (near Fethard).[26] What is clear is that there were two separate runs of the sheet. That sold at Thurles gave details omitted from the Fethard version, while the column arrangement was reversed in the two productions. This apparent existence of a second print run, the correspondents' information that the 'people appeared to purchase with much avidity', and the fact that the pedlar at Thurles had 300 of these sheets in his possession, together suggest that there was a considerable demand in the unlikely territory of south and mid Tipperary for news of Henry Hunt's activities. Was such interest generated by pre-existing familiarity with news from radical England available in the mainstream press?

Was it because popular grievances in Munster created a popular receptivity to Hunt's campaign against excessive taxation and administrative corruption?[27] Perhaps so, but contemporary reports from military men posted locally indicate that rural Tipperary was relatively tranquil in the late teens of the nineteenth century and that when disturbances did erupt in the early 1820s these were centred, not on political demands, but on grievances regarding tithe and land.[28] On the other hand, there was some faint echoing of Hunt's brand of political radicalism even in provincial Ireland. A printed 'Address to Irishmen', signed 'Hibernicus', was seized in the town of Clonmel a month after the confiscation of the pedlar's handbills at Thurles and Fethard and forwarded by a nervous mayor to Dublin Castle. Replete with references to despotism and 'Erin's Lovely Land', it was a garbled combination of calls for political reform and the relief of economic distress, not fundamentally different from Hunt's programme in the other island. Though it set alarm bells ringing with its proclamation that 'the day is nigh at hand' – a favourite line in popular subversive songs, especially those recalling the 1798 Rebellion – it was essentially a call for a meeting to petition parliament. The Castle did agree with the mayor that the author should be found – an indication that these handbills were taken seriously since their sentiments – unlike those of pamphlets – could be made available to the lower orders for the modest output of a halfpenny or a penny.[29] But the Castle also sensibly decided that there was no imminent danger of disturbance, perhaps surmising (as today's historian does) that it was the popular penchant for sensationalism that attracted the buyers at Thurles and Fethard to the handbill's flamboyant account of 'hundreds of footmen', 'bands of music' and 'The Immortal Memory of the Reformers Massacred at Manchester', in the same way that the public were attracted to those songs of shipwrecks, murders and executions that figured so prominently in the chapbooks of the time.[30]

The case of the Hunt handbills is also revealing insofar as it suggests that the gap between more elite pamphlet and newspaper production on the one hand, and that of cheap single-sheet pieces on the other, is partly artificial. First, the same printers could be involved in the production of more than one type of medium, the office of the radical *Cork Gazette,* for instance, following the newspaper's suppression in September 1797, printing Paine's works in pamphlet form. Secondly, the single sheet was frequently, in terms of its content, the offspring of large mainstream productions. Thus, the Fethard and Thurles handbill accounts of Hunt's London meeting were (as indicated on the Thurles version) taken directly from a report in the *Dublin Evening Post,* which in turn seem to have been closely modelled on that published in the London *Examiner*.[31]

While most of the print items discussed so far involved prose accounts, rhyme and song also played a considerable part in both disseminating and suppressing what were considered to be radical ideas. The United Irishmen certainly saw the sung word as a vital part of popular radicalization, one of the *Northern Star's* most successful series satirizing conservatives' fears of political minstrelsy: 'Tis songs that is most to be dreaded of all things. Singing ... is a d—d bad custom; it infects a whole country and makes them half-mad'.[32]

Paddy's Resource, the collection of revolutionary songs that the society published in the mid-1790s, was intended to thus 'infect' as wide a public as possible with the message of equality, secularism and republicanism through songs like 'Freedom Triumphant', 'Plant, Plant the Tree' and 'Dermot's Delight' that rejoiced in the collapse of 'despotic sway' and 'church delusion'.[33] Loyalists retorted with counter-publications like *A Collection of Constitutional Songs* printed in two volumes and distributed by Edwards of Cork in 1799 and old reliables like 'Lilliburlero' and 'The Protestant Boys' and more recent numbers like 'Down, in reply to Up' and 'Crops, Quit Exercising Pikey' – a more flippant number than 'Croppies Lie Down' but almost identical in its sentiments.[34] Such publications were both sophisticated and expensive. The first issue of *Paddy's Resource* cost 1s.1d. (one shilling and one penny) and while the price of the Constitutional song book was not indicated, its size (120 pages) and the high quality of its print and paper suggest that it was quite costly – putting them outside the range of the plebeian purchaser.[35]

Urban centres, with more cash flow and immediate access to press-borne news than was the case in rural areas, proved the most receptive to such musical evangelism. This, as Curtin points out, is just what was intended by the United Irish movement whose mission was to radicalize in the Irish context those groups that proved the backbone of revolution in France, i.e. the middle and artisan classes.[36] Urban receptivity to sung radical ideas was clear even before the United Irishmen published their song book, a performance at Dublin's Theatre Royal in 1792 being disturbed by 'infamous incendiaries calling out for seditious tunes [and] songs' while ballad singers spread the 'levelling spirit' through the streets.[37] *Paddy's Resource* worked on this popular predilection for subversive songs by providing a large repertoire of such compositions, and these seem to have penetrated well beyond Belfast and Dublin. Distributed and sung among the Wicklow rebels, they were claimed in Wexford to have served as a macabre accompaniment to the execution of informers and they continued to worry the custodians of order into the new century.[38] In 1804, for instance, the refrain – 'To the tune of equality, boys, let us dance round Liberty's Tree in the morning' – was heard emanating from a public house on Newry's Canal Street and the seriousness with which the incident was regarded was clear in the lengthy report sent to Dublin Castle. It detailed who had sung the refrain, the clasping of hands that accompanied its singing, and the seditious toast that followed it – 'May those that intend to invade us come in a breast [*sic*]' – not something to be ignored in the year when the French threat was particularly strong.[39]

Though the progress or slowness of anglicization in a region must also have limited the popular appeal of such evangelical political songs, it is clear from the widespread use of English in such diverse media as threatening notices (usually of an agrarian character), official proclamations, bishops' pastorals and newspaper advertisements, that language – like cost – was not an entirely impenetrable barrier.[40] Indeed, bilingualism seems to have been quite extensive, and the links between Gaelic- and English-language culture are clear in what looks like a widespread familiarity with songs in both languages. This was especially true in parts of South Leinster and Munster where good land, commercial farming, improving transport networks and rising literacy existed alongside increasing politicization and, at the same time, a surviving familiarity with Irish-language poetry and song.[41] This bridging of the cultural divide is clear in some surviving poetry notebooks from the region. One was compiled in east Cork around 1830 by Owen Sheehy, the other owned by Michael Hayes of Caherguillamore near Bruff on the edge of Limerick's Golden Vale. Compiled around 1840, this lovingly assembled notebook included pieces in both Irish and English extending onwards chronologically from the early eighteenth century, and ranging from *aisling* poetry through pieces by Byron to home-made compositions lamenting the fall of Napoleon.[42]

Whether in the Irish or the English language, the tenor of the poems and songs in these notebooks raise questions as to how radical – if at all – was popular opinion among the Irish *cosmhuintir*. Just like the popular songs available in print and in the oral tradition over the previous thirty years, they were certainly full to the brim with radical catch phrases imported from *Paddy's Resource*. The revellers in Newry in 1804 had sung 'to the tune of equality', while the printed notice circulated in Clonmel a few months earlier had called on 'the People to be ready to join their [French] Friends, who were coming to give them Liberty'. This wording was directly parallel to that of a contemporary Irish song from the same area, 'Sliabh na mBan', that was probably composed a few years earlier as a lament for the failed rising at Carrigmoclear in 1798 and that promised the imminent arrival of '*an Frannchach faobhrach is a loingeas*' – the keen Frenchman with his fleet.[43] Such cross-fertilization between print propaganda and popular song was not uncommon, indicating seepage of contemporary political events into popular consciousness. Some of these songs were essentially non-political but included references to the hoped-for French invader in such a fleeting manner that the offending lines would have eluded the ears of anyone unfamiliar with the song or with the cultural milieu of singer and audience. Thus, the widely sung multiple versions of 'An Spailpín Fánach' (The Wandering Day Labourer), which was essentially a diatribe against grinding farmers, slipped in a line about

Colours na bhFrancach ós cionn mo leapan
Agus Pike agam chun sáite

(The French colours over my bed and a pike in my possession for thrusting.)[44]

But despite such political allusions, and despite the ongoing references in both contemporary newspaper files and in the records of the Dublin Castle administration to 'seditious' songs and notices, there was little trace in the early nineteenth century of song-borne political radicalism in the French or United Irish sense. For instance, when John Callaghan, an itinerant potato digger, was arrested in the east Cork barony of Imokilly in late 1821 for activities described as 'seditious', his covert activities were more likely linked with the Rockitism, essentially agrarian and sectarian and without even a token smattering of political radicalism.[45] Similarly, though the Slane notice urging its readers to 'B Ready' for Bonaparte was described as 'seditious', it was, just like the 'Spailpín Fánach' song, fundamentally an expression of anti-farmer feelings that had nothing to do with political radicalism.[46] In fact, popular songs' constant references to the French and to Bonaparte were an indication that the outlook of the lower levels of the Irish population, particularly in rural areas, was essentially conservative.

If, as Kevin Whelan expressed it, 'the United Irishmen's necks were set in concrete, staring relentlessly forward' into a world of secularism and equality, most popular songs, like Lot's wife, looked longingly backwards.[47] This fascination with the past was patent among culturally aware individuals within the *cosmhuintir*. Scribe, teacher and sometimes farm labourer, Micheál Óg Ó Longáin of Whitechurch outside Cork transcribed genealogy, *Fiannaíocht* (the hero tales of the mythical Fianna) and devotional works for his elite patrons.[48] At a less exalted intellectual level, Michael Hayes, a large farmer from Caherguillamore, prefaced his poetry notebook with a list of the birth dates and times of his family members – hardly an elite genealogy but still an indicator of that concern with rootedness and family continuities that characterized the more elevated genealogies of others. The same past-centred focus appeared in the same individuals' own poetical work and in their personal collecting of songs. The poetry of Ó Longáin, though he was probably himself a United Irishman, was rooted primarily in the Jacobite tradition with the dominant motif being dispossession of the *Gael* by the *Gall* or foreigner. Hayes and Sheehy – more collectors than poets – showed a considerable familiarity with the work of eighteenth-century poets and carefully wrote down poems by Seamus Ó Choindealbhain, Eoghan Rua Ó Suilleabháin, Seán Ó Coileáin, Seán Clárach Mac Domhnall and William Rua Mac Coitir.[49]

If these individuals were to some extent the cultural elite of the *cosmhuintir* and possibly atypical, there are strong indications that their fixation with the past was shared by the broader population – though the focus in this case was not on the dispossession of 'the Gael' but on a far more recent event from the past, i.e. the rebellion of 1798. Whether the events of the rebellion were truly 'remembered', or whether they were formed over time into a narrative that all agreed to believe, is not clear.[50] What is clear is that in popular songs, both printed and orally transmitted, there was a simultaneous focus on past, present and future: the past had seen the cruel suppression of 'the people'; the present witnessed their continued persecution; and the future would see them avenged. When William Newenham reported to Dublin Castle in April 1819 that he had recently received a threatening notice including the words: 'Do you remember all you ever done [sic] in your time and every poor fellow you punished?', he explained that this referred to his suppression of disturbances in Galway twenty years previously in 1798.[51] A few years later, Thomas Crofton Croker, collecting songs in Munster, described a similar popular capacity to nurse past grievances:

> At the present day, the common malediction in the mouth of every Irish peasant is 'the curse of Cromwell', [this] being the strongest expression for entire ruin and desolation, and minute circumstances that occurred nearly two centuries since, areas fresh in popular recollection as the events of the preceding year.'[52]

What inspired popular songs, therefore, was not the creation of a *new* radical social and political order *à la française*, but the desire to restore a largely imagined world of the past and to punish those who had destroyed that world. The south Tipperary song, 'Sliabh na mBan' threatened '*go gcuirfhidh Gaeil boicht arís 'na gceart*' – 'that the oppressed Irish will be restored to their rightful place' – while the English-language songs, largely oral but fortunately for the historian transcribed (how accurately is unclear) by concerned observers, had the same theme of restoration and revenge.[53] 'The Boys You Know', sung at a wedding gathering in Moynalty in County Meath in 1816, managed to use images and notions drawn from French radicalism to specifically 'Irish' ends:

> We are the [free] born sons of Ireland,
> We fight for liberty
> And in the House of Lords in Dublin
> We will plant our Irish tree.

The gesture to radical abstractions complete, the song turned its attention to the main business in hand, i.e. revenge for the 1798 Rebellion:

> Our country lads they are loyal still
> And on them we'll depend,
> There is Louth and Meath will join hands
> And march to our friends.
> And if any of their English b—s
> Offend us on our way,
> With sword and pistol we will conquer
> And shew them Irish play.[54]

Perhaps the singing of such songs, composed locally and obviously performed with considerable verve, were a sign of some residual political radicalism in rural areas. One is, however, tempted to conclude, in view of the relative absence of political cases at successive assizes, that what lay behind the songs was simply a combination of machismo (frequently fanned by alcohol and the mixed or convivial company in which they were sung), local pride and a stronger desire to settle old scores than to tamper with the political system.[55] The sectarian element in the popular songs – the antithesis of the radical United Irish message – was part of this concentration on old scores. Even – or perhaps particularly – when the rebellion was raging in Wexford, songs were reputedly being sung that had nothing to do with equality and fraternity but were 'scurrilously abusive of the Protestant religion [and] were publicly sung by drinkers in tipling houses and ballad-singers in the streets' – a feature that continued for at least half a century thereafter.[56] Just as the popular songs' sectarianism showed that there was little interest in radical egalitarianism, so too in a different way did their penchant for heroes. While *Paddy's Resource* eschewed the adulation of individuals in favour of abstract principles like democracy and egalitarianism, the locally produced songs – especially those in English – were unequivocally hero-centred. The heroes could be either home grown like Fr Murphy (unequalled by 'Julius Caesar, Alexander or renowned King Arthur') or of truly international status like Napoleon, whose death was lamented by a farmer songwriter in one parish in south Limerick in February 1820:

> Old Erin would be free by his princely emulation
> Catholic Emancipation he would really restore
> No homage to the boors whose cruel domination
> Our poverty increases each day more and more.[57]

The more closely popular songs are examined, the more it seems that politics of any sort – let alone radicalism – was at the very bottom of the popular agenda. This is particularly clear when we look at the popular and emasculated English-language translations of eighteenth-century Irish-language songs. The original Irish versions – haunting songs of dispossession like 'Seán Ó Dhuibhir a' Ghleanna' (John O'Dwyer of the Glen) and powerful *aislingí* with Jacobite sentiments like 'An Druimfhionn Donn Dílis' (The Little Brown-Backed Cow) – were almost certainly very much alive in the oral tradition, but the popular English print culture of the towns, while retaining the rhythm and presumably the air of the originals, turned them into ill-translated doggerels with absolutely no political subtext. 'John O'Dwyer A Glana' when printed on broadside by Geoghegan of Athlone, was transformed into a love song about 'dear Anna', the only gesture towards the original being two disembodied lines proclaiming: "Tis home we'll steer in sorrow / For royalty is banished'.[58]

Others ended up as comic songs with something of a stage Irish character, the 'Druimfhionn Donn Dílis' changing from an emotive lament in which Ireland was portrayed as a brown-backed cow and the Stuart claimant to the throne as her herd, into a semi-comic song about a poor man whose cow was drowned:

> Arrah pox on you, Drumion Dubh,
> What made you die?
> Or why did you leave me,
> For what or for why?[59]

This absence of the political from the bastard offspring of eighteenth-century Irish poetry was even more remarkable in the original English-language popular songs that poured from the printing presses in provincial cities like Cork, Waterford and Limerick. Turned out largely in chapbooks – single-sheet productions folded and cut so as to give six to eight separate pages of songs – these were easily distributed by pedlars and 'flying stationers'. Goggin of Limerick was the chapbook printer *par excellence* in the late eighteenth and early nineteenth century, to be followed closely by Kelly of Waterford. Of the nearly 400 chapbooks that survive from these and other print shops, the vast majority were collections of non-political numbers – love songs (a few from Burns), comic songs, bawdy songs and songs of place, with some more nostalgic numbers from Moore. Typical was the selection in a locally printed chapbook sent into Dublin Castle from Castlebar in 1820, with its six songs – 'The Irish Maid', 'The Country Maid', 'Rosebud of Summer', 'Gra Galmachree', 'Shamrock of Erin so Green' and 'Eveleen's Bower' – all distinctly non-political.[60]

A handful of the chapbook songs – probably no more than 5 per cent of the total – might be loosely construed as political, and by far the greater number were loyal, but not of the virulent 'Croppies Lie Down' genre. The tenor of most might be described as a sort of rollicking machismo – like 'The Boys of Tanderagee' with political overtones. Typical were 'A New Song on the Tipperary Militia', 'Darby's Escape from Castlebar' and 'The Louth Heroes, or the Scourge of Croppies'.[61] Whether the political hue of these songs was determined by the political outlook of the printer or the nature of popular demand is not now clear. The loyalism of the chapbook songs or, at least, their lack of radicalism, may have been a reflection of the Goggins' elevated and consistently rising social and political status in the local affairs of Limerick city. The family controlled large amounts of land and property in the city and its liberties, and its successive generations included freemen, church wardens and members of the market jury – hardly the stuff of which radicals were made, and very different political animals from the Dublin printers and booksellers who were members of the Dublin United Irishmen in the same period.[62] But popular taste was also a vital consideration in what, unlike the evangelical mission of United Ireland, was primarily a business enterprise. Goggin's broad range of printing, like that of his contemporaries in Cork, reflected his capacity to identify and respond to the demands of the market, and the output of his warehouse in 1790 (since he was a supplier as well as a printer) included 'histories, manuals, penny books, spelling books, primers [sic], large and small pictures'.[63] Goggin's loyalist songs – and they formed only a tiny proportion of the whole selection – were obviously a response to a demand for loyal songs in Limerick city and beyond. 'The Gallant Limerick Militia', based on the local militia's victory over the rebels at the battle of Coloney, was typical:

> You stout Irish heroes that ne'er was dismayed
> Or of any enemy was never yet afraid;
> Attend to my story, while I shall unfold
> Our intrepid Limerick boys who are stout hearts of gold.
> The fifth of September, the year eighty-nine
> The Rebels and French both together did join
> Near the town of Sligo our force to subdue,
> While balls they in showers were pouring like rain,
> We stood them like Trojans and never did flinch,
> Tho' they were ten to one boys, we ne'er gave an inch.[64]

Was this a loyal and anti-radical song? It would certainly appear so, with its denigration of rebels and French as being essentially the opposite of Irish – a theme that appeared in other urban popular songs of the same period, such as the Cork-produced 'Groves of Blackpool' that celebrated the Cork City Militia's record at 'beatin' [sic] the rebels'.[65] But on closer examination, it is clear that the main theme of these songs was not loyalty or anti-radicalism but local pride and machismo – 'our intrepid Limerick boys' and 'those brave Irish heroes that sprang from the Groves of Blackpool'. This introversion is hardly surprising. The same essentially local note dominated the popular – and largely orally transmitted – songs from the other side of the political divide. The several 'Fr Murphy of County Wexford' songs that emerged from the rebellion in the south-east, and were only committed to writing in the 1840s by R. R. Madden, seem to have been shaped less by any sentiments of nationalism or radicalism than by essentially local experiences and memories. There was some brief allusion to Irishness, but only in the vaguest sense: the Wexford men were portrayed as triumphing over a 'British King' and – even more importantly – over the Ancient Britons, a regiment remembered with loathing in Wicklow and Wexford for its harrying of the local population before the rebellion was suppressed.[66] The predominant note was local: familiar place names (Monaseed, Camolin, Gorey, Kilcavan) provided the main appeal of these compositions and ensured their survival into the succeeding century, while the final stanza was firmly rooted in county pride – 'Success attend you, brave County Wexford / Who shook off the yoke and to battle did run'. But if there was no sign of nation or of radicalism in such a song, it was nonetheless capable of rousing strong emotions, a potential that can be seen in its closing lines. The vital parting shot – 'Let them not think we gave up our arms / For every man has a pike or gun' – epitomized the tendency of popular songs to look backwards and forwards at the same time, nursing the grievances of the past while planning revenge in the future.[67]

So to what extent did popular song and cheap print media together spread or combat radicalism among the Irish *cosmhuintir* in the decades immediately following the French Revolution? The United Irishmen envisaged that a combination of missionary zeal and effective dissemination was all that was required to imbue 'the people' with egalitarian idealism. Upholders of the status quo, for their part, used much the same means to the opposite end, fighting print with print and song with song. Neither side was successful, but the over-optimistic radicals were probably the more disappointed of the two. As Curtin put it, the 'United Irish failed to leave deep ideological footprints'.[68] There was certainly some degree of radicalization as revolutionary newspapers like the *Northern Star,* the *Press* and the *Cork Gazette* spread their ideas through town and countryside, as handbills spread political awareness, and as songs from books like *Paddy's Resource,* with its intention to 'fan the Patriotic flame', found their way into the popular repertoire.

But the apparent radicalization was only surface deep. Catchphrases about reform and equality were no indication of any fundamental changes in popular attitudes. Outside times of intense political excitement, the ongoing tensions deriving from religious animosities and competition for land proved far more important than any new-fangled ideas about the rights of man. Tastes in popular song were the ultimate proof of the failure of radicalization: The songs from *Paddy's Resource* do not seem to have made it into the notebooks in which culturally-aware individuals carefully transcribed their favourite songs. Nor do they appear to have found a niche in the thriving chapbook trade which mirrored popular musical tastes in the first half of the nineteenth century. Neither are they to be found (insofar as the sources allow us to judge) in the oral tradition where both Irish and English language songs were built not on an optimistic view of a future world of brotherhood and equality but one where the dispossession and defeats of the past would be avenged.

9 RADICAL POETRY AND THE LITERARY MAGAZINE: STALKING LEIGH HUNT IN THE REPUBLIC OF LETTERS

Dan Wall

In his landmark study *Literary Magazines and British Romanticism*, Mark Parker convincingly argues that the literary magazine became the 'preeminent literary form' of the 1820s and 1830s, and that the study of literary magazines is especially important to the study of the literature of the period because of the way in which each individual magazine projected what he calls 'a different version of Romanticism', thus further complicating what is already a problematic and highly contested term.[1] A particularly important part of his argument is that during the 1820s, literary magazines assumed an increasingly apolitical stance in their treatment of literature, the most notable example being the *New Monthly*, which is described by Parker as 'a timid, socially ambiguous exploration of domestic comfort and private feeling'.[2] However, elsewhere in his study Parker identifies two literary magazines which alternate between political discussion and literary criticism, namely the *London Magazine*, and *Blackwood's Edinburgh Magazine*. If viewed in those terms, these publications appear to highlight a transition towards less overt political discussions within the literary magazine by the 1820s. However, *Blackwood's* treatment of Leigh Hunt, when considered in detail, throws new light upon the extent to which *Blackwood's* was in fact prepared to enter into an often spirited discussion of politics, and highlights the profound impact which these political impulses had upon the magazine's reception of poetry. Furthermore, the implications of Hunt's treatment at the hands of his Blackwoodian critics tells us a great deal about how Edinburgh-based publications, in particular *Blackwood's*, self-consciously defined themselves against London's literary culture as the 1820s approached. What is also apparent from the so-called 'Cockney School' attacks upon Hunt and the other members of his coterie is a clear sense of how literary magazines in this period began to differentiate themselves from newspapers such as the *Examiner*, of which Hunt was editor.

It may be helpful to consider the *Examiner* as being an example of the type of publication that, along with pamphlets and single-sheet publications, gained considerable influence during the late eighteenth century, in that it provided a forum for political discussion, as well as a channel for the dissemination of poetry and overtly political writing. At the 'United Islands?' symposia hosted by Queen's University Belfast in 2008 and 2009 this type of political transmission rightly loomed large on the agenda, since the level of engagement between radical ideas and the literary magazine increased significantly between 1770 and 1820. One of the most notable examples of radical poetry's engagement with the public sphere in the 1780s and 1790s occurs with Burns' interaction with, for example, the *Edinburgh Evening Courant*, the *Edinburgh Herald* and the *Caledonian Mercury*, as well as with Belfast-based newspapers such as the *Northern Star*, and the *Belfast News-Letter*. Publications such as these were, certainly, overtly political in terms of their character and anticipated readership in a way that literary magazines were generally not by the 1820s. They essentially offered an open forum for the discussion of progressive politics, as well as poetry expressing similar sentiments, but it is important to remember, as Liam McIllvanney suggests in his book *Burns the Radical*, that these publications are in fact articulations of a number of different *radicalisms*,[3] just as early nineteenth-century literary magazines assume, enact and articulate a variety of *romanticisms*, to return to Parker's analysis. The political discussions featured in newspapers and pamphlets of the late eighteenth century highlight the kaleidoscopic nature of radicalism in the period treated by these symposia, and as anxieties regarding how to define radicalism in this period begin to surface, as they did at both Belfast symposia, a more nuanced understanding of the political and generic complexion of the various publications engaged in discourses of radicalism seems ever more important. For example, McIllvanney points out that the Belfast-based *Northern Star* carried Burns's most overtly political poetry, in keeping with its strongly radical character, while the *Belfast News-Letter* was, in fact, a far more cautious publication, with a particular stronghold in 'areas of Church of Ireland dominance', and which consequently shied away from these parts of Burns's corpus.[4] This is hugely significant, in that it indicates the ability of late eighteenth- and early nineteenth-century publications, whatever their particular brand of progressive or radical politics, to fashion their own identities according to their particular political position or constituent audience, or audiences. Conversely, many of the conservative periodicals established in response to their radical counterparts encountered great difficulties in establishing their own individual identities, and thus found it difficult to gain a foothold in the literary marketplace. The *British Critic*, for example, was established in 1793, at the height of the French Revolution debates, to, in the words of the Welsh Churchman Thomas Rees, 'uphold the tenets of the Established Church and the Tory Politics of the ruling government'.[5] More significantly, it was also designed to nullify the liberal political opinions of the *Monthly*, *Critical* and *Analytical Review*. The same can also be said of the *Antijacobin Review and Magazine*, which was founded in 1798, although that publication was also explicitly designed to maintain the political line held by the *Anti-Jacobin; or Weekly Examiner*. The *British Critic* ultimately became a dedicated theological magazine, while the *Antijacobin* folded in the 1820s, and it appears likely that the reasons for the demise of both publications ultimately lay in their failure to offer an imaginative and entertaining articulation of conservative values in the way that the *Quarterly Review* and *Blackwood's Magazine* eventually succeeded in doing. Additionally, as John O. Hayden has suggested in his wide-ranging survey of periodicals between 1802 and 1824, the decline of the *British Critic* also stemmed from a lack of independence due to the amount of conservative political patronage that it attracted.[6] Such a view was clearly articulated by Francis Hodgson in a letter to William Gifford, editor of the *Quarterly*, in a letter written in 1809.[7] The *Antijacobin* evidently suffered from a similar problem, in that it became primarily concerned with religious discussions which were of interest only to a limited constituency of its readers. The domination of such articles was ultimately reflected in its change of title to the *Antijacobin Review and True Churchman's Magazine* in its thirty-sixth edition. It is therefore important to note that while scholars undertake a valuable search for radical voices between 1770 and 1820, in periodical terms at least, the emergence of coherent and commercially successful conservative voices was clearly not without its setbacks.

Prior to the foundation of the *Edinburgh Review* in 1802, the most significant periodicals in existence were arguably the *Monthly* and the *Critical Review*. The particular breakthrough achieved by the *Edinburgh Review* was that it firmly established Edinburgh as a rival to London in the articulation of liberal opinion. Francis Jeffrey succeeded in reinvigorating the notion of the literary critic as a 'judge' of aesthetic merit, and in doing so he directly influenced, or possibly even inspired, the fearless tone of *Blackwood's*, the great rival to his own magazine. *Blackwood's* began to make its mark in October 1817, after a false start under the editorship of Thomas Pringle and James Cleghorn in April of that year, and immediately began positioning itself as the outspoken Tory alternative to the *Edinburgh Review*, although it is possible that the outspoken and scurrilous tone of the *British Critic* during the 1790s might also have provided a template for *Blackwood's*. Central to the creation of the identity of *Blackwood's* as a magazine was its adoption of theatrical techniques, such as an exaggerated tone, pseudonymous personae and the complete appropriation and subversion, and on occasion even the assimilation, of the identities of its competitors and of those it held in contempt. This might explain the lack of overt political discussion in the pages of *Blackwood's*; Mark Parker observes that the magazine only adhered to two or three steadfast Tory principles, but offers a convincing case for saying that these were only ever unconsciously expressed within its pages.[8] Consequently, the Whig *Edinburgh Review* was frequently constructed by *Blackwood's* as being far more liberal than it was in reality, and in attacking the cultural and political influence of Edinburgh's Whig élites over post-Enlightenment Edinburgh, charges of godlessness and a lack of respect for Scottish history and culture were often made which were in fact far removed from the reality of the *Edinburgh*'s position.

The lack of overt political discussion with the pages of *Blackwood's Edinburgh Magazine* does not, therefore, indicate a complete lack of political engagement. Rather, it was in fact another example of the magazine's sleight of hand. Central to this innovative and enigmatic approach to politics was the notion that the magazine was about to revolutionize the periodical marketplace, a point noted by David Higgins in relation to John Gibson Lockhart's article from March 1818, entitled 'On the Periodical Criticism of England'. Higgins argues that

> The foundation of *Blackwood's* success was its self-promotion and Lockhart's article was the first of a number of attempts by its writers to suggest that it was a new type of journal. It was important for the magazine to differentiate itself from the *Quarterly* as well as the *Edinburgh*, even though *Blackwood's* was on the same side as the former in terms of politics.[9]

Higgins connects the substance of Lockhart's article with remarks made by William Maginn (and possibly John Wilson) in 'Preface', from *Blackwood's* April 1826 issue, published following Lockhart's departure for London in order to take up the editorship of the *Quarterly*, in which the authors reaffirmed the magazine's place at the heart of a 'revolution' in periodical literature in 1817:

> The whole periodical criticism of Britain underwent a revolution. Principles were laid down and applied to passages from our living poets. People were encouraged to indulge their emotions, that they might be brought to know their nature. That long icy chill was shook off their fancies and imaginations, and here, too, in Criticism as in Politics, they began to feel, think, and speak, like free men.[10]

This is may seem to be Blackwoodian self-promotion at its most brazen, but the notion of a conservative 'revolution' in the 'Republic of Letters', as proclaimed by the authors of *Blackwood's* 1826 'Preface', is particularly significant. The key contributors to the magazine from October 1817 onwards had certainly seen themselves as emancipating literary criticism from the tyranny of Jeffrey and his fellow Whigs, and portrayed this struggle by consciously appropriating the rhetoric and spirit of more radical political newspapers, pamphlets and journals, including Leigh Hunt's *Examiner*. However, in order for claims of a Blackwoodian revolution in the periodical marketplace to appear credible, it was necessary for *Blackwood's* to not be seen engaging in direct political debate with its adversaries. Instead, the contributors to the magazine chose to allow its political sympathies to surface predominantly through its often outspoken discussions of literature and culture. Therefore, in its style and tone, if not in its politics, *Blackwood's Edinburgh Magazine* can certainly be considered revolutionary.

The misrepresentation and subversion of the *Edinburgh Review*'s position and tone in Edinburgh's literary and political landscape was just one of the markers of the success of *Blackwood's Edinburgh Magazine* in positioning itself in what was clearly a highly competitive marketplace for literary magazines. Its treatment of Leigh Hunt, on the other hand, constitutes a much more striking act of political, literary and geographical definition. For *Blackwood's*, the Leigh Hunt/John Keats coterie also 'officially' encompassed Shelley and Hazlitt, and became known within its pages as 'The Cockney School'. John Gibson Lockhart, writing under the pseudonym 'Z', produced the attacks upon Hunt, the first of which appeared in the August 1818 issue of *Blackwood's*. 'On the Cockney School of Poetry' even now retains its reputation as one of the most withering reviews ever written. The article, which was the first of a series which effectively ran until December 1822, famously also attacked John Keats in a strikingly harsh manner. As editor of the radical newspaper, the *Examiner*, Leigh Hunt stood for everything political to which *Blackwood's* was opposed. Kevin Gilmartin is therefore correct in suggesting that, for *Blackwood's*, radicalism entailed the 'utter destruction of the present state of things,' though it was seldom discussed directly in its pages.[11] The apparent lack of attention generally paid by *Blackwood's* to the subtleties of politics is evident in its failure to distinguish clearly between the political opinions of Hunt and one of his associates, Hazlitt. Nicholas Roe points out that 'unlike Hazlitt, Hunt was no Bonapartist, and although the *Examiner* always spoke of Napoleon as a great man, it was careful to hold him up as a "betrayer of freedom."'[12] To *Blackwood's*, however, such political nuances were apparently meaningless.

Hunt was specifically used by Lockhart to define the 'Cockney School', when he coined the term in the first article.[13] Lockhart's use of the term 'school' is in fact a playful reference to Hazlitt's incorporation of Wordsworth and Coleridge (both of whom were championed by Lockhart in *Blackwood's*) into the 'Lake School' (and coining of that term) in his *Edinburgh Review* article of April 1817. Later, in his 'Letter from Z to Mr Leigh Hunt', from *Blackwood's* January 1818 issue, Lockhart clearly set out his objections to Hunt:

> The charges which I have brought against your literary life and conversation are these: 1. The want and the pretence of scholarship; 2. A vulgar style in writing; 3. A want of respect for the Christian religion; 4. A contempt for kingly power, and an incessant mode of attacking the government of your country; 5. Extravagant admiration of yourself, the Round Table, and your own poems; 6. Affectation; 7. A partiality for indecent subjects, and an immoral manner of writing concerning the crime of incest, in your poem of *Rimini*; 8. I have asserted that you are a poet vastly inferior to Wordsworth, Byron, and Moore![14]

What is significant here is the lack of prominence given to politics as a cause of Lockhart's displeasure; it is only number four on his list, even though it is clearly a major issue for Lockhart. It is also the only overt mention of politics in Lockhart's treatment of Hunt, for as the 'Cockney School' series progressed, Lockhart would concentrate primarily upon the quality of the poetry produced by Hunt and his associates, and he would consistently judge it to be poor.

Although written from a hard-line Tory stance, the most striking aspect of the first 'Cockney School' article is the extent to which it deliberately downplays its political motives. Instead, Lockhart alternates between highly personal invective and a more methodical deconstruction of Hunt's literary abilities. Lockhart subjects Hunt's *Rimini* to eviscerating scrutiny, bemoaning the poem's incestuous subject matter, while citing it as evidence of the moral deficiencies of the Cockney 'sect'. This is, in fact, essential to Lockhart's construction of Hunt's circle, and the 'Cockney School' in general, as a band of pretentious sycophants ruled by Hunt, the so-called 'King of the Cockneys' from his castle at 13 Lisson Grove, London.[15] As Jeffrey Cox notes, Lockhart's use of the term 'Cockney' denotes moral collapse and wantonness, and was defined in terms of early nineteenth-century slang by Francis Grose's *Dictionary of the Vulgar Tongue* in 1811 (Grose's *Dictionary* was originally published in 1785).[16] More importantly, the geographical association of Hunt with the radical literary culture of London in such a negative manner indicates an attempt to distinguish the Edinburgh-based Toryism of *Blackwood's* from the politically dangerous, morally corrosive and artistically bankrupt literary circles of London, and 'south Britain' more generally.

Lockhart's fashioning of the 'Cockneys' as 'vulgar poetasters', whose poetry was not only incoherent and sometimes tainted with the odour of radical politics, but which was often downright indecent, helped to maintain the façade of immorality established by the 'Cockney' label. Special attention was paid by Lockhart to the discrediting of Hunt's opinions, largely because Hunt, unlike Keats, was also widely known for his editorial work. The degree to which Hunt became synonymous with the *Examiner* in fact earned him the nickname '*Examiner* Hunt'.[17] In periodical terms, Hunt's public status as editor of the *Examiner* made him an obvious target, and contrasted starkly with the anonymity and pseudonymous writing which characterized *Blackwood's*. The association of Hunt with the world of newspaper editing (and the editing of a radical newspaper at that), constitutes another act of self-fashioning and subversion by *Blackwood's*, in that it shows the magazine consciously distancing itself from what it implies to be disreputable form of literary activity. There is also a tacit recognition of the radicalism of the *Examiner* on the part of Lockhart here, as the primary aim of Lockhart's review is to associate Hunt with supposedly 'dangerous' politics, and to suggest that this in turn resulted in his production of 'bad' poetry.

In his attacks upon Hunt, Lockhart was reacting strongly to the supposed dissemination of the morally and politically corrosive ideas of his coterie through print. The connection was an indirect one, but it was firmly implanted by Lockhart in the minds of *Blackwood's* readers; the association made in this review is that 'radical' politics were the consequence of a fundamental immorality which was subsequently reflected in his poetry. Lockhart, by dismissing Hunt's abilities as a poet, as well as his supposed lack of moral principles, was in fact covertly attacking Hunt's politics. Hunt, in particular, was a 'marked' man for Lockhart because he was so publicly associated with the radical press. At the same time, Lockhart reassures his readers that 'bad' poetry of the sort produced by Hunt was incapable of expressing potentially dangerous radical sentiments. However, the sense remains that Lockhart believed that Hunt's radical journalism posed such a threat that it had to be repeatedly associated with the immorality and incoherence supposedly to be found in Hunt's poetry. This accounts for the severity of the attacks upon Hunt, and later Hazlitt, in the pages of *Blackwood's*, as well as the personal nature of those attacks.

The absence of overt political discussion continues in the second article in the series, 'On the Cockney School of Poetry No. II'.[18] Here Lockhart appears to moderate his tone in order to critique Hunt's *Rimini* in great depth, employing detailed comparisons with Byron's representation of incest in 'Parisina' and with classical representations of incest, such as that by Sophocles in *Oedipus Rex*. Predictably, Hunt is accused by Lockhart of having divested the subject of incest of its moral gravity. Through its failure to conform to his lofty moral standards, Lockhart classifies the poem as one which threatens to corrupt those unable to identify Hunt's poetic deficiencies. The conclusion of the article is therefore a moral and social one, and avoids any direct mention of politics:

> The story of *Rimini* can indeed do no harm to any noble spirit. We never saw a lady lift it up, who did not immediately throw it down again in disgust. But the lofty spirits of the earth are not the only ones; and we confess, that we think that poet deserving of chastisement, who prostitutes his talents in a manner that is likely to corrupt milliners and apprentice boys.[19]

There is clearly a political motivation behind Lockhart's criticism of *Rimini*, but this is subordinated by him when he chooses to focus upon the moral and stylistic defects of the poem, which impede any potential seditious messages and render it politically harmless. As Michael Eberle-Sinatra has argued, Lockhart attempted to exert control over the readership of the poem by 'attacking Hunt through calumny of character and ridicule of the language of the poem'.[20] Following the second 'Cockney School' article, Lockhart continued baiting Hunt. There was a response to Hunt's complaints about his treatment by *Blackwood's* in the *Examiner*. In 'Letter to Leigh Hunt, King of the Cockneys' from the May

1818 issue of *Blackwood's*, Lockhart reasserted his charges of immorality, literary pretentiousness, ungodliness and seditious impulses against Hunt's entire coterie. As was already the case as far as Hunt's journalism was concerned, Lockhart's dislike of Hunt's poetry had by this point become inseparable from his dislike of his politics, and it seems to be the case that often Lockhart could not distinguish between the two. In his article 'On the Cockney School of Poetry No. III', Lockhart wrote that as far as Hunt was concerned 'there can be no radical distinction between the private and public character of a poet. If a poet sympathises with and justifies wickedness in his poetry, he is a wicked man.'[21] The judgement made by Lockhart upon Hunt's supposed immorality can be found in Lockhart's references to Hunt's journalism as well as in his appraisals of Hunt's poetry. The intention of Lockhart's review is clearly to connect the two, and to discredit both without actually entering into a direct discussion of political principles. Thanks to Hunt's involvement with the *Examiner*, the attacks made by Lockhart on his poetry are evidently more politically motivated than those made upon Keats, whose poetry was primarily associated by Lockhart with the perceived immorality which had also tainted Hunt.

Lockhart's review of Shelley's *The Revolt of Islam* provides a useful point of comparison here, in that it highlights the extent to which Hunt was a particularly marked man for Lockhart. In his analysis of Shelley's poetry, Lockhart appears to overcome his disapproval of Shelley's radical views, which he clearly identified as 'pernicious' and 'those of the Cockney School'. Although it is undoubtedly the case that Lockhart did not entirely separate Shelley's politics from his poetry, as David Higgins has suggested,[22] he was nonetheless prepared to overlook the former in favour of the latter. Lockhart praised Shelley as 'strong, nervous, original; well entitled to take his place near to the great creative masters of the age'. This constitutes an uncharacteristically charitable judgement on Lockhart's part, for, as Paul Foot has observed, the inherently radical notion of 'divine equality' is clearly emphasized in the poem through Cythna's speech following the revolt of Islam.[23] Lockhart's judgement seems all the more remarkable since Shelley eventually echoed similar sentiments in his 1820 political pamphlet, 'A Philosophical View of Reform'. Although it remained unpublished, the political content of Shelley's pamphlet underscores the close relationship between radical print culture and poetry, and suggests that in his praise for Shelley's poetry, Lockhart was deploying a different set of critical criteria. Certain aspects relating to the poem's structure were criticized by him, but it is important to note that Lockhart picked out Shelley's portrayal of the relationship between Laon and Cythna for particular praise.[24] It is therefore clear that Shelley, in stark contrast to Hunt and Keats, had managed to impress Lockhart with his poetical abilities. Furthermore, a comparison with Lockhart's appraisal of Hunt reveals a much deeper personal and political antipathy towards the so-called 'King of the Cockneys', which constituted an attack upon radical print culture as well as on radical poetry. Hunt's treatment within the pages of *Blackwood's* appears all the more striking given Lockhart's explicit aversion to overt political discussion in his articles, as is articulated in a letter to William Blackwood from 1824:

> I have always wished and avowed our wish too, that this Magazine should be ... free of political discussion. We wd. admit Bingham or Cobbett at pleasure to write half a sheet every month for us, assuming, however, of course, our own right to conquer & destroy their effusions in our own way.[25]

The significance of all of this is considerable. Lockhart's attack upon Hunt forms part of one of the great acts of self-definition on the part of a literary magazine in the early nineteenth century. It is also one of the great theatrical moves played out in this period, since it revolved around a pseudonymous attempt by Lockhart to define the public identity of Leigh Hunt, suggesting that by the 1820s a conservative periodical had not only found a highly effective and unique voice of its own, but that it was also able to assimilate the tone of its political adversaries, as well as manipulating their public image when required. The manner in which *Blackwood's* (under Lockhart's direction) achieved this is also significant, in that it did so by peppering its reviews of Hunt's work with highly personal and implicitly political attacks in a way which, as Parker has suggested, was unusual for literary magazines during the 1820s. The *Blackwood's* attacks on Hunt ultimately formed part of a calculated attempt by *Blackwood's* to formulate a coherent, Edinburgh-based conservative identity which self-consciously attempted to define itself against the supposedly decadent, morally corrupt and poetically deficient effusions of London-based radicals. Leigh Hunt therefore emerged as the ultimate embodiment of *Blackwood's* political adversaries, and the magazine went out of its way to pay particular attention to him. As a result, Hunt found himself an unwilling participant in an elaborate and highly public game of personal invective, poetry and politics.

NOTES

Brown, 'Introduction'

1. *Report of the Trial of the King versus Hurdy Gurdy* (Dublin: [n.p.], 1794), p. 35.
2. Ibid., p. 15.
3. Ibid., p. 20.
4. Ibid., pp 15–16.
5. Ibid., pp 16–17.
6. J. Larkin (ed.), *The Trial of William Drennan* (Dublin, Irish Academic Press, 1990); *A Full Report of all the Proceedings on the Trial of the Rev. William Jackson, at the bar of His Majesty's Court of King's Bench, Ireland, on an Indictment for High Treason* (Dublin: J. Exshaw, 1795).
7. *A Full and Accurate Report of the Trial of James Bird, Roger Hamill and Casimir Dela-Hoyde, merchants; Patrick Kenny, Bartholomew Walsh, Matthew Read and Patrick Tiernan, before the Honourable Mr Justice Downes* (Dublin: H. Fitzpatrick, 1794), title page.
8. On the Defenders see J. Smyth, *The Men of no Property: Irish Radicals and Popular Politics in the Late Eighteenth Century* (Houndsmills: Palgrave, 1998) and L. M. Cullen, 'The Political Structures of the Defenders', in H. Gough and D. Dickson (eds), *Ireland and the French Revolution* (Dublin: Irish Academic Press, 1990), pp. 117–38; on the social critique see in particular J. Quinn, 'The United Irishmen and Social Reform', *Irish Historical Studies*, 31 (1998), pp. 188–201.
9. J. Fay, *The Trial of John Fay Esq of Navan in the County of Meath* (Dublin: Brett Smith, 1794).
10. For a British analysis of this fear, see D. Herzog, *Poisoning the Minds of the Lower Orders* (Princeton, NJ: Princeton University Press, 1998).
11. *Report of the Trial of the King versus Hurdy Gurdy*, p. 23.
12. Ibid., p. 25.
13. A. De Tocqueville, *The Old Régime and the French Revolution* (Garden City, NY: Doubleday, 1955).
14. For instance see R. Darnton, *The Forbidden Best-Sellers of Pre-Revolutionary France* (London: HarperCollins, 1996), pp. 169–246.
15. C. A. Bayley, *Empire and Information: Intelligence Gathering and Social Communication in India, 1780–1870* (Cambridge: Cambridge University Press, 1990).
16. R. Chartier, 'The Two Frances: The History of a Geographical Idea', in R. Chartier, *Cultural History: Between Practices and Representations* tr. L. G. Cochrane (Cambridge:

Polity Press, 1993), pp. 172–200; B. Bradshaw and J. Morrill (eds), *The British Problem: State Formation in the Atlantic Archipelago* (Houndsmills: Macmillan, 1996). See also J. G. A. Pocock, *The Discovery of Islands: Essays in British History* (Cambridge: Cambridge University Press, 2005).
17. L. Colley, *Britons: Forging the Nation, 1707–1837* (London: Pimlico, 1994).
18. K. Wilson, *The Sense of the People: Politics, Culture and Imperialism in England, 1715–1785* (Cambridge: Cambridge University Press, 1995).
19. M. Löffler, *Welsh Responses to the French Revolution: Press and Public Discourse 1789–1802* (Cardiff: University of Wales Press, 2012).
20. E. P. Thompson influentially viewed Methodism as a spiritual bulwark against radical reform in the here and now. See E. P. Thompson, *The Making of the English Working Class* (1963; London: Penguin, 1991), pp. 385–441.
21. M. Brown, 'Was there an Irish Enlightenment: The Case of the Anglicans', in R. Butterwick, S. Davies and G. Sánchez Espinosa (eds), *Peripheries of the Enlightenment*, SVEC (Oxford: Oxford University Press, 2008), pp. 49–64; M. Brown, 'The Biter Bitten: Ireland and the Rude Enlightenment', *Eighteenth–Century Studies*, 45:3 (2012), pp. 393–407; M. Brown, 'Configuring the Irish Enlightenment: Reading the *Transactions of the Royal Irish Academy*', in J. Kelly and M. J. Powell, *Clubs and Societies in Eighteenth-Century Ireland* (Dublin: Four Courts Press, 2010), pp. 163–178. For a survey of the literature on 1798 see T. Bartlett, D. Dickson, D. Keogh and K. Whelan (eds), *1798: A Bicentenary Perspective* (Dublin: Four Courts Press, 2003).
22. The link with France has been given its proper due in M. Elliot, *Partners in Revolution: The United Irishmen and France* (New Haven, CT: Yale University Press, 1982).
23. B. Harris, *The Scottish People and the French Revolution* (London: Pickering & Chatto, 2008); B. Harris (ed.), *Scotland in the Age of the French Revolution* (Edinburgh: John Donald, 2005). See also E. W. McFarland, *Ireland and Scotland in the Age of Revolution: Planting the Green Bough* (Edinburgh: Edinburgh University Press, 1994).
24. R. Porter, *Enlightenment: Britain and the Creation of the Modern World* (London: Penguin, 2000).
25. J. Barrell, *Figurative Treason, Fantasies of Regicide, 1793–1796* (Oxford: Oxford University Press, 2000).
26. See D. Gahan, 'Class, Religion and Rebellion: Wexford in 1798', in J. Smyth (ed.), *Revolution, Counter-Revolution and Union: Ireland in the 1790s* (Cambridge: Cambridge University Press), pp. 83–98.
27. D. Dickson, 'Smoke without Fire? Munster and the 1798 Rebellion', in Bartlett, Dickson, Keogh and Whelan (eds), *1798: A Bicentenary Perspective*, pp. 147–73.
28. J. Ellul, 'Politicisation and Political Solutions', in K. S. Templeton Jr (ed.), *The Politicization of Society* (Indianapolis, IN: Liberty Fund, 1979), pp. 209–47, on p. 216.
29. Ibid., pp. 231–2.
30. Ibid., pp. 220–1.
31. See J. C. D. Clark, *English Society, 1660–1832: Religion, Ideology and Politics during the Ancien Regime* (Cambridge: Cambridge University Press, 2000), pp. 527–47.
32. G. O'Brien, 'The Unimportance of Public Opinion in Eighteenth-Century Britain and Ireland', *Eighteenth-Century Ireland*, 8 (1993), pp. 115–27, on p. 115.
33. Ibid., p. 126.
34. See P. Higgins, *A Nation of Politicians: Gender, Patriotism and Political Culture in Late Eighteenth-Century Ireland* (Madison, WI: University of Wisconsin Press, 2010), pp.

70–81. See also P. Fagan, 'The Dublin Catholic Mob, 1700–1750', *Eighteenth-Century Ireland*, 4 (1989), pp. 133–42.
35. On instructions in this period see V. Morley, *Irish Opinion and the American Revolution* (Cambridge; Cambridge University Press, 2002), pp. 216–17, 224 and 241. See ibid., p. 245 for a case in which 'a prominent independent MP Denis Daly objected to the instructions he had received from his county Galway constituents on the grounds that many of the freeholders who had signed them were Catholics'. This was the same man who organized an earlier set of instructions as he 'was anxious to appear to be acting under pressure from his constituents'. Ibid., p. 224. That yielding to such pressure might be an acceptable excuse for taking a particular tack on a contentious issue does suggest that public opinion was given some credit, however.
36. T. C. Barnard, 'Considering the Inconsiderable: Electors, Patrons and Irish Elections, 1656–1761', in D. W. Hayton (ed.), *The Irish Parliament in the Eighteenth Century: The Long Apprenticeship* (Edinburgh: Edinburgh University Press, 2001), pp. 107–26. For a particular instance of a contested election, see for example, E. Magennis, 'Patriotism, Popery and Politics: The Armagh By-Election of 1753', in A. J. Hughes and W. Nolan (eds), *Armagh, History and Society: Interdisciplinary Essays on the History of an Irish County* (Dublin: Geography Publications, 2001), pp. 485–504.
37. For O'Brien's assessment see O'Brien, 'The Unimportance of Public Opinion', p. 120.
38. Quoted in Morley, *Irish Opinion and the American Revolution*, p. 78.
39. T. Barnard, *The Kingdom of Ireland, 1641–1760* (Houndsmills: Palgrave Macmillan, 2004), p. 104.
40. Details are drawn from N. Garnham, 'Local Elite Creation in Early Hanoverian Ireland: The Case of the County Grand Jury', *Historical Journal*, 42:3 (September 1999), pp. 623–42, on pp. 625–7.
41. Ibid., p. 628.
42. N. Garnham, *The Militia in Eighteenth-Century Ireland: In Defence of the Protestant Interest* (Woodbridge: Boydell, 2012).
43. Morley, *Irish Opinion and the American Revolution*, pp. 61–2.
44. Ibid., p. 14.
45. Barnard, *The Kingdom of Ireland*, pp. 56–7.
46. Ibid., p. 183.
47. C. I. McGrath and C. Fauske (eds), *Money, Power, and Print: Interdisciplinary Studies of the Financial Revolution in the British Isles* (Newark, DE: University of Delaware Press, 2008).
48. E. Magennis, 'Coal, Corn and Canals: Parliament and the Dispersal of Public Moneys 1695–1772', in Hayton (ed.), *The Irish Parliament in the Eighteenth Century*, pp. 71–86, on pp. 76, 83.
49. For these developments see C. I. McGrath, 'Central Aspects of the Eighteenth-Century Constitutional Framework in Ireland', *Eighteenth-Century Ireland*, 16 (2001), pp. 9–34.
50. Barnard, *The Kingdom of Ireland*, p. 49.
51. Ibid., p. 74.
52. Magennis, 'Coal, Corn and Canals', p. 86.
53. N. Garnham, 'Criminal Legislation in the Irish Parliament, 1692–1760', in Hayton (ed.), *The Irish Parliament in the Eighteenth Century*, pp. 55–70, on p. 63.
54. For a full list see ibid., p. 66.
55. Statistics are taken from J. Kelly, *Poynings' Law and the Making of Law in Ireland, 1660–1800* (Dublin: Four Courts Press, 2007), p. 159.

56. On this process more generally see G. Sartori, 'Liberty and Law', in Templeton (ed.), *The Politicization of Society*, pp. 249–311.
57. D. M. Dozer, 'History as Force', in Templeton (ed.), *The Politicization of Society*, pp. 341–72, on pp. 343.
58. Ibid., pp. 351, 352.
59. Ibid., p. 352.
60. Earlier fears centred less on an indigenous uprising than on a Jacobite invasion backed by French forces.
61. Helpful in the formulating of this paragraph was S. J. Connolly, 'Precedent and Principle: The Patriots and their Critics', in S. J. Connolly (ed.), *Political Ideas in Eighteenth-Century Ireland* (Dublin: Four Courts Press, 2000), pp. 130–58.
62. J. D. Lukacs, 'The Monstrosity of Government', in Templeton (ed.), *The Politicization of Society*, pp. 391–408, on p. 404.
63. Ibid., p. 400.
64. Ibid., p. 400.
65. Ibid., p. 393.
66. Intriguingly, Lukacs himself disagrees, seeing the future as shaped by an anarchic criminality reminiscent of Burke's nightmares concerning the levelling lawlessness of the Revolution. See ibid., pp. 406–7.
67. Clark, *English Society*, pp. 8, 9. His trenchant assault on careless vocabulary also includes the term 'Enlightenment'. See ibid., p. 9.
68. Ibid., p. 8.
69. Darnton, *The Forbidden Bestsellers of Pre-Revolutionary France*, p. 198.
70. B. D. Shaffer, 'Violence as a Product of Imposed Order', in Templeton (ed.), *The Politicization of Society*, pp. 447–99, on p. 450.
71. Ibid., p. 450.
72. See N. Garnham, 'How Violent was Eighteenth-Century Ireland?', *Irish Historical Studies*, 30 (1997), pp. 377–92.
73. Shaffer, 'Violence as a Product of Imposed Order', pp. 490–1.
74. Ibid., p. 489.
75. On this division see F. A. Hayek, 'Kinds of Order in Society', in Templeton (ed.), *The Politicization of Society*, pp. 501–23.
76. For a version of this thesis applied to the French Revolution see R. Chartier, 'Time to Understand: The Frustrated Intellectuals', in *Cultural History*, pp. 127–50.
77. Harris, *The Scottish People and the French Revolution*, pp. 24, 25.
78. *Report of the Trial of the King versus Hurdy Gurdy*, pp. 7–8.
79. F. M. Jones, this volume, pp. 46–7.
80. Jones, this volume, p. 37.
81. M. J. Powell, this volume, p. 53.
82. Powell, this volume, p. 62.
83. Powell, this volume, p. 61.
84. B. Harris, this volume, p. 77.
85. Recent recoveries include L. MacIlvanney, *Burns the Radical: Poetry and Politics in Late Eighteenth-Century Scotland* (East Linton: Tuckwell Press, 2002); A. Noble and P. Scott Hogg (eds), *The Canongate Burns* (Edinburgh: Canongate, 2003), introduction.
86. C. A. Whatley, this volume, p. 94.
87. E. Wyn James, this volume, p. 107.
88. Ibid, p. 112.

89. M. Philp, 'The Fragmented Ideology of Reform', in M. Philp (ed.), *The French Revolution and British Popular Politics* (Cambridge, Cambridge University Press, 1991), pp. 50–78.
90. M. Löffler, this volume, p. 128.
91. N. Ó Ciosáin, this volume, p. 136.
92. M. Cronin, this volume, p. 157.
93. Ibid.
94. *Report of the Trial of the King versus Hurdy Gurdy*, p. 45.
95. Ibid., p. 47.

1 Jones, '"England's Men Went Head to Head with their Own Brethren": The Welsh Ballad-Singers and the War of American Independence'

1. This chapter is based on a Welsh essay, entitled '"Gwŷr Lloeger aeth benben â'u brodyr eu hunen": Y Baledwyr Cymraeg a Rhyfel Annibyniaeth America', published in *Y Traethodydd*, 166:699 (2011), pp. 197–225. I am grateful to the editor, Dr Brynley F. Roberts, for permission to reproduce large parts of that essay in English, and to the editors and publishers of this present volume for their willingness to publish this translation.
2. Two versions of the poem have been preserved, one in National Library of Wales (hereafter NLW) MS 173E, pp. 79–80, and the other in NLW, Cwrtmawr MS 35B, pp. 118–21. The Cwrtmawr copy introduces the poem in a compressed form which could be considered as more final. On the other hand, it should be noted that the version in NLW 173E came into the possession of Edward Jones (Bardd y Brenin), a fact which might suggest that Dafydd Samwell considered it complete at one time at least.
3. See R. Middlekauff, *The Glorious Cause: The American Revolution, 1763–1789* (rev. edn, Oxford: Oxford University Press, 2007), p. 558.
4. A petition to the king from the Lord Mayor, aldermen and liverymen of the City of London (5 July 1775). Quoted by T. Bickham, *Making Headlines: The American Revolution as Seen through the British Press* (DeKalb, IL: Northern Illinois University Press, 2009), p. 84.
5. 'cynnal y Gyfraeth'.
6. 'ymysg y rhai gwirion, / yn codi ymryson, yn hyfion ddi hêdd'; 'ffoledd y Werin / Yn llês i rai cymm'in' eu Camwedd'.
7. 'araithu'; 'Ymhob rhyw Ddiodtu'; 'yn ymlyd am chwedlau / Celwyddog Bapurau ar forau fawr waith'. These are the only quotations taken from the version in NLW 173E, pp. 79–80. All other quotations are from Cwrtmawr 35B, pp. 118–21. For a portrayal of London life, showing the popularity of debating clubs and public debates during the year 1780, see D. T. Andrew, 'Popular Culture and Public Debate: London 1780', *Historical Journal*, 39:2 (1996), pp. 405–23.
8. 'Politics in Wales begin with the American Revolution', claimed Gwyn Alf Williams, noting that 'Even the John Bull balladmongers were disturbed by what they saw as a civil war'. In this, Williams was following the lead given by Jenkins, who had argued during the 1930s 'that there is hardly any sign of political thought' ('[nad] oes nemor arwydd o *feddwl* politicaidd') in the Welsh mindset nor in the work of the ballad-singers before the American War of Independence. R. T. Jenkins, *Hanes Cymru yn y Bedwaredd Ganrif ar Bymtheg: Y Gyfrol Gyntaf (1789–1843)* (Caerdydd [Cardiff]: Gwasg Prifysgol Cymru, 1933), p. 5; G. A. Williams, *When Was Wales? A History of the Welsh* (London: Penguin, 1991; 1st edn, 1985), p. 167.

9. S. Conway, *The British Isles and the War of American Independence* (Oxford: Oxford University Press, 2000), p. 135.
10. E. Roberts, 'Cerdd o Gwynfan a galar yr holl Dobaccwyr ar Trwynau Snisin yr hwn a godwyd yn ei bris o achos y Gwrthryfel yr Americaniaid a Lloegr' (A song giving the complaint and lament of all the tobacconists and snuff-noses, following a rise in prices because of the conflict between the Americans and England) (Trefriw, 1776) (JHD 296ii).
11. H. Jones, 'Cerdd newydd; neu Gwŷnfan Teyrnas Loeger ar Drigolion America, am eu bod yn gwrthryfela i'w herbyn; ar Ddyll Anfoniad Mam at ei Phlant' (A new song: or the complaint of the kingdom of England to the inhabitants of America, since they rebel against them; in the form of the letter of a Mother to her children) (n.p., n.d.) (JHD 683i); and H. Jones, 'Cerdd o Attebiad y Plant i'w Mam; neu Anfoniad Americans i Loeger' (A song giving the children's response to their mother; or the letter of the Americans to England) (n.p., n.d.) (JHD 683ii); E. Roberts, 'Yn adrodd hanes y Gwrthryfel sydd rhwng Lloegr Hen a Lloegr Newydd, sef America' (Recounting the story of the conflict between Old England and New England, namely America) (Trefriw, 1777) (JHD 300ii).
12. W. Smith, *Pregeth ar helynt bresennol America* (Brysto: W. Pine, 1775).
13. T. R. Adams, *American Independence: The Growth of an Idea. A Bibliographical Study of the American Political Pamphlets Printed Between 1764 and 1776 Dealing with the Dispute Between Great Britain and Her Colonies* (Providence, RI: Brown University Press 1965), pp. 144–7.
14. For Smith, see further J. B. Bell, *A War of Religion: Dissenters, Anglicans and the American Revolution* (Basingstoke: Palgrave Macmillan, 2008), pp. 180–3; and *ODNB*.
15. 'fel y byddai yn arwydd trag'wyddol eu bod o'r un genedl, ac a hawl i'r un breintiau gwledig a chrefyddol a'u brodyr o'r llwythau eraill'. Smith, *Pregeth ar helynt bresennol America*, p. 7.
16. 'y waedd yn eu herbyn yn ddiattreg. Ni phetrusodd *Penboethiaid* y dydd hwnnw eu cyhoeddi'n *wrthryfelwyr* yn erbyn y Duw byw ... [a] Gan hynny holl gyn'lleidfa'r brawdlwythau, y rhai yr oedd eu harosfa yng Nghanaan a ymga[s]glasant ynghyd i ryfel yn erbyn eu cig a'u gwaed eu hunain'. Ibid.
17. '(ac o fy Nuw na chafai'r 'siampl ei dilyn ymysg brawdlwythau ein Hisrael ni yn y famwlad)'. Ibid.
18. 'Gilead Americanaidd'; 'gorchwyl ... o dduwioldeb a chariad'; 'ei gamddeall'; 'brytanaidd Isr[a]el'. Ibid., pp. 7, 10.
19. 'Yn ddibris o anghyfleusdra'n lle'; 'heb ein gwasgi gan ofn'. Ibid., p. 10.
20. Ibid., p. 11.
21. 'allorau'; '[eu] hundeb a'[u] cariad'. Ibid., p. 12.
22. 'hyd yn oed ein gwrthodiad [i dalu trethi] yn brawf digonol o'n parch i'r allor ei hun'. Ibid., pp. 12, 13.
23. 'brodyr'. Ibid., p. 14.
24. 'aduno ... aelodau'; 'fel unig ddiogelwch rhydd-did a phrotestaniaeth'; 'y teyrnasoedd hynny ag sydd elynion rhydd-did, gwirionedd a thosturi'. Ibid., p. 15.
25. 'wlad ëang hon, mewn oesoedd i ddyfod, [wedi] ei llanw a'i haddurno a phobl rinweddol a doeth; yn mwynhau RHYDD-DID ai holl berthynol fendithion'; 'ei gorchuddio a rhywogaeth o ddynion gwaelach na gwylltiaid yr anialwch, am eu bod hwy unwaith "yn gwybod y pethau a berthynent i'w happusrwydd a'u heddwch, ond wedi goddef iddynt gael eu cuddio oddi wrth eu llygaid"'. Ibid., p. 18.
26. T. Paine, 'American Crisis I', in T. Paine, *Rights of Man, Common Sense and Other Political Writings*, ed. M. Philp (1995; Oxford: Oxford University Press, 2008), p. 67.

27. 'fod grym pob gwladwriaeth, dan Dduw, yn gynnwysedig yn eu HUNDEB'; 'gwendidau, ac hyd yn oed ... gwahanol feddyliau'. Smith, *Pregeth ar helynt bresennol America*, pp. 18, 21.
28. Anon., *Dechreuad, cynnydd, a chyflwr presennol, y dadl rhwng pobl America a'r llywodraeth. Wedi ei gyfiaethu o'r Saesnaeg er budd i'r Cymru* (Trefriw: D. Jones, 1776).
29. 'llawer o son am y rhyfel, ac sydd rhwng y Wlad yma, ac America; a llawer heb wybod yn iawn yr achos o hono'. Ibid., p. 2.
30. 'byddai'r hanes yn fuddiol i'r Cymru, yn eu Hiaith eu hunain'; 'fod y Cymraeg a osodais yntho, yn ddealladwy i bawb'. Ibid.
31. 'Nid oedd mor digon o Lythrennau, / I wneud hwn heb ynddo Feiau'. Ibid., p. 16.
32. 'uwchlaw pob cynnulliadau pleidiol'. Smith, *Pregeth ar helynt bresennol America*, p. 10.
33. J. Shipley, *A Sermon Preached Before the Incorporated Society for the Propagation of the Gospel in Foreign Parts* (London, 1773), in P. H. Smith (ed.), *English Defenders of American Freedoms 1774–1778: Six Pamphlets Attacking British Policy* (Washington: Library of Congress, 1972), pp. 17–27.
34. J. Shipley, *A Speech Intended to Have Been Spoken By the Bishop of St. Asaph, on the Bill for Altering the Charters of the Colony of Massachusetts Bay* (London, 1774), in Smith (ed.), *English Defenders of American Freedoms*, pp. 29–43.
35. Smith (ed.), *English Defenders of American Freedoms*, p. 11.
36. Ibid., p. 9 and *ODNB*.
37. T. R. Adams, *The American Controversy: A Bibliographical Study of the British Pamphlets About the American Disputes, 1764–1783*, 2 vols (Providence, RI and New York: Brown University Press, 1980), vol. 1, p. 326.
38. 'Gan ddarfod i'r dalenau canlynol, ddyfod im llaw, yn y dafodiaith Saesnaeg'. Anon., *Dechreuad, cynnydd, a chyflwr presennol, y dadl rhwng pobl America a'r llywodraeth*, p. 2.
39. Ibid., pp. 21–4.
40. On the wide range of English-language pamphlets published see the bibliographical studies by Adams (p. 174, n. 13 and p. 175, n. 37 above).
41. 'attebiad'. H. Jones, 'Cerdd newydd; neu Gwŷnfan Teyrnas Loeger ar Drigolion America, am eu bod yn gwrthryfela i'w herbyn; ar Ddyll Anfoniad Mam at ei Phlant' (JHD 683i); H. Jones, 'Cerdd o Attebiad y Plant i'w Mam; neu Anfoniad Americans i Loeger' (JHD 683 ii). These two poems were published in a single ballad pamphlet. The year 1777 has been noted at the foot of the second poem.
42. Anon., *Dechreuad, cynnydd, a chyflwr presenol, y dadl rhwng pobl America a'r llywodraeth*, p. 22.
43. See Middlekauff, *The Glorious Cause*, pp. 276, 278.
44. 'Os yn rhyfel y daw'.
45. 'Gall Crist roi inni esmwythder yr un fath â llong Peder'; 'mae llaw'r Hollalluog / Yn gre' ac yn drugarog, Eneiniog, i ni'.
46. 'dallu na'n cefnu mewn cur'.
47. 'ateb'.
48. 'gŵr ifanc sy'n byw yn America'; 'pwyntiau'.
49. 'Eich ŷd a'ch ymenyn, awch cyndyn, a'ch caws'; 'Siwgwr, dail dwndwr neu De; / Rum, Brandi, a Gwin'.
50. 'Rhoi treth ar bob Sîr o America dîr'.
51. 'gŵr ifanc'.
52. *ODNB*; E. S. Morgan, *Benjamin Franklin* (New Haven, CT: Yale University Press, 2002), pp. 74–5.

53. 'Ni ddaw mo ŷd Cymru yr wi'n tyngu i'r wlâd honn'.
54. 'Bydd lladdiad, hyll weiddi, all ofni pob llu, / Pob Cymru, pob teulu pob tâd'.
55. 'Nid un blaid ... a ddarfu bechu yn erbyn Iesu'; 'Y ddwyblaid a ddarfu ddiblo a gwyro er llwydo eu llun'. H. Jones, 'Cerdd newydd ym mherthynas y Rhyfel presennol yn America; yn gosod allan mae Oferedd yw Daroganau a Brudiau, ac yn dangos mae Ordinhad Duw yw'r cwbl' (A new song in relation to the present war in America, positing that prognostications and prophecies are frivolous, and that all is God's ordinance) (Wrecsam, n.d.) (JHD 281i).
56. 'Opiniwne a ffalster'; 'gwargledwch diystyried'.
57. 'sywedydd hoff'.
58. 'yn ddychrynadwy i amryw wledydd yn America, swn mawr am Ryfeloedd a Marwolaeth ar wyr enwog yn y parthau hynny or byd hwn; oblegid fod y Diffyg yn eu Deheulain hwynt'. J. Prys, *Dehonglydd y Sêr* (Amwythig [Shrewsbury], 1777), p. 17.
59. 'Cof-restr'; 'Pan ddech. rhyfel rhwng *Lloegr* ac *America*'. W. Williams, 'Rhai Gwersi a gyfansoddwyd er mwyn i bob Enw o Grist'nogion i daer weddio am Heddwch rhwng Lloegr ac America', M. William, *Britanus Merlinus Liberatus: Sef, Amgylchiadau Tymhorol ac Wybrennol: Neu, Almanac am y Flwyddyn o Oed ein Iachawdwr, 1777* (Caerfyrddin [Carmarthen], 1777).
60. '[t]aer weddio am Heddwch rhwng LLOEGR ac AMERICA', in ibid., p. 37.
61. 'Hen Ffraingc a Spain [yn] disgwyl cael rhyw ysglyfaeth draw'.
62. 'Gan fod pob gradd o ddynion a'u llygaid ar rhyfel annaturiol presennol [yno]'. M. William, *Britanus Merlinus Liberatus: Sef, Amgylchiadau Tymhorol ac Wybrennol: Neu, Almanac am y Flwyddyn o Oed ein Iachawdwr, 1778* (Caerfyrddin [Carmarthen], 1778), p. 41. For the interest of newspaper readers in the geography of the American colonies, see Bickham, *Making Headlines*, p. 54.
63. '[t]raul at y rhyfel presennol 1777'; 'a gynhyllir oddiar Drigolion y deyrnas trwy Dreth, Toll, Stampiau, &c'. William, *Britanus Merlinus Liberatus: Sef, Amgylchiadau Tymhorol ac Wybrennol: Neu, Almanac am y Flwyddyn o Oed ein Iachawdwr, 1778*, p. 12.
64. J. Prys, *Dehonglydd y Sêr, Neu Almanac Newydd* (Amwythig [Shrewsbury]: Stafford Pryse, 1779).
65. '[P]edwar Chwarter y Flwyddyn'. Ibid., p. 7.
66. 'Un o scrifenyddion seryddiaeth Lloegr'. Ibid.
67. 'A Lloegr gref yn llygru'i grym'. See C. L. Griffith, 'Am y Rhyfel' (About the war), in 'Wiliam Phylip, ei Fywyd a'i Waith' (PhD dissertation, University of Wales, 1999), p. 578. The proverb is found in various forms in Casgliad Bleddyn (William Jones) in NLW 8397B, and W. Hay, *Diarhebion Cymru* (Lerpwl [Liverpool]: Gwasg y Brython, 1955)), p. 152. I am grateful to Dr Ann Parry-Owen for these references.
68. H. Jones, 'Cerdd newydd ym mherthynas y Rhyfel presennol yn America; yn gosod allan mae Oferedd yw Daroganau a Brudiau, ac yn dangos mae Ordinhad Duw yw'r cwbl' (JHD 281i).
69. 'sydd wedi ordeinio lladd a mwrdro'; 'peri ein puro er llunio i ni wellhad'.
70. H. Hughes, 'Carol Plygain' (Matin carol), in NLW 18B, pp. 530–3.
71. 'Ddychwel[yd] o'[u] rhyfyg sy'n rhy fawr'.
72. F. M. Jones, *'The Bard is a Very Singular Character': Iolo Morganwg, Marginalia and Print Culture* (Cardiff: University of Wales Press, 2010), pp. 99–102.
73. Bickham, *Making Headlines*, pp. 120–1. The Chester and Shrewsbury newspapers were accessible to the ballad-writers of north Wales, or at least able to influence public opinion in their part of the world. In fact, by the 1780s, there were scores of newspapers available

in Wales and the Midlands, and Hannah Barker, a historian of the period's newspapers, believes that these two regions were served by a 'concentration of papers ... probably as dense ... as anywhere else outside the capital'. Reporting national and international news was an important part of these papers' remit. H. Barker, *Newspapers, Politics and Public Opinion in Late Eighteenth-Century England* (Oxford: Clarendon Press, 1998), pp. 95–7, 115, 122. Note, however, that Barker challenges those historians who have argued that the relationship between the provincial papers and the London press was a purely parasitic one. For the 'Welsh' features of the *Chester Chronicle* during the 1790s, see M. Löffler, 'Cerddi Newydd gan John Jones, "Jac Glan-y-gors"', *Llên Cymru*, 33 (2010), pp. 143–50.

74. For a comprehensive collection of contemporary newspaper reports relating to Jones's landing at Whitehaven, among other exploits, see D. C. Seitz, *Paul Jones: His Exploits in English Seas During 1778–1780. Contemporary Accounts Collected from English Newspapers with a Complete Bibliography* (New York: E. P. Dutton and Company, 1917). One report, from the *General Advertiser and Morning Intelligencer*, 7 September 1780, suggests that Jones had Welsh blood. There may, therefore, be some basis to the similar claim by Ellis Roberts in the ballad discussed here, 'O rybydd ir Cymru fod un pol Jones am Landio i gyffinie ein Gwlad, hefo 8 o Longe am ladd i gyd Frodur o achos rhyfel America: Yr hwn sydd i hun o enedigaeth o wlad fon medd rhai' (Of warning to the Welsh that a certain Paul Jones is about to land on the boundaries of our country, with eight ships, intent on killing his brothers because of the American war; he was himself born in Anglesey, some say) (Trefriw, 1778) (JHD 309ii).

75. See Seitz, *Paul Jones*, passim, and Bickham, *Making Headlines*, p. 129.

76. 'o achos rhyfel America'.

77. Compare E. Wynne, *Gweledigaetheu y Bardd Cwsc*, ed. A. Lewis (Caerdydd [Cardiff]: Gwasg Prifysgol Cymru, 1976), p. 10; H. Morys, 'Ar y rhyfel yn Fflandars' (Regarding the war in Flanders), in H. Morys, *Eos Ceiriog, Sef Casgliad o Bêr Ganiadau Huw Morus*, ed. W. Davies, 2 vols (Gwrecsam: I. Painter, 1823), vol. 1, pp. 233–6.

78. 'Brenin Annwn'.

79. 'Tân gwyllt a Phowder gloewddu / I losgi Cymru benddu'n boeth'.

80. See Seitz, *Paul Jones*, p. 43, which quotes a report from the *London Evening Post*, 21 September 1779.

81. See, for example, Seitz, *Paul Jones*, p. 5, which quotes a report in the *Morning Post and Daily Advertiser*, 28 April 1778, regarding Jones's attack on Whitehaven, noting: 'It appears that this infernal plan ... was laid at Brest, where for a considerable sum of money, *Paul* or *Jones*, (the latter is only an addition to his name) engaged to burn the shipping and town of Whitehaven; for which purpose he was convoyed through the channel by a French frigate of 38 guns'.

82. See Seitz, *Paul Jones*, p. 107 (*London Evening Post*, 19 October 1779); p. 117 (*London Evening Post*, 28 October 1779).

83. Seitz, *Paul Jones*, p. 118 (*Morning Post and Daily Advertiser*, 29 October 1779); p. 158 (*General Advertiser and Morning Intelligencer*, 7 September 1780). Seitz's bibliography shows that Jones was transformed from being a threatening, evil figure to being a romantic hero who made appearances in melodramatic plays and romances. See, for example, ibid., pp. 216, 217.

84. 'geill Duw bendigied gadwr hen Frutaniad / Na ddel y bwriad hwn i ben'.

85. On the comparison between recruitment for the American War and the later conflicts of the 1790s and 1800s against Revolutionary and Napoleonic France, see Conway, *The*

British Isles and the War of American Independence, pp. 19, 21, 23, 24, 29. For ballads responding to militarization in the latter period, see F. M. Jones, *Welsh Ballads of the French Revolution 1793–1815* (Cardiff: University of Wales Press, 2012).
86. 'oferddynion'. E. Roberts, 'O Rybydd i bawb ymbaratoi Sydd heb leico gweithio I ddiangc ymaith rhag eu preso' (Of warning to everyone who does not like to work to prepare themselves to escape lest they should be impressed) ([Caerfyrddin], n.d.) (JHD 610i).
87. E. Roberts, '[Cerdd] O Gyngor ir Merched rhag priodi'r un Dyn di ana yn y flwyddyn hon. Rhag iddo flino ar ei gwmpeini a myned i B[r]eifetirio neu'n filisia neu'r Maniwar neu ryw le anghyspell arall' ([A song] of advice to the girls against marrying any uninjured man this year, lest he should tire of his company and go off to privateer or to the militia or a man-of-war, or some other God-forsaken place) (Trefriw, 1778) (JHD 307ii). The ballad was reprinted by E. Evans, Brecon, in 1781.
88. Ellis Roberts, '[Cerdd] O hanes y blindere a fu yn Mon ac Arfon yn amser y bu Captain Trodn [yn] Pressio gyda'i Army drygionus' ([A song] about the troubles that took place in Anglesey and Caernarvonshire at the time that Captain Trodn came to impress with his evil army) (Trefriw, [1780]) (JHD 326ii).
89. 'Rhag cael ei lâdd yn farw', 'A thagu ei wddw'.
90. Conway, *The British Isles and the War of American Independence*, pp. 135–6.
91. NLW 12421D, no. 26, Thomas Pennant to [John Lloyd], 15 October 1775.
92. T. Pennant, *American Annals: or, Hints and queries for Parliament men, 1775–78* (Darlington, 1778), in NLW 12706E, pp. 101–8. This is a printed version of the text, glued into the manuscript.
93. T. Pennant, *Free Thoughts on the Militia Laws ... addressed to the Poor Inhabitants of North Wales* (London: Printed for B. White, 1781). This was reprinted as an appendix to *The Literary Life of the Late Thomas Pennant, Esq. By Himself* (London: B. and J. White, and R. Faulder, 1793), pp. 73–87. The work is introduced as an address to 'My Dear Countrymen', ibid., p. 73.
94. See NLW, Cwrtmawr MS 71E, pp. 21–34.
95. Ibid., p. 17.
96. Reports by R. P. Arden (dated 3 December 1781) and W. Walton (dated 6 December 1781) are found in ibid. pp. 29, 33–4.
97. Note, however, that there was some patriotic singing in praise of the militia – a new institution in many parts of Wales in this period, as noted above on p. 40. See for example the poem by E. Roberts, 'O Ffarwel ir Militia Cymru' (Of farewell to the militia of Wales) (Trefriw, 1783) (JHD 346i); and E. Roberts, 'O fawl i Falisia Sir Fon' (Of praise to the militia of Anglesey) (Bala, n.d.) (JHD 485i). These poems display some of the features most common to Welsh Napoleonic militia songs, including providing lists of corps county-by-county and referring to their aristocratic leaders.
98. See H. Jones, 'Cerdd newydd ym mherthynas y Rhyfel presennol yn America; yn gosod allan mae Oferedd yw Daroganau a Brudiau, ac yn dangos mae Ordinhad Duw yw'r cwbl' (JHD 281i), discussed above on pp. 36–7.
99. B. Porteus, *A Charge Delivered to the Clergy of the Diocese of Chester* (Chester: J. Poole, 1779), p. 26, quoted by Conway, *The British Isles and the War of American Independence*, pp. 116–17.
100. J. Toulmin, *The American War Lamented* (London: J. Johnson, 1776), pp. 12, 14, quoted by Conway, *The British Isles and the War of American Independence*, p. 116. The full text of this pamphlet, *The American War Lamented. A Sermon Preached at Taunton, February the 18th and 25th, 1776* (London, 1776), is found in H. T. Dickinson (ed.), *British Pam-*

phlets on the American Revolution, 1763–1785, 8 vols (London: Pickering & Chatto, 2007, 2008), vol. 4, pp. 327–52.
101. 'euogrwydd y wladwriaeth'; 'Golwg ar ein pechod, fel rhan o bechod y wladwriaeth, a'n dysg ni i lefain am fendith ar gerydd yr Arglwydd'. P. Williams, *Galwad Gan Wyr Eglwysig, Ar Bawb ffyddlon, i gyd-synio mewn Gweddi, yn enwedig Tra parhao'r Rhyfel presennol. Wedi ei gyfiethu (sic) i'r Gymraeg ... Er mwyn annog y Cymru i gyd uno mewn Gwaith mor fuddiol, a Dyledswydd mor angenrheidiol, yn amser trallod*, 2nd edn (Caerfyrddin [Carmarthen]: Ioan Ross, 1781). Two editions of the pamphlet were published by Ross in the same year. See G. M. Roberts, *Bywyd a Gwaith Peter Williams* (Caerdydd [Cardiff]: Gwasg Prifysgol Cymru dros Gyngor yr Eisteddfod Genedlaethol, 1943), p. 191.
102. 'dynion mewn llawer cwr o'r deyrnas ... mor ddieithr i fywyd a grym Crist'nogrwydd, ag yn Niffeithwch *Affrica*, neu gras-dir *Arabia*'. Williams, *Galwad Gan Wyr Eglwysig*, p. 13.
103. 'trywanu'n cyfeillion, dryllio'n plant, lladd y gwyr ieuaingc, a threisio'n gwragedd o flaen ein llygaid!'; 'Pabyddiaeth a chaethiwed'; 'ein crefydd a'n rhyddid'. Ibid., pp. 15–16.
104. H. Jones, *Gair yn ei amser, neu, Lythyr-annerch i'r cyffredin Gymry* (Mwythig: Argraphwyd gan T. Wood, 1782), pp. 9–16. On this pamphlet within the context of the life and career of Hugh Jones, see A. Price, '"Pulling aside the veil": Aspects of the Life and Work of Hugh Jones (1749–1825), Maesglasau', *Journal of the Merioneth Historical and Record Society*, 15:3 (2008), pp. 284–92, esp. p. 286.
105. Ibid., pp. 13–14.
106. 'Balchder'. H. Jones, 'Ymffrost balchder, o'i anrhydedd ai wrthiau: a'i ddrygioni, o ddechreuad y Byd i'r awr honn' (The boast of Pride about his honour, resistance and mischief, from the beginning of the world to this hour) (Trefriw, 1779) (JHD 314i). The character of Pride comes to the stage in the 1768 interlude, *Y Farddoneg Fabilonaidd*, by T. Edwards (Twm o'r Nant). See T. Edwards, *Gwaith Thomas Edwards (Twm o'r Nant)*, ed. I. Foulkes (Liverpool: I. Foulkes, 1874), pp. 158–61.
107. E. Roberts, 'Cerdd I Ddeisyf ar bawb yn Amser Rhyfel i roi eu Hymddiried yn yr Arglwydd, ac nid mewn amldra o ddynion' (A song to beseech everyone to put their trust in the Lord during a time of war, and not in a multitude of men) (n.p., [1779]) (JHD 605); H. Jones, 'Cerdd newydd ym mherthynas y rhyfel bresennol sydd yn America, gan gyffelybu yr ymbleidio neu'r sectiau yn y deyrnas yma â rhyfel yr America i'r goleuni gogleddol sydd i'w weled yn yr wybr ers 66 o flynyddoedd' (A new song in relation to the present war in America, comparing the Dissent or the sectarianism in this country and the American war to the northern light which has been seen in the skies for the past sixty-six years) (Caer, n.d.) (JHD 221i).
108. 'mendi[o] oll ein buchedd trigolion Brydain buredd'.
109. On Ellis Roberts's prolificacy as a ballad-writer see S. M. Rosser, 'Baledi Newyddiadurol Elis y Cowper', in G. H. Jenkins (ed.), *Cof Cenedl XXIII: Ysgrifau ar Hanes Cymru* (Llandysul: Gwasg Gomer, 2008),), pp. 67–99, esp. pp. 78–80; G. Morgan, 'Baledi Dyffryn Conwy', *Canu Gwerin*, 20 (1997), pp. 2–12, esp. p. 4. Other poets who published ballads relating to the American War of Independence are Thomas Edwards (Twm o'r Nant), for whom see further below; John Edwards, author of 'Cerdd o Goffadwriaeth am ein hen ffrind Tobacco, oherwydd ei fod gwedi mynd yn brin ac yn ddryd' (A song in remembrance of our old friend, Tobacco, because he has become rare and expensive) (Wrecsam, n.d.) (JHD 291ii); H. Eryri, 'Achwyniad Hywel o'r Yri wrth Wragedd Gwynedd am dderbyniad Morgan Rondl, a gwrthodiad Sir John Haidd o'r Gadair Senyddol' (The complaint of Hywel of the Yri to the wives of Gwynedd regarding the reception of Morgan Rondl and the rejection of Sir John Barley-corn from the parlia-

mentary chair) (Trefriw, 1780) (JHD 325ii); and M. Prichard, 'Yn rhoi hanes fel y darfu i'r Ffrangcod speilio'r Llongau Pyst Caergybi wrth ddyfod adre or Iwerddon' (Giving the story of how the French plundered the postal ships of Holyhead on their way home from Ireland) (Trefriw, 1780) (JHD 327i); and M. Prichard, 'I Filwyr Sir Gaernarfon ar ei trosglwyddiad o Gaergybi Ymôn, ir Gwersyll sy'n y Cosheath yng Nghent' (To the soldiers of Caernarvonshire upon their transferral from Holyhead in Anglesey to the camp which is in Coxheath in Kent) (Trefriw, 1780) (JHD 327ii). Hugh Jones, Maesglasau, composed free-metre poems in ballad style relating to the war. See 'Cerdd Ynghylch yr amryfusedd presennol rhwng Lloegr ac America' (A song regarding the current disagreement between England and America) and 'Cerdd, O Ddeusyfiad am Heddwch ac Undeb, rhwng Lloegr Hên â'r Newydd' (A song asking for peace and unity between Old and New England), in H. Jones, *Gardd y Caniadau: neu lyfr yn cynnwys ynddo garolau a cherddi ar amriw destunau, diddan a difrifol* (Mwythig: T. Wood, 1776), pp. 55–9, 60–3. These poems are discussed in G. Tibbot, 'Hugh Jones, Maesglasau', *Journal of the Merioneth Historical and Record Society*, 7:2 (1974), pp. 121–39, esp. p. 135; and Price, 'Pulling aside the veil', p. 286.

110. See A. C. Lake, *Huw Jones o Langwm* (Caernarfon: Gwasg Pantycelyn, 2009), p. 49.
111. See Jones, *Welsh Ballads of the French Revolution*.
112. For statistics relating to publishers of Welsh ballads responding to the American War of Independence, see Jones, 'Gwŷr Lloeger aeth benben â'u brodyr eu hunen', p. 218.
113. C. Jones, *Tymmhorol, ac wybrennol Newyddion, Neu Almanac Newydd, Am y Flwyddyn o Oedran ein Iachawdwr, 1783. Ym mha un y cynhwysir amryw bethau nad oes yma mo'r lle i'w henwi* (Mwythig, 1783), pp. 14–17. I am grateful to Dr Marion Löffler for drawing my attention to the presence of the poem in this almanac.
114. 'yn'r Ysgol'.
115. 'Merchants hyfryd'; 'dim am ŷd Oddiyma ir mor'.
116. 'Dihareb wir sydd bena, / [M]ae Lloegr hen Ymlygra, / [E]i hunan dyna ei hânaf'.
117. Regarding the great frustration of Chester traders during the period see also J. Edwards, 'Cerdd o Goffadwriaeth am ein hen ffrind Tobacco, oherwydd ei fod gwedi mynd yn brin ac yn ddryd' (JHD 291ii): 'Dymuniad pawb ac wllus da, / Am ffordd yn rhydd cin dechre'r hâ, / I forwur Caer i 'Merica, i fynd ar Llongc iw Llwn[?c]' (May everyone wish with good will / for a free passage before the beginning of the summer / for the Chester sailors to take their ships to America to their havens).
118. 'Smyglers cyfrwys iawn'; 'medru ymwthio i'r Tai, werthu Tea'.
119. 'llygaid gan las lwyn, / A chlustiau Crwŷn gan gae crin'.
120. One woman-poet who voiced her opinion about the American war was Mrs Parry from Plas yn y Fa[e]rdre, in the parish of Llandrillo, Merioneth. See 'Carol Plygen i'w ganu ar "Susanna"' (Matin carol to be sung on 'Susanna'). C. A. Charnell-White (ed.), *Beirdd Ceridwen: Blodeugerdd Barddas o Ganu Menywod hyd tua 1800* (Cyhoeddiadau Barddas, 2005), pp. 298–301, 407–8.

2 Powell, 'Scottophobia versus Jacobitism: Political Radicalism and the Press in Late Eighteenth-Century Ireland'

1. C. Fox, 'Swift's Scotophobia', *Bullán: An Irish Studies Journal*, 6 (2002), pp. 43–65; E. R. Davies, 'The Injured Lady, the Deluded Man, and the Infamous Creature: Swift and the 1707 Act of Union', in D. A. Valone and J. M. Bradbury (eds), *Anglo-Irish Identities, 1571–1845* (Lewisburg, PA: Bucknell University Press, 2008).
2. J. G. Simms, *Jacobite Ireland 1685–91* (London: Routledge, 1970); S. J. Connolly, *Religion, Law and Power: The Making of Protestant Ireland 1660–1760* (Oxford: Oxford University Press, 1992); T. Bartlett, *The Fall and Rise of the Irish Nation: The Catholic Question 1690–1830* (Dublin: Gill and Macmillan, 1992); E. Ó Ciardha, *Ireland and the Jacobite Cause, 1685–1766: A Fatal Attachment* (Dublin: Four Courts Press, 2000); Morley, *Irish Opinion and the American Revolution* (2007); G. Nobbe, *The North Briton: A Study in Political Propaganda* (New York: Columbia University Press, 1939); J. Brewer, 'The Misfortunes of Lord Bute: A Case-Study in Eighteenth-Century Political Argument and Public Opinion', *Historical Journal*, 16 (1973), pp. 3–43; Colley, *Britons*; P. D. G. Thomas, *John Wilkes: A Friend to Liberty* (Oxford: Oxford University Press, 1996); A. Rounce, '"Stuarts without End": Wilkes, Churchill, and Anti-Scottishness', *Eighteenth-Century Life*, 29:3 (2005), pp. 20–38; J. Sainsbury, *John Wilkes: The Lives of a Libertine* (Aldershot: Ashgate, 2006); A. Cash, *John Wilkes: The Scandalous Father of Civil Liberty* (New Haven, CT: Yale University Press, 2006); C. O'Halloran, *Golden Ages and Barbarous Nations: Antiquarian Debate and Cultural Politics in Ireland, c. 1750–1800* (Cork: Cork University Press/Field Day, 2004); D. Moore, 'James Macpherson and "Celtic Whiggism"', *Eighteenth-Century Life*, 30:1 (2005), pp. 1–24.
3. McFarland, *Ireland and Scotland in the Age of Revolution*; Harris, *The Scottish People and the French Revolution*; K. Whelan, *The Tree of Liberty: Radicalism, Catholicism and the Construction of Irish Identity 1760–1830* (Cork, Cork University Press/Field Day, 1996); D. Keogh and N. Furlong (eds), *The Mighty Wave: Aspects of the 1798 Rebellion in Wexford* (Dublin: Four Courts Press, 1996).
4. D. Armitage, 'Greater Britain: A Useful Category of Historical Analysis?', *American Historical Review*, 104:2 (1999), pp. 427–45; J. G. A. Pocock, 'The New British History in Atlantic Perspective: An Antipodean Commentary', *American Historical Review*, 104:2 (1999), pp. 490–500. An early example of the pan-Celtic approach (from the left) is T. Nairn, *The Break-Up of Britain: Crisis and Neo-Nationalism 1965–75* (London: New Left, 1977). Also see M. Pittock, *Celtic Identity and the British Image* (Manchester: Manchester University Press, 1999).
5. M. J. Powell, 'Celtic Rivalries: Ireland, Scotland and Wales in the British Empire, 1707–1801', in H. Bowen (ed.), *Wales and the British Empire* (Manchester: Manchester University Press, 2012), pp. 62–86. For an interpretation that places both the Scots and the Irish at the centre of imperial reform see J. R. Snapp, 'An Enlightened Empire: Scottish and Irish Imperial Reformers in the Age of the American Revolution', *Albion*, 33:3 (2001), pp. 388–403. According to Snapp, many Scottish imperial officials envisioned 'an empire of diverse subjects under a firm but benevolent central authority', ibid., p. 399. It should be noted, however, that as supporters of Anglo-Irish Union, Snapp's Irish exemplars, William Knox and Arthur Dobbs, were not in tune with broader patriot opinion.
6. For Scotland and the British Empire see J. M. Mackenzie, 'Essay and Reflection: On Scotland and the Empire', *International History Review*, 15:4 (1993), pp. 714–39.

7. Colley, *Britons*, pp. 105–32; Brewer, 'The Misfortunes of Lord Bute', pp. 3–43; Rounce, 'Stuarts without End', pp. 20–38.
8. Brewer, 'The Misfortunes of Lord Bute', pp. 8, 31.
9. P. Clark, *British Clubs and Societies 1580–1800* (Oxford: Oxford University Press, 2000), p. 99.
10. *Pennsylvania Evening Herald*, 30 April 1785.
11. For the Free Citizens of Dublin see M. J. Powell and J. Kelly, *Clubs and Societies in Eighteenth-Century Ireland*.
12. *Hibernian Journal*, 14–16 October 1776; *Universal Advertiser*, 16 March 1754, 20 December 1757; *London Evening Post*, 4 November 1777; *Hibernian Journal*, 15–17 January 1776.
13. See, for example, an account of festivities in Dublin and Tipperary in *Pue's Occurrences*, 18–21 April 1752; T. Barnard, *Making the Grand Figure: Lives and Possessions in Ireland, 1641–1770* (New Haven, CT: Yale University Press, 2004), p. 28.
14. *Hibernian Journal*, 14–16 October 1776.
15. Ibid.
16. *Freeman's Journal*, 17 December 1763.
17. Ibid., 13 June 1769.
18. Ibid., 19 June 1770.
19. M. Taylor, 'John Bull and the Iconography of Public Opinion in England *c.* 1712–1929', *Past and Present*, 134 (1992), pp. 93–128, on p. 103.
20. M. J. Powell, *Britain and Ireland in the Eighteenth-Century Crisis of Empire* (Basingstoke: Palgrave, 2003), pp. 95–139.
21. *Freeman's Journal*, 20 March 1770.
22. *Hibernian Journal*, 5–7 March 1777.
23. Brewer, 'The Misfortunes of Lord Bute', pp. 21–2.
24. Quoted in C. Nicolson, 'A Plan "To Banish all the Scotchmen": Victimization and Political Mobilization in Pre-Revolutionary Boston', *Massachusetts Historical Review*, 9 (2007), pp. 55–102, on p. 70.
25. Quoted in Snapp, 'An Enlightened Empire', p. 402.
26. Rush also noted that the 'black broth of Sparta, and the barley broth of Scotland, have been alike celebrated for their beneficial effects upon the minds of young people', D. J. D'Elia, 'Benjamin Rush: Philosopher of the American Revolution', *Transactions of the American Philosophical Society*, 64:5 (1974), pp. 1–113, on pp. 29–31, 79.
27. Nicolson, 'A Plan "To Banish all the Scotchmen"', p. 72.
28. Ibid., pp. 55, 68. Not that the Scots were always demonized – Nicholson notes that American Whigs used the history of Anglo-Scottish tensions – even down to the Jacobite rebellion – to bolster their cause, ibid., p. 70.
29. *Limerick Chronicle*, 22 March 1779.
30. *Dublin Evening Post*, 4 August 1778.
31. Quoted in Morley, *Irish Opinion and the American Revolution* (2007), p. 126, *Hibernian Journal*, 19 July 1775.
32. *Hibernian Journal*, 17–19 February 1777.
33. J. Pollock, *The Letters of Owen Roe O'Neill* (Dublin, 1779), p. 35; [F. Jebb], *The Letters of Guatimozin* (Dublin, 1779), p. 41. I am very grateful to Dr Michael Brown for these references.
34. *Finn's Leinster Journal*, 11–15 March 1775.

35. *Dublin Morning Post*, 16 October 1784. Also see N. Schaeffer, 'Charles Churchill's Political Journalism', *Eighteenth-Century Studies*, 9:3 (1976), pp. 406–28.
36. *Hibernian Journal*, 18–21 October 1776.
37. *Dublin Evening Post*, 17 September 1778; Colley, *Britons*, p. 130. Also see Mackenzie, 'On Scotland and the Empire', pp. 716–24.
38. *Hibernian Journal*, 18–21 October 1776.
39. Ibid., 17–19 February 1777.
40. Ibid., 10–12 March 1777.
41. For the Aldermen of Skinner's Alley see M. J. Powell, 'The Aldermen of Skinner's Alley: Ultra-Protestantism before the Orange Order', in Powell and Kelly (eds), *Clubs and Societies*, pp. 203–23.
42. E. C. Black, 'The Tumultuous Petitioners: The Protestant Association in Scotland, 1778–1780', *Review of Politics*, 25:2 (1963), pp. 183–211.
43. *Limerick Chronicle*, 1 March 1779.
44. Ibid., 25 February 1779.
45. *Freeman's Journal*, 27–9 June 1782.
46. Black, 'The Tumultuous Petitioners', p. 196.
47. *Volunteer Evening Post*, 22–4 April 1784.
48. Ibid., 9–12 April, 23–5 September 1785.
49. Davis, 'The Injured Lady', p. 134.
50. *Volunteer Evening Post*, 29–31 March 1785.
51. Ibid., 5–7 May 1785.
52. Brewer, 'The Misfortunes of Lord Bute', pp. 20–2; Schaeffer, 'Charles Churchill's Political Journalism', pp. 416–8; G. Rudé, 'The London "Mob" of the Eighteenth Century', *Historical Journal*, 2:1 (1959), pp. 1–18.
53. Cash, *John Wilkes*, p. 73.
54. *Freeman's Journal*, 27–30 July 1776.
55. *Dublin Evening Post*, 19 February 1784.
56. [Jebb], *Letters of Guatimozin*, p. 41.
57. *Dublin Morning Post*, 5 October 1784.
58. For more on the popular reaction to Twiss' tour see M. J. Powell, *Piss-Pots, Printers and Public Opinion in Eighteenth-Century Dublin: Richard Twiss's Tour in Ireland* (Dublin: Four Courts Press, 2009).
59. *Hibernian Journal*, 28–30 August, 1776.
60. W. Preston, *A Congratulatory Poem on the Late Successes of the British Arms: Congratulatory Poem; particularly the Triumphant Evacuation of Boston* (Dublin, 1776), pp. 6–9; W. Preston, *The Female Congress; or, the Temple of Cotytto: A Mock Heroic Poem, in Four Cantos* (London, 1779), p. 33.
61. R. D. Y. C. *Fidêfract; an Heroic Poem. In Four Cantos. In the Hudibrastic Style* (Dublin, 1778), pp. 16, 30.
62. Ibid., p. 34.
63. Rounce, 'Stuarts without End', pp. 29–30; Schaeffer, 'Charles Churchill's Political Journalism', pp. 415, 417.
64. D. Moore, 'James Macpherson and "Celtic Whiggism"', p. 8.
65. O'Halloran, *Golden Ages*, pp. 28–39.
66. Quoted in M. McCraith, 'The Saga of James MacPherson's "Ossian"', *Linen Hall Review*, 8 (1991), pp. 5–9, on p. 5.
67. Ibid., p. 6.

68. *Hibernian Journal*, 9–11 October 1776.
69. Ibid., 16–18 October 1776.
70. C. T. Bowden, *A Tour through Ireland* (Dublin, 1791), p. 21.
71. *Hibernian Magazine*, August 1776, p. 553.
72. *Hibernian Journal*, 16–18 October 1776.
73. McCraith, 'The Saga of James MacPherson's "Ossian"', p. 8.
74. *Londonderry Journal*, 20 September 1776; *Belfast News-Letter*, 10–13 December 1776.
75. Ó Ciardha, *Ireland and the Jacobite Cause*; Morley, *Irish Opinion and the American Revolution* (2007), pp. 6, 46–7, 64–5, 110–13.
76. Morley, *Irish Opinion and the American Revolution* (2007), pp. 46–7.
77. Ó Ciardha, *Ireland and the Jacobite Cause*; E. Ó Ciardha, 'The Stuarts and Deliverance in Irish and Scots-Gaelic Poetry, 1690–1760', in S. J. Connolly (ed.), *Kingdoms United? Ireland and Great Britain from 1500. Integration and Diversity* (Dublin: Four Courts Press, 1998), pp. 78–94; S. J. Connolly, 'Jacobites, Whiteboys and Republicans: Varieties of Disaffection in Eighteenth-Century Ireland', *Eighteenth-Century Ireland*, 18 (2003), pp. 63–79; D. Hayton, Review of E. Ó Ciardha, *Ireland and the Jacobite Cause*, *Eighteenth-Century Ireland*, 18 (2003), pp. 154–60; J. Kelly, *The Liberty and Ormond Boys: Factional Riot in Eighteenth-Century Dublin* (Dublin: Four Courts Press, 2005), p. 48. For a response by Morley, see 'The Continuity of Disaffection in Eighteenth-Century Ireland', *Eighteenth-Century Ireland*, 22 (2007), pp. 189–205.
78. Morley, *Irish Opinion and the American Revolution* (2007), p. 11.
79. Morley, 'The Continuity of Disaffection', p. 189.
80. M. J. Powell, 'The Society of Free Citizens and other Popular Political Clubs, 1749–1789', in Kelly and Powell (eds), *Clubs and Societies*, pp. 244–63.
81. *Hibernian Journal*, 7 May 1784.
82. Ibid., 12–14 January 1786.
83. Ibid., 1–3 June 1784.
84. Ibid., 19–22, 22–4 June 1784.
85. Morley, 'The Continuity of Disaffection', p. 203.
86. Morley, *Irish Opinion and the American Revolution*, pp. 108–9.
87. Morley, 'The Continuity of Disaffection', p. 201.
88. L. Colley, 'Whose Nation? Class and National Consciousness in Britain 1750–1830', *Past and Present*, 113 (1986), pp. 96–117, on p. 112.
89. *Hibernian Journal*, 18–21 October 1776.
90. *Volunteer Evening Post*, 3–5 June 1784. By 1784 Home's role as private secretary to Lord Bute in 1758 was of less import than the threat posed by dissent in both Scotland and Ireland. Charles Churchill had earlier warned that the performance of *Tamerlane* (an Irish favourite) on William III's birthday would be replaced by 'Home's Douglass and the Gentle Shepherd', Schaeffer, 'Charles Churchill's Political Journalism', p. 417.
91. *Volunteer Evening Post*, 3–15 April 1784.
92. *Dublin Morning Post*, 30 September 1784.

3 Harris, 'Lord Daer, Radicalism, Union and the Enlightenment in the 1790s'

1. Daer probably met Lavoisier initially in 1783, on his first visit to France.
2. R. Holmes, *The Age of Wonder: How the Romantic Generation Discovered the Beauty and Terror of Science* (London: Harper Press, 2008), p. 245.
3. Quoted in M. Jay, *The Atmosphere of Heaven: The Unnatural Experiments of Dr Beddoes and His Sons of Genius* (New Haven, CT and London: Yale University Press, 2009), p. 4.
4. *Morning Chronicle*, 16 March 1795. He was buried in Exeter Cathedral.
5. For helpful reflections on this theme, see M. Brown, 'A Scottish Literati in Paris: The Case of Sir James Hall', *Journal of Irish and Scottish Studies*, 2:1 (2008), pp. 73–100, esp. 75–6.
6. Colley, 'Whose Nation? Class and National Consciousness in Britain 1750–1830', pp. 97–117, esp. 112–3.
7. Although see my *The Scottish People and the French Revolution*; ibid., 'Scottish–English Connections in British Radicalism in the 1790s', in T. C. Smout (ed.), *Anglo-Scottish Relations from 1603 to 1900* (Oxford: Oxford University Press, 2005), pp. 189–212.
8. For the British convention, see esp. A. Goodwin, *The Friends of Liberty: The English Democratic Movement in the Age of the French Revolution* (London: Hutchison & Co., 1979), ch. 8; J. Barrell, *Imagining the King's Death: Figurative Treason, Fantasies of Regicide, 1793–1796* (Oxford: Oxford University Press, 2000).
9. E. Hughes, 'The Scottish Reform Movement and Charles Grey, 1792–94: Some Fresh Correspondence', *Scottish Historical Review*, 35:119 (1956), pp. 26–41, on pp. 26–7.
10. Ibid., p. 33.
11. Ibid., p. 35.
12. His exact words were: 'In short, thinking we have been the worse of every connection hitherto with you, the Friends of Liberty in Scotland have almost universally been enemies to Union with England. Such is the fact, whether the reasons be good or bad. *I for one should still be of that opinion did I not look upon it that a thorough Parliamentary Reform would necessarily place us in a much better situation and higher in this political sphere* whilst at the same time it would relieve you from vermin from this country who infect your court, your parliament, and every establishment. (My emphasis.) Ibid., p. 35.
13. Ibid., p. 36.
14. A fire in 1940 destroyed the library at St Mary's Isle, family home of the Earls of Selkirk, and thus any private papers.
15. For Palgrave school, see W. McCarthy, *Anna Letitia Barbauld: Voice of the Enlightenment* (Baltimore, MD: Johns Hopkins University Press, 2008), pp. 165–89.
16. 'Letter of Anna Letitia Barbauld to John Aikin', 16 August 1787, Hornel Library, Broughton House, Kirkcudbright, MS15/21, f. 15. The same letter refers to a pair of leather balls of the kind used by printers to ink type which Daer had made himself and given to Anna, which she particularly cherished for that reason.
17. That Vaughan and Daer were in frequent contact seems likely. It was through Daer that Vaughan conveyed a copy of a privy council report on American corn insects to Thomas Jefferson in Paris in the spring of 1789. See T. Jefferson, *The Papers of Thomas Jefferson, vol. 15, 27 Mar. 1789–30 Nov. 1789*, ed. J. P. Boyd (Princeton, NJ: Princeton University Press, 1958), pp. 102–3. Both were members of the Coffee House Philosophical Society, for which see below, p. 186, n. 30.
18. McCarthy, *Anna Letitia Barbauld*, p. 171.

19. See G. MacIntyre, *Dugald Stewart: The Pride and Ornament of Scotland* (Brighton: Sussex Academic Press, 2003).
20. Daer attended Stewart's mathematics class in 1783. MacIntyre, *Dugald Stewart*, p. 37.
21. He visited, for example, in 1801, 1813 and 1817.
22. See *The Papers of Thomas Jefferson, vol. 15*, pp. 90–7, Richard Price to Thomas Jefferson, Hackney, London, 6 May 1789, where Price notes: 'This letter will, I hope, be carry'd to you by Mr Dugald Stewart Professor of Moral Philosophy at Edinburgh and a very able man who is this day setting out for Paris with Lord Dare [sic] in order to be present there at the time of the meeting of the three estates.'
23. T. Jefferson to J. Adams, 14 March 1820, quoted in MacIntyre, *Dugald Stewart*, p. 73. Daer was used by Jefferson to carry a letter back to Richard Price in London. *The Papers of Thomas Jefferson, vol. 15*, pp. 279–80, 329–31.
24. On Stewart's 'optimism', which distinguished his thought and teaching in important ways from Smith and Hume, see esp. K. Haakonssen, 'From Moral Philosophy to Political Economy: The Contribution of Dugald Stewart', in V. Hope (ed.), *Philosophers of the Scottish Enlightenment* (Edinburgh: Edinburgh University Press, 1984), pp. 211–32. It is conceivable that through Stewart, Daer became connected to the Earl of Shelburne's Bowood circle, but I currently know of no evidence which might corroborate this.
25. A. C. Chitnis, *The Scottish Enlightenment and Early Victorian English Society* (London: Croom Helm, 1986), esp. pp. 23–6; M. Brown, 'Dugald Stewart and the Problem of Teaching Politics in the 1790s', *Journal of Irish and Scottish Studies*, 1:1 (2007), pp. 89–126; B. Lenman, *Integration, Enlightenment, and Industrialization: Scotland 1746–1832* (London: Edward Arnold, 1981), p. 110.
26. The phrase is D. Winch's in D. Winch, 'Dugald Stewart and his Pupils', in S. Collini, D. Winch and J. Burrow, *The Noble Science of Politics: A Study in Nineteenth-Century Intellectual History* (Cambridge: Cambridge University Press, 1983), pp. 25–61, on p. 33.
27. See J. Veitch, 'Memoir of Dugald Stewart', in Sir W. Hamilton (ed.), *Collected Works of Dugald Stewart*, 11 vols (Edinburgh, 1854–60), vol. 10, pp. lxx–lxxv.
28. Although appointed to the chair in 1779, Walker did not begin to lecture until 1782. M. D. Eddy, 'The University of Edinburgh Natural History Class Lists 1782–1800', *Archives of Natural History*, 30:1 (2003), pp. 97–117, esp. 100.
29. C. W. J. Withers, '"Both Useful and Ornamental": John Walker's Keepership of Edinburgh University's Natural History Museum, 1779–1803', *Journal of the History of Collections*, 5:1 (1993), pp. 65–77; List of subscribers for the purchase of Mr Weir's Museum, Edinburgh University Library, Special Collections, La III. 352/2, Weir was an Edinburgh painter.
30. See Lord Daer to Joseph Black, London, 9 August 1785, EUL, Gen. 874/IV/19–20, EUL, where Daer describes himself as Black's 'late pupil'. For the relationship to Beddoes, see esp. L. Stewart, 'Putting on Airs: Science, Medicine, and Polity in the Late Eighteenth Century', in T. Levere and G. L'E. Turner, *Discussing Chemistry and Steam: The Minutes of a Coffee House Philosophical Society 1780–1787* (Oxford: Oxford University Press, 2002), pp. 236–7. Trevor Levere has suggested that Daer was a friend of Priestley. See T. H. Levere, 'Natural Philosophers in a Coffee House: Dissent, Radical Reform and Pneumatic Chemistry', in P. Wood (ed.), *Science and Dissent in England 1688–1945* (Aldershot: Ashgate, 2004), pp. 131–46, on p. 137. That he was connected to Priestley and his Birmingham circle seems very plausible given his connections and interests, although there is no direct proof of this. A letter, nevertheless, from the Rev. Thomas Houlbooke to Thomas Wedgwood reads: 'A Mr Douglas, Br. to Ld. Dare enquired after

you & Dr Darwin and desired his compliments to you and your Br. he said Mr Wedgwood and I did not ask him which. he is a very sensible young Man a great Naturalist and a friend to Liberty – as you may suppose when I inform you he is gone to France with Sr. James Hall his Br. in Law to see free Men.' (University of Keele, Wedgwood Archives, 17651-20, 1761A-20). The brother referred to was almost certainly John, who shared his eldest brother's political views. I am very grateful to Professor Levere for a personal communication on this matter, and for supplying the above reference.

31. 'Letter from Thomas Charles Hope to Dr Joseph Black, Glasgow, 14 July 1789', EUL. Gen. 873/111/153-4,
32. Levere and Turner, *Discussing Chemistry and Steam*, p. 22.
33. L. Stewart, 'The Public Culture of Radical Philosophers in Eighteenth Century London', in Wood (ed.), *Science and Dissent*, p. 121.
34. Stewart, 'Putting on Airs', p. 236.
35. J. M. Bumsted, *Lord Selkirk: A Life* (East Lansing, MI: Michigan State University Press, 2009), p. 55.
36. [T. Douglas, fifth Earl of Selkirk] *A Letter Addressed to John Cartwright, Esq., Chairman of the Committee at the Crown and Anchor, on the Subject of Parliamentary Reform* (London and Edinburgh, 1809).
37. I have as yet been unable to consult the minutes of the society held in the Edinburgh University Library. I have relied instead on extracts from these reproduced in D. Wood, 'Constant in Edinburgh: Eloquence and History', *French Studies*, 11:2 (1986), pp. 151-66.
38. *History of the Speculative Society of Edinburgh from its Institution in 1764* (Edinburgh, 1845).
39. This may possibly have been a gesture of familial respect, given that his father's tutor at university in Glasgow had been Francis Hutcheson.
40. Wood, 'Constant in Edinburgh', p. 154.
41. For Daer's membership of the RSE, see Levere, 'Natural Philosophers', p. 137. For the Poker Club, see MacIntyre, *Dugald Stewart*, p. 122. The last known meeting of the club was in January 1784.
42. The minutes of the Speculative Society for 8 March 1785 record, 'Lord Daer & Mr Sibthorpe have left this place.' This presumably explains why he was not a member of the Edinburgh University Chemical Society, which comprised those members of Black's class with a special interest in chemistry. J. Kendall, 'The First Chemical Society, the First Chemical Journal, and the Chemical Revolution', *Proceedings of the Royal Society of Edinburgh: Section A (Mathematics and Physical Sciences)*, 63 (1949-52), pp. 346-58.
43. For details, see T. Murray, *The Literary History of Galloway* (Edinburgh, 1822), p. 307; S. Smith, *General View of the Agriculture of Galloway* (London, 1810). See also E. J. Cowan, 'Agricultural Improvement and the Formation of Early Agricultural Societies in Dumfries and Galloway', *Transactions of the Dumfries and Galloway Natural History and Antiquarian Society*, 53 (1977-8), pp. 157-67.
44. See e.g. G. O. Elder, *Kirkcudbright: The Story of an Ancient Royal Burgh* (Castle Douglas, 1898), pp. 32-4.
45. See D. E. Marsden, 'The Development of Kirkcudbright in the Late Eighteenth Century: Town Planning in a Galloway Context', *Transactions of the Dumfriesshire and Galloway Natural History and Antiquarian Society*, ser. 3, 72 (1997), pp. 89-96.
46. For his membership of the RSA, see *Morning Herald*, 18 June 1792; *Proceedings of the Association for Promoting the Discovery of the Interior Parts of Africa* (London, 1790), p. 4.

47. Bumsted, *Lord Selkirk*, pp. 14–15, 24–8, 33, 24–35, 37, 46–7.
48. *London Chronicle*, 29 October 1789.
49. D. E. Ginter, *The Whig Organization of the General Election of 1790* (Berkeley, CA: University of California Press, 1967), pp. 154–5, 201, 221–2.
50. *Public Advertiser*, 26 June 1790; *Gazetteer, or New Daily Advertiser*, 25 June 1790.
51. *Lloyd's Evening Post*, 17 October 1791; *London Chronicle*, 28 January 1792.
52. *The Right of the Eldest Sons of the Peers of Scotland to Represent the Commons of that Part of Great Britain in Parliament*, Considered (London, 1790), pp. 4–5. In England, the Duke of Norfolk claimed the right to stand as a freeholder at the Surrey election in 1790, interpreted by one newspaper as 'the first overt act of a democratic spirit among the British nobility' and linked explicitly to Daer's parallel effort in Scotland. *General Evening Post*, 3 July 1790.
53. *Star*, 9 March 1792.
54. Katherine Plymley diary (24 April–10 May 1792), 1066/10, Shropshire Record Office, Ludlow. I am grateful to Kathryn Gleadle for this reference.
55. Harris, *The Scottish People and the French Revolution*, pp. 82–6.
56. Ibid., p. 93.
57. *ODNB*.
58. Two of his letters to the Friends of the People were subsequently published in pamphlet form and widely circulated in radical circles, north and south of the border. Harris, *The Scottish People and the French Revolution*, p. 264, n. 129.
59. National Records of Scotland, Edinburgh, Home Office (Scotland) Papers, RH 2/4/209, f. 33.
60. *Morning Post & Daily Advertiser*, 15 July 1791.
61. T. Hardy to Lord Daer, 14 July 1792, British Library, Add MS 27,817, f. 15.
62. Copy of private letter from Hardy to Daer, 8 Sept. 1792, BL, Add MS 27,814, f. 184.
63. For his presence at meetings of the Friends of the Liberty of the Press, see *Morning Post*, 22 April 1793.
64. Minute Book of the Society for Constitutional Information, The National Archives, Kew, TS 11/962, f. 66. Other Scottish members of the SCI included Thomas Christie, Dr William Maxwell, friend of Burns and Hugh, Lord Sempill. Sempill was another of Stewart's students in Edinburgh.
65. Minute Book of the SCI, TS 11/962, TNA, ff. 77r, 81v, 139v. Daer's fellow stewards were Lord Edward Fitzgerald, John Frost, Lord Semphill and Captain Harwood. Daer met Millar in 1784 at a dinner for Edmund Burke, then in Glasgow for his institution as rector of the university.
66. *Star*, 16 May 1792.
67. See e.g. *Public Advertiser*, 14, 26 May 1792.
68. Katherine Plymley diary, 24 April–10 May 1792, Shropshire Record Office, Ludlow, 1066/10. I am grateful to Kathryn Gleadle for this reference.
69. Hall and Daer were ideological and intellectual bedfellows, sharing strong opposition to the slave trade, and deep interest in scientific matters, agricultural improvement and technological innovation.
70. The diaries are in the National Library of Scotland (MSS 6329–32).
71. Brown, 'A Scottish Literati in Paris', p. 67.
72. Diary of Sir James Hall of Dunglass, 24 June–7 August 1791, National Library of Scotland, Edinburgh, MS 6332, ff. 75, 79.

73. Fascinating evidence regarding the possible impact of the visit on Lord Selkirk survives in the diary of William Dickson, agent of the London Abolition Society, who met Selkirk in Scotland in March 1792. Dickson recorded: 'His Lordship a very sensible man but swears a very little – warm in his temper – his voice exactly Burke's – his political principles exactly the opposite – He is a great friend to Liberty and to the poor, whose rights he holds sacred & I love and venerate him – He is for every man having some share of political weight – he knows how the poor fare as also does Lady Selkirk – says he know not how they lived before potatoes introduced – will suffer no man to kill any thing on the Isle [i.e. St Mary's Isle] – Protects every thing that has life'. William Dickson, 'Diary of a Visit to Scotland, 5 January–19 March 1792 on Behalf of the Committee for the Abolition of the Slave Trade', Friends House, London, Temp MSS Box 10/14, entry for 18 March 1792.
74. See Appendix A, 'The Minutes of the Proceedings of the First General Convention of the Delegates from the Societies of the Friends of the People throughout Scotland', in H. W. Meikle, *Scotland and the French Revolution* (Glasgow, 1912), pp. 241–2, 244; minutes of the third general convention, NAS. JC 26/280, ff. 37, 41–2.
75. Harris, 'Scottish-English Connections', pp. 194–5.
76. See p. 185, n. 8, above.
77. Harris, *The Scottish People and the French Revolution*, pp. 101–3, on which the following paragraphs are based.
78. 'Letter from Calder, Cromarty, to William Skirving, 4 September 1793', NAS, JC26/280, bundle 1, item 22.
79. 'Hints on the Question of Union suggested by Class No. 3', NAS, JC 26/280, loose papers.
80. The best recent discussion of this episode is Barrell, *Imagining the King's Death*, pp. 252–84.
81. *Morning Chronicle*, 16 March 1795.
82. The failure of the Whig Association of the Friends of the People to expel Daer from its membership was raised during the trial of Thomas Hardy in March 1795.
83. Harris, 'Scottish-English Connections', pp. 203–8.
84. See e.g. McFarland, *Ireland and Scotland in the Age of Revolution*.
85. 'Report by "J. B.", 29 Oct. 1793', TNA, PRO 30/8/317, For this address, see 'Copy of Address from the Four Societies of the United Irishmen of Belfast', NAS, JC26/280, bundle 2, item 1.
86. *Reminiscences of Edinburgh 60 Years Ago, By John Howell* (1854), MS Acc 5779, NLS.
87. A. Page, *John Jebb and the Enlightenment Origins of British Radicalism* (Westport, CT and London: Praeger, 2003), esp. pp. 254–9.
88. Quoted in J. Livesy, *Civil Society and Empire: Ireland and Scotland in the Eighteenth Century Atlantic World* (New Haven, CT and London: Yale University Press, 2009), p. 4.
89. JC 26/280, bundle 11, NAS.
90. 'Copy of letter from William Skirving, the "Surprise" transport, 17 Apr. 1794', Minute Book of the SCI, TNA, TS 11/962, ff. 176–7.
91. Appendix A, 'The Minutes of the Proceedings', in Meikle, *Scotland and the French Revolution*, p. 246.
92. P. B. Ellis and S. Mac a'Ghobhainn, *The Scottish Insurrection of 1820* (Edinburgh: John Donald, 2001), pp. 56, 299–300.

4 Whatley, 'The Political and Cultural Legacy of Robert Burns in Scotland and Ulster, c. 1796–1859'

1. C. McGinn, 'Vehement Celebrations: The Global Celebration of the Burns Supper Since 1801', in M. Pittock (ed.), *Robert Burns in Global Culture* (Lanham, MD: Bucknell University Press, 2011), pp. 189–203; and see, for example, *Centenary Book of the Burns Club of Dumfries* (Dumfries: Courier & Herald Press, 1920).
2. *Times*, 26 January 1859; *Illustrated London News*, 29 January 1859; A. Rigney, 'Embodied Communities: Commemorating Robert Burns, 1859', *Representations*, 115 (Summer 2011), pp. 71–101, on pp. 71–2, 75.
3. R. Quinault, 'The Cult of the Centenary, c. 1784–1914', *Historical Research*, 71 (1998), pp. 303–23.
4. Anon, *Burnomania: The Celebrity of Robert Burns Considered: In a Discourse Addressed to all Real Christians of Every Denomination. To Which are Added, Epistles in Verse, Respecting Peter Pindar, Burns etc* (Edinburgh: J. Ogle, 1811).
5. See, for example, K. Simpson, *The Protean Scot: The Crisis of Identity in Eighteenth Century Scottish Literature* (Aberdeen: Aberdeen University Press, 1988).
6. See A. Rigney, 'Plenitude, Scarcity and the Circulation of Cultural Memory', *Journal of European Studies*, 35 (2005), pp. 11–27, on pp. 14–18.
7. J. Rodger and G. Carruthers, 'Introduction' in J. Rodger and G. Carruthers (eds), *Fickle Man: Robert Burns in the 21st Century* (Dingwall: Sandstone Press, 2009), pp. 1–10.
8. McIlvanney, *Burns the Radical*, p. 231.
9. C. Baraniuk, '"No bardolatry here": The Independence of the Ulster-Scots Poetic Tradition', in F. Ferguson and A. R. Holmes (eds), *Revising Robert Burns and Ulster: Literature, Religion and Politics, c. 1770–1920* (Dublin: Four Courts Press, 2009), pp. 64–82.
10. F. Ferguson, '"Burns the Conservative": Revising the Lowland Scottish Tradition in Ulster Poetry', in Ferguson and Holmes, *Revising Robert Burns and Ulster*, pp. 83–105, on p. 86.
11. A. Noble, 'Introduction', in A. Noble and P. S. Hogg (eds), *The Canongate Burns* (Edinburgh: Canongate, 2001), p. x; see too A. Noble, 'Versions of Scottish Pastoral: The Literati and the Tradition 1780–1830', in T. Markus (ed.), *Order in Space and Society: Architectural Form and its Context in the Scottish Enlightenment* (Edinburgh: Mainstream, 1982), pp. 263–311.
12. Harris, *The Scottish People and the French Revolution*, pp. 82–6.
13. See Lord H. Cockburn, *An Examination of the Trials for Sedition which have Hitherto Occurred in Scotland*, 2 vols (Edinburgh: David Douglas, 1838).
14. H. J. C. Grierson (ed.), *The Letters of Sir Walter Scott, 1819–21* (London: Constable & Co, 1934), pp. 1–3, 16–18, 29–33, 38–47.
15. Lord H. Cockburn, *Journal of Henry Cockburn, Being a Continuation of the Memorials of his Time, 1831–1854*, 2 vols (Edinburgh, 1874), vol. 2, pp. 2–6.
16. W. H. Fraser, 'The Scottish Context of Chartism', in T. Brotherstone (ed.), *Covenent, Charter, and Party: Traditions of Revolt and Protest in Modern Scottish History* (Aberdeen: Aberdeen University Press, 1989), pp. 66–77, on pp. 63, 67–75.
17. P. Joyce, *Visions of the People: Industrial England and the Question of Class, 1848–1914* (Cambridge: Cambridge University Press, 1991), p. 65; R. McWilliam, *Popular Politics in Nineteenth-Century England* (London and New York: Routledge, 1998), pp. 67–9.
18. See for example, W. H. Fraser, *Conflict and Class: Scottish Workers 1700–1838* (Edinburgh: John Donald, 1988); J. D. Young, *The Rousing of the Scottish Working Class*

(London: Croom Helm, 1979), alludes to Scottish plebeian radicals around 1820 sharing 'Robert Burns' vision of a new epoch in man's struggle for freedom', but provides no supporting evidence.
19. J. Erskine, 'Scotia's Jewel: Robert Burns and Ulster, 1786–c. 1830' in Ferguson and Holmes (eds), *Revising Robert Burns and Ulster*, pp. 22–32; McIlvanney, *Burns the Radical*, pp. 230–2.
20. McFarland, *Ireland and Scotland in the Age of Revolution*, pp. 6, 76.
21. An exception is R. J. Finlay, 'Heroes, Myths and Anniversaries in Modern Scotland', *Scottish Affairs*, 18 (Winter 1997), pp. 108–25, on pp. 110–14.
22. *Celebrity of Robert Burns*, pp. 7–8, 65, 75.
23. M. Lynch, *Scotland: A New History* (London: Century, 1991), p. 357.
24. R. J. Finlay, 'The Burns Cult and Scottish Identity in the Nineteenth and Twentieth Centuries', in K. Simpson (ed.), *Love & Liberty: Robert Burns, A Bicentenary Celebration* (East Linton: Tuckwell Press, 1997), pp. 69–78, on p. 74; I. Lindsay, 'Scotland and Burns', *Perspectives*, 20 (Winter 2008–9), pp. 11–13.
25. R. F. Foster, *Modern Ireland, 1600–1972* (London: Allen Lane, 1988), pp. 342, 388–9.
26. Rigney, 'Embodied Communities', pp. 87–8.
27. McIlvanney, *Burns the Radical*, p. 226.
28. *Scotsman*, 27 January 1859.
29. See M. Roberts, 'Burns and the Masonic Enlightenment', in J. C. Carter and J. H. Pittock (eds), *Aberdeen and the Enlightenment* (Aberdeen: Aberdeen University Press, 1988), pp. 331–8, on p. 337.
30. Baraniuk, 'No bardolatry here', p. 66; Erskine, 'Scotia's Jewel', pp. 30–1.
31. McIlvanney, *Burns the Radical*, pp. 238–40.
32. N. Leask, '"The Shadow Line": James Currie's "Life of Burns" and British Romanticism', in C. Lamont and M. Rossington (eds), *Romanticism's Debatable Lands* (London: Palgrave, 2007), pp. 64–79, on p. 64.
33. See, for example, A. Stewart, *Reminiscences of Dunfermline and Neighbourhood, Illustrative of Dunfermline Life, Sixty Years Ago* (Edinburgh: Scott & Ferguson, 1886), pp. 201–2.
34. Harris, *The Scottish People and the French Revolution*, pp. 165–6.
35. F. Ferguson, J. Erskine and R. Dixon, 'Commemorating and Collecting Burns in the North of Ireland, 1844–1902', in Ferguson and Holmes (eds), *Revising Robert Burns and Ulster*, pp. 127–47, on p. 133; McIlvanney, *Burns the Radical*, pp. 225–6.
36. E. J. Cowan and M. Paterson (eds), *Folk in Print: Scotland's Chapbook Heritage 1750–1850* (Edinburgh: Birlinn, 2007), pp. 11–14, 31–2.
37. A. Somerville, *The Autobiography of a Working Man* (London: Turnstile Press, 1951 edn), pp. 43–5.
38. Erskine, 'Scotia's Jewel', pp. 33–4.
39. P. Connell and N. Leask, 'What is the People?', in P. Connell and N. Leask (eds), *Romanticism and Popular Culture in Britain and Ireland* (Cambridge: Cambridge University Press, 2009), pp. 3–48, on p. 26.
40. D. Vincent, *Bread, Knowledge & Freedom: A Study of Nineteenth-Century Working Class Autobiography* (London and New York: Methuen, 1981), pp. 135–6.
41. J. Barrell, 'Rus in Urbe', in Connell and Leask (eds), *Romanticism and Popular Culture*, pp. 109–27, on pp. 113–4.
42. L. David, 'Burns and Transnational Culture', in G. Carruthers (ed.), *The Edinburgh Companion to Robert Burns* (Edinburgh: Edinburgh University Press, 2009), pp. 151–3.

43. K. Simpson, 'Burns and Independence', in G. Ross Roy (ed.), *Robert Burns & America: A Symposium* (Columbia, SC: University of South Carolina, 2001), pp. 11–22, on p. 15.
44. C. McGuirk, 'The "Rhyming Trade": Fergusson, Burns and the Marketplace', in R. Crawford (ed.), *'Heaven-Taught Fergusson': Robert Burns's Favourite Scottish Poet* (East Linton: Tuckwell Press, 2003), pp. 135–59, on pp. 142–6; C. A. Whatley, 'Burns: Work, Kirk and Community in Later Eighteenth-Century Scotland', in K. Simpson (ed.), *Burns Now* (Edinburgh: Canongate, 1994), pp. 92–116, on pp. 94–101; C. Kidd, 'Burns and Politics', in G. Carruthers (ed.), *The Edinburgh Companion to Robert Burns* (Edinburgh: Edinburgh University Press, 2009), pp. 61–73, on p. 71; M. Pittock, 'Nibbling at Adam Smith', in Rodger and Carruthers (eds), *Fickle Man*, pp. 118–31, on p. 125.
45. P. Aitchison and A. Cassell, *The Lowland Clearances: Scotland's Silent Revolution 1760–1830* (East Linton: Tuckwell Press, 2003), pp. 90–107.
46. W. Thom, *Rhymes and Recollections of A Hand-Loom Weaver* (London: Stewart and Murray, 1845), p. 14.
47. N. Murray, *The Scottish Hand Loom Weavers 1790–1850: A Social History* (Edinburgh: John Donald, 1978), pp. 168–72.
48. See T. Leonard (ed.), *Radical Renfrew: Poetry from the French Revolution to the First World War* (Edinburgh: Polygon, 1990).
49. L. J. Saunders, *Scottish Democracy, 1815–1840: The Social and Intellectual Background* (Edinburgh: Oliver & Boyd, 1950), p. 260.
50. T. C. Smout, *A Century of the Scottish People, 1830–1950* (London: Collins, 1986), p. 19; A. B. Campbell, *The Lanarkshire Miners: A Social History of their Trade Unions, 1775–1874* (Edinburgh: John Donald, 1979), pp. 160–1.
51. B. Maidment, *The Poorhouse Fugitives: Self-Taught Poets and Poetry in Victorian Britain* (Manchester: Carcanet, 1987), p. 162.
52. Maidment, *The Poorhouse Fugitives*, pp. 27–30.
53. See, for example, *Morning Chronicle*, 17 May 1816; *Caledonian Mercury*, 10 June 1819, 2 February 1832.
54. E. F. Biagini, *Liberty, Retrenchment and Reform: Popular Liberalism in the Age of Gladstone, 1860–1880* (Cambridge: Cambridge University Press, 1992), pp. 6, 84–93, 144–7; Smout, *A Century of the Scottish People*, pp. 248–9.
55. R. Brown, *Paisley Burns Clubs, 1805–1893* (Paisley and London: Alexander Gardner, 1893), pp. 96–7.
56. W. H. Fraser, *Dr John Taylor, Chartist Ayrshire Revolutionary* (Ayr: Ayrshire Archaeological and Natural History Society, 2006), pp. 25–7; *Chartism in Scotland* (Pontypool: Merlin Press, 2010), pp. 180–1.
57. *Caledonian Mercury*, 29 April 1819; *Manchester Times and Guardian*, 29 January 1842.
58. *Caledonian Mercury*, 29 April 1819.
59. C. Craig, 'The Making of a Scottish Literary Canon', in B. Bell (ed.), *The Edinburgh History of the Book in Scotland, Volume 3: Ambition and Industry, 1800–1880* (Edinburgh: Edinburgh University Press, 2007), pp. 266–77, on pp. 266–7.
60. H. Duncan to Duke of Buccleuch, 20 December 1813, and Duke of Buccleuch to Duncan, 30 December 1813, National Archives of Scotland, Buccleuch MSS, GD 224/653/4.
61. James Currie to John Syme, 1 September 1796, Mitchell Library, Currie Correspondence, Envelope 5 (1). I am grateful to Dr Rhona Brown, University of Glasgow, for this reference.

62. R. H. Cromek, *Reliques of Robert Burns, Consisting Chiefly of Original Letters, Poems and Critical Observations on Scottish Songs* (London: Cadell and Davies, 1808), pp. vi–xi.
63. For this section of the chapter see J. Wilson, *On the Genius and Character of Burns* (New York: Wiley and Putnam, 1845 edn), pp. 1–222.
64. W. Harvey, *Scottish Chapbook Literature* (New York: Burt Franklin, 1971 edn), pp. 116–20.
65. Leask, 'The Shadow Line', pp. 64–79; Craig, 'Making of a Scottish Literary Canon', p. 267.
66. Leask, 'The Shadow Line', p. 73.
67. C. Emsley, *Crime, Police and Penal Policy: European Experiences 1750–1940* (Oxford: Oxford University Press, 2007), pp. 135–6, 141.
68. Noble, 'Introduction', p. liii.
69. A. Tyrrell, 'Paternalism, Public Memory and National Identity in Early Victorian Scotland: The Robert Burns Festival at Ayr in 1844', *History*, 90:1 (2005), pp. 42–61, on p. 44.
70. Vincent, *Bread, Knowledge & Freedom*, pp. 55, 186–7.
71. Saunders, *Scottish Democracy*, p. 52; and see too, contemporaneous local histories such as A. Mercer, *The History of Dunfermline* (Dunfermline: John Miller, 1828), pp. 192–3.
72. Harris, *The Scottish People and the French Revolution*, pp. 38–9, 85–6; J. Crawford, 'Recovering the Lost Library Community: The Example of Fenwick', *Library History*, 23 (September, 2007), pp. 201–12, on pp. 205–6; and D. Gilmour, *Reminiscences of The Pen Folk, Paisley Weavers of Other Days* (Edinburgh and Paisley: Alex Gardner, 1879), pp. 25–8, 32–40.
73. See A. R. Holmes, 'Presbyterian Religion, Poetry and Politics in Ulster, *c.* 1770–1850', in Ferguson and Holmes (eds), *Revising Robert Burns and Ulster*, pp. 37–63.
74. Joyce, *Visions of the People*, p. 77; J. Belchem, *Popular Radicalism in Nineteenth-Century Britain* (Basingstoke: Macmillan, 1996), p. 126; Biagini, *Liberty*, pp. 87–8.
75. Ferguson, Erskine and Dixon, 'Commemorating and Collecting Burns', p. 134.
76. P. Burke, *Popular Culture in Early Modern Europe* (Aldershot: Wildwood House, 1988 edn), pp. 279–81; C. A. Whatley, *Scottish Society, 1707–1830: Beyond Jacobitism, towards Industrialisation* (Manchester: Manchester University Press, 2000), pp. 328–30.
77. Aitchison and Cassell, *Lowland Clearances*, pp. 73–89.
78. A. Black, *Gilfillan of Dundee, 1813–1878: Interpreting Religion and Culture in Mid-Victorian Scotland* (Dundee: Dundee University Press, 2006), pp. 171–2.
79. M. Chase, *Chartism: A New History* (Manchester: Manchester University Press, 2007).
80. Wilson, 'On the Genius and Character of Burns', p. xxx.
81. For an analysis of the political force of 'The Address of Beelzebub', see M. Butler, 'Burns and Politics', in R. Crawford (ed.), *Robert Burns and Cultural Authority* (Edinburgh: Edinburgh University Press, 1997), pp. 86–112, on pp. 91–2.
82. Tyrrell, 'Paternalism, Public Memory and National Identity', p. 57.
83. *Pilgrimage to The Shrine of Burns During the Festival with the Gathering of the Doon and other Poetical Pieces, By An Indian Officer* (Edinburgh: M'Dowall, Greig & Wahler, 1846), pp. 9–10.
84. Ferguson, Erskine, and Dixon, 'Commemorating and Collecting Burns', pp. 131–5.
85. *Belfast News-Letter*, 13 August 1844.
86. C. MacKay, *Forty Years Recollections of Life, Literary and Public Affairs*, 2 vols (London: Chapman & Hall, 1877), vol. 1, p. 259.
87. *Scotsman*, 10 August 1844.
88. *Glasgow Herald*, 28 June 1844.

89. T. Crawford, *Boswell, Burns and the French Revolution* (Edinburgh: Saltire Society, 1990), pp. 61–3.
90. For the 1805 date I am grateful to Kirsteen McCue, Centre for Robert Burns Studies, University of Glasgow; K. Bowan and P. A. Pickering, '"Songs for the Millions": Chartist Music and Popular Aural Tradition', *Labour History Review*, 74:1 (April 2009), pp. 44–63, on p. 55.
91. MacKay, *Forty Years Recollections*, p. 253.
92. J. Burnett, 'The Banner of Liberty: Symbols and the Celebration of the 1832 Reform Bill in Scotland', *Review of Scottish Culture*, 21 (2009), pp. 87–103, on p. 96.
93. Chase, *Chartism*, p. 143.
94. I. McCalman, *Radical Underworld: Prophets, Revolutionaries and Pornographers in London, 1795–1840* (Oxford: Oxford University Press, 1993), p. 211.
95. M. Vicinus, *The Industrial Muse: A Study of Nineteenth-Century Working-Class Literature* (London: Barnes & Noble, 1974), pp. 107–8.
96. Chase, *Chartism*, p. 56.
97. *Northern Star*, 24 August 1844.
98. *Belfast News-Letter*, 9 August 1844.
99. *Northern Star*, 26 August 1843.
100. *Glasgow Herald*, 28 June 1844.
101. *Northern Star*, 24 August 1844.
102. Tyrrell, 'Paternalism, Public Memory and National Identity', p. 43.
103. *Belfast News-Letter*, 6 September 1844.
104. G. Gilfillan, *The National Burns, Including The Airs of All the Songs and an Original Life of Burns*, 2 vols (Glasgow and London: William Mackenzie, 1879–80), vol. 1, p. cxix.
105. *Scotsman*, 27 January 1859; *Caledonian Mercury*, 25 January 1859.
106. G. Gilfillan, *The Martyrs and Heroes of the Scottish Covenant* (Edinburgh and London: Gall & Inglis, 1863 edn), pp. 228–30.
107. *Lloyd's Weekly Newspaper*, 30 January 1859.
108. *Illustrated London News*, 29 January 1859.
109. *Freeman's Journal and Daily Commercial Advertiser*, 31 December 1864.
110. *Scotsman*, 28 January 1859.
111. Much of what is said in this paragraph is based upon Ferguson, Erskine and Dixon, 'Commemorating and Collecting Burns', pp. 135–47.
112. *Scotsman*, 26 January 1859.
113. *Belfast News-Letter*, 25 January 1859.
114. *Scotsman*, 28 January 1859.
115. Ferguson, Erskine and Dixon, 'Commemorating and Collecting Burns', pp. 139, 147.

5 James, '"Blessèd Jubil!": Slavery, Mission and the Millennial Dawn in the Work of William Williams of Pantycelyn

1. T. Beynon, *Howell Harris, Reformer and Soldier* (Caernarfon: Calvinistic Methodist Bookroom, 1958), p. 50; E. Welch, *Spiritual Pilgrim: A Reassessment of the Life of the Countess of Huntingdon* (Cardiff: University of Wales Press, 1995), pp. 44, 54, 56.
2. D. C. Jones, *'A Glorious Work in the World': Welsh Methodism and the International Evangelical Revival, 1735–1750* (Cardiff: University of Wales Press, 2004), pp. 1–4, 20–32, 44–7.

3. E. Evans, Review of *Queen of the Methodists* (B. S. Schlenther), *Cylchgrawn Hanes* (Journal of the Historical Society of the Presbyterian Church of Wales), 22 (1998), pp. 77–82, on p. 81.
4. Welch, *Spiritual Pilgrim*, p. 54, cf. pp. 125–6.
5. On Harris, see G. F. Nuttall, *Howel Harris 1714–1773: The Last Enthusiast* (Cardiff: University of Wales Press, 1965); E. Evans, *Howel Harris, Evangelist* (Cardiff: University of Wales Press, 1974); G. Tudur, *Howell Harris: From Conversion to Separation 1735–1750* (Cardiff: University of Wales Press, 2000).
6. R. G. Gruffydd, 'The Revival of 1762 and William Williams of Pantycelyn', in E. Roberts and R. G. Gruffydd, *Revival and Its Fruit* (Bridgend: Evangelical Library of Wales, 1981), pp. 19–40, on pp. 21–2.
7. Welch, *Spiritual Pilgrim*, pp. 64, 88–9.
8. Welch, *Spiritual Pilgrim*, pp. 112–16; G. F. Nuttall, *The Significance of Trevecca College 1768–91* (London: Epworth Press, 1969), pp. 4–6.
9. J. Julian (ed.), *A Dictionary of Hymnology*, rev. edn (London: John Murray, 1915), p. 77; J. R. Watson, *An Annotated Anthology of Hymns* (Oxford: Oxford University Press, 2002), p. 228. The hymn is an English reworking of a Welsh-language hymn published by Williams in 1762.
10. Gruffydd, 'The Revival of 1762 and William Williams of Pantycelyn', pp. 23, 25–6.
11. K. Jenkins, 'Williams Pantycelyn', in B. Jarvis (ed.), *A Guide to Welsh Literature c. 1700–1800* (Cardiff: University of Wales Press, 2000), pp. 256–78, on p. 273; D. G. Jones, 'Some Recent Trends in Welsh Literature', in J. E. C. Williams (ed.), *Literature in Celtic Countries* (Cardiff: University of Wales Press, 1971), pp. 175–92, on pp. 182–4.
12. Bearing in mind the predominance of pilgrimage as a theme in Pantycelyn's hymns, it is interesting to see James Abbington, in a paper entitled 'Unsung Hymns by Black and Unknown Bards: Charles Albert Tindley (1851–1933)', delivered at the International Hymn Conference in Opole, Poland in 2009, emphasizing the recurring image of 'the pilgrim' in the work of Tindley, the 'father of African American hymnody'.
13. For good introductions in English to Williams and his work, see E. Evans, *Bread of Heaven: The Life and Work of William Williams, Pantycelyn* (Bridgend: Bryntirion Press, 2010) and G. T. Hughes, *Williams Pantycelyn* (Cardiff: University of Wales Press, 1983). See also the bibliography in K. Jenkins, 'Williams Pantycelyn', pp. 277–8. His key role in the development of the Welsh hymn is discussed in E. W. James, 'The Evolution of the Welsh Hymn', in I. Rivers and D. L. Wykes (eds), *Dissenting Praise: Religious Dissent and the Hymn in England and Wales* (Oxford: Oxford University Press, 2011), pp. 229–68.
14. [A. C. H. Seymour], *The Life and Times of Selina Countess of Huntingdon*, 2 vols (London: W. E. Painter, 1839), vol. 1, pp. 84–5; vol. 2, pp. 98–100, 107–8, 112–14; G. M. Roberts, *Y Per Ganiedydd*, vol. 1 (Llandysul: Gwasg Aberystwyth, 1949), pp. 148–50. See also E. Welch, 'Three Letters from William Williams, Pantycelyn, to Lady Huntingdon', *Journal of the Historical Society of the Presbyterian Church of Wales*, 53:3 (September 1968), pp. 56–61.
15. Quoted (in Welsh) in [T. Charles], 'Buchwedd a Marwolaeth y Parch. William Williams, o Bant y Celyn, Sir Gaerfyrddin', *Trysorfa*, 2:11 (January 1813), pp. 443–54, on p. 448.
16. R. Bennett, *Howell Harris and the Dawn of Revival*, tr. from Welsh by G. M. Roberts, 2nd English edn (Bridgend: Evangelical Press of Wales, 1987), p. 86; Welch, *Spiritual Pilgrim*, pp. 131–2.

17. F. Cook, *Selina Countess of Huntingdon* (Edinburgh: Banner of Truth Trust, 2001), pp. 316–17.
18. Welch, *Spiritual Pilgrim*, pp. 133–4.
19. See, for example, J. Coffey, 'Evangelicals, Slavery & the Slave Trade: From Whitefield to Wilberforce', *Anvil*, 24:2 (2007), pp. 97–119, on pp. 97–101; Cook, *Selina Countess of Huntingdon*, p. 316.
20. Welch, *Spiritual Pilgrim*, pp. 144–5. Whitefield made provision for the instruction of the black slaves at Bethesda in the Christian faith ([Seymour], *The Life and Times of Selina Countess of Huntingdon*, vol. 2, pp. 251–2, 265) and the Countess of Huntingdon made similar provision (Welch, *Spiritual Pilgrim*, pp. 139, 142; [Seymour], *The Life and Times of Selina Countess of Huntingdon*, vol. 2, pp. 262, 272). It is difficult to accept B. S. Schlenther's assertion, in his *Queen of the Methodists* (Durham: Durham Academic Press, 1997), p. 91, that 'Lady Huntingdon's concern even for the salvation of slaves was strangely muted'; in the case of Bethesda, all evidence suggests that any blame for neglect in this matter, and for the increase in the number of slaves at the orphanage and their treatment in general, should be laid at the door of her staff there, and in particular the person in charge, William Piercy, rather than the Countess herself, who had only very intermittent contact with Bethesda, because of the distances involved, not to mention the American War of Independence – see Welch, *Spiritual Pilgrim*, ch. 8 and ch. 10; Schlenther, *Queen of the Methodists*, pp. 87–91; [Seymour], *The Life and Times of Selina Countess of Huntingdon*, vol. 2, pp. 267–70.
21. For a balanced discussion of George Whitefield and slavery, see A. A. Dallimore, *George Whitefield*, vol. 1 (London: Banner of Truth Trust, 1970), pp. 207–8, 482–3, 495–501, 508–9, 588; vol. 2 (Edinburgh: Banner of Truth Trust, 1980), pp. 219, 367–8, 520–1. See also Whitefield's letter, 'To the inhabitants of Maryland, Virginia, North and South-Carolina, concerning their Negroes' (1740), reprinted in M. M. Smith and T. Lockley (eds), *Slavery in North America: From the Colonial Period to Emancipation*, vol. 1 (London: Pickering & Chatto, 2009), pp. 223–6.
22. *An Elegiac Poem, on the Death of that Celebrated Divine, and Eminent Servant of Jesus Christ, the Reverend and Learned George Whitefield, Chaplain to the Right Honourable the Countess of Huntingdon* (Boston, MA: Ezekiel Russell and John Boyles, [1770]), p. 7. Wheatley addresses the Countess thus in the elegy: 'Great COUNTESS! we *Americans* revere / Thy name, and thus condole thy grief sincere: / We mourn with thee, that TOMB obscurely plac'd, / In which thy Chaplain undisturb'd doth rest.' A revised version of the elegy was included in the volume of Wheatley's poems, *Poems on Various Subjects, Religious and Moral*, published in London in 1773 and dedicated to the Countess of Huntingdon. In the 1773 edition the line 'If you will chuse to walk in grace's road' is replaced by 'Wash'd in the fountain of redeeming blood'. In a variant of the couplet on a broadside circulated in London, the liberation discourse is more explicit: 'If you will walk in Grace's heavenly Road, / He'll make you free, and Kings, and Priests to God'; see H. Thomas, *Romanticism and Slave Narratives* (Cambridge: Cambridge University Press, 2000), p. 216.
23. N. C. Jones, *Gweithiau Williams Pant-y-Celyn*, vol. 1 (Treffynnon [Holywell]: P. M. Evans & Son, 1887), p. 489. There is an irony in the phrase used here in Welsh by Williams Pantycelyn for 'blessed holy gospel', namely 'efengyl wen fendigaid', as the adjective '[g]wen' can mean 'white' as well as 'holy, blessed; fair, splendid'.
24. D. W. Bebbington, *Evangelicalism in Modern Britain* (London: Unwin Hyman, 1989), p. 71.

25. R. Robinson, *Slavery Inconsistent with the Spirit of Christianity* (Cambridge: J. Archdeacon, 1788), p. 3; quoted in B. Stanley, 'Baptists, Anti-Slavery and the Legacy of Imperialism', *Baptist Quarterly*, 42:4 (October 2007), pp. 284–96, on p. 285. The words in italics are direct quotations from the Bible.
26. Coffey, 'Evangelicals, Slavery & the Slave Trade', p. 101.
27. R. Wheeler, *The Complexion of Race: Categories of Difference in Eighteenth-Century British Culture* (Philadelphia, PA: University of Pennsylvania Press, 2000), pp. 5, 15–16.
28. Bebbington, *Evangelicalism in Modern Britain*, p. 5.
29. Coffey, 'Evangelicals, Slavery & the Slave Trade', pp. 101, 102, 103.
30. Bebbington, *Evangelicalism in Modern Britain*, pp. 71–2; Coffey, 'Evangelicals, Slavery & the Slave Trade', pp. 107–8; E. W. James, 'Welsh Ballads and American Slavery', *Welsh Journal of Religious History*, 2 (2007), pp. 59–86, on pp. 71–85 (an electronic version of this article is to be found on the Welsh Ballads website).
31. [Charles], 'Buchwedd a Marwolaeth y Parch. William Williams', p. 448.
32. W. I. Morgan, 'George Owen, Llwyn-gwair, a'i Deulu', *Bathafarn*, 22 (1967), pp. 37–48; 23 (1968), pp. 14–24.
33. A. H. Williams (ed.), *John Wesley in Wales 1739–1790* (Cardiff: University of Wales Press, 1971), pp. 87, 94, 97, 100, 115, 121, 125.
34. Morgan, 'George Owen, Llwyn-gwair, a'i Deulu', *Bathafarn*, 22 (1967), p. 41; K. Buckley, 'Did John Wesley really come to Meidrim', *Capel*, 17 (Autumn 1992), pp. 2–3, on p. 3.
35. G. M. Roberts (ed.), *Hanes Methodistiaeth Galfinaidd Cymru: Cyfrol II. Cynnydd y Corff* (Caernarfon: Llyfrfa'r Methodistiad Calfinaidd, 1978), p. 125.
36. G. M. Roberts, *Y Per Ganiedydd*, vol. 2 (Llandysul: Gwasg Aberystwyth, 1958), p. 82. A story based on this tradition was published by the Welsh short-story writer, D. J. Williams (1885–1970), in his collection, *Storïau'r Tir Glas* ([Aberystwyth]: Gwasg Aberystwyth, 1936). A variant of the tradition says that Pantycelyn composed the hymn after having to turn back while travelling from Llwyn-gwair to the Methodist meeting house at Woodstock on the other side of the Preseli hills because of the mist (*Y Goleuad*, 3 November 1989, p. 1). Another source says his inspiration was seeing the dawn break over the Frenni mountain, on the eastern side of the Preseli hills: [G. P. Griffiths (ed.)], *Handbook to the Great Missionary Exhibition* (Swansea: Lewis Evans, 1907), p. 68.
37. Roberts, *Y Per Ganiedydd*, vol. 1, pp. 21, 39, 149, 185; vol. 2, pp. 82–3, 96; 'Hen Gapel y Gyfylchi', *Yr Adolygydd*, 2:4 (March 1852), pp. 496–507, on pp. 499–500; D. Davies, 'Capel y Gyfylchi', *Y Drysorfa*, 62 (1892), pp. 142–6, on pp. 143, 144; D. Davies, 'Yma a Thraw ym Morgannwg', *Cymru*, 16 (1899), pp. 252–9, on pp. 254–5, 257; G. Thomas, *Lloffyn Olaf o Faes Hynafiaethau Capel y Gyfylchi* (Treorchy: T. J. Davies, [1900]), pp. 34–7, 44, 85, 119; W. S. Williams, 'Capel y Gyfylchi', *Y Drysorfa*, 87 (1917), pp. 304–7, on pp. 306–7; T. Beynon, *Braslun o Hanes Gyfylchi a Jerusalem, Pontrhydyfen* (Port Talbot: D. W. Jones, 1926), pp. 30, 40; R. L. Brown, 'Capel y Gyfylchi', *Afan Uchaf: The Journal of the Cymer Afan and District Historical Society*, 1 (1978), pp. 25–46, on p. 29; 'Some More Notes on Gyfylchi Chapel', *Afan Uchaf*, 2 (1979), pp. 58–9, on p. 58. (In passing, it may be of interest to note that the actor Richard Burton (Richard Walter Jenkins, 1925–84) was from Pont-rhyd-y-fen.)
38. [Seymour], *The Life and Times of Selina Countess of Huntingdon*, vol. 2, pp. 112–14. (The name 'Llwyn-gwair' is spelt 'Languire' in Seymour's volume.)
39. 'travel' means travail.
40. See Matthew 4:16; Luke 1:79, 2:32.

41. See Isaiah 8:8. In John Bunyan's *The Pilgrim's Progress* (London: Nath. Ponder, 1678), the Delectable Mountains, which provide a resting place for pilgrims on their way to the Celestial City, are also called Immanuel's Land.
42. See Exodus 15:15; Psalm 108:9. Moab and Philistia were the lands of traditional enemies of the Israelites, the one to the east and the other to the west of the southern Israelite kingdom of Judah.
43. S. Lewis, *Williams Pantycelyn* (London: Foyle's Welsh Depôt, 1927); R. T. Jones, *Saunders Lewis a Williams Pantycelyn* (Swansea: University College of Swansea, 1987). See also G. T. Hughes, 'Pantycelyn a'r Piwritaniaid', in D. Ll. Morgan (ed.), *Meddwl a Dychymyg Williams Pantycelyn* (Llandysul: Gwasg Gomer, 1991), pp. 31–54.
44. See G. H. Jenkins, *Protestant Dissenters in Wales, 1639–1689* (Cardiff: University of Wales Press, 1992), pp. 15–16, 77; M. W. Thomas, *Morgan Llwyd* (Cardiff: University of Wales Press, 1984); D. Ll. Morgan, 'Morgan Llwyd a'r Iddewon', in J. E. C. Williams (ed.), *Ysgrifau Beirniadol XXI* (Denbigh: Gwasg Gee, 1996), pp. 81–96; G. W. Owen, *Cewri'r Cyfamod* (Bangor: Centre for the Advanced Study of Religion in Wales, Bangor University, 2008), ch. 3. Llwyd was heavily influenced by Fifth Monarchism.
45. I. H. Murray, *The Puritan Hope: A Study in Revival and the Interpretation of Prophecy* (London: Banner of Truth Trust, 1971), pp. 52–5, 187; Bebbington, *Evangelicalism in Modern Britain*, pp. 62–3, 81–5, 191.
46. G. H. Hughes (ed.), *Gweithiau William Williams Pantycelyn. Cyfrol II. Rhyddiaith* (Cardiff: University of Wales Press, 1967), pp. 164, 171–9; D. A. Hughes, 'William Williams Pantycelyn's Eschatology as Seen Especially in his *Aurora Borealis* of 1744', *Scottish Bulletin of Evangelical Theology*, 4:1 (Spring 1986), pp. 49–63, on pp. 50–2, 59.
47. See Hughes, 'William Williams Pantycelyn's Eschatology', p. 56, and Evans, *Bread of Heaven*, pp. 237–8, for Williams Pantycelyn's reaction to the Lisbon and other earthquakes of 1755–6, where he states that they cannot signify the end of the world, since all the events that Scripture promised would occur in the 'last days', including the evangelization of the whole world, had not yet come to pass.
48. T. Evans, *The History of Modern Enthusiasm* (London: W. Owen and W. Clarke, [1752]), p. 75. In the preface to the second, enlarged edition, published in 1757, he returns to the matter, accusing 'deluding and deluded *Methodistical* Teachers' of pretending 'to foretel that the *Glorious Millenium* begins to dawn upon the World, when the Wicked shall all be destroyed, and *they* (the Saints) shall alone bear Dominion' (p. xii).
49. Trevecka Letters, no. 1381, Calvinistic Methodist Archives, MS Aberystwyth, National Library of Wales (the punctuation and orthography have been revised). For a transcript of the letter, see G. Tibbott, 'Un o Lythyrau Anghyhoeddedig Williams, Pantycelyn', *Journal of the Historical Society of the Presbyterian Church of Wales*, 20:4 (December 1935), pp. 131–7, on pp. 132–4. See also Hughes, 'William Williams Pantycelyn's Eschatology', pp. 54, 61; Evans, *Bread of Heaven*, pp. 57–9.
50. NLW 4798E, f. 57, MS Aberystwyth, National Library of Wales (the punctuation and orthography have been revised). For a transcript of the letter, see Roberts, *Y Per Ganiedydd*, vol. 1, pp. 161–2.
51. Murray, *The Puritan Hope*, p. 51.
52. D. A. Hughes, *Meddiannu Tir Immanuel: Cymru a Mudiad Cenhadol y Ddeunawfed Ganrif* (Bridgend: Evangelical Library of Wales, 1990), p. 26.
53. Quoted in Murray, *The Puritan Hope*, p. 132.
54. James, 'Welsh Ballads and American Slavery', pp. 62–3; E. W. James, 'Williams Pantycelyn a Gwawr y Mudiad Cenhadol', in G. H. Jenkins (ed.), *Cof Cenedl XVII* (Llandysul:

Gwasg Gomer, 2002), pp. 65–101, on pp. 86–9; Hughes, *Meddiannu Tir Immanuel*, pp. 12–21; Hughes, 'William Williams Pantycelyn's Eschatology', pp. 56–8; Evans, *Bread of Heaven*, pp. 163–71, 238–9, 308.

55. On these missionary ventures, see G. F. Nuttall, 'The Students of Trevecca College 1768–1791', *Transactions of the Honourable Society of Cymmrodorion*, Session 1967: part 2 (1968), pp. 249–77, on pp. 255–9; [Seymour], *The Life and Times of Selina Countess of Huntingdon*, vol. 2, ch. 40 and ch. 41; Welch, *Spiritual Pilgrim*, ch. 8 and ch. 10; A. Harding, *The Countess of Huntingdon's Connexion* (Oxford: Oxford University Press, 2003), pp. 205–9; Cook, *Selina Countess of Huntingdon*, ch. 24; and (for a more controversial appraisal) Schlenther, *Queen of the Methodists*, ch. 6. In a letter to the Countess, Williams Pantycelyn expresses his wish 'that the Lord may prosper his work in the Colledge [at Trefeca] and by those that were sent to America' (Welch, 'Three Letters from William Williams, Pantycelyn, to Lady Huntingdon', pp. 60–1).

56. Hughes, 'William Williams Pantycelyn's Eschatology', pp. 49–53, 58–63; Evans, *Bread of Heaven*, pp. 232–42; Hughes, *Williams Pantycelyn*, pp. 70–5. B. S. Schlenther notes that the Countess of Huntingdon's belief in the imminence of the Millennium led to her encouraging relevant publications in the early 1770s (*Queen of the Methodists*, pp. 86, 93, n. 21), and Pantycelyn's *Aurora Borealis* fits well into that category.

57. Hughes, *Gweithiau William Williams Pantycelyn. Cyfrol II. Rhyddiaith*, p. 179 (my translation into English of this sentence and the volume's subtitle). G. F. Nuttall in his volume, *The Welsh Saints 1640–1660* (Cardiff: University of Wales Press, 1957), pp. 48–9, suggests that the use of the imagery of summer being close at hand for the imminent Millennium, which is frequently found in Morgan Llwyd's works, may be 'peculiarly Llwydian'. It is possible, therefore, that Llwyd is the inspiration for that imagery in Pantycelyn's work.

58. Pantycelyn refers to Eliot in the section of his *Pantheologia* which discusses Native Americans. See Hughes, *Meddiannu Tir Immanuel*, pp. 9, 17–19; Hughes, 'William Williams Pantycelyn's Eschatology', pp. 56–7.

59. [Seymour], *The Life and Times of Selina Countess of Huntingdon*, vol. 1, pp. 298–9, 411–13; W. DeLoss Love, *Samson Occom and the Christian Indians of New England*, new edn (Syracuse, NY: Syracuse University Press, 2000), ch. 8. His name is sometimes spelt Occum. His sermon on the execution of Moses Paul (who like Occom belonged to the Mohegan tribe) was published in English in 1772, and is regarded as an important milestone in the history of publishing by Native Americans. A Welsh translation of that sermon was published by the radical Baptist minister and abolitionist, Morgan John Rhys (or Rhees; 1760–1804) in 1789. For Rhys's abolitionist activities, see James, 'Welsh Ballads and American Slavery', pp. 67–8; H. M. Davies, *Transatlantic Brethren* (Bethlehem, PA: Lehigh University Press/London: Associated University Presses, 1995); E. W. James, 'Morgan John Rhys a Chaethwasiaeth Americanaidd', in D. G. Williams (ed.), *Canu Caeth: Y Cymry a'r Affro-Americaniaid* (Llandysul: Gwasg Gomer, 2010), pp. 2–25.

60. Welch, *Spiritual Pilgrim*, pp. 169–71, 173; [Seymour], *The Life and Times of Selina Countess of Huntingdon*, vol. 2, pp. 273–4.

61. Welch, *Spiritual Pilgrim*, p. 135; Cook, *Selina Countess of Huntingdon*, p. 319.

62. It was also impeded significantly by tensions between the students and William Piercy, the man in charge at Bethesda, who sought to prevent them from evangelizing the Native Americans. These tensions led to all five students leaving Bethesda by 1775; see Cook, *Selina Countess of Huntingdon*, pp. 322–3, 325–6, 328; Schlenther, *Queen of the*

Methodists, p. 94, n. 35; Davies, *Transatlantic Brethren*, p. 169; Hughes, *Meddiannu Tir Immanuel*, pp. 40–1.
63. Cook, *Selina Countess of Huntingdon*, p. 327. Coincidentally, in the following century, a Welshman from the Trefeca area, Evan Jones (1788–1872), and his son, John Buttrick Jones (1824–76), conducted significant missionary work among the Cherokee. See W. G. McLoughlin, *Champions of the Cherokees: Evan and John B. Jones* (Princeton, NJ: Princeton University Press, 1990).
64. Welch, *Spiritual Pilgrim*, pp. 139, 142; [Seymour], *The Life and Times of Selina Countess of Huntingdon*, vol. 2, p. 262; W. M. Price, 'The Countess of Huntingdon and Missionary Enterprise', *Journal of the Historical Society of the Presbyterian Church of Wales*, 27:3 (September 1942), pp. 130–1, on p. 130.
65. Phillis Wheatley paid a visit to London in 1773, but did not meet the Countess, as she was at Trefeca at the time: Welch, *Spiritual Pilgrim*, p. 144; Thomas, *Romanticism and Slave Narratives*, pp. 205–6. It is interesting to see Phillis Wheatley, in a letter to the Native American minister, Samson Occom, using the same imagery of light 'chasing' darkness as Williams Pantycelyn in his 'O'er those gloomy hills of darkness'. In her letter (published in the *Connecticut Gazette*, 11 March 1774), she says, in discussing the 'natural Rights' of black people, 'that the divine Light is chasing away the thick Darkness which broods over the Land of Africa'.
66. A. Potkay and S. Burr (eds), *Black Atlantic Writers of the Eighteenth Century* (Basingstoke: Macmillan Press, 1995), includes substantial selections from the narratives of Ukawsaw Gronniosaw, John Marrant, Olaudah Equiano and Quobna Ottobah Cugoana and details of their publishing history. Adam Potkay, in his introduction to that volume, draws particular attention to the fact that the appearance of George Whitefield, 'as character and as symbol, [is] an important motif of black autobiography': 'Whitefield himself – as a preacher and as a man – is a crucial presence in early black Atlantic autobiography' (pp. 8–9). It is also striking that theologically the authors of these 'slave narratives' espouse Calvinism rather than Arminianism (p. 8), despite the strong opposition of the Arminian Methodist leader, John Wesley, to slavery, as compared to the Calvinistic Methodist, George Whitefield.
67. Harding, *The Countess of Huntingdon's Connexion*, pp. 209, 376; Welch, *Spiritual Pilgrim*, p. 142; Schlenther, *Queen of the Methodists*, p. 91; 'Margate and Jeremiah', in Smith and Lockley (eds), *Slavery in North America: From the Colonial Period to Emancipation*, vol. 1, pp. 289–301.
68. Cook, *Selina Countess of Huntingdon*, p. 440; G. W. Kirby, *The Elect Lady* (Croydon: Countess of Huntingdon Connexion, 1972), p. 60; J. Saillant, 'Hymnody and the Persistence of an African-American Faith in Sierra Leone', *Hymn*, 48:1 (January 1997), pp. 8–17.
69. H. M. Davies, 'Morgan John Rhys and James Bicheno: Anti-Christ and the French Revolution in England and Wales', *Bulletin of the Board of Celtic Studies*, 29:1 (November 1980), pp. 111–27.
70. T. Fulford, *Romantic Indians: Native Americans, British Literature, and Transatlantic Culture 1756–1830* (Oxford: Oxford University Press, 2006), ch. 7.
71. G. Carr, *William Owen Pughe* (Cardiff: University of Wales Press, 1983), ch. 6.
72. D. E. Jenkins, *The Life of Thomas Charles*, vol. 2 (Denbigh: Llewelyn Jenkins, 1908), ch. 38; F. P. Jones, *Radicaliaeth a'r Werin Gymreig yn y Bedwaredd Ganrif ar Bymtheg* (Cardiff: University of Wales Press, 1977), pp. 23–8.
73. Hughes, *Meddiannu Tir Immanuel*, p. 24.

74. J. H. Morris, *Hanes Cenhadaeth Dramor y Methodistiaid Calfinaidd Cymreig* (Caernarfon: Llyfrfa y Cyfundeb, 1907), p. 9. That year, 1795, also saw the translation into Welsh of the hymn 'O'er those gloomy hills of darkness', a translation which would become very popular. It was made by Pantycelyn's son, John Williams (1754–1828), who was master of Trefeca College from 1786 to 1791. For the Welsh text and a discussion of the translation, see James, 'Williams Pantycelyn a Gwawr y Mudiad Cenhadol', pp. 77–9.

75. It is worth emphasizing that, in addition to its worldwide influence, the overseas missionary movement also impacted heavily on the religious, social and intellectual life of Wales, as regards activities, perceptions and globalization, making places like Madagascar and the Khasia Hills of north-east India as familiar to large sections of the Welsh population as Manchester and Birmingham, and making the missionary collection boxes and Sunday-school gift books on missionary topics an integral part of Welsh chapel life for generations. As Aled Gruffydd Jones has underlined, the missionary movement would prove a significant element in the development of a body of Welsh travel writing, in the enhancement of the profile of women in religious and public life and in the growth of modernity and Welsh national consciousness: A. G. Jones, '"Meddylier am yr India": Tair Taith y Genhadaeth Gymreig yn Sylhet, 1887–1947', *Transactions of the Honourable Society of Cymmrodorion 1997*, 4 (1998), pp. 84–110; A. G. Jones, 'The Other Internationalism? Missionary Activity and Welsh Nonconformist Perceptions of the World in the Nineteenth and Twentieth Centuries', in C. Williams, N. Evans and P. O'Leary (eds), *A Tolerant Nation? Exploring Ethnic Diversity in Wales* (Cardiff: University of Wales Press, 2003), pp. 49–60.

76. B. Stanley, *The Bible and the Flag: Protestant Missions and British Imperialism in the Nineteenth and Twentieth Centuries* (Leicester: Apollos, 1990), pp. 74–8; Bebbington, *Evangelicalism in Modern Britain*, pp. 191–4.

77. Stanley, *The Bible and the Flag*, p. 77; cf. Bebbington, *Evangelicalism in Modern Britain*, pp. 84–5.

78. See Bebbington, *Evangelicalism in Modern Britain*, ch. 2; Stanley, *The Bible and the Flag*, pp. 61–3; M. A. G. Haykin and K. J. Stewart (eds), *The Emergence of Evangelicalism: Exploring Historical Continuities* (Nottingham: Apollos, 2008); E. W. James, 'Griffith Jones (1684–1761) of Llanddowror and His "Striking Experiment in Mass Religious Education" in Wales in the Eighteenth Century', in R. Siegert (ed.), *Volksbildung durch Lesestoffe im 18. und 19. Jahrhundert/Educating the People through Reading Material in the 18th and 19th Centuries* (Bremen, Germany: Edition Lumière, 2012), pp. 275–89.

79. James, 'Welsh Ballads and American Slavery', p. 73.

80. Potkay and Burr (eds), *Black Atlantic Writers of the Eighteenth Century*, p. 10. It hardly needs emphasizing that such ambiguity is a commonplace in African-American 'spirituals'.

81. On the Welsh involvement in slavery and the abolition movement, see A. Llwyd, *Black Wales: A History of Black Welsh People* (Cardiff: Hughes a'i Fab, 2005); C. Evans, *Slave Wales: The Welsh and Atlantic Slavery, 1660–1850* (Cardiff: University of Wales Press, 2010); James, 'Welsh Ballads and American Slavery'.

82. James, 'Morgan John Rhys a Chaethwasiaeth Americanaidd', p. 19.

83. 'Cof-nodau o Gymdeithasfa (Association) a gynhaliwyd yn Machynlleth, Ebrill 15 a'r 16, 1795', *Trysorfa Ysbrydol*, 1:3 (October 1799), pp. 164–70, on pp. 169–70 (my translation); see also R. W. James, 'Ymateb y Methodistiad Calfinaidd Cymraeg i'r Chwyldro Ffrengig', *Cylchgrawn Hanes* (Journal of the Historical Society of the Presbyterian Church of Wales), 12–13 (1988/9), pp. 35–60, on p. 38.

84. R. T. Jenkins, *Hanes Cymru yn y Bedwaredd Ganrif ar Bymtheg* (Cardiff: University of Wales Press, 1933), p. 51. (It should perhaps be explained that the Welsh Methodists, who were almost exclusively Calvinist in theology in the eighteenth century, finally seceded from the Established Church in 1811, and would become known as the Welsh Calvinistic Methodist Connexion, subsequently the Calvinistic Methodist or Presbyterian Church of Wales.)
85. Saillant, 'Hymnody and the Persistence of an African-American Faith in Sierra Leone', pp. 8–17.

6 Löffler, 'Serial Literature and Radical Poetry in Wales at the End of the Eighteenth Century'

1. *Chester Chronicle*, 27 July 1798.
2. The English literary device of 'hardening' voiced consonants to denote Welshness is based on the phonetic feature of 'calediad' associated with the Welsh dialect of the Tawe valley in south-west Wales. See S. E. Thomas, 'A Study of Calediad in the Upper Swansea Valley', in M. J. Ball (ed.), *The Use of Welsh: A Contribution to Sociolinguistics* (Clevedon: Multilingual Matters, 1988), pp. 85–96.
3. T. Eagleton, *The Function of Criticism: From The Spectator to Post-Structuralism* (London: Verso, 1984), p. 36.
4. L. Miskell, *Intelligent Town: An Urban History of Swansea, 1780–1855* (Cardiff: University of Wales Press, 2006), p. 18.
5. J. Williams, *Digest of Welsh Historical Statistics*, 2 vols (Aberystwyth: University College of Wales, 1985), vol. 1, pp. 62–7; P. Jenkins, 'Wales', in P. Clark (ed.), *Cambridge Urban History of Britain, Volume 2 1540–1840* (Cambridge: Cambridge University Press, 2000), pp. 133–47, esp. pp. 133–6; G. H. Jenkins, *The Foundations of Modern Wales 1642–1780* (Oxford: Oxford University Press, 1987), pp. 286–9.
6. D. J. V. Jones, *Before Rebecca: Popular Protests in Wales 1793–1835* (London: Allan Lane, 1973), pp. 60–6.
7. G. A. Williams, 'Druids and Democrats: Organic Intellectuals and the First Welsh Nation', in G. A. Williams, *The Welsh in their History* (London and Canberra: Helm Croom, 1982), pp. 31–64.
8. M. H. Thuente, *The Harp Re-strung: The United Irishmen and the Rise of Irish Literary Nationalism* (Syracuse, NY: Syracuse University Press, 1994), pp. 125, 133–69.
9. J. Barrell,*'Exhibition Extraordinary!' Radical Broadsides of the Mid 1790s* (Nottingham: Trent Editions, 2001), pp. vii–x.
10. For the working of the press in late eighteenth-century Wales, see Löffler, *Welsh Responses to the French Revolution*, pp. 3–5.
11. A. Jones, 'The Newspaper Press in Wales, 1804–1945', in P. H. Jones and E. Rees (eds), *A Nation and its Books: A History of the Book in Wales* (Aberystwyth: National Library of Wales, 1998), pp. 209–19.
12. R. Prichard, 'Rhyfedd-fyrr Olygiad yn Nrych y Drindod', in D. Jones (ed.), *Blodeu-gerdd Cymry* (Y Mwythig: Stafford Prys, 1759), p. 425. I am grateful to E. Wyn James for this reference.
13. R. Roberts, 'Yn gosod allan y moddion am y Rhyfeloedd presennol rhyngom a'r Ffrangcod, a dull grefydd Babaidd, ar King George Delight' (s. l., *c.* 1794).

14. E. Williams [I. Morganwg], *The Correspondence of Iolo Morganwg*, eds G. H. Jenkins, F. M. Jones and D. C. Jones, 3 vols (Cardiff: University of Wales Press, 2007), vol. 1, pp. 789, 801–2, 811; Tomos Glyn Cothi's seditious notebook, 'Y Gell Gymysg', National Library of Wales (hereafter NLW) MS 6238A, *passim*; 'Diary, &c., of John Davies, Ystrad', NLW MS 12350A., *passim*.
15. W. D. Leathart, *The Origin and Progress of the Gwyneddigion Society of London instituted M.DCC.LXX* (London: Hugh Pierce Hughes, 1831); R. T. Jenkins and H. M. Ramage, *The History of the Honourable Society of Cymmrodorion and of the Gwyneddigion and Cymreigyddion Societies (1751–1951)* (London: Honourable Society of Cymmrodorion, 1951); G. Carr, 'The London Welsh', in Jones and Rees (eds), *A Nation and its Books*, pp. 147–57. For the contribution of Iolo Morganwg to metropolitan literature, see M.-A. Constantine and E. Edwards, '"Bard of Liberty": Iolo Morganwg, Wales and Radical Song', in J. Kirk, A. Noble and M. Brown (eds), *United Islands? The Languages of Resistance* (London: Pickering & Chatto, 2012), pp. 63–79.
16. For the significance of the revival of the eisteddfod, see P. Morgan, *The Eighteenth Century Renaissance* (Llandybïe: Christopher Davies, 1981), pp. 63–6.
17. For content and circulation of these newspapers see Löffler, *Welsh Responses to the French Revolution*, pp. 8–26.
18. H. Barker, *Newspapers, Politics, and Public Opinion in Late Eighteenth-Century England* (Oxford: Oxford University Press, 1998), p. 122.
19. Its editor Thomas Wood was in close contact with loyalist Welsh poets like Thomas Jones (Rhaiadr). See Löffler, *Welsh Responses to the French Revolution*, p. 11.
20. Regular as well as occasional bardic names have been an integral part of Welsh culture since early modern times. Throughout, authors and poets will therefore be referred to by the bardic names with which they signed and by which most of them are still known in Wales.
21. *Chester Chronicle*, 1 August 1794. The poets are discussed, respectively, in E. Edwards, *English-Language Poetry from Wales 1789–1805* (Cardiff: University of Wales Press, 2013) and C. Charnell-White, *Welsh Poetry of the French Revolution 1789–1805* (Cardiff: University of Wales Press, 2012).
22. *Morning Chronicle*, 26 September 1793.
23. E. Williams, *Poems, Lyric and Pastoral*, 2 vols (London: J. Nichols, 1794), vol. 2, pp. 160–8.
24. *Chester Chronicle*, 25 July 1794.
25. J. B. Edwards, 'John Jones (Jac Glan-y-gors): Tom Paine's Denbighshire Henchman?', *Denbighshire Historical Society Transactions*, 51 (2002), pp. 95–112. The best source for the life and letters of Glan-y-gors is still M. P. Jones, 'John Jones of Glan-y-gors', *Transactions of the Honourable Society of Cymmrodorion* (1911), pp. 60–94.
26. Jones, 'John Jones of Glan-y-gors', pp. 72–3. Text and translation of this pamphlet will be published in M. Löffler (with B. Jenkins), *Political Pamphlets and Sermons from Wales 1790–1806*, a forthcoming volume in the University of Wales series on Wales and the French Revolution.
27. *Chester Chronicle*, 21 November 1794; Löffler, 'Cerddi Newydd gan John Jones', pp. 143–50.
28. *Chester Chronicle*, 4 March 1796.
29. This may be a topical reference to an attack on the King's carriage reported in the *Chester Chronicle*, 12 February 1796.

30. *Chester Chronicle*, 11 March 1796. Note that 'Bywyd RHYDD', i.e. a 'FREE life', in the original Welsh was changed to the less incriminating 'LOVE, CHARITY and PEACE' in the English version.
31. Translation and the transfer of (revolutionary) ideas are the theme of M. Löffler and H. Williams, *Translating the French Revolution in Wales*, a forthcoming volume in the University of Wales series on Wales and the French Revolution.
32. J. Jones [J. Glanygors], *Cerddi Jac Glan-y-Gors*, ed. E. G. Millward (Cyhoeddiadau Barddas, 2003), p. 101.
33. Annotated texts and translations in Löffler, *Welsh Responses to the French Revolution*, pp. 146–51.
34. *Chester Chronicle*, 21 August 1795.
35. *Chester Chronicle*, 28 December 1792.
36. Löffler, *Welsh Responses to the French Revolution*, pp. 5–6.
37. See, e.g. G. Howel, *Tymmhorol, ag wybrenol newyddion, neu almanac newydd* (Amwythig [Shrewsbury]: J. Eddowes, 1766), p. 3.
38. G. Howel, *Tymmhorol, ag wybrenol newyddion, neu Almanac newydd* (Amwythig [Shrewsbury]: J. Eddowes, 1770), p. 6; (Dublin, 1794), pp. 23–4. The latter was most probably printed illegally in north Wales.
39. T. Edwards, 'Cerdd yn cynnwys ymddiddan rhwng gwraig y Siopwr a gwraig yr Hwsmon, ynghylch hwyl y bŷd presennol. I'w ganu ar Mentra Gwen', in C. Jones, *Tymmhorol, ac wybrennol Newyddion, neu almanac newydd* (Mwythig: J. Eddowes, 1783), pp. 14–17.
40. A *cywydd* is a form of strict-metre Welsh poetry which dates back to the fourteenth century. There is no English equivalent form.
41. 'Cywydd o hanes Pensylfania yn America, wnaed yno gan Hugh Gryffydd gwr anwyd ac a fagwyd yn Sir Feirionydd, yn rhoddi eglurdeb am gynyrch a ffrwythlondeb y tir, a moesau'r trigolion, &c.', in J. Prys, *Dehonglydd y Sêr neu Almanac Newydd* (1779), pp. 13–16.
42. S. Dafydd, 'Cywydd i ddau offeiriad am feddwi', in C. Jones, *Tymmhorol, ac wybrennol newyddion, neu almanac newydd* (Mwythig: J. Eddowes, 1787), pp. 13–16; M. William, *Britanus Merlinus Liberatus* (Caerfyrddin [Carmarthen]: I. Ross, 1780), p. 6.
43. I. H. Tague, 'Eighteenth-Century English Debates on a Dog Tax', *Historical Journal*, 51 (2008), pp. 901–20.
44. Anon, 'Breuddwyd Sion o'r Bryn, Llandilo-Fawr, a'i Gi Ciwpit', in J. Harris, *Vox Stellarum & Planetarum* (Caerfyrddin [Carmarthen]: I. Ross, 1798), p. 30. Löffler, *Welsh Responses to the French Revolution*, pp. 86–7.
45. M. William, *Britanus Merlinus Liberatus* (Aberhonddu: W. a G. North, 1796), p. 32. Annotated text in Löffler, *Welsh Responses to the French Revolution*, p. 74.
46. J. Harris, *Vox Stellarum et Planetarum* (Caerfyrddin [Carmarthen]: I. Ross, 1796), p. 8–10. Annotated text and translation in Löffler, *Welsh Responses to the French Revolution*, pp. 80–6.
47. J. J. Evans, 'Y Cylchgronau Cymraeg Cynharaf', *Yr Ymofynnydd*, 52:11 (1942), pp. 162–4. See also C. McKenna, 'Aspects of Tradition Formation in Eighteenth-Century Wales', in J. F. P. Nagy (ed.), *Memory and the Modern in Celtic Literature: CSANA Yearbook 5* (Dublin: Four Courts Press, 2006), pp. 37–60.
48. G. H. Jenkins, 'The Eighteenth Century', pp. 109–22; E. Rees, 'The Welsh book trade from 1718 to 1810', in Jones and Rees (eds), *A Nation and its Books*, pp. 123–34; E. M. White, 'Popular Schooling and the Welsh Language 1650–1800', in G. H. Jenkins (ed.), *The Welsh Language before the Industrial Revolution* (Cardiff: University of Wales Press, 1997), pp. 317–42.

49. *The Welsh Piety* (London, 1749–50), p. 38, cited in Jones and Rees (eds), *A Nation and its Books*, p. 113.
50. Anon, 'Rhamant y Byd, neu Ddammeg Rheynart', *Trysorfa Gwybodaeth*, 2 (1770), p. 104.
51. Richard, Lewis and William Morris from Anglesey were key figures of the Welsh cultural renaissance. See G. Morgan, 'The Morris Brothers', in B. Jarvis (ed.), *A Guide to Welsh Literature*, c. *1700–1800* (Cardiff: University of Wales Press, 2000), pp. 64–80; Jenkins and Ramage, *The History of the Honourable Society of Cymmrodorion and of the Gwyneddigion and Cymreigyddion Societies*, pp. 16–45.
52. D. Rh. Phillips, 'The "Eurgrawn Cymraeg" of 1770', *Journal of the Welsh Bibliographical Society*, 5:1 (1937), pp. 49–56, on p. 54; Richard Morris to Hugh Hughes, 17 April 1770, in *Additional Letters of the Morrises of Anglesey (1735–1786)*, ed. H. Owen, 2 vols (London: Honourable Society of Cymmrodorion, 1949), vol. 2, p. 767.
53. Richard Morris to Evan Evans, 23 June 1770', ibid., p. 768.
54. Phillips, 'The "Eurgrawn Cymraeg" of 1770', pp. 55–6; Löffler, *Welsh Responses to the French Revolution*, pp. 27–8.
55. For a detailed treatment of the three serials, see Löffler, *Welsh Responses to the French Revolution*, pp. 28–34.
56. M.-A. Constantine, 'The Welsh in Revolutionary Paris', in M.-A. Constantine and D. Johnston (eds), *'Footsteps of Liberty and Revolt': Essays on Wales and the French Revolution* (Cardiff: University of Wales Press, 2013), in press.
57. M. ab I. Rhus [Morgan John Rhys], *Y Drefn o Gynnal Crefydd yn Unol-Daleithiau America* (Caerfyrddin [Carmarthen]: I. Ross, 1794); D. Davies, *The Influence of the French Revolution on Welsh Life and Literature* (Carmarthen: W. Morgan Evans, 1926), pp. 23–46. The most recent works on aspects of his career are Davies, 'Morgan John Rhys and James Bicheno: Anti-Christ and the French Revolution in England and Wales', pp. 111–27; E. W. James, '"Seren Wib Olau": Gweledigaeth a Chenhadaeth Morgan John Rhys (1760–1804)', *Trafodion Cymdeithas Hanes y Bedyddwyr* (2007), pp. 5–37.
58. G. H. Jenkins, '"A Very Horrid Affair": Sedition and Unitarianism in the Age of Revolutions', in R. R. Davies and G. H. Jenkins (eds), *From Medieval to Modern Wales: Historical Essays in Honour of Kenneth O. Morgan and Ralph A. Griffiths* (Cardiff: University of Wales Press, 2004), pp. 175–96; M. Löffler, 'The "Marseillaise" in Wales', in Constantine and Johnston (eds), *'Footsteps of Liberty'*, in press.
59. T. Roberts, *Cwyn yn Erbyn Gorthrymder* (Llundain: John Jones, 1798), p. v. Text and translation of this pamphlet will be published in M. Löffler (with B. Jenkins), *Political Pamphlets and Sermons from Wales 1790–1806*.
60. Löffler, *Welsh Responses to the French Revolution*, pp. 41, 33, 278.
61. C. Kidd, 'Wales, the Enlightenment and the New British History', *Welsh History Review*, 25:2 (2010), pp. 209–30.
62. 'Amrywiol ddamweiniau y'nghodiad a gostyngiad rhyddid wladwriaethol o'r cynfyd hyd ei sefydliad ym Mrydain (a dynnwyd allan o draethawd Gwallter Mechain)', *Y Geirgrawn*, 6 (1796), pp. 176–9.
63. *Cynghanedd* is the complex Welsh system of alliteration used in formal Welsh poetry. Its genres are *cywydd*, *awdl* (ode) and *englyn*.
64. M. J. Rhys, 'Arwyddion yr Amserau', *Cylchgrawn Cynmraeg*, 2 (1793), pp. 119–20.
65. See Löffler, *Welsh Responses to the French Revolution*, pp. 188–93.
66. Poeta Rusticus, 'Englynion i'r Geirgrawn', *Y Geirgrawn*, 1 (1796), p. 64.
67. I. E., 'Cywydd i'r Drindod', *Y Geirgrawn*, 4 (1796), pp. 126–7.

68. Dafydd Ddu o'r Eryri, 'Awdlau ar destunau y Gwyneddigion i'r Eisteddfodau yn B.A. 1789, 1790, 1791. Sef, Ystyriaeth ar Oes Dyn, Rhyddid, a Gwirionedd', *Cylch-grawn Cynmraeg*, 1 (1793), pp. 50–4.
69. E. Burke, 'To Charles-Jean-François Depont', in *On Empire, Liberty and Reform: Speeches and Letters. Edmund Burke*, ed. D. Bromwich (New Haven, CT: Yale University Press, 2000), p. 410.
70. Dafydd Ddu o'r Eryri, 'Awdlau ar destunau y Gwyneddigion i'r Eisteddfodau yn B.A. 1789, 1790, 1791', p. 52.
71. Anon, 'At Orchychwylwyr y Cylchgrawn', *Cylch-grawn Cynmraeg*, 3 (1793), p. 148. Annotated text and translation in Löffler, *Welsh Responses to the French Revolution*, pp. 205–9.
72. 'Ar Lŷs Ifor Hael, o Faes Haleg yn Swydd Fonwy; o waith y Parchedig Evan Evans (neu Evan Brydydd hîr) o Lan Rheidiol, yn Swydd Garedigion', *Cylch-grawn Cynmraeg*, 2 (1793), p. 98. Ieuan Brydydd Hir was the celebrated eighteenth-century poet who published the first collection of medieval Welsh poetry, *Some Specimens of the Poetry of the Ancient Bards* (London: Dodsley, 1764). See McKenna, 'Aspects of Tradition Formation in Eighteenth-Century Wales', pp. 52–8.
73. 'To Ifor the Liberal', in Williams, *Poems, Lyric and Pastoral*, vol. 1, pp. 192–8. See D. Walford Davies,'"At Defiance": Iolo, Godwin, Coleridge, Wordsworth', in G. H. Jenkins (ed.), *A Rattleskull Genius: The Many Faces of Iolo Morganwg* (Cardiff: University of Wales Press), pp. 147–72, on pp. 169–71.
74. G. Bowen and Z. Bowen, *Hanes Gorsedd y Beirdd* (Cyhoeddiadau Barddas, 1991), p. 31.
75. I. Morganwg, 'Cywydd hanes Hywel, un a fu hael yn ei dlodi, ac a droes yn gybydd angor pan gafwys gyfoeth', *Cylch-grawn Cynmraeg*, 5 (1794), pp. 270–1.
76. For Tomos Glyn Cothi, see Löffler, *Welsh Responses to the French Revolution*, p. 30.
77. *Politics for the People*, 2:4 (1794), 3–5; M. Scrivener, *Poetry and Reform: Periodical Verse from the English Democratic Press* (Detroit, MI: Wayne State University Press), pp. 88–90; Welsh text, translation and discussion in Löffler, *Welsh Responses to the French Revolution*, pp. 46–9, 229–33.
78. Tomos Glyn Cothi, 'HYMN i'w chanu ar ddydd ympryd gan gyfeillion dynolryw', *Miscellaneous Repository*, 1 (1795), pp. 16–18. Annotated text and translation in Löffler, *Welsh Responses to the French Revolution*, pp. 225–8.
79. Jenkins, 'A Very Horrid Affair', p. 189; NLW MS 21373D.
80. M. Vovelle, 'La Marseillaise: War or Peace', in P. Nora (ed.), *Realms of Memory: The Construction of the French Past. Volume III: Symbols*. English-language edn ed. L. D. Kritzman, tr. A. Goldhammer (New York and Chichester: Columbia University Press, 1998), pp. 29–74.
81. Gwilym, 'Can Rhyddid', *Y Geirgrawn*, 4 (1796), pp. 127–8.
82. Annotated text and translation in Löffler, *Welsh Responses to the French Revolution*, pp. 276–9.
83. For a detailed analysis of the translation and its journey, see Löffler, 'The "Marseillaise" in Wales', in press.
84. According to Vovelle, 'La Marseillaise: War or Peace', p. 37, the seventh verse was added by an unknown author in late 1792 because 'the young had begun to play an increasingly important part in civic celebrations'. It had not appeared in English translation.
85. Gwilym, 'Can Rhyddid', pp. 127–8. This English translation is my rendering of the Welsh song and not an English translation of the French original.
86. Löffler, 'The "Marseillaise" in Wales', pp. 101–6.

87. D. Stansfield, 'Agweddau ar fywyd a gwaith Dafydd Saunders', *Trafodion Cymdeithas Hanes y Bedyddwyr* (2008), pp. 35–51.
88. D. Saunders, 'Golwg ar yr rhyfel presenol; Ac ar fynediad dynion i *America*, ynghyd a'r fantais o fyned yno', *Y Geirgrawn*, 9 (1796), pp. 287. Annotated text and translation in Löffler, *Welsh Responses to the French Revolution*, pp. 293–8.
89. 'Transport and Communication', in E. D. Evans, *A History of Wales 1660–1815* (Cardiff: University of Wales Press, 1976), pp. 169–78; Jenkins, *The Foundations of Modern Wales 1642–1780*, pp. 296–9.
90. H. Walters, 'The Periodical Press to 1914', in Jones and Rees (eds), *A Nation and its Books*, pp. 197–207.

7 Ó Coisáin, 'Popular Song, Readers and Language: Printed Anthologies in Irish and Scottish Gaelic, 1780–1820'

1. J. S. Donnelly, 'Propagating the Cause of the United Irishmen' *Studies*, 69 (1980), p. 5–23.
2. N. Curtin, *The United Irishmen: Popular Politics in Ulster and Dublin 1791–1798* (Oxford: Clarendon, 1994), pp. 174–227; Whelan, *The Tree of Liberty*, pp. 65–77.
3. Donnelly, 'Propagating', p. 7; Whelan, *Tree of Liberty*, pp. 71–4; on reading aloud in general in this period, see N. Ó Ciosáin, *Print and Popular Culture in Ireland 1750–1850* (Houndsmills: Palgrave Macmillan, 1997), pp. 186–91 and R. Schenda, 'Leggere ad alta voce: fra analfabetismo e sapere libresco', *La Ricerca Folklorica*, 15 (1987), pp. 5–10.
4. Donnelly, 'Propagating', p. 20; T. Dunne, 'Subaltern Voices? Poetry in Irish, Popular Insurgency and the 1798 Rebellion', *Eighteenth-Century Life*, 22:3 (November 1998), pp. 31–44; G. Fitzgerald, 'Estimates for Baronies of Minimum Level of Irish Speaking amongst Successive Decennial Cohorts', *Proceedings of the Royal Irish Academy*, 84 (1984), pp. 117–55.
5. *Northern Star*, 16–20 April 1795.
6. B. Ó Buachalla, *I mBéal Feirste Cois Cuain* (Baile Átha Cliath: An Clóchomhar 1968), pp. 31–4 and Thuente, *The Harp Re-Strung*, pp. 94–6 both stress the revivalist aspects of this publication.
7. W. Stokes, *Projects for Reestablishing the Internal Peace and Tranquility of Ireland* (Dublin: Moore, 1799), pp. 45–6; W. Stokes, *Observations on the Necessity of Publishing the Scriptures in the Irish Language* (Dublin: Watson, 1806).
8. *An Soisgeal do reir Lucais, agus Gniovarha na Neasbal/The Gospel According to St Luke, and the Acts of the Apostles* (Dublin: Watson, 1799); Ó Buachalla, *I mBéal Feirste*, p. 37; Ó Ciosáin, *Print and Popular Culture*, pp. 138–9, 159; I. Whelan, *The Bible War in Ireland* (Madison, WI: University of Wisconsin Press, 2005), pp. 98–104.
9. Whelan, *Bible Wars*, passim; V. E. Durkacz, *The Decline of the Celtic Languages: A Study of Linguistic and Cultural Conflict in Scotland, Wales and Ireland from the Reformation to the Twentieth Century* (Edinburgh: John Donald, 1983), pp. 118–19.
10. For simplicity, I will use 'Irish' to refer to Irish Gaelic and 'Gaelic' to refer to Scottish Gaelic.
11. Durkacz, *The Decline of the Celtic Languages*, p. 120.
12. D. Dewar, *Observations on the Character, Customs, and Superstitions of the Irish* (London: Gale and Curtis, 1812), p. 139; D. Dewar, *Laoidhean o'n Scrioptur Naomha/A Collection of Gaelic Hymns* (London: A. Paris, 1806).

13. *The Psalms of David in the Irish Language/Psalma Dhaibhi Rígh Israel* (London: R. Watts, 1836); on MacLeod's Irish travels, see J. N. MacLeod, *Memorials of the Rev. Norman MacLeod D. D.* (Edinburgh: D. Douglas, 1898); on the role of the Psalms in Gaelic religious culture, see for example D. Meek, 'Gaelic and the Churches', in C. MacLean and K. Veitch (eds), *Scottish Life and Society: Religion* (Edinburgh: John Donald, 2006), pp. 369–70.
14. The figure of 10,000 for Welsh in the nineteenth century as shown in figure 7.2 derives from a figure of 8,500 given in the *Report of the Royal Commission on Land in Wales* of 1896, which is most probably an underestimate – see eg. P. H. Jones, 'A Golden Age Reappraised: Welsh-Language Publishing in the Nineteenth Century', in P. Isaac and B. McKay (eds), Images and Texts: Their Production and Distribution in the Eighteenth and Nineteenth Centuries (Winchester: St. Paul's Bibliographies, 1997) pp. 121–41; for the figures for 1750–1800 in figure 7.1, see G. H. Jenkins, *The Foundations of Modern Wales 1642–1780* (Oxford: Oxford Univesity Press, 1987), p. 409; G. H Jenkins, 'The Cultural Uses of the Welsh Language 1660–1800', in G. H Jenkins (ed.) *The Welsh Language before the Industrial Revolution* (Cardiff: University of Wales Press, 1997), on p. 371; all books in Welsh up to 1820 are listed in E. Rees, *Libri Walliae: A Catalogue of Welsh Books and Books printed in Wales 1546–1820* (Aberyswyth: National Library of Wales, 1987); the Scottish Gaelic figures represent items of 4 pages or more, excluding dictionaries and grammars, but including reading primers, listed in M. Ferguson and A. Matheson, *Scottish Gaelic Union Catalogue: A List of Books Printed in Scottish Gaelic from 1567 to 1973* (Edinburgh: National Library of Scotland, 1984); for Irish, there is an initial bibliography of devotional works in M. McKenna, 'A Textual History of The Spiritual Rose', *Clogher Record*, 14 (1991), pp. 52–73, but this is far from listing even all devotional books. It only includes two out of nearly twenty pre-Famine editions of Ó Súilleabháin's Pious Miscellany (see below), for example. I have used this list as a basis and added to it. See also E. R. Dix and S. Ó Casaide, *A List of all the Books, Pamphlets, etc. Printed wholly or partly in Irish ... to 1820* (Dublin; An Cló-Chumann, 1905) and R. de Hae and B. Ní Dhonnchadha, *Clár Litridheacht na nua-Gaeilge 1850–1936*, 3 vols (Dublin: Government Publication Office, 1938–40).
15. N. Ó Ciosáin, 'Printing in Irish and O'Sullivan's *Miscellany*', in G. Long (ed.), *Books Beyond the Pale: Aspects of the Provincial Book Trade in Ireland before 1850* (Dublin: Rare Books Group of the Library Association of Ireland, 1996), pp. 87–99; Ú. nic Enrí, *An Cantaire Siúlach: Tadhg Gaelach* (An Daingean: Sagart, 2001); D. Meek, 'Ath-sgrudadh: Dughall Bochanan', *Gairm: An Raitheachan Gaidhlig*, 147 (1989), pp. 269–80 and ibid., 148 (1989), pp. 319–31; N. Ó Ciosáin, 'Pious Miscellanies and Spiritual Songs: Devotional Publishing and Reading in Irish and Scottish Gaelic, 1760–1900', in J. Kelly and C. Mac Murchaidh (eds), *Linguistic Frontiers in Eighteenth and Nineteenth-Century Ireland* (Dublin: Four Courts Press, 2012), pp. 267–82.
16. S. Kidd, 'Social Control and Social Criticism: The Nineteenth-Century *còmhradh*', *Scottish Gaelic Studies*, 20 (2000), pp. 67–87; on the Irish improvement literature in English, Ó Ciosáin, *Print and Popular Culture*, ch. 8, and H. O'Connell, *Ireland and the Fiction of Improvement* (Oxford: Oxford University Press, 2006); on Hannah More's tracts, see S. Pedersen, 'Hannah More meets Simple Simon: Tracts, Chapbooks and Popular Culture in late Eighteenth-Century England', *Journal of British Studies*, 25 (1986), pp. 84–113.
17. I do not know of any comprehensive analysis of any of these lists. There is a detailed discussion of the seventy-one Glasgow-based subscribers to the 1790 edition of Duncan Ban MacIntyre's collection in R. Black, 'Some Notes from my Glasgow Scrapbook,

1500–1800', in S. M. Kidd (ed.), *Glasgow: Baile Mòr nan Gàidheal/City of the Gaels* (Glasgow: Roinn Na Ceiltis Oilthigh Ghlaschu, 2007), pp. 36–45.
18. The full titles are *Orain Ghaidhealach, agus Bearla air an eadar-theangacha le Coinneach Mac'Coinnich* [Songs in Gaelic, and in English translated by Kenneth MacKenzie] (1792) and *Comhchruinneacha do dh'orain taghta, Ghaidhealach, nach robh riamh roimhe clo-bhuailte gus a nis, air an tional o mheodhair, air feadh gaidhealtachd a's eileine na h-Alba* [A collection of Gaelic songs that were never previously printed, collected from memory from the Gaidhealtachd and islands of Scotland] (1813).
19. The list is in R. C. Cole, *Irish Booksellers and English Writers* (London: Continuum International Publishing, 1986), pp. 226–31.
20. I do not have a detailed local knowledge of this area, so that I was not able to identify all of the places and may well have misidentified others. The general pattern is consistent, however.
21. MacCoinnich, *Orain*, p. 175; J. MacKenzie, *Sar-Obair nam Bard Gaelach or, The Beauties of Gaelic Poetry* (Glasgow: John Muir, 1841), pp. 270–1. The latter part of the story, if true, has not affected the survival of the work, and the *Eighteenth Century Short Title Catalogue* lists three copies in libraries in Scotland, six in England, one in Ireland and four in North America. There are other copies not listed, such as those in Glasgow University Library and Trinity College, Dublin.
22. Figures 7.3 and 7.4 were drawn especially for this chapter. However, they have subsequently been used in my essay 'Pious Miscellanies and Spiritual Songs: Devotional Publishing and Reading in Irish and Scottish Gaelic, 1760–1900', J. Kelly and C. Mac-Murchaidh (eds), *Linguistic and Cultural Frontiers: English and Irish, 1650–1850* (Dublin: Four Courts Press, 2012), pp. 267–82.
23. R. Black, 'The Gaelic Academy: The Cultural Commitment of the Highland Society of Scotland', *Scottish Gaelic Studies*, 14:2 (1986), pp. 1–38, on p. 8.
24. J. F. Campbell, *Leabhar na Féinne: Heroic Gaelic Ballads Collected in Scotland Chiefly from 1512 to 1871* (London: for the author, 1872), p. xxx. 'O Patrick Turner, I have much praised you. If I met you in Gleann Ruadh, I'd spend the price of a lamb in drink for you.'
25. Black, 'Some Notes from my Glasgow Scrapbook', p. 36.
26. MacCoinnich, *Orain*, p. 88, 'Oran do na Caoraich Mhoire'.
27. On the contemporary reception of the O'Daly books, see N. Ó Ciosáin, 'Creating a New Reading Public?: Printing in Irish 1880–1920', in C. Hutton (ed.), *The Irish Book in the Twentieth Century* (Dublin: Irish Academic Press, 2004), pp. 5–15. This is not to say that these collections were never bought or read by Irish speakers, and some texts from O'Daly's books were recorded orally in County Cork in the early twentieth century – see N. Ó Ciosáin, 'Bacaigh agus Boccoughs: fianaise ar chultúr na Gaeilge sa naoú céad déag' in D. Ó Giolláin and S. Ó Cadhlaigh (eds), *Léann an Dúchais: féilscríbhinn Ghearóid Uí Chrualaoich* (Cork: Cló Ollscoil Chorcaigh, 2012), pp. 116–28.
28. J. Leerssen, *Mere Irish and Fíor-Ghael: Studies in the Idea of Irish Nationality, Its Development and Literary Expression Prior to the Nineteenth Century* (Amsterdam & Philadelphia, PA: John Benjamins Publishing Company, 1986), pp. 363–5.
29. C. Brooke, *Reliques of Irish Poetry: Consisting of Heroic Poems, Odes, Elegies, and Songs, Translated into English Verse* (Dublin: Bonham, 1789), p. x.
30. D. Dickson, 'Paine and Ireland', in D. Dickson, D. Keogh and K. Whelan (eds), *The United Irishmen: Republicanism, Radicalism and Rebellion* (Dublin: Lilliput, 1993), pp. 136–50; Cole, *Irish Booksellers*, pp. 226–31; R. B. Sher, *The Enlightenment and the*

Book: Scottish Authors and Their Publishers in Eighteenth-Century Britain, Ireland, and America (Chicago, IL: University of Chicago Press, 2006), p. 470ff.
31. Northern Star, 16–20 April 1795.
32. Curtin, The United Irishmen, p. 193.
33. J. R. R. Adams, The Printed Word and the Common Man: Popular Culture in Ulster, 1700–1900 (Belfast: Institute of Irish Studies, 1987), pp. 86–90.
34. Stokes, Observations, pp. 5–6; M. Tynan, Catholic Instruction in Ireland 1720–1950: The O'Reilly/Donlevy Catechetical Tradition (Dublin: Four Courts Press, 1985).
35. J. Smyth, The Men of No Property: Irish Radicals and Popular Politics in the late Eighteenth Century (Dublin: Gill and Macmillan, 1992), pp. 66–8.
36. A. Stewart and D. Stewart, Cochruinneacha taoghta de shaothair nam bard gaeleach, 2 vols (Duneidin: T. Stiuart, 1804), vol. 2, pp. 470–8.
37. A New Gaelic Song-book, composed by Duncan Campbell, from Argyle-shire .../Nuadh Orain Ghailach, air n dianadh le Donnchadh Chaimbeull e Sheuraemachd Earraghaidheal (Cork, 1798); J. Flahive, 'Duncan Campbell: A Scottish-Gaelic Bard in Eighteenth-Century Cork', Journal of the Cork Historical and Archaeological Society, 113 (2008), pp. 80–9.
38. E. McFarland, 'Scotland and the 1798 Rebellion', in Bartlett, Dickson, Keogh and Whelan (eds), 1798: A Bicentenary Perspective, pp. 565–576, on p. 569.
39. Campbell, New Gaelic Song-book, pp. 131–2.
40. McFarland, 'Scotland and the 1798 Rebellion', p. 568.

8 Cronin, 'Broadside Literature and Popular Political Opinion in Munster, 1800–1820'

1. G. Sheridan, 'Irish Periodicals and the Dissemination of French Enlightenment Writings in the Eighteenth Century' in Bartlett, Dickson, Keogh and Whelan (eds), 1798: A Bicentenary Perspective, pp. 28–51.
2. N. Curtin, The United Irishmen: Popular Politics in Ulster and Dublin 1791–1798 (Oxford: Clarendon, 1998), pp. 181–89, 212–25.
3. Curtin, United Irishmen, p. 192; Freeman's Journal, 2 June 1792, 5 January 1793; T. Paine, Agrarian Justice, opposed to Agrarian Law, and to Agrarian Monopoly, being a Plan for Meliorating the Condition of Man by Creating in Every Nation a National Fund (Cork: Gazette Office, 1797).
4. A Hint to the Jacobines [sic] of Great Britain and Ireland, more particularly Addressed to the Young Reformers of the Day (Cork: Edwards, 1793); T. Townsend, Considerations on the Theoretical Spirit of the Times ... Liberty and Equality (Cork: Edwards, 1793), A Summary Defence of the Right Hon. Edmund Burke. In Two Letters (Cork: Edwards, 1796); R. Watson, An Apology for the Bible in a Series of Letters Addressed to Thomas Paine, Author of a Book entitled The Age of Reason (Cork: Edwards, 1796); Rev. T. D. Hincks, Letters Addressed to the Inhabitants of Cork (Cork: Haly, 1795).
5. A Remonstrance Addressed to the Lower Orders of Roman Catholics, in the Diocess [sic] of Cloyne and Ross by the Rev. Doctor Coppinger (Cork: Harris, 1798); A Pastoral Letter to the Catholic Clergy of the United Dioceses of Waterford and Lismore, by the Right Reverend Doctor Hussey (Waterford: Ramsey, 1797).

6. K. Whelan, 'The Republic in the Village' in Whelan, *The Tree of Liberty*, pp. 59–98, on p. 61; Dickson, 'Smoke without Fire? Munster and the 1798 Rebellion', pp. 56, 62, 163. The *Cork Gazette* circulated from 1792 to 1797.
7. Hincks, *Letters Addressed to the Inhabitants of Cork*, p. iv.
8. The average price of a Dublin or provincial newspaper was two pence in 1797, four pence in 1799 and five pence in 1819. *Freeman's Journal*, 5 December 1797, 3 December 1799, 16 September 1819; *Finn's Leinster Journal*, 1 December 1819; G. O'Brien, 'Spirit, Impartiality and Independence: *The Northern Star* 1792–1797', *Eighteenth Century Ireland: Iris an dá chultúr*, 13 (1998), pp. 7–23, on p. 15.
9. D. Dickson, *Old World Colony: Cork and South Munster 1630–1830* (Madison, WI: Wisconsin Press, 2005), p. 662. Dickson's figures apply to agricultural labourers; lower than those of unskilled urban workers and considerably less than those of skilled artisans.
10. Curtin, *The United Irishmen*, p. 177; O'Brien, 'Spirit, Impartiality and Independence', p. 17.
11. *Freeman's Journal*, 2 June 1793; Smyth, *Men of No Property*, pp. 159–61; R. O'Donnell, *Rebellion in Wicklow 1798* (Dublin: Irish Academic Press, 1998), p. 46.
12. Rebellion Papers, National Archives of Ireland (cited hereafter as RP) 1797, 620/30/198, Maurice Tracy, Carlow, to Dublin Castle, 26 May 1797.
13. *Freeman's Journal*, 19 August 1811.
14. O'Brien, 'Spirit, Impartiality and Independence', pp. 16–19; U. Callaghan, 'Newspaper Printing and Print Culture in Eighteenth-Century Limerick' (PhD dissertation, Mary Immaculate College, University of Limerick), p. 27.
15. *Freeman's Journal*, 11 December 1792, 4 October 1796; State of the Country Papers, 1016/42, O. Wynne, Sligo, 24 May 1797; 10917/10, Lord Longueville, Mallow, 28 April 1798; 1017/65, Major General Henry Johnson, Fermoy, 5 February 1799; 1020/45, General Sir C Ross, Youghal, 5 May 1801; 1025/22, Wogan Browne, Naas, 29 July 1803.
16. Countryman, *To the People of Ireland, South*, (Limerick: no printer, 1798), *Eighteenth-Century Collections Online*. Gale, University of Limerick at http://find.galegroup.com/ecco/infomark [accessed 5 April 2010].
17. SOC1801 1020/50. John Beevor, Newtownbarry, to Dublin Castle, 18 October 1801.
18. SOC 1809, 1228/12. Mr Jacob, Mortalstown Castle, Fethard Co Tipperary to Dublin Castle, 29 January 1809.
19. Curtin, *United Irishmen*, p. 192.
20. SOC, 1803, 1025/41, William Gethin, Slane, to Dublin Castle, 3 June 1803.
21. *Cosmhuintir*, literally means 'the people at the bottom', and can be roughly translated as the 'lower classes' though the term is probably more applicable in the rural than in the urban context.
22. Smyth, *Men of No Property*, p. 161; RP 1797, 620/30/198, Maurice Tracy, Carlow, to Dublin Castle, 26 May 1797.
23. SOC 1025/59, Richard Jones to Dublin Castle, 1 November 1803.
24. *Freeman's Journal*, 5 September 1816, 19 January 1818, 16, 17, 24 September 1819; *Leinster Journal*, 25 September 1819.
25. SOC 1817, 1831/3, 7 March 1817.
26. SOC 1819, 2083/32, Major Wilcocks, Cashel, to Dublin Castle 4 November 1819; 1819, 2083/34, Rev. William Archdall, Fethard, to Dublin Castle 3 November 1819.
27. Thompson, *The Making of the English Working Class* (Harmondsworth: Pelican, 1968), pp. 662–70.

28. SOC 1819, 2083/49, Major Wilcocks to Dublin Castle, 4 November 1819, regarding conditions among the lower classes; *Freeman's Journal,* 11 December 1821.
29. SOC 1819 2083/41, William Chaytor, Mayor of Clonmel to Dublin Castle, 11 December 1819.
30. M. Murphy, 'The Ballad Singer and the Role of the Seditious Ballad in Nineteenth-Century Ireland: Dublin Castle's View', *Ulster Folklife,* 25 (1979), pp. 79–102; E. O'Brien, 'Irish Voices in Nineteenth-Century English Street Ballads', *Canadian Journal of Irish Studies,* 28:2, 1 (Fall 2002–Spring 2003), pp. 154–67.
31. *Examiner* (London), 19 September 1819.
32. J. Porter, *Billy Bluff and Squire Firebrand* (Belfast: Northern Star, 1796) quoted in Curtin, *United Irishmen,* p. 186.
33. G. D. Zimmermann, *Songs of Irish Rebellion: Political Street Ballads and Rebel Songs 1780–1900* (Dublin: Allen Figgis, 1967), pp. 125–9.
34. *A Collection of Constitutional Songs, to which is Prefixed a Collection of New Toasts and Sentiments written on Purpose for this Work, Volume 1* (Cork: Edwards, 1799), pp. 59, 66; *A Collection of Constitutional Songs, Volume II, to which is annexed an historical account of the Battle of the Boyne, July, 1690* (Cork: Edwards, 1800).
35. *Paddy's Resource: Being a Select Collection of Original and Modern Patriotic Songs, Toasts and Sentiments, Compiled for the Use of the People of Ireland.* (Belfast: Northern Star, 1795).
36. Curtin, *United Irishmen,* pp. 286–7.
37. *Freeman's Journal,* 11 December 1792; Curtin, *United Irishmen,* p. 193.
38. O'Donnell, *Rebellion in Wicklow,* p. 46; Zimmermann, *Songs of Irish Rebellion,* p. 18; R. Musgrave, *Memoirs of the Different Rebellions in Ireland,* 1, 3rd edn (Dublin: Marchbank, 1802), p. 565.
39. SOC 1804, 1028/7, John Goddard, Newry, to Dublin Castle, 22 March 1804.
40. The Irish language publication of the United Irish movement, *Bolg an tSolair,* included the originals and translations of a number of Irish songs, but none of these were political in any way. *Bolg an tSolair, or Gaelic Magazine containing Laoi na Sealga or the Famous Fenian Poem called The Chase, with a Collection of Choice Irish Songs translated by Miss Brooke* (Belfast: Northern Star Office, 1795).
41. K. Whelan, 'An Underground Gentry? Catholic Middlemen in Eighteenth-Century Ireland', in *The Tree of Liberty,* pp. 27–37.
42. Owen Sheehy, Poems in Irish, National Library of Ireland, MS 662; Michael Hayes' Notebook, National Library of Ireland MS G494.
43. SOC 1803, 1025/59, Richard Jones to Dublin Castle, forwarding informations of John and Anne Russell, 1 November 1803; N. Tóibín, *Duanaire Déiseach* (Baile Atha Cliath: Sáirséal agus Dill, 1978), pp. 35–40.
44. P. Breathnach, *Fuínn na Smól* (Baile Atha Cliath: Brún agus Ó Nualláin, 1913). part 2, p. 16.
45. *Freeman's Journal,* 6 December 1821; J. S. Donnelly, *Captain Rock: The Irish Agrarian Rebellion of 1821–1824* (Cork: Collins, 2009).
46. SOC 1803, 1025/41, William Gethin, Slane, to Dublin Castle, 3 June 1803.
47. Whelan, 'Republic in the Village', p. 61.
48. National Library of Ireland, Ms. G 154, Ms G 158, English and Irish verse scraps by Micheál Óg Ó Longáin in his own hand; Ms G 161, Ossianic tales and poetry compiled by William Breatyhnach of Carraic Beg 1812–13; Ms G 182, Ossianic and other Irish poetry, Padruig Ua Guarann 1818.
49. B. Ó Buachalla, 'From Jacobite to Jacobin' in Bartlett, Dickson, Keogh and Whelan (eds), *1798: A Bicentenary Perspective,* pp. 85–97; Dunne, 'Subaltern Voices? Poetry in

Irish, Popular Insurgency and the 1798 Rebellion', pp. 38–9; T. Dunne, '"Tá Gaedhil bhocht cráidhte": Memory, Tradition and the Politics of the Poor in Gaelic Poetry and Song', in L. M. Geary (ed.), *Rebellion and Remembrance in Modern Ireland* (Dublin: Four Courts Press, 2001), pp. 93–111, on p. 96; R. Ó Foghludha, *Mil na hÉigse* (Baile Atha Cliath: Brún agus Ó Nualláin Teo., 1945), pp. 99–111, 129–48, 190–95, 300–16.

50. For a discussion of popular memories of the 1798 rebellion in pre-famine Ireland, see M. Cronin, 'Memory, Story and Balladry: 1798 and its Place in Popular Memory in Pre-Famine Ireland', in Geary (ed.), *Rebellion and Remembrance*, pp. 112–34.
51. SOC 1819, 2083/16. William Newenham to Dublin Castle, 30 April 1819.
52. T. Crofton Croker, *Researches in the South of Ireland* (London: Murray, 1824), p. 11.
53. Erionnach (G. Sigerson), *The Poets and Poetry of Munster: A Selection of Irish Songs by the Poets of the Last Century* (Dublin: O'Daly, 1860), pp. 76–81.
54. SOC 1816, 1764/12.
55. *Finn's Leinster Chronicle*, 7, 14 August 1819. The crimes tried at the Summer Assizes in south Leinster and east Munster were predominantly murder, highway robbery and sheep-stealing.
56. J. Gordon, *History of the Rebellion in Ireland in the Year 1798* (London: Hurst, 1803), p. 14.
57. 'Come All You Warriors', Zimmermann, *Songs of Irish Rebellion*, p. 14; Michael Hayes' Notebook, National Library of Ireland, Ms. G494, verses written by Nicholas Hayes, Cahir Guillamore, parish of Grange and Bruff, 26 February 1820.
58. Madden Ballads, Cambridge University Library, M.8367;
59. British Library Broadside Ballads, Ms. 835.m.10/32.
60. SOC 1820, 2175/58.
61. Most chapbooks, like that taken up at Castlebar, included no political number. Those printed by Kelly of Waterford were equally devoid of politics while the songs printed by Goggin included roughly 7 per cent that were political. British Library Ms. 11622.df.19. (1–33); 11622.df.34.(3); 11622.df.51.(17–19); 11622.de.15 (1, 14–20)
62. William Goggin, who was made a freeman in 1788 and died in 1811, was an extensive property owner and a long serving member of the market jury; his son, Stephen, also a freeman and member of the Market Jury was also Church Warden of St Mary's Parish, and George Morgan Goggin was made a freeman in 1823; E. R. McC Dix, *Irish Bibliographical Pamphlets, No. V: List of Books, Pamphlets and Newspapers printed in Limerick from the Earliest Period to 1800* (Limerick: Guy, 1907), p. 11; Whelan, 'The Republic in the Parish', p. 63.
63. 'The north country maid, to which are added, The Irish Morsho, The rakes of Mallow, The young man's folly, A new song on Cappoquin', (Limerick: Goggin, *c.* 1790).
64. 'The Gallant Limerick Militia'. The identification of the year of victory as 'eighty-nine' rather than 'ninety-eight' was probably less a matter of historical inaccuracy than of the need to keep the rhyme consistent.
65. D. Casey, *Cork Lyrics or Scraps from the Beautiful City, Consisting of Election Squibs, 'Corporate Ballads', Fancy Ball Songs, Humorous Effusions* (Cork: Nash, 1857), pp. 125–7.
66. L. Cullen, *'98 in Wicklow: The Story as written by Brother Luke Cullen*, ed. M. Ronan (Wexford: Wexford People, 1938), p. 10.
67. 'Come All You Warriors' and 'Father Murphy or the Wexford Men of '98'. Zimmermann, *Songs of Irish Rebellion*, pp. 142–8.
68. Curtin, *United Irishmen*, p. 286.

9 Wall, 'Radical Poetry and the Literary Magazine: Stalking Leigh Hunt in the Republic of Letters'

1. M. Parker, *Literary Magazines and British Romanticism* (Cambridge: Cambridge University Press, 2000), pp. 1, 136.
2. Ibid., p. 137.
3. McIllvanney, *Burns the Radical*, p. 232.
4. Ibid., pp. 232–3.
5. J. O. Hayden, *The Romantic Reviewers 1802–1824* (Chicago, IL: Chicago University Press, 1969), pp. 45–6.
6. Ibid., p. 45.
7. See ibid.
8. Parker, *Literary Magazines*, p. 137.
9. D. Higgins, *Romantic Genius and the Literary Magazine: Biography, Celebrity, Politics* (London; Routledge, 2005), p. 16.
10. W. Maginn (and possibly J. Wilson), 'Preface', *Blackwood's Edinburgh Magazine*, 19 (January 1826), pp. i–xxviii, on p. xxii.
11. K. Gilmartin, *Print Politics: The Press and Radical Opposition in Early Nineteenth Century England* (Cambridge: Cambridge University Press, 1996), p. 13.
12. N. Roe, *Fiery Heart: The First Life of Leigh Hunt* (London: Pimlico, 2005), p. 207.
13. Hayden, *The Romantic Reviewers*, p. 176.
14. J. G. Lockhart, 'Letter from "Z" to Mr. Leigh Hunt', *Blackwood's Edinburgh Magazine*, 2 (January 1818), pp. 414–17, on p. 415.
15. J. Cox, *Poetry and Politics in the Cockney School: Keats, Shelley, Hunt and their Circle* (Cambridge: Cambridge University Press, 1998), p. 25.
16. Ibid., p. 24.
17. J. R. Thompson, *Leigh Hunt* (Boston, MA: Twayne, 1977), p. 20.
18. J. G. Lockhart, 'On the Cockney School of Poetry', No. 2, *Blackwood's Edinburgh Magazine*, 2 (November 1817), pp. 194–201, on p. 194.
19. Ibid., p. 201.
20. M. Eberle-Sinatra, *Leigh Hunt and the London Literary Scene: A Reception History of his Major Works 1805–1828* (London: Routledge, 2005), p. 87.
21. J. G. Lockhart, 'On the Cockney School of Poetry', No. 3, *Blackwood's Edinburgh Magazine*, 3 (July 1818), pp. 453–6, on p. 454.
22. Higgins, *Romantic Genius and the Literary Magazine*, p. 117.
23. P. Foot, *Red Shelley* (London: Bookmarks, 1984), p. 90.
24. T. Redpath, *The Young Romantics and Critical Opinion 1807–1824* (London: Harrap, 1973), p. 48.
25. J. G. Lockhart, letter to William Blackwood, Summer 1824, Blackwood Archive, NLS, MS. 4012, f. 38

WORKS CITED

Ab I. Rhus, M. [Morgan John Rhys], *Y Drefn o Gynnal Crefydd yn Unol-Daleithiau America* (Caerfyrddin [Carmarthen]: J. Ross, 1794).

Adams, J. R. R., *The Printed Word and the Common Man: Popular Culture in Ulster, 1700–1900* (Belfast: Institute of Irish Studies, 1987).

Adams, T. R., *American Independence: The Growth of an Idea. A Bibliographical Study of the American Political Pamphlets Printed Between 1764 and 1776 Dealing with the Dispute Between Great Britain and Her Colonies* (Providence, RI: Brown University Press 1965).

—, *The American Controversy: A Bibliographical Study of the British Pamphlets About the American Disputes, 1764–1783*, 2 vols (Providence, RI and New York: Brown University Press, 1980).

Anon., *Dechreuad, cynnydd, a chyflwr presennol, y dadl rhwng pobl America a'r llywodraeth. Wedi ei gyfiaethu o'r Saesneg er budd i'r Cymru* (Trefriw: D. Jones, 1776).

Aitchison, P. and A. Cassell, *The Lowland Clearances: Scotland's Silent Revolution 1760–1830* (East Linton: Tuckwell Press, 2003).

Andrew, D. T., 'Popular Culture and Public Debate: London 1780', *Historical Journal*, 39:2 (1996), pp. 405–23.

Armitage, D., 'Greater Britain: A Useful Category of Historical Analysis?', *American Historical Review*, 104:2 (1999): pp. 427–45.

Baraniuk, C., '"No bardolatry here": The Independence of the Ulster-Scots Poetic Tradition', in Ferguson and Holmes (eds), *Revising Robert Burns and Ulster*, pp. 64–82.

Barker, H., *Newspapers, Politics, and Public Opinion in Late Eighteenth-Century England* (Oxford: Oxford University Press, 1998).

Barnard, T., *Making the Grand Figure: Lives and Possessions in Ireland, 1641–1770* (New Haven, CT: Yale University Press, 2004).

—., *The Kingdom of Ireland, 1641–1760* (Houndsmills: Palgrave Macmillan, 2004).

Barnard, T. C., 'Considering the Inconsiderable: Electors, Patrons and Irish Elections, 1656–1761', in D. W. Hayton (ed.), *The Irish Parliament in the Eighteenth Century: The Long Apprenticeship* (Edinburgh: Edinburgh University Press, 2001), pp. 107–26.

Barrell, J., *Imagining the King's Death: Figurative Treason, Fantasies of Regicide 1793–1796* (Oxford: Oxford University Press, 2000).

—, *'Exhibition Extraordinary!' Radical Broadsides of the Mid 1790s* (Nottingham: Trent Editions, 2001).

—, 'Rus in Urbe', in Connell and Leask (eds), *Romanticism and Popular Culture*, pp. 109–27.

Bartlett, T., *The Fall and Rise of the Irish Nation. The Catholic Question 1690–1830* (Dublin: Gill and Macmillan, 1992).

Bartlett, T., Dickson, D., Keogh, D. and K. Whelan (eds), *1798: A Bicentenary Perspective* (Dublin: Four Courts Press, 2003).

Bayley, C. A., *Empire and Information: Intelligence Gathering and Social Communication in India, 1780–1870* (Cambridge: Cambridge University Press, 1990).

Bebbington, D. W., *Evangelicalism in Modern Britain* (London: Unwin Hyman, 1989).

Belchem, J., *Popular Radicalism in Nineteenth-Century Britain* (Basingstoke: Macmillan, 1996).

Bell, B. (ed.), *The Edinburgh History of the Book in Scotland, Volume 3: Ambition and Industry, 1800–1880* (Edinburgh: Edinburgh University Press, 2007).

Bell, J. B., *A War of Religion: Dissenters, Anglicans and the American Revolution* (Basingstoke: Palgrave Macmillan, 2008).

Bennett, R., *Howell Harris and the Dawn of Revival*, tr. from Welsh by G. M. Roberts, 2nd English edn (Bridgend: Evangelical Press of Wales, 1987).

Beynon, T., *Braslun o Hanes Gyfylchi a Jerusalem, Pontrhydyfen* (Port Talbot: D. W. Jones, 1926).

—, *Howell Harris, Reformer and Soldier* (Caernarfon: Calvinistic Methodist Bookroom, 1958).

Biagini, E. F., *Liberty, Retrenchment and Reform: Popular Liberalism in the Age of Gladstone, 1860–1880* (Cambridge: Cambridge University Press, 1992).

Bickham, T., *Making Headlines: The American Revolution as Seen through the British Press* (DeKalb, IL: Northern Illinois University Press, 2009).

Bird, J., *A Full and Accurate Report of the Trial of James Bird, Roger Hamill and Casimir DelaHoyde, merchants; Patrick Kenny, Bartholomew Walsh, Matthew Read and Patrick Tiernan, before the Honourable Mr Justice Downes* (Dublin: H. Fitzpatrick, 1794).

Black, A., *Gilfillan of Dundee, 1813–1878: Interpreting Religion and Culture in Mid-Victorian Scotland* (Dundee: Dundee University Press, 2006).

Black, E. C., 'The Tumultuous Petitioners: The Protestant Association in Scotland, 1778–1780', *Review of Politics*, 25:2 (1963), pp. 183–211.

Black, R., 'The Gaelic Academy: The Cultural Commitment of the Highland Society of Scotland', *Scottish Gaelic Studies*, 14 (1986), pp. 1–38.

—, 'Some Notes from my Glasgow Scrapbook, 1500–1800', in S. M. Kidd (ed.), *Glasgow: Baile Mòr nan Gàidheal/City of the Gaels* (Glasgow: Roinn Na Ceiltis Oilthigh Ghlaschu, 2007), pp. 36–45.

Bowan, K. and P. A. Pickering, '"Songs for the Millions": Chartist Music and Popular Aural Tradition', *Labour History Review*, 74:1 (April 2009), pp. 44–63.

Bowen, G. and Z. Bowen, *Hanes Gorsedd y Beirdd* (Cyhoeddiadau Barddas, 1991).

Braithwaite, H., 'From the See of St Davids to St Paul's Churchyard: Joseph Johnson's Cross-Border Connections', in D. W. Davies and L. Pratt (eds), *Wales and the Romantic Imagination* (Cardiff: University of Wales Press, 2007), pp. 53–5.

Breathnach, P., *Fuínn na Smól* (Baile Atha Cliath: Brún agus Ó Nualláin, 1913).

Brewer, J., 'The Misfortunes of Lord Bute: A Case-Study in Eighteenth-Century Political Argument and Public Opinion', *Historical Journal*, 16 (1973): pp. 3–43.

Brooke, C., *Reliques of Irish Poetry: Consisting of Heroic Poems, Odes, Elegies, and Songs, Translated into English Verse* (Dublin: Bohnam, 1789).

Brotherstone, T. (ed), *Covenant, Charter and Party: Traditions of Revolt and Protest in Modern Scottish History* (Aberdeen: Aberdeen University Press, 1989).

Brown, M., 'Dugald Stewart and the Problem of Teaching Politics in the 1790s', *Journal of Irish and Scottish Studies*, 1:1 (2007), pp. 87–126.

—, 'A Scottish Literati in Paris: The Case of Sir James Hall', *Journal of Irish and Scottish Studies*, 2:1 (2008), pp. 73–100.

—, 'Was there an Irish Enlightenment? The Case of the Anglicans', in R. Butterwick, S. Davies and G. Sánchez Espinosa (eds), *Peripheries of the Enlightenment*, SVEC (Oxford: Oxford University Press, 2008), pp. 49–64.

—, 'Configuring the Irish Enlightenment: Reading the *Transactions of the Royal Irish Academy*', in J. Kelly and M. J. Powell (eds), *Clubs and Societies in Eighteenth-Century Ireland* (Dublin: Four Courts Press; 2010), pp. 163–78.

—, 'The Biter Bitten: Ireland and the Rude Enlightenment', *Eighteenth-Century Studies*, 45:3 (2012), pp. 393–407.

Brown, R., *Paisley Burns Clubs, 1805–1893* (Paisley and London: Alexander Gardner, 1893).

Brown, R. L., 'Capel y Gyfylchi', *Afan Uchaf: The Journal of the Cymer Afan and District Historical Society*, 1 (1978), pp. 25–46.

[—], 'Some More Notes on Gyfylchi Chapel', *Afan Uchaf: The Journal of the Cymer Afan and District Historical Society*, 2 (1979), pp. 58–9.

Buckley, K., 'Did John Wesley really come to Meidrim', *Capel*, 17 (Autumn 1992), pp. 2–3.

Bumsted, J. *Lord Selkirk: A Life* (East Lansing, MI: Michigan State University Press, 2009).

Bunyan, J., *The Pilgrim's Progress* (London: Nath. Ponder, 1678).

Burke, E., *On Empire, Liberty and Reform. Speeches and Letters*, ed. D. Bromwich (New Haven, CT: Yale University Press, 2000).

Burke, P., *Popular Culture in Early Modern Europe* (Aldershot: Wildwood House, 1988) [2nd edn 1994; 3rd edn 2009].

Burnett, J., 'The Banner of Liberty: Symbols and the Celebration of the 1832 Reform Bill in Scotland', *Review of Scottish Culture*, 21 (2009), pp. 87–103.

Butler, M., 'Burns and Politics', in Crawford (ed), *Robert Burns and Cultural Authority*, pp. 86–112.

Callaghan, U., 'Newspaper Printing and Print Culture in Eighteenth-Century Limerick', (PhD dissertation, Mary Immaculate College, University of Limerick).

Campbell, A. B., *The Lanarkshire Miners: A Social History of their Trade Unions, 1775–1874* (Edinburgh: John Donald, 1979).

Campbell, D., *A New Gaelic Song-book, composed by Duncan Campbell, from Argyle-shire .../ Nuadh Orain Ghailach, air n dianadh le Donnchadh Chaimbeull e Sheuraemachd Earraghaidheal* (Cork: Cronin, 1798).

Campbell, J. F., *Leabhar na Féinne: Heroic Gaelic Ballads Collected in Scotland Chiefly from 1512 to 1871* (London: for the author, 1872).

Carr, G., *William Owen Pughe* (Cardiff: University of Wales Press, 1983).

—, 'The London Welsh', in P. H. Jones and E. Rees (eds), *A Nation and its Books: A History of the Book in Wales* (Aberystwyth: National Library of Wales, 1998), pp. 147–57.

—, 'William Owen Pughe and the London Societies', in B. Jarvis (ed.), *A Guide to Welsh Literature c. 1700–1800* (Cardiff: University of Wales Press, 2000), pp. 168–88.

—, 'An Uneasy Partnership: Iolo Morganwg and William Owen Pughe', in G. H. Jenkins (ed.), *A Rattleskull Genius: The Many Faces of Iolo Morganwg* (Cardiff: University of Wales Press, 2005), pp. 443–60.

Carruthers, G. (ed.), *Edinburgh Companion to Robert Burns* (Edinburgh: Edinburgh University Press, 2009).

Carter, J. C. and J. H. Pittock (eds), *Aberdeen and the Enlightenment* (Aberdeen: Aberdeen University Press, 1988).

Casey, D., *Cork Lyrics or Scraps from the Beautiful City, Consisting of Election Squibs, 'Corporate Ballads', Fancy Ball Songs, Humorous Effusions* (Cork: Nash, 1857), pp. 125–7.

Cash, A., *John Wilkes: The Scandalous Father of Civil Liberty* (New Haven, CT: Yale University Press, 2006).

Charnell-White, C. A. (ed.), *Beirdd Ceridwen: Blodeugerdd Barddas o Ganu Menywod hyd tua 1800* (Abertawe: Cyhoeddiadau Barddas, 2005).

—, *Welsh Poetry of the French Revolution 1789–1805* (Cardiff: University of Wales Press, 2012).

[Charles, T.], 'Buchwedd a Marwolaeth y Parch. William Williams, o Bant y Celyn, Sir Gaerfyrddin', *Trysorfa*, 2:11 (January 1813), pp. 443–54.

Chartier, R. 'The Two Frances: The History of a Geographical Idea', in R. Chartier, *Cultural History: Between Practices and Representations*, tr. L. G. Cochrane (Cambridge: Polity, 1993), pp. 172–200 [first published Oxford: Blackwell, 1988].

—, 'Time to Understand: The Frustrated Intellectuals', in R. Chartier, *Cultural History*, pp. 127–50.

Chase, M., *Chartism: A New History* (Manchester: Manchester University Press, 2007).

Chester Chronicle.

Chitnis, A. C., *The Scottish Enlightenment and Early Victorian English Society* (London: Croom Helm, 1986).

Clark, J. C. D., *English Society.1660–1832: Religion, Ideology and Politics during the Ancien Regime* (Cambridge: Cambridge University Press, 2000).

Clark, P., *British Clubs and Societies 1580–1800* (Oxford: Oxford University Press, 2000).

Cockburn, H., *An Examination of the Trials for Sedition which have Hitherto Occurred in Scotland*, 2 vols (Edinburgh: David Douglas, 1838).

Coffey, J., 'Evangelicals, Slavery & the Slave Trade: From Whitefield to Wilberforce', *Anvil*, 24:2 (2007), pp. 97–119.

'Cof-nodau o Gymdeithasfa (Association) a gynhaliwyd yn Machynlleth, Ebrill 15 a'r 16, 1795', *Trysorfa Ysbrydol*, 1:3 (October 1799), pp. 164–70.

Cole, R. C., *Irish Booksellers and English Writers* (London: Continuum International Publishing, 1986).

Colley, L., 'Whose Nation? Class and National Consciousness in Britain 1750–1830', *Past and Present*, 113 (1986): pp. 96–117.

—, *Britons: Forging the Nation 1707–1837* (London: Pimlico, 1994).

Connell, P. and N. Leask (eds), *Romanticism and Popular Culture in Britain and Ireland* (Cambridge: Cambridge University Press, 2009).

Connell, P. and N. Leask, 'What is the People?', in Connell and Leask (eds), *Romanticism and Popular Culture*, pp. 3–48.

Connolly, S. J., *Religion, Law and Power: The Making of Protestant Ireland 1660–1760* (Oxford: Oxford University Press, 1992).

—, 'Precedent and Principle: The Patriots and their Critics', in S. J. Connolly (ed.), *Political Ideas in Eighteenth-Century Ireland* (Dublin: Four Courts Press, 2000), pp. 130–58.

—, 'Jacobites, Whiteboys and Republicans: Varieties of Disaffection in Eighteenth-Century Ireland', *Eighteenth-Century Ireland*, 18 (2003): pp. 63–79.

Constantine, M.-A.,'"This Wilderness Business of Publication": The Making of *Poems, Lyric and Pastoral* (1794)', in Jenkins (ed.), *A Rattleskull Genius*, pp. 123–45.

—, 'The Welsh in Revolutionary Paris', in M.-A. Constantine and D. Johnston (eds), *'Footsteps of Liberty and Revolt': Essays on Wales and the French Revolution* (Cardiff: University of Wales Press, 2013), in press.

—, and E. Edwards, '"Bard of Liberty": Iolo Morganwg, Wales and Radical Song', in J. Kirk, A. Noble and M. Brown (eds), *United Islands? The Languages of Resistance* (London: Pickering & Chatto, 2012), pp. 63–76.

Conway, S., *The British Isles and the War of American Independence* (Oxford: Oxford University Press, 2000).

Cook, F., *Selina Countess of Huntingdon* (Edinburgh: Banner of Truth Trust, 2001).

Cowan, E. J., 'Agricultural Improvement and the Formation of Early Agricultural Societies in Dumfries and Galloway', *Transactions of the Dumfries and Galloway Natural History and Antiquarian Society*, 53 (1977–8), pp. 157–67.

Cowan, E. and M. Paterson (eds), *Folk in Print: Scotland's Chapbook Heritage 1750–1950* (Edinburgh: Birlinn, 2007).

Cox, J., *Poetry and Politics in the Cockney School: Keats, Shelley, Hunt and their Circle* (Cambridge: Cambridge University Press, 1998).

Craig, C., 'The Making of a Scottish Literary Canon', in Bell (ed), *Edinburgh History of the Book*, pp. 266–77.

Crawford, J., 'Recovering the Lost Library Community: The Example of Fenwick', *Library History*, 23 (September, 2007), pp. 201–12.

Crawford, R. (ed.), *Robert Burns and Cultural Authority* (Edinburgh: Edinburgh University Press, 1997).

—, '*Heaven Taught Fergusson*': *Robert Burns's Favourite Scottish Poet* (East Linton: Tuckwell Press, 2003).

Crawford, T., *Boswell, Burns and the French Revolution* (Edinburgh: Saltire Society, 1990).

Crofton Croker, T., *Researches in the South of Ireland* (London: Murray, 1824).

Cromek, R. H., *Reliques of Robert Burns, Consisting Chiefly of Original Letters, Poems and Critical Observations on Scottish Songs* (London: Cadell and Davies, 1808).

Cronin, M., 'Memory, Story and Balladry: 1798 and its Place in Popular Memory in Pre-Famine Ireland', in L. M. Geary (ed.), *Rebellion and Remembrance in Modern Ireland* (Dublin: Four Courts Press, 2000), pp. 112–34.

Cugoana, [Q.] O., *Thoughts and Sentiments on the Evil and Wicked Traffic of the Slavery and Commerce of the Human Species. Humbly Submited to the Inhabitants of Great-Britain by Ottabah Cugoano, a Native of Africa* (London, 1787).

Cullen, L., '*98 in Wicklow: the Story as written by Brother Luke Cullen*, ed. M. Ronan (Wexford: Wexford People, 1938).

Cullen, L. M. 'The Political Structures of the Defenders', in H. Gough and D. Dickson (eds), *Ireland and the French Revolution* (Dublin: Irish Academic Press, 1990), pp. 117–38.

Curtin, N., *The United Irishmen: Popular Politics in Ulster and Dublin 1791–1798* (Oxford: Clarendon, 1994).

Cyfaill Dawnus (Dublin, 1794).

Cylch-grawn Cynmraeg; Neu Drysorfa Gwybodaeth (Trefecca, Carmarthen, 1793–4).

Dallimore, A. A., *George Whitefield*, vol. 1 (London: Banner of Truth Trust, 1970).

—, *George Whitefield*, vol. 2 (Edinburgh: Banner of Truth Trust, 1980).

Darnton, R., *The Forbidden Best-Sellers of Pre-Revolutionary France* (London; HarperCollins, 1996), pp 169–246.

David, L., 'Burns and Transnational Culture', in Carruthers (ed), *Edinburgh Companion to Robert Burns*, pp. 50–63.

Davies, D., 'Capel y Gyfylchi', *Y Drysorfa*, 62 (1892), pp. 142–6.

—, 'Yma a Thraw ym Morgannwg', *Cymru*, 16 (1899), pp. 252–9.

Davies, D., *The Influence of the French Revolution on Welsh Life and Literature* (Carmarthen: W. Morgan Evans, 1926).

Davies, D. W., '"At Defiance:" Iolo, Godwin, Coleridge, Wordsworth', in Jenkins (ed.), *A Rattleskull Genius*, pp. 147–72.

Davies, H. M., 'Morgan John Rhys and James Bicheno: Anti-Christ and the French Revolution in England and Wales', *Bulletin of the Board of Celtic Studies*, 29:1 (November 1980), pp. 111–27.

—, *Transatlantic Brethren* (Bethlehem, PA: Lehigh University Press/London: Associated University Presses, 1995).

D'Elia, D. J., 'Benjamin Rush: Philosopher of the American Revolution', *Transactions of the American Philosophical Society*, 64:5 (1974): pp. 1–113.

De Tocqueville, A., *The Old Régime and the French Revolution* (Garden City, NY: Doubleday, 1955).

Dewar, D., *Laoidhean o'n Scrioptur Naomha/A Collection of Gaelic Hymns* (London: A. Paris, 1806).

—, *Observations on the Character, Customs, and Superstitions of the Irish* (London: Gale and Curtis, 1812).

Dickinson, H. T. (ed.), *British Pamphlets on the American Revolution, 1763–1785*, 8 vols (London: Pickering & Chatto, 2007, 2008).

Dickson, D., 'Paine and Ireland', in D. Dickson, D. Keogh and K. Whelan (eds), *The United Irishmen: Republicanism, Radicalism and Rebellion* (Dublin: Lilliput, 1993), pp. 136–50.

—, 'Smoke without Fire? Munster and the 1798 Rebellion', in Bartlett, Dickson, Keogh and Whelan (eds), *1798: A Bicentenary Perspective* (Dublin: Four Courts Press, 2003), pp. 147–73.

—, *Old World Colony: Cork and South Munster 1630–1830* (Madison, WI: Wisconsin Press, 2005).

Dix, E. R. McC., *Irish Bibliographical Pamphlets, No. V: List of Books, Pamphlets and Newspapers Printed in Limerick from the Earliest Period to 1800* (Limerick: Guy, 1907).

Dix, E. R. and S. Ó Casaide, *A List of all the Books, Pamphlets, etc. Printed wholly or partly in Irish ... to 1820* (Dublin; An Cló-Chumann, 1905).

Donnelly, J. S., 'Propagating the Cause of the United Irishmen', *Studies*, 69 (1980), pp. 5–23.

—, *Captain Rock: The Irish Agrarian Rebellion of 1821–1824* (Cork: Collins, 2009).

Dozer, D. M., 'History as Force', in K. S. Templeton Jr (ed.), *The Politicization of Society* (Indianapolis, IN: Liberty Fund, 1979), pp. 341–72.

Dunne, T., 'Subaltern Voices? Poetry in Irish, Popular Insurgency and the 1798 Rebellion', *Eighteenth Century Life*, 22:3 (November 1998), pp. 31–44.

—, '"Tá Gaedhil bhocht cráidhte": Memory, Tradition and the Politics of the Poor in Gaelic Poetry and Song', in L. M. Geary (ed.), *Rebellion and Remembrance in Modern Ireland* (Dublin: Four Courts Press, 2000), pp. 93–111.

Durkacz, V. E., *The Decline of the Celtic Languages: A Study of Linguistic and Cultural Conflict in Scotland, Wales and Ireland from the Reformation to the Twentieth Century* (Edinburgh: John Donald, 1983).

Eagleton, T., *The Function of Criticism: From The Spectator to Post-Structuralism* (London: Verso, 1984).

Eberle-Sinatra, M., *Leigh Hunt and the London Literary Scene: A Reception History of his Major Works 1805–1828* (London: Routledge, 2005).

Eddy, M. D., 'The University of Edinburgh Natural History Class Lists 1782–1800', *Archives of Natural History*, 30:1 (2003), pp. 97–117.

Edwards, E., *English-Language Poetry from Wales 1789–1805* (Cardiff: University of Wales Press, 2013).

Edwards, J., 'Cerdd o Goffadwriaeth am ein hen ffrind Tobacco, oherwydd ei fod gwedi mynd yn brin ac yn ddryd' (A song in remembrance of our old friend, Tobacco, because he has become rare and expensive) (Wrecsam, [n.d.]) (JHD 291ii).

Edwards, J. B., 'John Jones (Jac Glan-y-gors): Tom Paine's Denbighshire Henchman?', *Denbighshire Historical Society Transactions*, 51 (2002), pp. 95–112.

Edwards, T., *Gwaith Thomas Edwards (Twm o'r Nant)*, ed. I. Foulkes (Liverpool: I. Foulkes, 1874).

Elder, G. O., *Kirkcudbright: The Story of an Ancient Royal Burgh* (Castle Douglas, 1898).

Elliot, M., *Partners in Revolution: The United Irishmen and France* (New Haven, CT: Yale University Press, 1982).

Ellis, P. B. and S. Mac a'Ghobhainn, *The Scottish Insurrection of 1820* (Edinburgh: John Donald, 2001).

Ellul, J., 'Politicisation and Political Solutions', in K. S. Templeton Jr (ed.), *The Politicization of Society* (Indianapolis, IN: Liberty Fund, 1979), pp. 209–47.

Emsley, C., *Crime, Police and Penal Policy: European Experiences 1750–1940* (Oxford: Oxford University Press, 2007).

Equiano, O., *The Interesting Narrative of the Life of Olaudah Equiano, or Gustavus Vassa, the African* (London: The Author, [1789]).

Erionnach (Sigerson. G.), *The Poets and Poetry of Munster: A Selection of Irish Songs by the Poets of the Last Century* (Dublin: O'Daly, 1860), pp. 76–81.

Erskine, J., 'Scotia's Jewel: Robert Burns and Ulster, 1786–*c*. 1830', in Ferguson and Holmes (eds), *Revising Robert Burns and Ulster*, pp. 15–36.

Eryri, H., 'Achwyniad Hywel o'r Yri wrth Wragedd Gwynedd am dderbyniad Morgan Rondl, a gwrthodiad Sir John Haidd o'r Gadair Senyddol' (The complaint of Hywel of the Yri to the wives of Gwynedd regarding the reception of Morgan Rondl and the rejection of Sir John Barley-corn from the parliamentary chair) (Trefriw, 1780) (JHD 325ii).

Evans, C., *Slave Wales: The Welsh and Atlantic Slavery, 1660–1850* (Cardiff: University of Wales Press, 2010).

Evans, E., *Some Specimens of the Poetry of the Ancient Bards* (London: Dodsley, 1764).

Evans, E., *Howel Harris, Evangelist* (Cardiff: University of Wales Press, 1974).

—, Review of *Queen of the Methodists* (B. S. Schlenther), *Cylchgrawn Hanes* (Journal of the Historical Society of the Presbyterian Church of Wales), 22 (1998), pp. 77–82.

—, *Bread of Heaven: The Life and Work of William Williams, Pantycelyn* (Bridgend: Bryntirion Press, 2010).

Evans, E. D., *A History of Wales 1660–1815* (Cardiff: University of Wales Press, 1976).

Evans, J. J., 'Y Cylchgronau Cymraeg Cynharaf', *Yr Ymofynnydd*, 52:11 (1942), pp. 162–4.

Evans, T., *Drych y Prif Oesoedd* (Y Mwythig [Shrewsbury]: John Rhydderch, 1716); 2nd rev. edn ([1740]).

—, *The History of Modern Enthusiasm* (London: W. Owen and W. Clarke, [1752]); enlarged 2nd edn (1757).

Fagan, P., 'The Dublin Catholic Mob, 1700–1750', *Eighteenth-Century Ireland*, 4 (1989), pp. 133–42.

Fay, J., *The Trial of John Fay Esq of Navan in the County of Meath* (Dublin: Brett Smith, 1794).

Ferguson, F., '"Burns the Conservative": Revising the Lowland Scottish Tradition in Ulster Poetry', in Ferguson and Holmes (eds), *Revising Robert Burns and Ulster*, pp. 83–105.

Ferguson, F. and A. R. Holmes (eds), *Revising Robert Burns and Ulster: Literature, Religion and Politics*, c. *1770–1920* (Dublin: Four Courts Press, 2009).

Ferguson, F., J. Erskine and R. Dixon, 'Commemorating and Collecting Burns in the North of Ireland, 1844–1902', in Ferguson and Holmes (eds), *Revising Robert Burns and Ulster*, pp. 127–47.

Ferguson, M. and A. Matheson, *Scottish Gaelic Union Catalogue: A List of Books Printed in Scottish Gaelic from 1567 to 1973* (Edinburgh, National Library of Scotland, 1984).

Finlay, R., 'Heroes, Myths and Anniversaries in Modern Scotland', *Scottish Affairs*, 18 (Winter 1997), pp. 108–25.

—, 'The Burns Cult and Scottish Identity in the Nineteenth and Twentieth Centuries', in Simpson (ed.), *Love & Liberty*, pp. 69–78.

Fitzgerald, G., 'Estimates for Baronies of Minimum Level of Irish Speaking amongst Successive Decennial Cohorts', *Proceedings of the Royal Irish Academy*, 84 (1984), pp. 117–55.

Flahive, J., 'Duncan Campbell: A Scottish-Gaelic Bard in Eighteenth-Century Cork', *Journal of the Cork Historical and Archaeological Society*, 113 (2008), pp. 80–9.

Foot, P., *Red Shelley* (London: Bookmarks, 1984).

Franklin, C., 'The Welsh American dream: Iolo Morganwg, Robert Southey and the Madog legend', in G. Carruthers and A. Rawes (eds), *English Romanticism and the Celtic World* (Cambridge: Cambridge University Press, 2003), pp. 69–84.

Fraser, W. H., *Conflict and Class: Scottish Workers 1700–1838* (Edinburgh: John Donald, 1988).

—, 'The Scottish Context of Chartism', in Brotherstone (ed), *Covenant, Charter and Party*, pp. 66–77.

—, *Dr John Taylor, Chartist Ayrshire Revolutionary* (Ayr: Ayrshire Archaeological and Natural History Society, 2006).

—, *Chartism in Scotland* (Pontypool: Merlin Press, 2010).

Foster, R. F., *Modern Ireland, 1600–1972* (London: Allen Lane, 1988).

Fulford, T., *Romantic Indians: Native Americans, British Literature, and Transatlantic Culture 1756–1830* (Oxford: Oxford University Press, 2006).

Gahan, D., 'Class, Religion and Rebellion: Wexford in 1798', in Smyth (ed.), *Revolution, Counter-Revolution and Union*, pp. 83–98.

Garnham, N., 'Criminal Legislation in the Irish Parliament, 1692–1760', in Hayton (ed.), *The Irish Parliament in the Eighteenth Century*, pp. 55–70.

—, 'How Violent was Eighteenth-Century Ireland?', *Irish Historical Studies*, 30 (1997), pp. 377–92.

—, 'Local Elite Creation in Early Hanoverian Ireland: The Case of the County Grand Jury', *Historical Journal*, 42:3 (September 1999), pp. 623–42.

—, *The Militia in Eighteenth-Century Ireland: In Defence of the Protestant Interest* (Woodbridge: Boydell, 2012).

Geary, L. M. (ed.), *Rebellion and Remembrance in Modern Ireland* (Dublin: Four Courts Press, 2001).

Gilfillan, G., *The Martyrs and Heroes of the Scottish Covenant* (Edinburgh and London: Gall & Inglis, (1863 edn).

—, *The National Burns, Including the Airs of All the Songs and an Oriiginal Life of Burns*, 2 vols (Glasgow and London: William Mackenzie, 1879–80).

Gilmartin, K., *Print Politics: The Press and Radical Opposition in Early Nineteenth Century England* (Cambridge: Cambridge University Press, 1996).

Gilmour, D., *Reminiscences of the Pen Folk, Paisley Weavers of Other Days* (Edinburgh and Paisley: Alex Gardner, 1879).

Ginter, D. E., *The Whig Organization of the General Election of 1790* (Berkeley, CA: University of California Press, 1967).

Goodwillie, E., *The World's Memorials of Robert Burns* (Detroit, MI: Waverley Publishing Company, 1911).

Goodwin, A., *The Friends of Liberty: The English Democratic Movement in the Age of the French Revolution* (London: Hutchison & Co., 1979).

Grierson, H. J. C. (ed.), *The Letters of Sir Walter Scott, 1819–21* (London: Constable & Co, 1934).

Griffith, C. L., 'Wiliam Phylip, ei Fywyd a'i Waith' (PhD dissertation, University of Wales, 1999).

[Griffiths, G. P. (ed.)], *Handbook to the Great Missionary Exhibition* (Swansea: Lewis Evans, 1907).

Gronniosaw, U., *A Narrative of the Most Remarkable Particulars in the Life of James Albert Ukawsaw Gronniosaw, an African Prince* (Bath: W. Gye, 1772).

—, *Berr Hanes o'r Pethau Mwyaf Hynod ym Mywyd James Albert Ukawsaw Groniosaw, Tywysog o Affrica*, tr. into Welsh by William Williams of Pantycelyn (Aberhonddu [Brecon]: E. Evans, 1779).

Gruffydd, R. G., 'The Revival of 1762 and William Williams of Pantycelyn', in E. Roberts and R. G. Gruffydd, *Revival and Its Fruit* (Bridgend: Evangelical Library of Wales, 1981), pp. 19–40.

Haakonssen, K., 'From Moral Philosophy to Political Economy: The Contribution of Dugald Stewart', in V. Hope (ed.), *Philosophers of the Scottish Enlightenment* (Edinburgh: Edinburgh University Press, 1984), pp. 211–32.

Harding, A., *The Countess of Huntingdon's Connexion* (Oxford: Oxford University Press, 2003).

Harris, B., 'Scottish–English Connections in British Radicalism in the 1790s', in T. C. Smout (ed.), *Anglo-Scottish Relations from 1603 to 1900* (Oxford: Oxford University Press, 2005), pp. 189–212.

—, *The Scottish People and the French Revolution* (London: Pickering & Chatto, 2008).

— (ed.), *Scotland in the Age of the French Revolution* (Edinburgh: John Donald, 2005).

Harris, J., *Vox Stellarum et Planetarum* (Caerfyrddin [Carmarthen]: I. Ross, 1796).

—, *Vox Stellarum et Planetarum* (Caerfyrddin [Carmarthen]: I. Ross, 1798).

Harvey, W., *Scottish Chapbook Literature* (New York: Burt Franklin, 1971 edn).

History of the Speculative Society of Edinburgh from its Institution in 1764 (Edinburgh, 1845).

Hay, W., *Diarhebion Cymru* (Lerpwl [Liverpool]: Gwasg y Brython, 1955).

Hayden, J. O., *The Romantic Reviewers* (Chicago, IL: Chicago University Press, 1969).

Hayek, F. A., 'Kinds of Order in Society', in Templeton (ed.), *The Politicisation of Society*, pp. 501–23.

Haykin, M. A. G., and K. J. Stewart (eds), *The Emergence of Evangelicalism: Exploring Historical Continuities* (Nottingham: Apollos, 2008).

'Hen Gapel y Gyfylchi', *Yr Adolygydd*, 2:4 (March 1852), pp. 496–507.

Herzog, D., *Poisoning the Minds of the Lower Orders* (Princeton, NJ: Princeton University Press, 1998).

Higgins, D., *Romantic Genius and the Literary Magazine: Biography, Celebrity, Politics* (London: Routledge, 2005).

Higgins, P., *A Nation of Politicians: Gender, Patriotism and Political Culture in Late Eighteenth-Century Ireland* (Madison, WI: University of Wisconsin Press, 2010).

Holmes, A. R., 'Presbyterian Religion, Poetry and Politics in Ulster, *c.* 1770–1850', in Ferguson and Holmes (eds), *Revising Robert Burns and Ulster*, pp. 37–63.

Howel, G., *Tymmhorol, ag wybrenol newyddion, neu almanac newydd* (Amwythig [Shrewsbury]: J. Eddowes, 1766).

—, *Tymmhorol, ag wybrenol newyddion, neu Almanac newydd* (Amwythig [Shrewsbury]: J. Eddowes, 1770).

Hughes, D. A., 'William Williams Pantycelyn's Eschatology as Seen Especially in his *Aurora Borealis* of 1744', *Scottish Bulletin of Evangelical Theology*, 4:1 (Spring 1986), pp. 49–63.

—, *Meddiannu Tir Immanuel: Cymru a Mudiad Cenhadol y Ddeunawfed Ganrif* (Bridgend: Evangelical Library of Wales, 1990).

Hughes, E., 'The Scottish Reform Movement and Charles Grey, 1792–94: Some Fresh Correspondence', *Scottish Historical Review*, 35:119 (1956), pp. 26–41.

Hughes, G. H. (ed.), *Gweithiau William Williams Pantycelyn. Cyfrol II. Rhyddiaith* (Cardiff: University of Wales Press, 1967).

Hughes, G. T., *Williams Pantycelyn* (Cardiff: University of Wales Press, 1983).

—, 'Pantycelyn a'r Piwritaniaid', in D. Ll. Morgan (ed.), *Meddwl a Dychymyg Williams Pantycelyn* (Llandysul: Gwasg Gomer, 1991), pp. 31–54.

Jackson, W., *A Full Report of all the Proceedings on the Trial of the Rev. William Jackson, at the bar of His Majesty's Court of King's Bench, Ireland, on an Indictment for High Treason* (Dublin: J. Exshaw, 1795).

James, E. W., 'Williams Pantycelyn a Gwawr y Mudiad Cenhadol', in G. H. Jenkins (ed.), *Cof Cenedl XVII* (Llandysul: Gwasg Gomer, 2002), pp. 65–101.

—, '"Seren Wib Olau": Gweledigaeth a Chenhadaeth Morgan John Rhys (1760–1804)', *Trafodion Cymdeithas Hanes y Bedyddwyr* (2007), pp. 5–37.

—, 'Welsh Ballads and American Slavery', *Welsh Journal of Religious History*, 2 (2007), pp. 59–86.

—, 'Morgan John Rhys a Chaethwasiaeth Americanaidd', in D. G. Williams (ed.), *Canu Caeth: Y Cymry a'r Affro-Americaniaid* (Llandysul: Gwasg Gomer, 2010), pp. 2–25.

—, 'The Evolution of the Welsh Hymn', in I. Rivers and D. L. Wykes (eds), *Dissenting Praise: Religious Dissent and the Hymn in England and Wales* (Oxford: Oxford University Press, 2011), pp. 229–68.

—, 'Griffith Jones (1684–1761) of Llanddowror and His "Striking Experiment in Mass Religious Education" in Wales in the Eighteenth Century', in R. Siegert (ed.), *Volksbildung durch Lesestoffe im 18. und 19. Jahrhundert / Educating the People through Reading Material in the 18th and 19th Centuries* (Bremen, Germany: Edition Lumière, 2012), pp. 275–89.

James, R. W., 'Ymateb y Methodistiad Calfinaidd Cymraeg i'r Chwyldro Ffrengig', *Cylchgrawn Hanes* (Journal of the Historical Society of the Presbyterian Church of Wales), 12–13 (1988/9), pp. 35–60.

Jarvis, B. (ed.), *A Guide to Welsh Literature* c. 1700–1800 (Cardiff: University of Wales Press, 2000).

Jenkins, D. E., *The Life of Thomas Charles*, vol. 2 (Denbigh: Llewelyn Jenkins, 1908).

Jenkins, G. H., *The Foundations of Modern Wales 1642–1780* (Oxford: Oxford University Press, 1987).

—, 'The Eighteenth Century', in Jones and Rees, *A Nation and its Books*, pp. 109–22, on pp. 110–11.

—, *Protestant Dissenters in Wales, 1639–1689* (Cardiff: University of Wales Press, 1992).

—, 'The Cultural Uses of the Welsh Language 1660–1800', in G. H Jenkins (ed.) *The Welsh Language before the Industrial Revolution* (Cardiff: University of Wales Press, 1997), pp. 369–406.

—, '"A Very Horrid Affair": Sedition and Unitarianism in the Age of Revolutions', in R. R. Davies and G. H. Jenkins (eds), *From Medieval to Modern Wales: Historical Essays in Honour of Kenneth O. Morgan and Ralph A. Griffiths* (Cardiff: University of Wales Press, 2004), pp. 175–96.

Jenkins, G. H. (ed.), *A Rattleskull Genius: The Many Faces of Iolo Morganwg* (Cardiff: University of Wales Press, 2005).

Jenkins, K., 'Williams Pantycelyn', in B. Jarvis (ed.), *A Guide to Welsh Literature* c. 1700–1800, pp. 256–78.

Jenkins, P., 'Wales', in P. Clark (ed.), *Cambridge Urban History of Britain, Volume 2: 1540–1840* (Cambridge: Cambridge University Press, 2000), p. 133–47.

Jenkins, R. T., *Hanes Cymru yn y Bedwaredd Ganrif ar Bymtheg: Y Gyfrol Gyntaf (1789–1843)* (Caerdydd [Cardiff]: University of Wales Press, 1933).

Jenkins, R. T. and H. M. Ramage, *A History of the Honourable Society of Cymmrodorion and of the Gwyneddigion and Cymreigyddion Societies (1751–1951)* (London: Honourable Society of Cymmrodorion, 1951).

Johnson, N. E., 'Fashioning the Legal Subject: Narratives from the London Treason Trials of 1794', *Eighteenth-Century Fiction*, 21: 3 (2009), pp. 413–43.

Jones, A., 'The Newspaper Press in Wales, 1804–1945', in Jones and Rees (eds), *A Nation and its Books*, pp. 209–19.

Jones, A. G., '"Meddylier am yr India": Tair Taith y Genhadaeth Gymreig yn Sylhet, 1887–1947', *Transactions of the Honourable Society of Cymmrodorion 1997*, 4 (1998), pp. 84–110.

—, 'The Other Internationalism? Missionary Activity and Welsh Nonconformist Perceptions of the World in the Nineteenth and Twentieth Centuries', in C. Williams, N. Evans and P. O'Leary (eds), *A Tolerant Nation? Exploring Ethnic Diversity in Wales* (Cardiff: University of Wales Press, 2003), pp. 49–60.

Jones, C., *Tymmhorol, ac wybrennol Newyddion, Neu Almanac Newydd* (Mwythig: J. Eddowes, 1783).

—, *Tymmhorol, ac wybrennol Newyddion, Neu Almanac Newydd, Am y Flwyddyn o Oedran ein Iachawdwr, 1783. Ym mha un y cynhwysir amryw bethau nad oes yma mo'r lle i'w henwi* (Mwythig, 1783).

—, *Tymmhorol, ac wybrennol Newyddion, Neu Almanac Newydd* (Mwythig: J. Eddowes, 1787).

Jones, D. (ed.), *Blodeu-gerdd Cymry* (Y Mwythig: Stafford Prys, 1759).

Jones, D. C., *'A Glorious Work in the World': Welsh Methodism and the International Evangelical Revival, 1735–1750* (Cardiff: University of Wales Press, 2004).

Jones, D. G., 'Some Recent Trends in Welsh Literature', in J. E. C. Williams (ed.), *Literature in Celtic Countries* (Cardiff: University of Wales Press, 1971), pp. 175–92.

Jones, D. V. J., *Before Rebecca: Popular Protests in Wales 1793–1835* (London: Allan Lane, 1973).

Jones, F. M., *'The Bard is a Very Singular Character': Iolo Morganwg, Marginalia and Print Culture* (Cardiff: University of Wales Press, 2010).

—, *Welsh Ballads of the French Revolution 1793–1815* (Cardiff: University of Wales Press, 2012).

Jones, F. P., *Radicaliaeth a'r Werin Gymreig yn y Bedwaredd Ganrif ar Bymtheg* (Cardiff: University of Wales Press, 1977).

Jones, H. [Llangwm], 'Ymffrost balchder, o'i anrhydedd ai wrthiau: a'i ddrygioni, o ddechreuad y Byd i'r awr honn' (The boast of Pride about his honour, resistance and mischief, from the beginning of the world to this hour) (Trefriw, 1779) (JHD 314i).

—, 'Cerdd newydd; neu Gwŷnfan Teyrnas Loeger ar Drigolion America, am eu bod yn gwrthryfela i'w herbyn; ar Ddyll Anfoniad Mam at ei Phlant' (A new song: or the complaint of the kingdom of England to the inhabitants of America, since they rebel against them; in the form of the letter of a Mother to her children) (n.p., n.d.) (JHD 683 i).

—, 'Cerdd o Attebiad y Plant i'w Mam; neu Anfoniad Americans i Loeger' (A song giving the children's response to their mother; or the letter of the Americans to England) (n.p., n.d.) (JHD 683 ii).

—, 'Cerdd newydd ym mherthynas y rhyfel bresennol sydd yn America, gan gyffelybu yr ymbleidio neu'r sectiau yn y deyrnas yma â rhyfel yr America i'r goleuni gogleddol sydd i'w weled yn yr wybr ers 66 o flynyddoedd' (A new song in relation to the present war in America, comparing the Dissent or the sectarianism in this country and the American war to the northern light which has been seen in the skies for the past sixty-six years) (Caer, n.d.) (JHD 221i).

—, 'Cerdd newydd ym mherthynas y Rhyfel presennol yn America; yn gosod allan mae Oferedd yw Daroganau a Brudiau, ac yn dangos mae Ordinhad Duw yw'r cwbl' (A new song in relation to the present war in America, positing that prognostications and prophecies are frivolous, and that all is God's ordinance) (Wrecsam, n.d.) (JHD 281i).

Jones, H. [Maesglasau], *Gardd y Caniadau: neu lyfr yn cynnwys ynddo garolau a cherddi ar amriw destunau, diddan a difrifol* (Mwythig: T. Wood, 1776).

—, *Gair yn ei amser, neu, Lythyr-annerch i'r cyffredin Gymry* (Mwythig: Argraphwyd gan T. Wood, 1782).

Jones, J., *Cerddi Jac Glan-y-Gors,* ed. E. G. Millward (Cyhoeddiadau Barddas, 2003).

Jones, M. P., 'John Jones of Glan-y-gors', *Transactions of the Honourable Society of Cymmrodorion* (1911), pp. 60–94.

Jones, N. C., *Gweithiau Williams Pant-y-Celyn*, vol. 1 (Treffynnon [Holywell]: P. M. Evans & Son, 1887).

Jones, P. H., 'A Golden Age Reappraised: Welsh-Language Publishing in the Nineteenth Century', in P. Isaac and B. McKay (eds), *Images and Texts: Their Production and Distribution in the Eighteenth and Nineteenth Centuries* (Winchester: St. Paul's Bibliographies, 1997) pp. 121–41.

Jones, P. H. and E. Rees (eds), *A Nation and its Books: A History of the Book in Wales* (Aberystwyth: National Library of Wales, 1998).

Jones, R. T., *Saunders Lewis a Williams Pantycelyn* (Swansea: University College of Swansea, 1987).

Joyce, P., *Visions of the People: Industrial England and the Question of Class, 1848–1914* (Cambridge: Cambridge University Press, 1991).

Julian, J. (ed.), *A Dictionary of Hymnology*, rev. edn (London: John Murray, 1915).

Kelly, J., *The Liberty and Ormond Boys: Factional Riot in Eighteenth-Century Dublin* (Dublin: Four Courts Press, 2005).

—, *Poynings' Law and the Making of Law in Ireland, 1660–1800* (Dublin: Four Courts Press, 2007).

Kendall, J., 'The First Chemical Society, the First Chemical Journal, and the Chemical Revolution', *Proceedings of the Royal Society of Edinburgh: Section A (Mathematics and Physical Sciences)*, 63 (1949–1952), pp. 346–58.

Keogh D. and N. Furlong (eds), *The Mighty Wave: Aspects of the 1798 Rebellion in Wexford* (Dublin: Four Courts Press, 1996).

Kidd, C., 'Wales, the Enlightenment and the New British History', *Welsh History Review*, 25:2 (2010), pp. 209–30.

Kidd, S., 'Social Control and Social Criticism: the Nineteenth-Century *còmhradh*', *Scottish Gaelic Studies*, 20 (2000), pp. 67–87.

Kirby, G. W., *The Elect Lady* (Croydon: Countess of Huntingdon Connexion, 1972).

Lake, A. C., *Huw Jones o Langwm* (Caernarfon: Gwasg Pantycelyn, 2009).

Lamont, C. and M. Rossington (eds), *Romanticism's Debatable Lands* (London: Palgrave, 2007).

Larkin J. (ed.), *The Trial of William Drennan* (Dublin: Irish Academic Press, 1990).

Leask, N., '"The Shadow Line": James Currie's "Life of Burns" and British Romanticism', in Lamont and Rossington (eds), *Romanticism's Debatable Lands*, pp. 64–79.

Leathart, W. D., *The Origin and Progress of the Gwyneddigion Society of London instituted M.DCC.LXX* (London: Hugh Pierce Hughes, 1831).

Leerssen, J., *Mere Irish and Fíor-Ghael: Studies in the Idea of Irish Nationality, Its Development and Literary Expression Prior to the Nineteenth Century* (Amsterdam & Philadelphia, PA: John Benjamins Publishing Company, 1986).

Leonard, T. (ed.), *Radical Renfrew: Poetry from the French Revolution to the First World War* (Edinburgh: Polygon, 1990).

Levere, T. H., 'Natural Philosophers in a Coffee House: Dissent, Radical Reform and Pneumatic Chemistry', in P. Wood (ed.), *Science and Dissent in England 1688–1945* (Aldershot: Ashgate, 2004), pp. 131–46.

Lewis, S., *Williams Pantycelyn* (London: Foyle's Welsh Depôt, 1927).

Livesey, J., *Civil Society and Empire: Ireland and Scotland in the Eighteenth Century Atlantic World* (New Haven, CT and London: Yale University Press, 2009).

Llwyd, A., *Black Wales: A History of Black Welsh People* (Cardiff: Hughes a'i Fab, 2005).

Lockhart, J. G., 'On the Cockney School of Poetry', No. 2, *Blackwood's Edinburgh Magazine*, 2 (November 1817), pp. 194–201.

—, 'Letter from "Z" to Mr. Leigh Hunt', *Blackwood's Edinburgh Magazine*, 2 (January 1818), pp. 414–17.

—, 'On the Cockney School of Poetry', No. 3, *Blackwood's Edinburgh Magazine*, 3 (July 1818), pp. 453–6.

—, Letter to William Blackwood, Summer 1824, Blackwood Archive, NLS, MS. 4012, f. 38.

Löffler, M., *The Literary and Historical Legacy of Iolo Morganwg, 1826–1926* (Cardiff: University of Wales Press, 2007).

—, 'Cerddi Newydd gan John Jones, "Jac Glan-y-gors"', *Llên Cymru*, 33 (2010), pp. 143–50.

—, *Welsh Responses to the French Revolution: Press and Public Discourse 1789–1802* (Cardiff: University of Wales Press, 2012).

—, 'The "Marseillaise" in Wales', in M.-A. Constantine and D. Johnston (eds), *'Footsteps of Liberty and Revolt': Essays on Wales and the French Revolution* (Cardiff: University of Wales Press, 2013), pp. 93–112.

DeLoss Love, W., *Samson Occom and the Christian Indians of New England*, new edn (Syracuse, NY: Syracuse University Press, 2000).

Lukacs, J. D., 'The Monstrosity of Government', in Templeton (ed.), *The Politicisation of Society*, pp. 391–408.

Lynch, M., *Scotland: A New History* (London: Century, 1991).

Mac-an-Tuairneir, P., *Comhchruinneacha do dh'ain taghta Ghaidhealach, nach robh riamh roimhe clo-bhuailte gus a nis, air an tional o mheodhair, air feadh gaidhealtachd a's eileine na h-Alba* (Duneideonn: Stiubhart, 1813).

McCalman, I., *Radical Underworld: Prophets, Revolutionaries and Pornographers in London, 1795–1840* (Oxford: Oxford University Press, 1993).

McCarthy, W., *Anna Letitia Barbauld: Voice of the Enlightenment* (Baltimore, MD: Johns Hopkins University Press, 2008).

MacCoinnich, C., *Orain Ghaidhealach agus Bearla air an eadar-theangacha le Coinneach Mac'Coinnich* (Dunedainn, 1792).

McCraith, M., 'The Saga of James MacPherson's "Ossian"', *Linen Hall Review*, 8 (1991), pp. 5–9.

McFarland, E. W., *Ireland and Scotland in the Age of Revolution: Planting the Green Bough* (Edinburgh: Edinburgh University Press, 1994).

McFarland, E., 'Scotland and the 1798 Rebellion', in Thomas Bartlett, David Dickson, Daire Keogh and Kevin Whelan (eds.), *1798: A Bicentenary Perspective* (Dublin: Four Courts Press, 2003), pp. 565–76.

McGrath, C. I., 'Central Aspects of the Eighteenth-Century Constitutional Framework in Ireland', *Eighteenth-Century Ireland*, 16 (2001), pp. 9–34.

McGrath C. I. and C. Fauske (eds), *Money, Power, and Print: Interdisciplinary Studies of the Financial Revolution in the British Isles* (Newark, DE: University of Delaware Press, 2008).

McGuirk, C., 'The "Rhyming Trade": Ferguson, Burns and the Marketplace', in Crawford (ed.), *'Heaven Taught Fergusson'*, pp. 135–59.

McIlvanney, L., *Burns the Radical: Poetry and Politics in Late Eighteenth-Century Scotland* (East Linton: Tuckwell Press, 2002).

MacIntyre, G., *Dugald Stewart: The Pride and Ornament of Scotland* (Brighton: Sussex Academic Press, 2003).

MacKay, C., *Forty Years Recollections of Life, Literacy and Public Affairs*, 2 vols (London: Chapman & Hall, 1977).

McKenna, C., 'Aspects of Tradition Formation in Eighteenth-Century Wales', in J. F. P. Nagy (ed.), *Memory and the Modern in Celtic Literature: CSANA Yearbook 5* (Dublin: Four Courts Press, 2006), pp. 37–60.

McKenna, M., 'A Textual History of The Spiritual Rose', *Clogher Record*, 14 (1991), pp. 52–73.

MacKenzie, J., *Sar-Obair nam Bard Gaelach or, The Beauties of Gaelic Poetry* (Glasgow: John Muir, 1841).

Mackenzie, J. M., 'Essay and Reflection: On Scotland and the Empire', *International History Review*, 15:4 (1993): pp. 714–39.

MacLeod, J. N., *Memorials of the Rev. Norman MacLeod D. D.* (Edinburgh: D. Douglas, 1898).

McLoughlin, W. G., *Champions of the Cherokees: Evan and John B. Jones* (Princeton, NJ: Princeton University Press, 1990).

McWilliam, R., *Popular Politics in Nineteenth-Century England* (London and New York: Routledge, 1998).

Magennis, E., 'Coal, Corn and Canals: Parliament and the Dispersal of Public Moneys 1695–1772', in Hayton (ed.), *The Irish Parliament in the Eighteenth Century*, pp. 71–86.

—, 'Patriotism, Popery and Politics: The Armagh By-Election of 1753', in A. J. Hughes and W. Nolan (eds), *Armagh, History and Society: Interdisciplinary Essays on the History of an Irish County* (Dublin: Geography Publications, 2001), pp. 485–504.

Maginn, W. (and possibly J. Wilson), 'Preface', *Blackwood's Edinburgh Magazine*, 19 (January 1826), pp. i–xxviii.

Maidment, B., *The Poorhouse Fugitives: Self-Taught Poets and Poetry in Victorian Britain* (Manchester: Carcanet, 1987).

Markus, T. (ed.), *Order in Space and Society: Architectural Form and its Context in the Scottish Enlightenment* (Edinburgh: Mainstream, 1982).

Marrant, J., *A Narrative of the Lord's Wonderful Dealings with John Marrant, a Black* (London, 1785).

Marsden, D. E., 'The Development of Kirkcudbright in the Late Eighteenth Century: Town Planning in a Galloway Context', *Transactions of the Dumfriesshire and Galloway Natural History and Antiquarian Society*, ser. 3, 72 (1997), pp. 86–96.

Meek, D., 'Ath-sgrudadh: Dughall Bochanan', *Gairm: An Raitheachan Gaidhlig*, 147 (1989), pp. 269–80.

—, 'Ath-sgrudadh: Dughall Bochanan', *Gairm: An Raitheachan Gaidhlig* 148 (1989), pp. 319–31.

—, 'Gaelic and the Churches', in C. MacLean and K. Veitch (eds), *Scottish Life and Society: Religion* (Edinburgh: John Donald, 2006), pp. 369–70.

Meikle, H. W., *Scotland and the French Revolution* (Glasgow, 1912).

Mercer, A., *The History of Dunfermline* (Dunfermline: John Miller, 1828).

Middlekauff, R., *The Glorious Cause: The American Revolution, 1763–1789*, rev. edn (Oxford: Oxford University Press, 2007).

Millward, E. G. (ed.), *Cerddi Jac Glan-y-gors* (Cyhoeddiadau Barddas, 2003).

Miskell, L., *Intelligent Town: An Urban History of Swansea, 1780–1855* (Cardiff: University of Wales Press, 2006).

Mitchell, I., 'Willie Thom, Weaver Bard of Bon-Accord', *History Scotland*, 10:1 (Jan/Feb 2010), pp. 47–51.

Moore, D., 'James Macpherson and "Celtic Whiggism"', *Eighteenth-Century Life*, 30:1 (2005), pp. 1–24.

Morgan, D. Ll., 'Morgan Llwyd a'r Iddewon', in J. E. C. Williams (ed.), *Ysgrifau Beirniadol XXI* (Denbigh: Gwasg Gee, 1996), pp. 81–96.

Morgan, E. S., *Benjamin Franklin* (New Haven, CT: Yale University Press, 2002).

Morgan, G., 'Baledi Dyffryn Conwy', *Canu Gwerin*, 20 (1997), pp. 2–12.

—, 'The Morris Brothers', in Jarvis (ed.), *A Guide to Welsh literature c. 1700–1800*, pp. 64–80.

Morgan, P., *The Eighteenth Century Renaissance* (Llandybïe: Christopher Davies, 1981).

Morgan, W. I., 'George Owen, Llwyn-gwair, a'i Deulu', *Bathafarn*, 22 (1967), pp. 37–48.

—, 'George Owen, Llwyn-gwair, a'i Deulu', *Bathafarn*, 23 (1968), pp. 14–24.

Morley, V., *Irish Opinion and the American Revolution* (Cambridge; Cambridge University Press, 2002).

—, 'The Continuity of Disaffection in Eighteenth-Century Ireland', *Eighteenth-Century Ireland*, 22 (2007): pp. 189–205.

Morris, J. H., *Hanes Cenhadaeth Dramor y Methodistiaid Calfinaidd Cymreig* (Caernarfon: Llyfrfa y Cyfundeb, 1907).

Morris, L. et al., *Additional Letters of the Morrises of Anglesey (1735–1786)*, ed. H. Owen, 2 vols (London: Honourable Society of Cymmrodorion, 1949).

Morys, H., *Eos Ceiriog, Sef Casgliad o Bêr Ganiadau Huw Morus*, ed. W. Davies, 2 vols (Gwrecsam: I. Painter, 1823).

Murphy, M., 'The Ballad Singer and the Role of the Seditious Ballad in Nineteenth-Century Ireland: Dublin Castle's View', in *Ulster Folklife*, 25, 1979, pp. 79–102.

Murray, I. H., *The Puritan Hope: A Study in Revival and the Interpretation of Prophecy* (London: Banner of Truth Trust, 1971).

Murray, N., *The Scottish Hand Loom Weavers 1790–1850: A Social History* (Edinburgh: John Donald, 1978).

Musgrave, R., *Memoirs of the Different Rebellions in Ireland*, 1, 3rd edition (Dublin: Marchbank, 1802).

Nairn, T., *The Break-Up of Britain: Crisis and Neo-Nationalism 1965–75* (London: New Left, 1977).

National Library of Wales [hereafter NLW] MS 12350A. 'Diary, &c., of John Davies, Ystrad'.

NLW MS 6238A, 'Y Gell Gymysg'.

Nic Enrí, Ú., *An Cantaire Siúlach: Tadhg Gaelach* (An Daingean: An Sagart, 2001).

Nicolson, C., 'A Plan "To Banish all the Scotchmen": Victimization and Political Mobilization in Pre-Revolutionary Boston', *Massachusetts Historical Review*, 9 (2007): pp. 55–102.

Nobbe, G., *The North Briton: A Study in Political Propaganda* (New York: Columbia University Press, 1939).

Noble, A., 'Versions of the Scottish Pastoral: The Literati and the Tradition, 1780–1830', in Markus (ed.), *Order in Space and Society*, pp. 263–311.

Noble A. and P. Scott Hogg (eds), *The Canongate Burns* (Edinburgh: Canongate Classics, 2001, rev. edn. 2003).

Nuttall, G. F., *The Welsh Saints 1640–1660* (Cardiff: University of Wales Press, 1957).

—, *Howel Harris 1714–1773: The Last Enthusiast* (Cardiff: University of Wales Press, 1965).

—, 'The Students of Trevecca College 1768–1791', *Transactions of the Honourable Society of Cymmrodorion*, Session 1967: part 2 (1968), pp. 249–77.

—, *The Significance of Trevecca College 1768–91* (London: Epworth Press, 1969).

O'Brien, G., 'The Unimportance of Public Opinion in Eighteenth-Century Britain and Ireland', *Eighteenth-Century Ireland*, 8 (1993), pp. 115–27.

—, 'Spirit, Impartiality and Independence: *The Northern Star* 1792–1797', *Eighteenth Century Ireland: Iris an dá chultúr*, 13 (1998), pp. 7–23.

O'Brien, E., 'Irish Voices in Nineteenth-Century English Street Ballads', *Canadian Journal of Irish Studies*, 28:2/29:1 (Fall 2002–Spring 2003), pp. 154–67.

Ó Buachalla, B., *I mBéal Feirste Cois Cuain* (Baile Átha Cliath: An Clóchomhar 1968).

—, 'From Jacobite to Jacobin', in T. Bartlett, D. Dickson, D. Keogh and K. Whelan, (eds), *1798: A Bicentenary Perspective* (Dublin: Four Courts, 2003).

Ó Ciardha, É., 'The Stuarts and Deliverance in Irish and Scots-Gaelic Poetry, 1690–1760', in S. J. Connolly (ed.), *Kingdoms United? Ireland and Great Britain from 1500. Integration and Diversity* (Dublin: Four Courts Press, 1998), pp. 78–94.

—, *Ireland and the Jacobite Cause, 1685–1766: A Fatal Attachment* (Dublin: Four Courts Press, 2000).

Ó Ciosáin, N., 'Printing in Irish and O'Sullivan's *Miscellany*', in G. Long (ed.), *Books Beyond the Pale: Aspects of the Provincial Book Trade in Ireland before 1850* (Dublin: Rare Books Group of the Library Association of Ireland, 1996), pp. 87–99.

—, *Print and Popular Culture in Ireland, 1750–1850* (Houndsmills: Palgrave Macmillan, 1997).

—, 'Creating a New Reading Public?: Printing in Irish 1880–1920', in C. Hutton (ed.), *The Irish Book in the Twentieth Century* (Dublin: Irish Academic Press, 2004), pp. 5–15.

—, 'Bacaigh agus Boccoughs: fianaise ar chultúr na Gaeilge sa naoú céad déag', in Diarmuid Ó Giolláin and Stiofán Ó Cadhlaigh (eds), *Léann an Dúchais: féilscríbhinn Ghearóid Uí Chrualaoich* (Cork: Cló Ollscoil Chorcaigh, 2012), pp. 116–128.

—, 'Pious Miscellanies and Spiritual Songs: Devotional Publishing and Reading in Irish and Scottish Gaelic, 1760–1900', in J. Kelly and C. Mac Murchaidh (eds), *Linguistic Frontiers in Eighteenth and Nineteenth-Century Ireland* (Dublin: Four Courts Press, 2012), pp. 267–82.

O'Connell, H., *Ireland and the Fiction of Improvement* (Oxford: Oxford University Press, 2006).

O'Donnell, R., *Rebellion in Wicklow 1798* (Dublin: Irish Academic Press, 1998).

Ó Foghludha, R., *Mil na hÉigse* (Baile Atha Cliath: Brún agus Ó Nualláin Teo., 1945).

O'Halloran, C., *Golden Ages and Barbarous Nations: Antiquarian Debate and Cultural Politics in Ireland, c. 1750–1800* (Cork: Cork University Press/Field Day, 2004).

Owen, J. D., 'Morgan John Rhys yn ei gysylltiad a Threfecca', *Cylchgrawn Hanes y Methodistiaid Calfinaidd*, 7: 1 (1922), pp. 14–20.

Owen, G. W., *Cewri'r Cyfamod* (Bangor: Centre for the Advanced Study of Religion in Wales, Bangor University, 2008).

Page, A., *John Jebb and the Enlightenment Origins of British Radicalism* (Westport, CT and London: Praeger, 2003).

Paine, T., 'American Crisis I', in *Rights of Man, Common Sense and Other Political Writings*, ed. M. Philp (1995; Oxford: Oxford University Press, 2008).

Parker, M., *Literary Magazines and British Romanticism* (Cambridge: Cambridge University Press, 2000).

Pedersen, S., 'Hannah More meets Simple Simon: Tracts, Chapbooks and Popular Culture in late Eighteenth-Century England', *Journal of British Studies*, 25 (1986), pp. 84–113.

Pennant, T., *Free Thoughts on the Militia Laws ... addressed to the Poor Inhabitants of North Wales* (London: Printed for B. White, 1781).

—, *American Annals: or, Hints and queries for Parliament Men, 1775–78* (Darlington, 1778).

Phillips, D. Rh., 'The "Eurgrawn Cymraeg" of 1770', *Journal of the Welsh Bibliographical Society*, 5:1 (1937), pp. 49–56.

Philp, M., 'The Fragmented Ideology of Reform', in M. Philp (ed.), *The French Revolution and British Popular Politics* (Cambridge: Cambridge University Press, 1991), pp. 50–78.

Pittock, M., *Celtic Identity and the British Image* (Manchester: Manchester University Press, 1999).

—, 'Nibbling at Adam Smith', in Rodger and Carruthers (eds) *Fickle Man*, pp. 118–31.

Pocock, J. G. A., 'The New British History in Atlantic Perspective: An Antipodean Commentary, *American Historical Review*, 104:2 (1999): pp. 490–500.

—, *The Discovery of Islands: Essays in British History* (Cambridge: Cambridge University Press, 2005).

Porter, R., *Enlightenment: Britain and the Creation of the Modern World* (London: Penguin, 2000).

Potkay, A. and S. Burr (eds), *Black Atlantic Writers of the Eighteenth Century* (Basingstoke: Macmillan Press, 1995).

Powell, M. J., *Britain and Ireland in the Eighteenth-Century Crisis of Empire* (Basingstoke: Palgrave, 2003).

—, *Piss-Pots, Printers and Public Opinion in Eighteenth-Century Dublin: Richard Twiss's Tour in Ireland* (Dublin: Four Courts Press, 2009).

—, 'The Aldermen of Skinner's Alley: Ultra-Protestantism before the Orange Order', in M. J. Powell and J. Kelly (eds), *Clubs and Societies in Eighteenth-Century Ireland* (Dublin: Four Courts Press, 2010), pp. 203–23.

—, 'The Society of Free Citizens and other Popular Political Clubs, 1749–1789', in M. J. Powell and J. Kelly (eds), *Clubs and Societies in Eighteenth-Century Ireland* (Dublin: Four Courts Press, 2010), pp. 244–63.

Price, A., '"Pulling aside the veil": Aspects of the Life and Work of Hugh Jones (1749–1825), Maesglasau', *Journal of the Merioneth Historical and Record Society*, 15:3 (2008), pp. 284–92.

Price, W. M., 'The Countess of Huntingdon and Missionary Enterprise', *Journal of the Historical Society of the Presbyterian Church of Wales*, 27:3 (September 1942), pp. 130–1.

Prichard, M., 'I Filwyr Sir Gaernarfon ar ei trosglwyddiad o Gaergybi Ymôn, ir Gwersyll sy'n y Cosheath yng Nghent' (To the soldiers of Caernarvonshire upon their transferral from Holyhead in Anglesey to the camp which is in Coxheath in Kent) (Trefriw, 1780) (JHD 327ii).

—, 'Yn rhoi hanes fel y darfu i'r Ffrangcod speilio'r Llongau Pyst Caergybi wrth ddyfod adre or Iwerddon' (Giving the story of how the French plundered the postal ships of Holyhead on their way home from Ireland) (Trefriw, 1780) (JHD 327i).

Prys, J., *Dehonglydd y Sêr* (Amwythig [Shrewsbury]: Stafford Prys, 1777).

—, *Dehonglydd y Sêr neu Almanac Newydd* (Amwythig [Shrewsbury]: Stafford Prys, 1779).

Psalms of David in the Irish Language, The/Psalma Dhaibhi Rígh Israel (London: R. Watts, 1836).

Quinault, R., 'The Cult of the Centenary, c. 1784–1914', *Historical Research*, 71 (1998), pp. 303–23.

Quinn, J., 'The United Irishmen and Social Reform', *Irish Historical Studies*, 31 (1998), pp. 188–201.

Redpath, T., *The Young Romantics and Critical Opinion 1807–1824* (London: Harrap, 1973).

Rees, E., 'The Welsh Book Trade from 1718 to 1810', in Jones and Rees (eds), *A Nation and its Books*, pp. 123–34.

—, *Libri Walliae: A Catalogue of Welsh Books and Books printed in Wales 1546–1820* (Aberystwyth: National Library of Wales, 1987).

Rigney, A., 'Plenitude, Scarcity and the Circulation of Cultural Memory', *Journal of European Studies*, 35 (2005), pp. 11–27.

—, 'Embodied Communities: Commemorating Robert Burns, 1859', *Representations*, 115 (Summer 2011), pp. 71–101.

Roberts, E., 'Cerdd o Gwynfan a galar yr holl Dobaccwyr ar Trwynau Snisin yr hwn a godwyd yn ei bris o achos y Gwrthryfel yr Americaniaid a Lloegr' (A song giving the complaint and lament of all the tobacconists and snuff-noses, following a rise in prices because of the conflict between the Americans and England) (Trefriw, 1776) (JHD 296ii).

—, 'Yn adrodd hanes y Gwrthryfel sydd rhwng Lloegr Hen a Lloegr Newydd, sef America' (Recounting the story of the conflict between Old England and New England, namely America) (Trefriw, 1777) (JHD 300ii).

—, '[Cerdd] O Gyngor ir Merched rhag priodi'r un Dyn di ana yn y flwyddyn hon. Rhag iddo flino ar ei gwmpeini a myned i B[r]eifetirio neu'n filisia neu'r Maniwar neu ryw le anghyspell arall' ([A song] of advice to the girls against marrying any uninjured man this year, lest he should tire of his company and go off to privateer or to the militia or a man-of-war, or some other God-forsaken place) (Trefriw, 1778) (JHD 307ii).

—, 'O rybydd ir Cymru fod un pol Jones am Landio i gyffinie ein Gwlad, hefo 8 o Longe am ladd i gyd Frodur o achos rhyfel America: Yr hwn sydd i hun o enedigaeth o wlad fon medd rhai' (Of warning to the Welsh that a certain Paul Jones is about to land on the boundaries of our country, with eight ships, intent on killing his brothers because of the American war; he was himself born in Anglesey, some say) (Trefriw, 1778) (JHD 309ii).

—, 'Cerdd I Ddeisyf ar bawb yn Amser Rhyfel i roi eu Hymddiried yn yr Arglwydd, ac nid mewn amldra o ddynion' (A song to beseech everyone to put their trust in the Lord during a time of war, and not in a multitude of men) (n.p., [1779]) (JHD 605).

—, '[Cerdd] O hanes y blindere a fu yn Mon ac Arfon yn amser y bu Captain Trodn [yn] Pressio gyda'i Army drygionus' ([A song] about the troubles that took place in Anglesey and Caernarvonshire at the time that Captain Trodn came to impress with his evil army) (Trefriw, [1780]) (JHD 326ii).

—, 'O Ffarwel ir Militia Cymru' (Of farewell to the militia of Wales) (Trefriw, 1783) (JHD 346i).

—, 'O fawl i Falisia Sir Fon' (Of praise to the militia of Anglesey) (Bala, n.d.) (JHD 485i).

—, 'O Rybydd i bawb ymbaratoi Sydd heb leico gweithio I ddiangc ymaith rhag eu preso' (Of warning to everyone who does not like to work to prepare themselves to escape lest they should be impressed) ([Caerfyrddin], n.d.) (JHD 610i).

Roberts, G. M., *Bywyd a Gwaith Peter Williams* (Caerdydd [Cardiff]: Gwasg Prifysgol Cymru dros Gyngor yr Eisteddfod Genedlaethol, 1943).

—, *Y Per Ganiedydd*, vol. 1 (Llandysul: Gwasg Aberystwyth, 1949)

—, *Y Per Ganiedydd*, vol. 2 (Llandysul: Gwasg Aberystwyth, 1958).

— (ed.), *Hanes Methodistiaeth Galfinaidd Cymru: Cyfrol II. Cynnydd y Corff* (Caernarfon: Llyfrfa'r Methodistiad Calfinaidd, 1978).

Roberts, M., 'Burns and the Masonic Enlightenment', in Carter and Pittock (eds), *Aberdeen and the Enlightenment*, pp. 331–8.

Roberts, R., 'Yn gosod allan y moddion am y Rhyfeloedd presennol rhyngom a'r Ffrangcod, a dull grefydd Babaidd, ar King George Delight' (s.l., *c.* 1794).

Roberts, T., *Cwyn yn Erbyn Gorthrymder* (Llundain: John Jones, 1798).

Robinson, R., *Slavery Inconsistent with the Spirit of Christianity* (Cambridge: J. Archdeacon, 1788).

Rodger, J. and G. Carruthers (eds), *Fickle Man: Robert Burns in the 21st Century* (Dingwall: Sandstone Press, 2009).

Roe, N., *Fiery Heart: The First Life of Leigh Hunt* (London: Pimlico, 2005).

Rosser, S. M., 'Baledi Newyddiadurol Elis y Cowper', in G. H. Jenkins (ed.), *Cof Cenedl XXIII: Ysgrifau ar Hanes Cymru* (Llandysul: Gwasg Gomer, 2008), pp. 67–99.

Rounce, A., '"Stuarts without End": Wilkes, Churchill, and Anti-Scottishness', *Eighteenth-Century Life*, 29:3 (2005): pp. 20–38.

Roy, G. R. (ed.), *Robert Burns & America: A Symposium* (Columbia, SC: University of South Carolina, 2001).

Rudé, G., 'The London "Mob" of the Eighteenth Century', *Historical Journal*, 2:1 (1959): pp. 1–18.

Saillant, J., 'Hymnody and the Persistence of an African-American Faith in Sierra Leone', *Hymn*, 48:1 (January 1997), pp. 8–17.

Sainsbury, J., *John Wilkes: The Lives of a Libertine* (Aldershot: Ashgate, 2006).

Sartori, G., 'Liberty and Law' in Templeton (ed.), *The Politicization of Society*, pp. 249–311.

Saunders, L. J., *Scottish Democracy, 1815–1840: The Social and Intellectual Background* (Edinburgh: Oliver & Boyd, 1950).

Schaeffer, N., 'Charles Churchill's Political Journalism', *Eighteenth-Century Studies*, 9:3 (1976), pp. 406–28.

Schenda, R., 'Leggere ad alta voce: fra analfabetismo e sapere libresco', *La Ricerca Folklorica*, 15 (1987), pp. 5–10.

Schlenther, B. S., *Queen of the Methodists* (Durham: Durham Academic Press, 1997).

Scrivener, M., *Poetry and Reform: Periodical Verse from the English Democratic Press* (Detroit, MI: Wayne State University Press, 1992).

Seitz, D. C., *Paul Jones: His Exploits in English Seas During 1778–1780. Contemporary Accounts Collected from English Newspapers with a Complete Bibliography* (New York: E. P. Dutton and Company, 1917).

[Seymour, A. C. H.], *The Life and Times of Selina Countess of Huntingdon*, 2 vols (London: W. E. Painter, 1839).

Sher, R. B., *The Enlightenment and the Book: Scottish Authors and Their Publishers in Eighteenth-Century Britain, Ireland, and America* (Chicago, IL: University of Chicago Press, 2006).

Sheridan, G., 'Irish Periodicals and the Dissemination of French Enlightenment Writings in the Eighteenth Century', in T. Bartlett, D. Dickson, D. Keogh and K. Whelan (eds), *1798: A Bicentenary Perspective* (Dublin: Four Courts, 2003), pp. 28–51.

Simms, J. G., *Jacobite Ireland 1685–91* (London: Routledge, 1970).

Simpson, K., *The Protean Scot: The Crisis of Identity in Eighteenth Century Scottish Literature* (Aberdeen: Aberdeen University Press, 1988).

— (ed.), *Burns Now* (Edinburgh: Canongate, 1994).

—, (ed.), *Love & Liberty: Robert Burns, A Bicentenary Celebration* (East Linton: Tuckwell Press, 1997).

—, 'Burns and Independence', in Roy (ed.), *Robert Burns & America*, pp. 11–22.

Smith, P. H. (ed.), *English Defenders of American Freedoms 1774–1778: Six Pamphlets Attacking British Policy* (Washington: Library of Congress, 1972).

Smith, M. M. and T. Lockley (eds), *Slavery in North America: From the Colonial Period to Emancipation*, vol. 1 (London: Pickering & Chatto, 2009).

Smith, W., *Pregeth ar helynt bresennol America* (Brysto: W. Pine, 1775).

Smout, T. C., *A Century of the Scottish People, 1830–1950* (London: Collins, 1986).

Smyth, J., *The Men of No Property: Irish Radicals and Popular Politics in the Late Eighteenth Century* (Dublin: Gill and Macmillan, 1992).

Snapp, J. R., 'An Enlightened Empire: Scottish and Irish Imperial Reformers in the Age of the American Revolution', *Albion*, 33:3 (2001): pp. 388–403.

Soisgeal do reir Lucais, agus Gniovarha na Neasbal, An/The Gospel According to St Luke, and the Acts of the Apostles (Dublin: Watson, 1799).

Somerville, A., *The Autobiography of a Working Man* (London: Turnstile Press, 1951 edn).

Stanley, B., *The Bible and the Flag: Protestant Missions and British Imperialism in the Nineteenth and Twentieth Centuries* (Leicester: Apollos, 1990).

—, 'Baptists, Anti-Slavery and the Legacy of Imperialism', *Baptist Quarterly*, 42:4 (October 2007), pp. 284–96.

Stansfield, D., 'Agweddau ar fywyd a gwaith Dafydd Saunders', *Trafodion Cymdeithas Hanes y Bedyddwyr* (2008), pp. 35–51.

Stewart, A., *Reminiscences of Dunfermline and Neighbourhood, Illustrative of Dunfermline Life, Sixty Years Ago* (Edinburgh: Scott & Ferguson, 1886).

Stewart, A. and D. Stewart, *Cochruinneacha taoghta de shaothair nam bard gaeleach*, 2 vols (Duneidin: T. Stiuart, 1804).

Stewart, L., 'Putting on Airs: Science, Medicine, and Polity in the Late Eighteenth Century', in T. Levere and G. L'E. Turner, *Discussing Chemistry and Steam: The Minutes of a Coffee House Philosophical Society 1780–1787* (Oxford: Oxford University Press, 2002), pp. 236–7.

—, 'The Public Culture of Radical Philosophers in Eighteenth Century London', in Wood (ed.), *Science and Dissent*, pp. 113–29.

Stokes, W., *Projects for Reestablishing the Internal Peace and Tranquility of Ireland* (Dublin: Moore, 1799).

—, *Observations on the Necessity of Publishing the Scriptures in the Irish Language* (Dublin: Watson, 1806).

Tague, I. H., 'Eighteenth-Century English Debates on a Dog Tax', *Historical Journal*, 51 (2008), pp. 901–20.

Taylor, M., 'John Bull and the Iconography of Public Opinion in England *c.* 1712–1929', *Past and Present*, 134 (1992): pp 93–128.

Templeton, K. S., Jr (ed.), *The Politicization of Society* (Indianapolis, IN: Liberty Fund, 1979).

The Miscellaneous Repository: Neu, Y Drysorfa Gymmysgedig (Carmarthen, 1795).

Thom, W., *Rhymes and Recollections of a Hand-Loom Weaver* (London: Stewart & Murray, 1845).

Thomas, G., *Lloffyn Olaf o Faes Hynafiaethau Capel y Gyfylchi* (Treorchy: T. J. Davies, [1900]).

Thomas, H., *Romanticism and Slave Narratives* (Cambridge: Cambridge University Press, 2000).

Thomas, M. W., *Morgan Llwyd* (Cardiff: University of Wales Press, 1984).

Thomas, P. D. G., *John Wilkes: A Friend to Liberty* (Oxford: Oxford University Press, 1996).

Thomas, S. E., 'A Study of Calediad in the Upper Swansea Valley', in M. J. Ball (ed.), *The Use of Welsh: A Contribution to Sociolinguistics* (Clevedon: Multilingual Matters, 1988), pp. 85–96.

Thompson, E. P., *The Making of the English Working Class* (1963; London: Penguin, 1991).

—, *The Making of the English Working Class* (Harmondsworth: Pelican, 1968).

Thompson, J. R., *Leigh Hunt* (Boston, MA: Twayne, 1977).

Thuente, M. H., *The Harp Re-strung: The United Irishmen and the Rise of Irish Literary Nationalism* (Syracuse, NY: Syracuse University Press, 1994).

Tibbott, G., 'Un o Lythyrau Anghyhoeddedig Williams, Pantycelyn', *Journal of the Historical Society of the Presbyterian Church of Wales*, 20:4 (December 1935), pp. 131–7.

—, 'Hugh Jones, Maesglasau', *Journal of the Merioneth Historical and Record Society*, VII, part ii (1974), pp. 121–39.

Tóibín, N., *Duanaire Déiseach* (Baile Atha Cliath: Sáirséal agus Dill, 1978).

Toulmin, J., *The American War Lamented. A Sermon Preached at Taunton, February the 18th and 25th, 1776* (London: J. Johnson, 1776).

Trysorfa Gwybodaeth, neu Eurgrawn Cymraeg (Carmarthen, 1770).

Tudur, G., *Howell Harris: From Conversion to Separation 1735–1750* (Cardiff: University of Wales Press, 2000).

Tynan, M., *Catholic Instruction in Ireland 1720–1950: The O'Reilly/Donlevy Catechetical Tradition* (Dublin: Four Courts Press, 1985).

Tyrrell, A., 'Paternalism, Public Memory and National Identity in Early Victorian Scotland: The Robert Burns Festival at Ayr in 1844', *History*, 90:1 (2005), pp. 42–61.

Vicinus, M., *The Industrial Muse: A Study of Nineteenth Century Working-Class Literature* (London: Barnes & Noble, 1974).

Vincent, D., *Bread, Knowledge & Freedom: A Study of Nineteenth-Century Working Class Autobiography* (London and New York: Methuen, 1981).

Vovelle, M., 'La Marseillaise: War or Peace', in P. Nora (ed.), *Realms of Memory: The Construction of the French Past. Volume III: Symbols.* English-language edn ed. L. D. Kritzman, tr. Arthur Goldhammer (New York and Chichester: Columbia University Press, 1998), pp. 29–74.

Walters, H., 'The Periodical Press to 1914', in Jones and Rees (eds), *A Nation and its Books*, pp. 197–207.

Watson, J. R., *An Annotated Anthology of Hymns* (Oxford: Oxford University Press, 2002).

Welch, E., 'Three Letters from William Williams, Pantycelyn, to Lady Huntingdon', *Journal of the Historical Society of the Presbyterian Church of Wales*, 53:3 (September 1968), pp. 56–61.

—, *Spiritual Pilgrim: A Reassessment of the Life of the Countess of Huntingdon* (Cardiff: University of Wales Press, 1995).

Whatley, C. A., 'Burns: Work, Kirk and Community in Later Eighteenth-Century Scotland', in Simpson (ed), *Burns Now*, pp. 92–116.

—, *Scottish Society, 1707–1830: Beyond Jacobitism, towards Industrialiation* (Manchester: Manchester University Press, 2000).

Wheatley, P., *An Elegiac Poem, on the Death of that Celebrated Divine, and Eminent Servant of Jesus Christ, the Reverend and Learned George Whitefield, Chaplain to the Right Honourable the Countess of Huntingdon* (Boston, MA: Ezekiel Russell and John Boyles, [1770]).

—, *Poems on Various Subjects, Religious and Moral* (London: A. Bell, 1773).

—, Letter to Samson Occom dated 11 February 1774, *Connecticut Gazette*, 11 March 1774.

Wheeler, R., *The Complexion of Race: Categories of Difference in Eighteenth-Century British Culture* (Philadelphia, PA: University of Pennsylvania Press, 2000).

Whelan, I., *The Bible War in Ireland* (Madison, WI: University of Wisconsin Press, 2005).

Whelan, K., *The Tree of Liberty: Radicalism, Catholicism and the Construction of Irish Identity 1760–1830* (Cork: Cork University Press/Field Day, 1996).

—, 'The Republic in the Village', in Whelan, *The Tree of Liberty*, pp. 59–98.

—, 'An Underground Gentry? Catholic Middlemen in Eighteenth-Century Ireland', in Whelan, *The Tree of Liberty*, pp. 27–37.

White, E. M., 'Popular Schooling and the Welsh Language 1650–1800', in G. H. Jenkins (ed.), *The Welsh Language before the Industrial Revolution* (Cardiff: University of Wales Press, 1997), pp. 317–42.

William, M., *Britanus Merlinus Liberatus: Sef, Amgylchiadau Tymhorol ac Wybrennol: Neu, Almanac am y Flwyddyn o Oed ein Iachawdwr, 1777* (Caerfyrddin [Carmarthen], 1777).

—, *Britanus Merlinus Liberatus: Sef, Amgylchiadau Tymhorol ac Wybrennol: Neu, Almanac am y Flwyddyn o Oed ein Iachawdwr, 1778* (Caerfyrddin [Carmarthen], 1778).

—, *Britanus Merlinus Liberatus* (Caerfyrddin [Carmarthen]: I. Ross, 1780).

—, *Britanus Merlinus Liberatus* (Aberhonddu: W. a G. North, 1796).

Williams, A. H. (ed.), *John Wesley in Wales 1739–1790* (Cardiff: University of Wales Press, 1971).

Williams, D. J., *Storïau'r Tir Glas* ([Aberystwyth]: Gwasg Aberystwyth, 1936).

Williams, E., *Poems, Lyric and Pastoral*, 2 vols (London: J. Nichols, 1794).

—, [I. Morganwg], *The Correspondence of Iolo Morganwg*, eds G. H. Jenkins, F. M. Jones and D. C. Jones, 3 vols (Cardiff: University of Wales Press, 2007).

Williams, G. A., 'Druids and Democrats: Organic Intellectuals and the First Welsh Nation', in G. A. Williams, *The Welsh in their History* (London and Canberra: Croom Helm, 1982), pp. 31–64.

—, *Madoc: the making of a myth* (Oxford University Press: Oxford, 1987).

—, *When Was Wales? A History of the Welsh* (London: Penguin, 1991; 1st edn, 1985).

Williams, J., *Digest of Welsh Historical Statistics*, 2 vols (Aberystwyth: University College of Wales, 1985).

Williams, P., *Galwad Gan Wyr Eglwysig, Ar Bawb ffyddlon, i gyd-synio mewn Gweddi, yn enwedig Tra parhao'r Rhyfel presennol. Wedi ei gyfiethu (sic) i'r Gymraeg… Er mwyn annog y Cymru i gyd uno mewn Gwaith mor fuddiol, a Dyledswydd mor angenrheidiol, yn amser trallod* (2nd edn, Caerfyrddin [Carmarthen]: Ioan Ross, 1781).

Williams, W. (of Pantycelyn), Letter to Howel Harris, 7 December 1745: Trevecka Letters, no. 1381, Calvinistic Methodist Archives, MS Aberystwyth, National Library of Wales.

—, *A Favourite Hymn, Sung by Lady Huntingdon's Young Collegians. Printed by the Desire of Many Christian Friends* ([c. 1772]).

—, *Gloria in Excelsis: or Hymns of Praise to God and the Lamb* (Carmarthen: John Ross, 1772).

—, *Pantheologia, neu Hanes Holl Grefyddau'r Byd* (Caerfyrddin [Carmarthen]: E. and D. Powell, 1762–78/9).

—, *Ffarwel Weledig, Groesaw Anweledig Bethau* (Caerfyrddin [Carmarthen]: part 1, John Ross, 1763; part 2, John Ross, 1766; part 3, Rhys Thomas, 1769).

—, *Aurora Borealis* (Aberhonddu [Brecon]: E. Evans, 1774).

—, Letter to Thomas Charles, 14 September 1787: NLW 4798E, f. 57, MS Aberystwyth, National Library of Wales.

Williams, W. S., 'Capel y Gyfylchi', *Y Drysorfa*, 87 (1917), pp. 304–7.

Wilson, J. and R. Chambers, *The Land of Burns, A Series of Landscapes and Portraits, Illustrative of the Life and Writings of the Scottish Poet* (London and Glasgow: Blackie and Son, 1840).

Wilson, K., *The Sense of the People: Politics, Culture and Imperialism in England, 1715–1785* (Cambridge: Cambridge University Press, 1995).

Winch, D., 'Dugald Stewart and his Pupils', in S. Collini, D. Winch and J. Burrow, *The Noble Science of Politics: A Study in Nineteenth-Century Intellectual History* (Cambridge: Cambridge University Press, 1983), pp. 25–61.

Withers, C. W. J., '"Both Useful and Ornamental": John Walker's Keepership of Edinburgh University's Natural History Museum, 1779–1803', *Journal of the History of Collections*, 5:1 (1993), pp. 65–77.

Wood, D., 'Constant in Edinburgh: Eloquence and History', *French Studies*, 11:2 (1986), pp. 151–66.

Wynne, E., *Gweledigaetheu y Bardd Cwsc*, ed. A. Lewis (Caerdydd [Cardiff]: Gwasg Prifysgol Cymru, 1976).

Y Geirgrawn; Neu Drysorfa Gwybodaeth (Chester, 1796).

Young, J. D., *The Rousing of the Scottish Working Class* (London: Croom Helm, 1979).

Zimmermann, G. D., *Songs of Irish Rebellion: Political Street Ballads and Rebel Songs 1780–1900* (Dublin: Allen Figgis, 1967).

INDEX

1798 rebellion, 4–6, 18, 49, 149, 152–3

Abolitionist movement, 70, 109–12
Act of Union (1707), 74, 76–7
Adam's Weekly Courant, 114
Adams, John, 53
Adams, Thomas R., 30
Aikin, John, 65
Aldermen of Skinner's Alley Society, 54, 55
alienation, 14, 16
Alison, Sir Archibald, 86, 92–3
Almon, John, 52
Anderson, Christopher, 132
Antijacobin Review and Magazine, 161
anti-war poetry, 113, 115, 117–18, 124–7
Association for Discountenancing Vice, 131
astrology, 34–5, 117

Baker, Keith Michael, 12
Barbauld, Anna Letitia, 65
Barnard, Toby, 8
Barnes, Edward, 111
Barrell, John, 5, 83
    Imagining the King's Death, 73
Bate, Henry, 55
Bayley, Christopher, 3
Bebbington, David, 99
Beddoes, Thomas, 66–7
Belfast News-Letter, 88–9, 90, 92, 160
belief structures, 21–2
Bengel, J. A., 105
Berry, Walter, 71
Bickham, Troy, 32
Black, Joseph, 66–7
Black, Ronald, 140
Blacklock, Thomas, 56
Blackwood, William, 167

Blackwood's Edinburgh Magazine, 24, 159, 161–7
Bonaparte, Napoleon, 147, 151–2, 154, 163
Boswell, James, 56
Bowen, George, 100–1
Brainerd, David, 107
Braxfield, Lord, 64
Brewer, John, 49, 50–1
Brewster, Rev. Patrick, 90
British and Foreign Bible Society, 132
British Constitution, 25, 28
British Critic, 160–1
Brooke, Charlotte, *Reliques of Irish Poetry*, 130, 140–2
Brown, Matthew, 73–4
Browne, Arthur, 12
Buchanan, Dugald, *Laoidhe Spioradail*, 134
bureaucracy, 14
Burke, Edmund, 17, 56
'Burnomania', 79
Burns, Robert
    celebration of, 79, 84, 86–90, 92–4
    'Does Haughty Gaul', 85
    influence of, 80–2, 83–4
    and literary magazines, 160
    and Lord Daer, 63, 64
    monument to, 86, 90–1
    popularity of, 79, 82–3
    portrayal of, 80–1, 85, 89–90, 92–4
    'The Address of Beelzebub', 88
    'The Cotter's Saturday Night', 21, 85, 86–8
    'The Twa Dogs', 21, 83–4
Bute, Lord, 49, 50–1, 52, 53–4, 59
Butler, Rev. Thomas, 2
Byrne, Patrick, 141

'Ça Ira' (song), 1, 19–20
Caledonian Chronicle, 71
Callaghan, John, 152
Callendar, Alexander, 75
Cambrian, 114
Campbell, Duncan, *Nuadh Orain Ghailach*, 23, 143–4
Campbell, Ilay, 69
Carey, William, 109
Cartwright, Major John, 72
Castle party, 52
catechisms, 142–3
Catholicism
　and clash with establishment, 18
　and emergence of Republicanism, 15
　and French Revolution, 121
　and polarization of Enlightenment, 13–14
　and Protestant Association, 56–7
　and Relief Acts, 7, 55–7
　and Whiggism, 51, 53
Chapter House Philosophical Society, 67, 69
Charles, Thomas, 105, 109, 132
Chartism, 81, 84, 88, 90
Chartist Circular, 90
Chester Chronicle, 113, 114–17
Christie, Thomas, 71
Churchill, Charles, 54, 59
'Clapham Sect', 99, 108
Clark, J. C. D., 15
Cleghorn, James, 161
'Cockney School', 24, 159, 163–7
Colley, Linda, 49, 50–1, 64
　Britons: Forging the Nation, 4
Connolly, Sean, 60
'constitutional revolution', 10
Conway, Stephen, 26
Cork, 5–6
Cork Gazette, 145, 149
corruption, 35–7, 46, 54
Cothi, Tomos Glyn, 120, 126
　'HYMN to be sung on a day of fast by the friends of mankind', 124–5
Covenanters, 92, 94
Cowdroy, William, 116
Cox, Jeffrey, 164
Cox, Walter, *Irish Magazine*, 146
Craik, Professor G. L., 93

criminal legislation, 10–11
Croker, Thomas Crofton, 153
Cromek, R. H., *Reliques of Robert Burns*, 85
Cugoana, Quobna Ottobah, 108
Cullen, Louis, 5, 60
Culloden Volunteers, 53
Culloden, Battle of (1746), 51, 53
Cumberland, Duke of, 51
Cunningham, Waddell, 57
Currie, James, 85
　Works of Robert Burns, 82
Curtin, Nancy, 129, 142, 146, 150, 157
Cylch-grawn Cynmraeg, 123–4

Daer, Lord (Basil William Douglas)
　as abolitionist, 70
　death of, 64
　education of, 65–6
　and electoral reform, 69–70
　and French Revolution, 66, 72–3
　health of, 67, 75
　as landowner, 68–9
　and reform movement, 70–6
　and scientific discovery, 63–4, 66–7
　and Scottish Enlightenment, 63, 67–8
　and union, 21, 64–5, 68, 74–5, 76–7
Darnton, Robert, 16
Davies, David, 120–1
Davies, John, 114
Defenders, 2, 18, 49, 143
democratization, 7–8
Dewar, Daniel, *Observations on the Character, Customs, and Superstitions of the Irish*, 132
Disruption (1843), 81
distribution of political ideas, 19–20, 22–3
Donnelly, James, 129, 130
Dozer, Donald, 12
Drennan, William, 2
Dublin Evening Post, 54, 57, 149
Dublin Mercury, 62
Dublin Morning Post, 54, 57
Dudith, Andrew, 121
Duigenan, Patrick, 61
Dumfries Volunteers, 82
Dun, Alexander, 52
Dundas, Robert, 75
Dunne, Tom, 130

Durey, Michael, 19
Dyson, Jeremiah, 52

Eagleton, Terry, 113
Eberle-Sinatra, Michael, 165
Edinburgh Friends of the People, 70–1
Edinburgh Gazetteer, 71
Edinburgh Review, 24, 161–3
Edinburgh Speculative Society, 67
Edwards, Jonathan, 107
Edwards, Thomas, 'Ymddiddan rhwng Gwraig yr Hwsmon a Gwraig y Shiopwr', 45–7
Egmont, Battle of (1799), 135, 143
Elias, John, 111–12
Eliot, John, 107
Ellis, David, 37–8
Ellul, Jacques, 6–7
Emmet, Dr Thomas Addis, 67
Enfield, William, 65
Enlightenment, 3–5, 11, 13–14, 18–20, 110, 121
Equiano, Olaudah, 108
Erskine, David Stewart, 135
Erskine, Henry, 70
Eryri, Dafydd Ddu, 'Ode on Liberty', 123
Evans, Evan, 'On the Court of Ivor the Generous', 123–4
Evans, Thomas, 114
Examiner, 159–60, 162–6

Farge, Arlette, 12
Fay, John, 2
Ferguson, Adam, 66
financial revolution, 10
Fisher, Andrew, 84
Fitzgerald, Garrett, 130
Flood, Henry, 13
Foot, Paul, 166
Franklin, Benjamin, 29–30
   'Rattlesnakes for felons', 33
Free Citizens of Dublin, 51, 54
Freeman's Journal, 52, 56
freemasonry, 81–2
French, Richard, 12

Gaelic language texts, 130, 132–44
Garnham, Neal, 10

George III, King, 26, 51, 54
Gerrald, Joseph, 73–4, 75
Gifford, William, 161
Gilfillan, Rev. George, 92–3
Gilmartin, Kevin, 163
Glan-y-gors, Jac, 115–17, 122, 125
   'A Welsh hymn, to be sung on the fast-day', 116
   Seren Tan Gwmmwl, 121
Glasgow Argus, 89
Glorious Revolution (1688), 25, 28
Gordon, Lord George, 55–7
Grant, Peter, *Dain Spioradail*, 134
Grattan, Henry, 13
Grey, Charles, 64–5, 76
Gronniosaw, Ukawsaw, 108
Grose, Francis, *Dictionary of the Vulgar Tongue*, 164
Gryffydd, Hugh, 'Cywydd of the story of Pennsylvania in America', 118
'Gwilym', 'Song of Liberty', 125–6

Haddo, Lord, 69
Hall, Sir James, 72–3
Hamilton, Thomas, 86, 91
handloom weavers, 82–4
Hardiman, James, *Irish Minstrelsy*, 140
Hardy, Thomas, 71
Harney, Julian, 90, 91
Harp of Erin, 6, 145
Harris, Howel, 95–7, 104, 109
Harris, John, 'The Dream of John of the Hill, Llandeilo Fawr, and his Dog Cupid', 118–19
Hasting, Warren, 54
Hastings, Selina (Lady Huntingdon), 95–8, 99–100, 101, 106–9
Havel, Vaclav, 76
Hayden, John O., 161
Hayes, Michael, 151–2
Hayton, David, 60
Hely-Hutchinson, John, 8
Hereford Journal, 114
Hibernian Journal, 52, 54, 55, 58–9, 60
Higgins, David, 162
Hodgson, Francis, 161
Holmes, Richard, 63
Home, John, *Douglas*, 62

Hope, Thomas Charles, 67
Howe, General, 42
Howe, William, 25
Hughes, Dewi Arwel, 106
Hughes, Hugh, 37, 38
Hume, David, 53, 59
Hunt, Henry, 148–9
Hunt, Leigh, 159, 162–7
   Rimini, 24, 164–5
Hunter-Blair, Sir David, 87
Hurdy Gurdy (instrument), 1–2, 19–20, 24

Illustrated London News, 93
improvement schemes, 10

Jackson, William, 2
Jebb, Frederick, 54, 57
Jebb, John, 76
Jefferson, Thomas, 66
Jeffrey, Francis, 161
Jenkins, R. T., 26–7, 112
Johnson, Samuel, 59
   Dictionary of the English Language, 15
Jones, Cain, 45
Jones, Dafydd, 29, 30, 45
Jones, Edward, 26
Jones, Griffith, 119
Jones, Hugh, 33–4, 43–5
   'Cerdd newydd ym mherthynas y rhyfel presennol yr America', 36–7
   'Mother', 30–2
Jones, John Paul, 38–40, 43
'Juvenis', 117

Keats, John, 163, 166
Kelly, James, 11
Kidd, Colin, 83
Knox, John, 56

Lavoisier, Antoine Laurent, 63
   Traité Élémentaire de Chimie, 67
Leland, Thomas, 12
Lenman, Bruce, 66
Lewis, Saunders, *Williams Pantycelyn*, 103
Limerick Chronicle, 55–6, 146
Lindsey, Theophilus, 120
literary magazines, 159–61, 167
Llangeitho Revival (1762), 97, 105
Llwyd, Morgan, 103

Lockhart, John Gibson, 163–7
   'On the Periodical Criticism of England', 162
London Corresponding Society (LCS), 71–2, 73–5
London Magazine, 159
Louis XIV, King, 39
Louis XVI, 'King, 39
Lucas, Charles, 12, 51, 52
Lukacs, John D., 14
Lynch, Patrick, 131, 142

Macartney, Sir George, 51, 52
McDonald, Alexander, *Ais-eiridh na Sean Chánoin Albannaich*, 134
McDonald, Ranald, *Comh-chruinneachidh Orannaigh Gaidhealach*, 134
Macdowall, Rev., 92
McFarland, Elaine, 144
McIlvanney, Liam, 82
   Burns the Radical, 160
McIntyre, Duncan Ban, 134–5, 136, 140–1, 143
Mackenzie, Henry, 68
MacKenzie, Kenneth, *Orain Ghaidhealach*, 135–8, 140–1, 143
Macleod, Norman, 70, 132
   An Teachdaire Gaelach, 134
   Cuairteir nan Gleann, 134
MacNeven, William James, 141
Macpherson, James, 49, 50
   The Rights of Great Britain Asserted against the Claims of America, 59
Madden, R. R., 156
Magennis, Eoin, 10
Maginn, William, 162
Mansfield, Lord, 52, 54
Margarot, Maurice, 73–4, 75
Methodist Revival, 95–7, 104, 109
military presence, 9–10
military recruitment, 40–3
Millar, John, 72
mobilization, 7–8
Monks of the Screw, 58
Moore, James, 141
Morganwg, Iolo, 38, 122, 123–4
   'Ode on converting a sword into a pruning-hook', 115

Morley, Vincent, 9, 50, 60
Morning Chronicle, 75
Morning Herald, 55
Morris, Richard, 120
Morys, Huw, 39
Muir, Thomas, 75, 77
Murray, Iain H., *The Puritan Hope*, 103
Musgrave, Richard, *Memoirs of the Different Rebellions in Ireland*, 23

Natural History Museum, 66
New Burns Club, 84
New Monthly, 159
Newenham, Sir Edward, 52, 54
Newenham, William, 153
Nonconformity, 112
Nora, Pierre, 92
North Briton, 51, 52, 54
North Wales Gazette, 117
North, Lord, 25
Northern Star, 81, 90, 129–30, 142, 145–6, 150, 160

O'Brien, Gerard, 7–8
O'Brien, Gillian, 146
Ó Ciardha, Eamonn, 60
O'Connor, Arthur, 6
O'Connor, Feargus, 88
O'Conor, Charles, 12, 59
O'Daly, John
    Reliques of Irish Jacobite Poetry, 140–1
    The Poets and Poetry of Munster, 140–1
Ó Longáin, Micheál Óg, *Fiannaíocht*, 152
O'Sullivan, Timothy, 134
Occom, Samson, 107
Octennial Act (1768), 8
Owen, Robert, 88
Ozouf, Mona, 12

Paddy's Resource, 23, 150, 151, 154, 157
Paine, Thomas, 28, 49, 72–3, 109, 119, 145–6
    Age of Reason, 145
    Rights of Man, 89
Parker, Mark, *Literary Magazines and British Romanticism*, 159, 160–1
Parsons, Sir Laurence, 51

Particular Baptist Society for the Propagation of the Gospel Amongst the Heathen, 109
Patriot movement, 13
Pemberton, Handy, 60–1
Pennant, Thomas
    American Annals, 42
    Free Thoughts on the Militia Laws, 42–3
Philp, Mark, 22
Phylip, Wiliam, 36
Pine, William, 27, 29
Pitt, William, 119
'Poeta Rusticus', 122
political public opinion, 11–13
politicization
    and criminal legislation, 10–11
    and democratization, 7–8
    and distribution of ideas, 19–20, 22–3
    and military presence, 9–10
    and mobilization, 7–8
    and polarization of Enlightenment, 13–14
    and propaganda, 129–31
    and public opinion, 11–13
    and radicalization, 15–18
    rise of, 6–7
    and state expansion, 10–11
    and violence, 16–18
Pollock, Joseph, 54
Porter, Roy, 5
Porteus, Beilby, 43
Potkay, Adam, 111
premillennialism, 110
Presbyterianism, 20–1, 57, 62, 87, 92, 94
Preston, William, 59
    A Congratulatory Poem on the Late Successes of the British Arms, 58
    The Female Congress, 58
Priestley, Joseph, 65
    An Appeal to the Serious and Candid Professors of Christianity, 120
    Experiments and Observations on Different Kinds of Air, 63
Pringle, Thomas, 161
print culture, 22–4, 119–21, 142–3
print media, circulation of, 145–50, 157
Pritchard, Robert, 114
Wilson, Professor John, 85

propaganda, 129–31, 141–4
Protestant Ascendancy, 15–16
Protestant Association, 55–7
Prys, John, 34, 35–6
Pughe, William Owen, 109, 121
'Puritan Hope', 103–7, 109–10

Quarterly Review, 161–2

Radical War (1820), 84
Rees, Josiah, *Trysorfa Gwybodaeth, neu Eurgrawn Cymraeg*, 119–20
Rees, Thomas, 160
Reform Act (1832), 7
Relief Act (1778), 55–6
Relief Act (1782), 55–6
Religious Tract Society, 132
Rhys, Morgan John, 111
  'Signs of the Times', 122
Richardson, Robert, 82
Risiart, Dafydd, 119
Roberts, Ellis, 38–42, 44–5
Roberts, Thomas, 121
Robertson, William, 53
Robinson, Robert, 98
Rodger, Alexander, 'The Twa Weavers', 84
Ross, John, 43
Rounce, Adam, 51
Rowland, Daniel, 101
Royal Society of Edinburgh, 68
Rush, Benjamin, 53

Salopian Journal, 114
Samwell, David, 25–6
Sanderson, Elijah, 31–2
Saunders, Dafydd, 'Look at the present war', 126–8
scientific discovery, 63–4
Scott, Sir Walter, 80, 89
Scottish Friends of the People, 21, 71, 73
'self-actualisation', 17–18
Shaffer, Butler, 16–17
Sheares, Henry, 6
Sheares, John, 6
Sheehy, Owen, 151–2
Sheffield Society for Constitutional Information, 74
Shelley, Percy Bysshe
  'A Philosophical View of Reform', 166

Revolt of Islam, 24, 166
Sheridan, Richard Brinsley, 55
Shipley, Jonathan, 29–30
Shrewsbury Chronicle, 114
sin, 43–4
Sinclair, Charles, 73–4, 75
Skirving, William, 64, 73–4, 75–6
slave trade, 24, 70, 98–9, 108–12
Smith, William, *A Sermon On The Present Situation Of American Affairs*, 27–9
Society for Constitutional Information (SCI), 72, 73–4, 76
Society for the Education of the Native Irish through the medium of their own language, 131
Somerville, Andrew, 83
Southcott, Joanna, 109
Stanley, Brian, *The Bible and the Flag*, 110
state, 10–11, 17
Stewart, Dugald, 65–6, 76
Stewart, Larry, 67
Stokes, Whitley, 131, 141, 143
Styles, Ezra, 53
Swift, Jonathan, 49, 57
  'The Story of the Injured Lady', 50

Taylor, Dr John, 84
temperance, 93–4
Test and Corporation Acts (repeal of, 1828), 7
The Missionary Society, 109
The Rise, Progress, and Present State Of The Dispute, 29–30
Theophilus Evans, *The History of Modern Enthusiasm*, 104
Thom, William, *Recollections*, 83
Thomas, David, 121
Thompson, E. P., 5
Thompson, William, 90
Tlysau'r Hen Oesoedd, 119
Toulmin, Joshua, 43
Townshend, Lord, 51, 52
Trefeca College, 97, 101, 106–7
Turner, Patrick, *Comhchruinneacha do dh'ain taghta Ghaidhealach*, 135, 136, 138–41, 143
Twiss, Richard, 50, 58–60
Tyrell, Alex, 92

United Irish movement
    alliance with Defenders, 2, 18
    Bolg an tSolair, 130, 131, 140
    and Cork, 6
    and French Revolution, 4, 49, 151–2
    increased use of violence, 18
    political claims of, 17
    and propaganda, 129–31, 141–4
    repression of, 2, 15
    and song, 149–50, 152–4, 157

Vallencey, Charles, 12
Vaughan, Benjamin, 65
violence, 15, 16–18
Volunteer Evening Post, 56–7, 60, 62
Volunteer movement, 7, 9, 13–14, 55–6

'W. T. M.', 113
Wakefield, Gilbert, 121
Walker, Professor John, 66
War of the Two Kings (1688–91), 9
Watson, William, 131
Watt, Robert, 75
Wedderburne, Alexander, 54
Weir, Alexander, 66
Welch, Edwin, 95
Wesley, Charles, 95
Wesley, John, 100, 104
Wheatley, Phillis, 98
Wheeler, Roxann, 99
Whelan, Kevin, 129, 152

Whitefield, George, 97–8, 99, 104, 108
Wilkes, John, 49, 50–2, 56–7, 75–6
William, Mathew, 35, 37, 119
    Britanus Merlinus Liberatus, 34
Williams, Edward, 26, 114
Williams, Gwyn Alf, 26–7
Williams, Peter, 43
Williams, Peter Bailey, 121
Williams, William (Pantycelyn)
    and American War of Independence, 34–5, 37
    Aurora Borealis, 106–7, 110
    Ffarwel Weledig, Groesaw Anweledig Bethau, 106
    Gloria in Excelsis: or Hymns of Praise to God and the Lamb, 99–100
    'Guide me, O thou great Jehovah, Pilgrim through this barren land', 96, 97
    'O'er those gloomy hills of darkness', 22, 99–102, 103–4, 107–8, 109, 112
    Pantheologia, neu Hanes Holl Grefyddau'r Byd, 106
    and 'Puritan Hope', 104–6, 110
    and slave trade, 98–9, 108–9, 111–12
Wilson, Kathleen, *Sense of the People*, 4
Wilson, Professor John, 85–6, 88–90
Wynne, Ellis, 39
Wyvill, Christopher, 61, 76

Y Geirgrawn, 125, 128